D1717875

Optional-Narrator Theory

Frontiers of Narrative

SERIES EDITOR

Jesse E. Matz, Kenyon College

Optional-Narrator Theory

Principles, Perspectives, Proposals

EDITED BY SYLVIE PATRON

University of Nebraska Press | Lincoln

This book has received financial support from the
Université de Paris and the Paris Centre for Narrative Matters, ANR-18-IDEX-0001, IdEx Université
de Paris.

Library of Congress Cataloging-in-Publication Data
Names: Patron, Sylvie, 1969– editor.
Title: Optional-narrator theory: principles, perspectives, proposals / edited by Sylvie Patron.
Description: Lincoln: University of Nebraska Press,
2021. | Series: Frontiers of narrative | Includes bibliographical references and index.
Identifiers: LCCN 2020023684
ISBN 9781496223371 (hardback)
ISBN 9781496224507 (epub)
ISBN 9781496224514 (mobi)
ISBN 9781496224521 (pdf)
Subjects: LCSH: Narration (Rhetoric) | Discourse,
analysis, Narrative.
Classification: LCC PN212 .O68 2021 | DDC
808/.036—dc23
LC record available at
https://lccn.loc.gov/2020023684

Set in Minion Pro by Laura Buis.

Contents

Illustrations

Acknowledgments

I would like to thank all the members of the Advisory Board for their invaluable advice: Claire Badiou-Monferran (University Sorbonne nouvelle, France), Gregory Currie (University of York, UK), Andrew Kania (Trinity University, USA), Gilles Philippe (University of Lausanne, Switzerland), Marianne Wolff Lundholt (University of Southern Denmark), and Jan-Noël Thon (University of Tübingen, Germany).

My thanks also go to:

A. C. Spearing, with whom I have maintained a correspondence for a long time; it was after reading an article he sent me that I first had the idea for this volume;

Jonathan Culler and the organizers of the Biannual Conference of the Society for Novel Studies at Cornell University (May 31–June 2, 2018), where two panels on optional-narrator theories, chaired by Jonathan Culler and myself, were presented; they included six contributors to this volume;

Jonathan Culler again, for his invaluable advice and support throughout the preparation of this volume;

Ann Banfield, Bridget Barry, Brian Boyd, Jonathan Culler, Wayne Larsen, Anne-Marie Le Fée, Jesse E. Matz, Melissa McMahon, Gérard and Marie-Cécile Patron, A. C. Spearing, and Elizabeth Zaleski, for their help, their support, their re-reading, or their collaboration on different points.

Optional-Narrator Theory

Introduction

SYLVIE PATRON

The ubiquity of fictional narrators in fictional narratives has been a fundamental assumption that distinguishes narratology from previous narrative theories (see Barthes [1966] 1975; Genette [1972] 1980, and [1983] 1988; Bal [1978, 1985] 2017; Stanzel [1979] 1984; Prince [1982] 2012; Rimmon-Kenan [1983] 2002; Chatman 1990).[1] Ever since the first formulations of this assumption, however, voices have come forward to denounce over-simplifications and dangerous confusions of issues. "Only in cases where the narrative poet actually does 'create' a narrator, namely the first-person narrator of the first-person narrative, can one speak of the latter as a (fictive) narrator," declares Käte Hamburger ([1957, 1968] 1993, 140).[2] For a long time, Hamburger's perspective, but also those of S.-Y. Kuroda and Ann Banfield, who invoke Hamburger's legacy, have been marginalized by the power and dominance of narratological discourse and practices. Yet, as A. C. Spearing puts it, in reference to these marginalized voices, "If one reads any of these theorists, one thing noticeable is that they present *arguments* in favour of their views, whereas those who hold the majority view simply assert it or take it for granted."[3]

Terminology and Preliminaries

The theory according to which we can only speak of a fictional narrator in cases where the author creates or constructs this narrator through a process that is assumed to be intentional can be called and will be called in this volume the *optional-narrator theory of fictional narration*, or *optional-narrator theory* for short.[4] This theory was originally intended to account for the narration in novels or short stories, that is, literary fiction, but we will also see versions of optional-narrator theory in contributions devoted to other forms of fiction (cinematic, graphic, and so on), as well as contributions on other forms of literary narrative that predate the modern novel.

Optional-narrator theory is opposed to the *pan-narrator theory of fictional narration.*[5] The contributors to this volume use different terms for the narrator of pan-narrator theory that should be considered synonymous: "necessary narrator," "obligatory narrator," "imposed narrator," "fundamental narrator." As the expression *pan-narrator theory* implies, in this theory the fictional narrator is not an authorial choice but a prerequisite for thinking about all fictional narrative.[6]

The theory according to which we can only speak of a fictional narrator in cases where the author creates or constructs this narrator through a process that is assumed to be intentional also contains the implicit proposition that outside these cases it is useless and even potentially erroneous to refer to a narrator, that is, a fictional narrator. The optional-narrator theory also contains a "no-narrator theory of fictional narration," an expression that can also be found in Lars-Åke Skalin's contribution to this volume. Other contributors, however, indicate that they prefer to avoid this expression because it could create confusion: for example, the idea that the "no" in "no-narrator theory" means there is never a fictional narrator in fictional narratives.

Optional-narrator theory has a much clearer concept of the narrator than pan-narrator theory. The former takes the distinction between the author and the narrator seriously, whereas many pan-narrator theorists muddle this fundamental distinction, claiming, for example, that all narratives have a narrator on the grounds that all artifacts are the product of human activity (all novels are the product of a novel writer; all plays, of a playwright; and so on). Throughout this volume, the term "narrator" is meaningful only as a function of the binary opposition between author and narrator, unless the contributors are explicitly referring to the ordinary sense of this term, meaning "the person who narrates," in conversational narratives, for example.

Recent years have seen a growing interest in optional-narrator theory. Simultaneously, the proponents of pan-narrator theory have become more combative and have started to formulate arguments, or at least critically examine some of their opponents' arguments (see Zipfel 2015; I could not take into account J. Alexander Bareis's recent article on the subject [see Bareis 2020]). This double novelty, in summary, is the context of the theoretical discussions about the narrator in this volume.

The Strength of the Arguments

Frank Zipfel's article "Narratorless Narration? Some Reflections on the Arguments for and against the Ubiquity of Narrators in Fictional Narration" will serve as my point of departure. Zipfel is the first author, to my knowledge, who has tried to draw up an inventory of the arguments put forward by optional-narrator theorists against pan-narrator theory.[7] He distinguishes three arguments or sets of arguments:

1. *The language argument*, which may be better called the *linguistic argument*: "fictional heterodiegetic narration is considered as a mode of presentation that is completely different from fictional homodiegetic narration as well as from factual narration and is described as a non-communicative use of language" (Zipfel 2015, 45). Zipfel's terminology here is in keeping with pan-narrator theory;[8] the theorists concerned, essentially Kuroda and Banfield,[9] never, for their part, use the terms "heterodiegetic" and "homodiegetic." Zipfel's formulation is nevertheless acceptable if "heterodiegetic" and "homodiegetic" narration are replaced with "third-person" and "first-person" narration, and perhaps with the removal of "completely" from "completely different," which is a purposeful exaggeration.

2. *The transmedial narratology argument*: "due to the fact that parallels can be drawn between story presentation in feature film and story presentation in verbal heterodiegetic narration and against the background that most film theorists find it ill-advised to postulate that every feature film has a narrator, there seem to be good reasons for the assumption that there are fictional narrations (verbal as well as others) without a narrator" (45–46).

3. *The interpretation and fiction theory argument*: "this argument only refutes the concept of effaced narrators, claiming that we should only talk about a narrator when there are explicit features in the text that prompt the assumption that there is a narrator" (46).

Zipfel's presentation is interesting, but it is also very partial and partisan. In particular, Zipfel never interrogates the logical, semiotic, or pragmatic constraints that govern the relationships between the different arguments. He seems more eager to stress that in his view arguments 1 and 2 concern all "fictional heterodiegetic narration," whereas argument 3 concerns only "some fictional heterodiegetic narrations," namely those with "effaced narrators," as opposed to what pan-narrator theorists see as a manifest narrator in fictional third-person narrative—Stanzel's "auctorial narrator," for example. This is a way of stressing that arguments 1, 2, and 3 neutralize rather than complement each other.

By reviewing the extensive bibliography on the subject,[10] we can present the arguments used to reject the different versions of pan-narrator theory in a numbered list. I will then examine each of these arguments in greater or lesser detail. The disadvantage of the list is that it obscures the chronological dimension. It should therefore be pointed out that the oldest arguments are the linguistic ones, and those most often put forward today are the transmedial narratology, fiction theory, and interpretation arguments.

Arguments of a general or social kind

1. The ubiquity of fictional narrators in fictional narratives is a doctrinal proposition rather than a theoretical one, a kind of dogma of modern literary theory and criticism.

2. The ubiquity thesis is presented as a mark of critical sophistication, but it only creates clutter and, more seriously, hampers the development of the critical faculties, among secondary and tertiary students for example.

3. Pan-narrator theory is counterintuitive.

4. Pan-narrator theory is irrational and produces monsters (for example, the "omniscient narrator," the "nonactual nonfictional narrator").[11]

Arguments of a scientific and theoretical kind
Linguistic arguments

5.1. The communicational theory of narration, which defines narration as an act of communication between a narrator and a narratee, can account for only a subcategory of fictional narratives, taken here to mean verbal fictional narratives, which is to say encoded in language in the narrow sense.

5.2. There are noncommunicational uses of language.

5.3. The hypothesis of the omniscient narrator is an ad hoc hypothesis.

Transmedial narratology argument

6. The language-based, or rather, speech-act-based, approach to narrative, which defines narrative as the product of a speech act performed by a narrator and addressed to a narratee, can account for only a subcategory of fictional narratives, being taken here in the sense of verbal and nonverbal fictional narratives, encoded in various media, modes, or languages in the broad sense.

Fiction theory arguments

7.1. The arguments advanced in favor of pan-narrator theory are untenable, or at least largely insufficient.

7.2. The fictional narrator of pan-narrator theory is an inconsistent construction.

Interpretation arguments

8.1. The application of pan-narrator theory to the study of some fictional narratives generates "strange interpretations," or interpretations that ordinary competent readers would consider to be forced, erroneous, nonsensical, irrelevant, and sometimes even contradictory to the work under consideration.

8.2. Narratologists present relevant and often excellent interpretations of fictional narratives, but this is because they do not apply their theory in a strict way.

Arguments of a historical kind

Argument from literary history

9. Pan-narrator theory is an anachronistic theory, ill-suited to the study of certain fictional narratives, such as medieval narratives and narratives of the French classical period.

Arguments from the history and epistemology of literary theories

10.1. Pan-narrator theory is itself a historical construction alongside other theories of fictional narration.

10.2. Two different concepts of the narrator are at the origin of the modern, ubiquitous concept of the narrator.

10.3. The ubiquity of fictional narrators in fictional narratives is not an empirical discovery but a stipulation.

Arguments 1 and 2 are presented together in the first lines of a recent article by Brian Boyd, one of the contributors to this volume: "Modern literary study tends to accept both as a dogma and as a mark of critical sophistication that all narratives must have a narrator distinct from the author" (2017, 285). Boyd also quotes Dorothee Birke and Tilmann Köppe: the "idea that the narrator of a literary work must be sharply divided from its author . . . is a kind of First Principle, or dogma, of narrative analysis" (2015a, 3, quoted in Boyd 2017, 304n1). It is unstated but nevertheless very clear that not all theorists are obliged to conform to this dogma.

Argument 2 is found in Boyd, as we have seen, but it has also been made on several occasions by Marc Hersant, another contributor to this volume: "This theoretical framework [that of pan-narrator theory] . . . is still a source of dubious pleasure for secondary school students, who are used to distinguishing, in sibylline fashion, with no one understanding what is going on, 'the author' from 'the narrator'" (2011, 206; translation by Melissa McMahon, hereafter identified as "M.M."); "In this work [*Candide* by Voltaire] as in so many others, students [are] regularly invited to 'look for' signs of the presence of a 'narrator,' who is perhaps nothing but an invention of the theoretical and pedagogical doxa" (2015, 310n68; translation by M.M.). Boyd, for his part, perceives two stages in the students' thinking: "students naturally resist a doctrine that is unnecessary, counter to their experience, and internally contradictory, until they decide they had better submit to the authority of the 'experts' lest they be deemed naive by those who grade their work" (2017, 287). The chapter by Jonathan Culler, which opens this volume, and the one by Boyd, which comes after it, contain several passages that echo these remarks.

Argument 3, "Pan-narrator theory is counterintuitive," is not necessarily pertinent in itself, in light of everything Gaston Bachelard has written on intuition as an epistemological obstacle. It is only of interest in context because it contradicts the claim of pan-narrator theory to be more intuitive than optional-narrator theory, especially in its linguistic version: "the thesis that narrative sentences have speakers explains more phenomena more adequately, with less violence to the reader's intuitions" (McHale 1983, 22, quoted by Cohn 1999, 127). Argument 3 is reinforced by the second part of argument 4, "Pan-narrator theory is irrational and produces monsters," especially when it comes to "the omniscient narrator." If there are fictional narrators in all fictional narratives, then there are (fictional) omniscient narrators in third-person fictional narratives or at least in the majority of them. (I will return to the issue of the fictionality of the omniscient narrator.) Hamburger long ago stressed the inconsistency and the lack of explanatory power of the hypothesis of the omniscient narrator:

> Then thirty years later [after the publication of *Die Rolle des Erzählers in der Epik*, by Käte Friedemann], when Julius Petersen expands upon this aspect by comparing the narrator with a "director who stands between the persons on the stage and assigns them their places, movements and intonations," and, what is more, places this narrator "in the role of the psychologist" and has him "assume the tasks of the latter, so that responsibility for describing and portraying psychic processes falls on him"—it becomes all the more clear that we are dealing here with sometimes more, sometimes less adequate *metaphorical pseudo-definitions* which in literary jargon have become condensed and overused slogans, like the "authority" or the "omniscience of the narrator," or which have been mythologized in their comparison with God's omniscience. ([1957, 1968] 1993, 141)

We can find many quotations from classical structuralist narratology, as well as contemporary narratology or narratologies, that are vulnerable to the same criticisms. Genette: "the extreme delicacy of the feelings, which only an omniscient narrator, capable like God himself of seeing beyond actions and of sounding body and soul, can reveal" ([1972] 1980, 209). Cohn: "This anticipation is a clear indication of the narrator's temporal omniscience; he views the events from a distant perspective, looking over the entire time span he recounts. Only that telescopic perspective makes it possible for him to order and digest the events in the process of displaying them" (1978, 35). Cohn again: "a narrator's magic power allows him to see into sleeping minds quite as readily as into waking ones" (52). For Hamburger, there is no omniscience or magic power; there is only the work of the author, of which the reader is always conscious. Hamburger's criticisms, inspired by empiricism and rationalism, have been reiterated by Kuroda, who evokes "the epistemological or metaphysical opaqueness of the narrator theory of narration," "such a mystifying notion as the omniscient narrator," "such an enigmatic creature as the omniscient narrator" ([1976] 2014, 77, 78; [1987] 2014, 143). As for the "nonactual nonfictional narrator"—so named by Peter Alward (2007), but whose origins go back to at least Stanzel (see esp. [1979] 1984, 81 and 90)—I will mention it later in relation to the theory of fiction arguments. Suffice it to say here that this theoretical entity is severely criticized by both an optional-narrator theorist (Kania 2007) and a pan-narrator theorist (Zipfel 2015, 57): "Nonactual nonfictional narrators do not inhabit the real world, but they do not belong to a fictional world either. . . . I must admit that I do not know what to make of this third realm, which is neither real nor fictional and from which all heterodiegetic narrations are supposed to be told."

Arguments of a Scientific and Theoretical Kind

Among these arguments, the linguistic ones are of fundamental importance, even if they concern only verbal fictional narratives or, even more specific, one type of verbal fictional narrative. They are fundamental because they falsify the pan-narrator theory by means of the linguistic interpretation that can be given of it: "there is a fictional narrator in every fictional narrative" = "there is an *I* (and potentially a *you*) in every sentence of fictional narrative; and when this *I* (and potentially this *you*) is not explicit, it is implicit and could be made explicit without altering the meaning of the sentence." The linguistic arguments correspond to the main discoveries of Kuroda and Banfield, both of whom draw on some of Hamburger's propositions. These arguments have been reiterated by Marianne Wolff Lundholt (2008) within a different theoretical framework.

We can start with an observation by Kuroda, commenting on a famous quotation from Roland Barthes ([1966] 1975, 260: "Narrative, viewed as object, is the basis of a communication: there is a giver of narrative and a recipient of narrative," and so on):

This quotation represents an example of the most explicit, and frank, statements which recognize that a theory of narration having recourse to the notion of narrator must have its theoretical basis in the communicational theory of linguistic performance. Such recognition may not necessarily be made explicitly. However, so long as no alternative to the communicational theory of linguistic performance is proposed, it seems unavoidable to interpret the notion of narrator current in narrative theory within the communicational framework as Barthes does. (Kuroda [1976] 2014, 73)

The following division can be deduced from this. On the one side are the narratologists (Barthes, Genette), for whom communication is primary— it is a primitive fact, one that is not itself explained—and in whose work linguistic observations are secondary or nonexistent. On the other side are the linguists (Kuroda, Banfield), for whom language—linguistic competence and performance—is primary and who strive to analyze communicational as well as noncommunicational structures at the linguistic level. We can also add, firstly, that the linguists carry out their analyses on the level of the sentence and not of the narrative as a whole, which is why the formulation of argument 5.1 should be understood as a generalization of "The communicational theory of narration . . . can account for only the *sentences* of a subcategory of fictional narratives." Secondly, the linguists offer tests that make it possible to eliminate the hypothesis of the presence of an implicit narrator (one not observable at the linguistic level) in some sentences of fictional narratives, whether in Japanese (Kuroda) or in English and in French (Banfield).[12] These sentences can be generally characterized as sentences in the "free indirect style" (*style indirect libre*, as Charles Bally named it in 1912, even if the term has since taken on a broader meaning, with varied definitions and fields of application) or the "free indirect style in the third person and the past tense." A clearer and perhaps more useful description from the point of view that concerns us here would be "sentences that represent third-person subjectivity," for example, those that contain an exclamation attributed to the referent of a third-person pronoun. The linguistic tests proposed by Kuroda and Banfield show that no supposedly implicit *I* can be made explicit without changing the meaning of the sentence, the meaning of the sentences in question being tied to this very particular representation of third-person subjectivity.

The focus on explicit linguistic features, as well as the need for tests, is found again in the development of argument 5.3, "The hypothesis of the omniscient narrator is an ad hoc hypothesis." We can again quote Kuroda:

The omniscient narrator cannot be identified by a linguistic mechanism whose existence we can establish independently of the assumption of his existence in the way the narrator in the reportive style can. The omniscient narrator has no linguistic basis in the way that the narrator in the reportive style does. ([1973] 2014, 56)[13]

I return now to argument 5.2, "There are noncommunicational uses of language." Contrary to what Zipfel would have us believe when referring to "a mode of presentation that is completely different from fictional homodiegetic narration as well as from factual narration," third-person fictional narrative is not the only place we find a noncommunicational use of language. Noam Chomsky had already given the example of soliloquy ("communication with oneself, that is, thinking in words," 1975, 57), an example alluded to by Banfield ([1983] 2019, 66) and taken up by Kuroda ([1979] 2014 and [1980] 2014). Kuroda adds legislative texts ("legal decrees") and "the 'magical' use of language in primitive rituals" ([1979] 2014, 117). The idea is that language use can have other goals apart from a communicational one, and apart from the imitation of the communicational goal in the narration of fictional narrative.[14]

I will add a last point concerning the linguistic arguments: Banfield's theory notably gives a place to the notion of "authorial intrusion" in third-person fictional narrative: "A text may have occasional sentences in the first-person—so-called 'authorial intrusions'—without all sentences being ascribed to this narrator" ([2005] 2010, 396). The terminology used fits with the fact that any appearance of the "I" of the author or of a "here and now" referring to the time and place of his or her activity is experienced as a sudden and unexpected intervention, or one that breaks with the general regime of the text (precisely what we call an "intrusion").[15] Under these conditions, Zipfel's presentation of the linguistic argument—"fictional heterodiegetic narration is considered as a mode of presentation that is completely different from fictional homodiegetic narration as well as from factual narration and is described as a noncommunicative use of language"—reads as so lacking in nuance that it becomes flatly false.

Robert Kawashima's chapter in this volume rests on linguistic arguments that come directly from the work of Kuroda and Banfield.

Argument 6 is a more recent one: "The language-based, or rather, speech-act-based, approach to narrative . . . can account for only a sub-category of fictional narratives." It is deduced from Marie-Laure Ryan's propositions (see especially 2005, 2, and 2006, 4–5). Ryan refuses the reduction of narrative to verbal narrative (encoded in language in the narrow sense of the term), arguing from the empirical existence of numerous other forms of narrative: visual or audiovisual, musical, and so on. She also rejects the solution adopted by certain theorists of postulating the existence of a "cinematic narrator" (or a "dramatic narrator," a "comic-strip narrator," and so on), which she considers to be an ad hoc solution. She proposes a definition of narrative as a form of cognitive construction: "narrative is a certain type of mental image, or cognitive template which can be isolated from the stimuli that trigger its construction" (Ryan 2005, 4). According to her, the cognitive template that is constitutive of narrative is defined by the following features or conditions:

- narrative must be about a world populated by individuated existents;
- this world must be situated in time and undergo significant transformations, caused by nonhabitual physical events;
- some of the participants in the events must be intelligent agents, having a mental life and reacting emotionally to the states of the world; some of the events must be actions performed by these agents;
- the events must be part of a unified causal chain, leading to a closure (adapted from Ryan 2005, 4, and 2006, 8).

We can nevertheless see a contradiction in Ryan's transmedial theory, one that, as we shall see, is removed in Jan-Noël Thon's version. According to Ryan, the language-based, or rather, speech-act-based, approach to narrative is able to account for all verbal narratives apart from dramatic texts (see 2004a, 13; 2005, 11; 2006, 13; 2014a, 471; 2014b, 37–39, 46). When the verbal narrative is a fictional narrative, the act of the real narrator (the author) is duplicated by that of a fictional narrator, situated in the same fictional world as the characters. It is he or she who is supposed to satisfy the felicity conditions for the speech acts corresponding to the sentences of the text (see especially Ryan [2009] 2014a, 471). This proposition is false and contrary to the theory it is based on: John

Searle's theory of fictional discourse.[16] On the other hand, it can be considered as unnecessary from the perspective of the cognitive definition of narrative given above.

Ryan clearly adopts the position of film theorists such as David Bordwell (1985 and 2008), Paisley Livingston ([2001] 2013), Berys Gaut (2004), and Katherine Thomson-Jones (2007 and 2009), for whom the cinematic narrator is an ad hoc construction. The cinematic narrator, Ryan writes, was "postulated for purely formal reasons" by film theorists who were adherents of structuralism; it has no "imaginative reality for the spectator" (2004b, 196); "when we watch a fiction film . . . , the medium disappears from our mind; it is not part of our game of make-believe that somebody filmed the events" (2010, 18). But Ryan herself offers a description of what she calls "the impersonal narrator" in verbal fictional narratives that is vulnerable to all the objections made against the theory of the cinematic narrator:

> I would locate such narrators at the edge of the outer storyworld: they belong to this world logically because they situate themselves in this world by presenting it as "the real world," but they do not belong to it corporally because they are not individuated members of its population. (2014b, 38)

A footnote adds:

> Scholars who have denied the presence of a narrator in this case include Ann Banfield, Richard Walsh, and Henrik Skov Nielsen. I personally favor a compromise that makes the impersonal extradiegetic narrator a purely logical placeholder whose purpose is to relieve the author of the responsibility for the textual speech acts. (46n10)

Here we find the same weaknesses and dysfunctions that are pointed out in the theory of the cinematic narrator: the impersonal narrator is postulated for purely theoretical reasons by Ryan, who adheres to a revised version of Searle's theory of fictional discourse; it has no imaginative reality for the ordinary reader. Searle's theory does not require the hypothesis of an impersonal narrator, since there is already the pretense hypothesis, which relieves the author of having to conform to the constitutive rules of textual speech acts, especially the rule of sincerity. There are, moreover, other theories of fictional discourse in which it is not necessary to relieve the author of the responsibility for the textual statements (see Wolterstorff 1980; Pettersson 1990; Walsh 2007; Köppe and Stühring 2011; Gammelgaard et al., forthcoming).

Another version of the transmedial narratology argument, which eliminates the contradictions of Ryan's theory, can be found in Thon (2014 and 2016). Thon shares with film theorists the idea that "any narrator we might want to describe as a representational strategy of narrative works across media (not just film) will have to be 'perceivable' by or, rather, 'comprehensible' to, the recipients of that work (not just certain critics who may be heavily invested in 'perceiving' it due to their previous theoretical commitments)" (2016, 130). Thon proposes to define narrators as "narrating characters" to whom recipients may attribute the kind of narratorial representation that prototypically takes the form of verbal narration, whether in films, in comics, or in video games. He argues that this narratorial representation can be distinguished from "non-narratorial representation," which classically takes the form of audiovisual representation in films, verbal-pictorial representation in comics, or interactive representation in video games, and which is usually attributed not to narrators but to authors, who can be singular or collective. He relies on examples showing different strategies of narratorial representation in contemporary films, comics, and video games (165 and 167–220).

We can deduce from the work of Ryan and Thon that neither the definition of narrative nor the selection of the elements and the presentation of the story, for example, in terms of the order of events, necessitates the presence of a fictional narrator, whether in verbal or in multimodal fictional narratives.

Kai Mikkonen's chapter in this volume is based explicitly on a transmedial method (comparison) and transmedial arguments. Livingston's represents the point of view of film theory, which seems indispensable today to any discussion of narration in narrative fiction.

I will move now to a third set of arguments, which I have called, following Zipfel, the *theory of fiction arguments*. Argument 7.1 concerns the untenable or at least largely insufficient nature of the arguments advanced in favor of pan-narrator theory. It is presented in numerous articles: Gaut (2004); Kania (2005); Thomson-Jones (2007 and 2009); Davies (2010); and Köppe and Stühring (2011). Zipfel responds to it in his article of 2015.

The first argument advanced in favor of pan-narrator theory is the *analytic argument,* presented in Gaut and in Thomson-Jones as the "a priori argument." Even though it is formulated in different ways by different theorists, the structure of the analytic argument remains globally the same:

- Narration is an activity (an "activity of telling or showing a story," according to Thomson-Jones;[17] "speech acts," according to Tilmann Köppe and Jan Stühring);
- every activity implies an agent ("someone who utters them," according to Köppe and Stühring);
- therefore, narration implies an agent ("the utterer," according to Köppe and Stühring). It is this agent who is called the narrator in pan-narrator theory.

For Gaut, Kania, Thomson-Jones, Davies, and Köppe and Stühring, the analytic argument does not prove what it is supposed to prove, namely the existence of a fictional narrator in all fictional narratives. What it establishes is the existence, in all narratives, of a narrative agent who may be called a narrator but who is none other than the author. It says nothing, however, as to the ontological status of the narrator or, shall we say, of the second narrator in the case of fictional narratives. The conclusion that all narration implies a narrator does not necessarily lead to the conclusion that all fictional narration implies a fictional narrator. Put simply, "the a priori argument if successful proves the necessity of an actual author, not of a narrator" (Gaut 2004, 236).

A second argument advanced in favor of pan-narrator theory is the *ontological-gap argument.* It is presented under this name, but with slightly different content, in Kania, Davies, and Köppe and Stühring. Thomson-Jones, for her part, uses the expression "argument from means of access," which must be considered as synonymous with Kania's ontological-gap argument. The argument rests on two premises:

- It is reasonable to expect an explanation of how films or literary narratives are able to give us access, perceptually in the case of film, linguistically in the case of literary narrative, to information concerning fictional worlds (for brevity's sake, to fictional worlds). The obvious answer is that somebody gives us access to these fictional worlds;

- only fictional individuals can have access to fictional worlds and thus provide this access to other individuals.

The conclusion is that only a fictional person, the narrator, who, this time, is clearly characterized as fictional, can give us access to the fictional world of the film or of the literary narrative.

The ontological-gap argument is vulnerable to several criticisms. In Kania, Thomson-Jones, Davies, and Köppe and Stühring, two main ones can be identified. The first concerns the arguable nature of the first premise. Is it really reasonable to ask ourselves how films or literary narratives are able to give us access to fictional worlds? Kania draws firstly on George Wilson to remind us that there may be paradoxes or incoherencies at the very heart of fictional works; narratives where the narrator is a dead character come to mind (Wilson 1997, 309). He adds that it is more commonly indeterminate whether the narrator is supposed to be thinking the words we are reading, speaking them aloud, or has written them down, and in any case how we are supposed to have obtained a transcription or copy? The other main criticism of the ontological-gap argument is that postulating a fictional narrator does not resolve the problem of our access to the fictional world. The second premise suggests that a real person (the filmmaker, the author of the literary narrative) cannot have access to a fictional world, because he or she is situated on an ontological level different from that of the characters and events of this world. At the same time, the fictional narrator is on an ontologically different level from the one we occupy as readers, who are real people. We are thus still faced with the same problem: that of understanding how the narrator is supposed to bridge the gap between the real world and the fictional world of the film or the literary narrative in order to provide us with access to the fictional world.

One of the aims of Zipfel's article is to show that some of the refutations of the arguments for pan-narrator theory, especially in Köppe and Stühring, are not conclusive. We can quote, for example,

a sentence like "Of course it is perfectly possible for a non-fictional narrator to narrate a fictional narrative" [Köppe and Stühring 2011,

64] is not self-evident at all. In fact, when we say that a non-fictional narrator narrates a fictional narrative the meaning of the term "narrative" shifts because in this understanding the felicity conditions of narrative have changed. . . . Also the claim that "every fictional narrative is authored by some non-fictional narrator" becomes questionable. Of course it is sensible to say that every fictional narrative has an author, but it is not self-evident to say that the author of a fictional narrative is its narrator. In my opinion, to claim that the author of a letter, novel, or poem is its "narrator in the proper sense" because he is the person "whose intentions have to be understood if we are to understand what is being communicated to us" [Currie 2010, 66] is only one way of looking at things. (Zipfel 2015, 56)

This is an interesting thought. It might be asked, however, whether the divergences between Köppe and Stühring on the one hand and Zipfel on the other really concern essential points of the theory of fiction or simply the words used in the theory or theories. According to Zipfel, it is inaccurate to refer to the author of a fictional narrative as its narrator.[18]

Argument 7.2 posits that the fictional narrator of pan-narrator theory is an inconsistent construction. It can take a variety of forms:

- The adjective "fictional" is used in two different senses when we refer to the narrator of the first-person fictional narrative, who belongs to the same fictional world as the other characters, and when we refer to the narrator of the third-person fictional narrative, who is fictional only by presupposition, moreover by an undemonstrated presupposition. While the first narrator is undoubtedly fictional, the second one might more legitimately be termed "postulated" (by the theory and its theorists) or simply "theoretical" (see Patron 2010, 259–61; 2012, §2).
- Whereas the narrator of the first-person fictional narrative belongs to the same fictional world as the other characters, the narrator of the third-person fictional narrative belongs to "an imaginary space of narration." This narrator is imaginary, according to John Brenkman's formulations ([2000] 2005, 414–5), "in the simple sense that he does not 'exist,' either on the plane of reality of the story or that of the book," "no such space of witness ex-

ists within or outside the story world." This idea is also found in Kania, in relation to Alward's "nonactual nonfictional narrator": "there is no reason to suppose that there are some nonactual beings 'out there' somewhere who are epistemically related to fictional worlds the way we are epistemically related to possible worlds" (2007, 407), and in Zipfel (2015, 57), as we have seen ("I must admit that I do not know what to make of this third realm," and so on). This also applies to Ryan's "impersonal narrator."

- We can also invoke the notion of fictional truth: "within the category of fictional narration, we may distinguish between works in regard to which it is and is not fictionally true that the story is told or presented by a narrator" (Livingston [2001] 2013, 363). Kendall Walton also points out that the term "omniscient narrator" is misleading, "for it is not usually fictional that the narrator is omniscient—nor that he is perfectly honest or godlike or telepathic or clairvoyant or disincarnated or supernatural" (1990, 360).

Another version of argument 7.2 stresses the internal contradictions involved in positing a fictional narrator in the third-person fictional narrative:

The function of the narrator is to allow the narrative to be read as something known rather than something imagined, something reported as fact rather than something told as fiction. . . . But such a view of the matter suffers the embarrassment that some of the things such an extradiegetic heterodiegetic narrator is required to "know" are clear indices of the narrative's fictional status, and so they contradict this rationale for positing such an agent. (Walsh [1997] 2007, 73)

Argument 8.1, closely linked to the previous ones, posits that the application of pan-narrator theory to the study of some fictional narratives generates "strange interpretations,"[19] or interpretations that ordinary competent readers would consider to be forced, erroneous, nonsensical, irrelevant, and sometimes even contradictory to the work under consideration. Strange interpretations appear, for example, when questions posed from the internal perspective on the fictional narrative are substituted for questions that can only be satisfactorily answered from the external perspective. The most obvious example is that of questions concerning the omniscient narrator:

> The omniscient narrator is presumably a human being (the fictional teller is not usually an extraterrestrial or God). How could a mere human being gain access to all this knowledge, often the most intimate thoughts of people which they do not tell to anyone else? Or consider a novel about someone who dies alone, and we read of their dying thoughts; how could the narrator know such things? Clearly, a whole array of silly questions threatens; and a similar argument to that rehearsed against ascribing cinematic narrators should apply to show that implicit narrators are far less common in literature than one might suppose. (Gaut 2004, 247)[20]

We can also use the example of the reverse case, the "reticent" narrator. Thus Jonathan Culler writes in relation to Ernest Hemingway's "The Killers,"

> the critic finds herself obliged to explain why the omniscient narrator declines to tell us all the relevant things he must know—including the real names and full past histories of Al and Max. Imagining motivations for this refusal yields strange contortions, because such choices are properly explained as choices made by the author for artistic reasons. . . . The presumption of omniscience gives us, instead of Hemingway deciding whether to invent pasts for Al and Max, a scenario of an imagined narrator knowing all about them and deciding whether to reveal their pasts. The artistic choices are obfuscated by being transformed into decisions of an imagined narrator. (Culler [2004] 2006, 188)

It is appropriate to mention here the work of Greger Andersson, Per Klingberg, Tommy Sandberg, Lars-Åke Skalin, and Sten Wistrand, together sometimes called the "Örebro School," who have been notable in their efforts to promote and valorize the artistic work of the author, which is obfuscated if not completely obliterated in several versions of contemporary narratology (pan-narrator narratology, "natural narratology," "prototype narratology").

The chapters by Andersson and Skalin in this volume constitute a representative sample of the work of the Örebro School.

I also borrow from Andersson and Sandberg the following corollary argument, 8.2: "Narratologists present relevant and often excellent interpretations of fictional narratives, but this is because they do not apply their theory in a strict way" (adapted from Andersson and Sandberg 2018, 242). Andersson and Sandberg rely on examples from the major representatives of contemporary narratology, such as Liesbeth Korthals Altes and James Phelan. What Andersson and Sandberg call the "sameness theory" (an abbreviation for the theory of the sameness between fictional and nonfictional narratives) encompasses what we are here calling pan-narrator theory (see, for example, Andersson and Sandberg 2018, 246, 251–52; 2019, 379; Andersson, Klingberg, and Sandberg 2019, 13). Their suggestion that it would be better to rework the theory commonly adopted by narratologists so that the theoretical assertions are congruent with the analytical and interpretive practices is also valid for pan-narrator theory.

Arguments of a Historical Kind

Argument 9 stresses the misalignment between pan-narrator theory, which is a recent theory—indeed very recent on the scale of literary history—and the theory available at the time to the authors of fictional narratives, as well as to their first readers and critics. Vincenz Pieper and Brian Boyd express the same doubts in relation to Goethe's *Elective Affinities* in the first respect, and to Jane Austen's *Emma* in the second:

> Ignace Feuerlicht is right to point out that a fictional narrator, as some of the critics have described him, would have been noticed by Goethe's contemporaries. But the evidence suggests that they did not distinguish the narrator, who speaks and relates the narrative, from the author who created the work. For Böttinger, Abeken, Solger, and Conz amongst others, the story is narrated by the *poet* in his own person. Friedrich Spielhagen and Walter Benjamin, too, refer only to the poet and his characters. This is quite remarkable: Stöcklein, Barnes, Pascal, Blackall, Martínez, and others, claim to find something in the novel that none of these previous readers suspected to be there. Has narratology provided, as it is sometimes supposed to have done, a set of tools enabling critics to discover what previous-

ly escaped even some of the most attentive and well-informed readers? (Pieper 2015, 86)

The very idea of a narrator as anything other than a character had not been voiced in Austen's time, and the idea of a necessary non-authorial narrator in fictions without character-narrators did not become widespread until the 1960s and 1970s. Perhaps Austen was naively unaware of what she was doing, and so were her readers, until the last fifty years when a small minority was given the technical sophistication to see that neither Austen nor her other readers knew how fiction works. But I doubt it. (Boyd 2017, 291)

That pan-narrator theory is an anachronistic theory, ill-suited to the study of some fictional narratives has been amply demonstrated by A. C. Spearing's work on English medieval narratives and Marc Hersant's work on the narratives of the French classical period. For reasons of space, I must limit myself to a few remarks and quotations. I will take from Spearing the definition of pan-narrator theory as "the product of a body of academic thought about narrative that has developed over the last century and more, but especially over the last sixty years—thought based not on narrative in general but on post-1700 Western narratives in prose" (2015, 59). He counters it with his own interest in medieval narratives, adding that "in a recent book [he] argued that modern interpretation of them is often distorted by uncritical acceptance of the narrator concept as it appears in current narrative theory" (59; the book he refers to is Spearing 2012). From Hersant I will take the remark that "communicational theories, as is the case in Genette, tend to minimize . . . or even completely neutralize [the] opposition [between first-and third-person narratives]. Yet, in the organization of fictional genres in the seventeenth and eighteenth centuries, this is a distinction of primary importance." He adds that by contrast, some elements of Hamburger's theory, in particular the concept of feigning in first-person fictional narrative, "greatly illuminate . . . the prefatory metadiscourses of eighteenth-century novels and the topos of the found manuscript" (Hersant and Ramond 2015, 10; translation by M.M.).

The chapters by Spearing and Hersant in this volume, which continue these authors' previous work, represent the contribution of literary history to the debate between optional-narrator theory and pan-narrator theory.

All of the arguments presented up to this point are united in saying that pan-narrator theory is not the universal theory of narrative or fictional narrative that it claims to be but only a theory of a subcategory of fictional narratives. In other words, the operation and justification of pan-narrator theory appear very coherent and appropriate in the case of first-person narrative, and possibly of fictional narratives, such as Robbe-Grillet's *Jealousy*, that could plausibly be assimilated to this model. On the other hand, pan-narrator theory fails to account for fictional narratives that do not conform to this model, whether linguistically, ontologically, or from the point of view of the reader's experience. The arguments grouped under "10" offer an explanation of this fact, an explanation borrowed from the history and epistemology of literary theories.

Argument 10.1 posits that pan-narrator theory is itself a historical construction among other theories of fictional narration. "Historical" here is opposed to "natural"—there is nothing "natural," that is, spontaneous, intuitive, or unquestionable, about pan-narrator theory. There have been other theories of fictional narration, older than and different from pan-narrator theory.[21] As we have seen previously, it does not seem obvious that their representatives were wrong and the proponents of current pan-narrator theory right.

Argument 10.2 points out that two concepts of the narrator are at the origin of the modern concept of the narrator in pan-narrator theory. I will briefly repeat here the propositions I have already detailed in the introduction of my work on the narrator (Patron [2009] 2016) and in other books and articles (2015 and 2019; Patron in Gammelgaard et al., forthcoming), which appear again in my contribution to this volume. There is a first concept of the narrator that was introduced to account for the distinctive character of memoir-novels or first-person novels in the original sense of the term (I call this "the original concept of the narrator"), and a new concept of the narrator that comes from the German controversy over authorial intrusions at the end of the nineteenth century. The two concepts encapsulate very different issues or sets of issues, which is what allows us to speak of two different concepts. The original concept of the narrator goes hand in hand with a dualist or differentialist conception of fictional narrative, which considers first-person fictional narrative to be a specific case of fictional narrative. The new concept of the narrator, however, goes hand in hand with a monist conception of fictional narrative, which does not see any fundamental difference between first- and third-person fictional narratives or, in other words, which makes the effective, empirical difference between first- and third-person fictional narratives a secondary consideration.

We can represent the difference between the two concepts by saying that the first is an empirical concept: it is the result of observations and historical and critical data. The second, on the other hand, is a theoretical concept: it is relevant only within a determinate theoretical framework. In the case of Friedemann, it is a matter of defining the epic narrative in opposition to drama. In the case of Barthes, it is a matter of promoting an "immanent" approach to narrative. In the case of Genette, it is a matter of defining fictional narrative in opposition to nonfictional narrative, and so on.

Another way of representing this difference is to say that the first concept refers to the narrator as a creation of the author and that the second, on the other hand, is a purely theoretical creation, or a creation of theory. We find the same idea, expressed almost in the same terms, in Spearing:

> It would be generally and rightly agreed that the appropriate approach to novels ranging from, say, Ford Madox Ford's *The Good Soldier* to Kazuo Ishiguro's *The Remains of the Day* is through their narrators. In such cases the "presumed textually projected occupant" of the speech position from which "the narrative discourse originates" is no mere theoretical hypothesis but a literal reality. (2015, 69)[22]

Argument 10.3 posits that the ubiquity of fictional narrators in fictional narratives is not an "empirical discovery" but a "stipulation," (terms borrowed from Pieper 2015, 87). I provide historical evidence of this argument in my contribution to this volume. The argument can be varied or broken down in different ways: the fictionality of the narrator of the third-person fictional narrative is not an empirical discovery but a stipulation; the fact that the narrator of the third-person fictional narrative satisfies the felicity conditions for the speech acts corresponding to the sentences of the text is not an empirical discovery but a stipulation (and, as we have seen, an unwarranted stipulation, at least from Searle's perspective); and the fact that the narrator of the third-person fictional narrative gives us access to the fictional world is not an empirical discovery but a stipulation (and, as we have seen, an unwarranted and problematic stipulation from an ontological perspective).

The Contributions to the Volume

The volume is divided into two major parts: "Optional-Narrator Theory in Literary Studies" and "Optional-Narrator Theory before and beyond Literature." Opening the first part, Jonathan Culler's chapter, "Some Problems concerning Narrators of Novels and Speakers of Poems," develops a parallel between narrative theory and the theory of lyric poetry. In both cases, current theory presumes that the speaker of the text is not the author but a fictional figure whose identity, situation, and motives the reader is asked to reconstruct. But, as Culler shows, lyric poems often lack any signs of a speaker and many of their most salient features—rhythm, rhyme, or other kinds of formal patterns—are necessarily attributed to an author, not to a fictional speaker. In many cases, the hypothesis of a fictional speaker who is responsible for the content but not the form of the discourse adds nothing to the appreciation or understanding of the poem and raises questions that distract readers from the visible features of the text. The case of lyric poetry helps illustrate that there are literary genres, including some in which narrative plays a significant part, that contain good arguments for regarding fictional speakers or narrators as optional. We could speak of a *transgeneric argument*, to be added to the transmedial one.

Brian Boyd's contribution, "Implied Authors and Imposed Narrators—or Actual Authors?," demonstrates the importance of discarding the narrator of pan-narrator theory (the "Imposed Narrator" in his own terminology), firstly because this figure or function is "imposed, unnecessary, confused and confusing to those who discuss narrative" (54–55) but mostly because it obscures the real operation and pleasure of fiction. According to Boyd, when we read, we enjoy not only the fiction but also our imaginative complicity with the author: our attempts to infer the intentions behind each choice. The end of the chapter contains an argument that has not been previously presented, and that could be added to the "interpretation" arguments. I would formulate it as follows: The application of pan-narrator theory to the study of several works by the same author prevents us from properly analyzing the evolution of an author as a storyteller, since it ascribes a different narrator to each narrative, and there is no reason to suppose that the narrator of one narrative is older or more experienced than the narrator of another. This is what Boyd convincingly demonstrates in the case of Leo Tolstoy's *War and Peace* and *Anna Karenina*.

In "Real Authors, Real Narrators, and the Rhetoric of Fiction," Vincenz Pieper sees the poststructuralist approach represented by Barbara Herrnstein Smith as a means of moving beyond structuralism and naïve intentionalism in conceptualizing the relationships among text, author, and reader. He concludes that once the separation between the work itself and the author's writing practice is overcome, there is no longer any reason to retain the rigid assumption of a fictional narrator who is inherent to the work; the introduction of a fictional narrator is just one option among others. This position, in one form or another, and against different theoretical backdrops, is shared by all the contributors to this volume.

In "Voice and Time," a chapter that after twenty years echoes his famous article "On Voice" (2000), John Brenkman addresses the debate between optional-narrator theory and pan-narrator theory from the perspective of novel theory with an analysis of two works published close together in the 1920s: F. Scott Fitzgerald's *The Great Gatsby* and Ernest Hemingway's *The Sun Also Rises*. He reaffirms that "the *writing*-of-the-*telling* is the act and process whose nature, procedures and techniques ought to be the theoretical focus" (91) and highlights the tensions, both productive and antagonistic, between the novel theory and narratology. The concept of voice he advocates at the end of his chapter is deeply different from the voice of any actual or imaginary entity, and is characterized as "anonymous" and "novelistic, literary, aesthetic" (105).

I will not dwell on my own contribution, which has already been mentioned, where pan-narrator theory and optional-narrator theory are placed within the broader framework of the history and epistemology of literary theory.

The next section contains two chapters by Biblical scholars. In "Biblical Narrative and the Death of the Narrator," Robert Kawashima argues for the optional-narrator theory, basing his argument on the tense system governing Classical Biblical Hebrew prose narrative (Genesis to Kings). He shows that various syntactic features distinguish the registers of *histoire* (narration) and *discours* (discourse, speech) in Émile Benveniste's sense, a distinction also indicated by the distribution of tense forms, deictics, and expressive constructions, not to mention constraints on word order. All of these factors argue against the intervention of a narrator. In other words, Classical Biblical Hebrew narration should not be conceived of as transcribed speech. Kawashima then addresses the diachronic dimension of the typology of narratives with and without a narrator, understood as a speaker. In his powerful formulation, "First comes the archaic singer or rhapsode of ancient Near Eastern epics, e.g., *Gilgamesh*. Next, we find the Classical Biblical Hebrew author of biblical prose narrative. . . . The advent of the prose writer in ancient Israel signals the death of the epic narrator" (145–46). In the next chapter, Greger Andersson also discusses pan-narrator theory from the perspective of Biblical studies but concentrates less on linguistic aspects than on the interpretation of certain Biblical narratives in both Old and New Testaments. His central claim is that in spite of certain similarities, narratives can belong to different pragmatic frameworks and hence concepts like the narrator, omniscience, and so on take on different meanings in different contexts. The demonstration is based on the parable of the Good Samaritan, several examples from the books of Samuel and Nehemiah, and from Genesis. The results challenge the universality of narratology, the common distinction between fact and fiction, and the application of narratological concepts in the study of texts.

In the next section, devoted to literary history, A. C. Spearing continues his work on narrator theory and medieval English narratives. He reminds us that the purportedly universal theory proposed under current narratology, which regards the narrator as necessary to narrative, is largely derived from post-1700 Western prose narratives, many of which do have narrators characterized as distinct from their authors. Most medieval narratives do not, however, have such narrators. Freestanding first-person narratives are rare in English before the middle of the fourteenth century, and for non-first-person narratives the narrator/author opposition is generally inoperative because the stories told are not original inventions but have the authority of what already exists; the re-tellers of these stories are not potentially unreliable narrators but the poets themselves. Spearing discusses in depth two medieval English verse narratives for which the current concept of the narrator is irrelevant or distorting, or both: *King Horn* (anonymous), and Geoffrey Chaucer's *Book of the Duchess*. In the next chapter, Marc Hersant examines two narratives by the Marquis de Sade, *The Mystified Magistrate* and *The Misfortunes of Virtue* (the first version, from 1787), to show that Sadean fiction is the perfect illustration of a creation by an author who reigns alone over his narrations and produces his fictions without any mediation. The author who is solely responsible for the third-person narration that frames Justine's narrative in *The Misfortunes of Virtue*, for example, is also solely responsible for the narrative statements he attributes to his character, and finally solely responsible for the "enunciative gaps" that continually emphasize the artificiality and structural fragility of this voice.

Opening the second part, Mary Galbraith's contribution, "Silent Self and the Deictic Imaginary: Hamburger's Radical Insight," argues in support of optional-narrator theory by way of contemporary theories of the evolution of human consciousness and language, which find that on both a historical level and an existential one, nonverbal invention is prior to language and continuously present in human thought and communication. This accords with the ancient notion of mimesis as a unique human skill emerging in early childhood and giving rise to art. Galbraith argues that the representation of nonverbal childhood experience in literary narrative is inventive, mimetic, and ekphrastic: it is "a verbal *ekphrasis* of felt sense, [a] verbalization that emerges from direct reference to nonverbal phenomena" (208). The most critically acclaimed representations of childhood experience are those that foreground the experiential primacy and creativity of the figure of the child, as in two passages that Galbraith examines closely: one from "The Little Match Girl" and the other from "The Girl Who Trod on a Loaf," both by Hans Christian Andersen. Language in this form of narration is the mode of being of the fiction but not part of its fictional world. This conclusion is consistent with the notions of nonreportive style (Kuroda), the representation of nonreflective consciousness (Banfield), and the contention that fictional narration is a mimesis of creation rather than a mimesis of a reality statement (Hamburger).

In "Aesthetic Theory Meets Optional-Narrator Theory," Lars-Åke Skalin discusses the concept of the narrator in literary fiction from the point of view of an "artistic/aesthetic" theory and in dialogue with Hamburger's logic of literature. In Skalin's view, the artistic/aesthetic meaning of an artwork comes less from the events it represents, considered as a kind of information given by a narrator to a narratee, than from its interactional play with the audience. Looking at Hamburger's theory, he discusses specifically the thesis of the "absolute boundary" between first- and third-person narratives (only the latter of which pertains to "pure fiction"), drawing on examples from Joseph Conrad's *Heart of Darkness*.

In "The Vanishing Narrator Meets the Fundamental Narrator: On the Literary Historical and Transmedial Limitations of the Narrator Concept," Kai Mikkonen discusses the optional-narrator theory in the context of transmedial narratology and adaptation. More specifically, he explores the question of the narrator in Alphonse Daudet's *Tartarin de Tarascon* and in two contemporary modern French-language comic book adaptations of this novel. By comparing the choices of their narrative strategies and the various implications of narrative agency in these works, he examines the relevance or irrelevance of the concept of the narrator in the comic-book medium. Ultimately, the point of this comparison is to consider some of the general principles that apply to both the literary historical and the transmedial arguments for the optional-narrator theory.

The last chapter of the volume, "A Paradox of Cinematic Narration," by Paisley Livingston, belongs to the field of film theory and, more specifically, the philosophy of film. Livingston takes as his point of departure three incompatible propositions: "(1) Some cinematic works are narration; (2) A work is a narration only if it has one or more narrators; (3) Some of the cinematic works that are narrations have no narrator" (259). And he proposes to resolve the paradox by disambiguating the term "narrator." The result is a reaffirmation of the optional-narrator position. Livingston's chapter also includes a useful summary of the controversy surrounding the narrator in film studies and a careful analysis of the arguments pro and con.

Despite the different theoretical orientations of these scholars and the range of domains from which their narrative examples are taken, all of the contributors to this volume share the view that pan-narrator theory can no longer be accepted as something that goes without saying, and that henceforth students of narrative must take seriously whether to posit a narrator for the works they are analyzing. On a purely theoretical level, these contributors venture to think that with this volume, the burden of proof, which has rested with the pan-narrator theorists since the first formulations of pan-narrator theory, has perhaps become a little heavier.

Translated by Melissa McMahon with
the collaboration of Sylvie Patron

Notes

1. I understand the term "narratology" here as referring to the narratology inspired by structuralism, as well as Franz Stanzel's later theory ([1979] 1984), which seems to approach it.
2. The adjective "fictive" here has the sense of "fictional." In other words, it refers to not only the fact that the narrator does not exist in the real world of reference but also the fact that it exists in an alternative world or a "here and now" constructed by a text.
3. "What Is a Narrator?," lecture given at the University of Mannheim in 2015 (personal communication). See also Spearing (2015), in particular pp. 60–61, where the opposition between "argue" and "take for granted" can be found.
4. The first systematic use of this expression is found in Patron ([2009] 2016). It has been disseminated in the English-speaking world in reference to Köppe and Stühring (2011).
5. The first use of this expression is found in Köppe and Stühring (2011). Before that, the same phenomenon was called "narrator theory of narration," which comes from S.-Y. Kuroda ([1976] 2014, 73). See, for example, Spearing (2005; 2015).
6. I could refer to this theory as "narratology," the term here meaning both classical structuralist narratology and the dominant trends in contemporary narrative studies, but to respect the proclaimed multiplicity and diversity of narratology, I prefer to refer to what is criticized in this volume as "pan-narrator theory" or "pan-narrator narratology."
7. To be clear, Zipfel is a representative of pan-narrator theory.
8. For more details, see my contribution to this volume (sections "Gérard Genette's *Coup de Force*" and "Some Historical Errors of Genette's").
9. Zipfel mentions Hamburger and Banfield but not Kuroda.
10. See the general bibliography at the end of this volume.
11. See Alward (2007) and below.
12. I give a detailed example in my contribution to this volume (section "The Denial of Falsification").
13. In the category of narratives in the reportive style, Kuroda includes both first-person fictional narratives, in the historical sense of the term, and fictional narratives that could plausibly be assimilated to this model, that is, fictional narratives with a neutral or effaced narrator, considered to be "reporting" in the way the narrator of the first-person fictional narratives does, for example, in Alain Robbe-Grillet's *Jealousy*.
14. This idea is accepted by many linguists and cognitive scientists. See, for example, Segal (1995, 16–17), who sees himself as the spokesperson for the whole volume (Duchan et al. 1995).

15. On the concept of authorial intrusion, its history, and interpretations of it, see my contribution to this volume (sections "The German Controversy over Author-Intrusions at the End of the Nineteenth Century" and "The Original Narrator and the Neceessary Narrator: An Irresolvable Duality").

16. More precisely, it errs in extending to all fictional narratives the description Searle reserves for first-person narrative, which from Searle's perspective is a misinterpretation (see Patron [2009] 2016, 111–17 and 92n6, where I draw on correspondence with Searle dated 19 December 2007).

17. The couple *telling* and *showing* comes from Percy Lubbock ([1921] 1972), but it is used here in reference to the work of Seymour Chatman to account for the narration respectively in verbal narratives (apart from damatic texts) and in dramas and films.

18. Perhaps this claim should be qualified to say there are theoretical and critical contexts in which it can be accurate (or not as inaccurate, or not important) to refer to the author of a fictional narrative as its narrator, and contexts in which this terminology is inaccurate for the reasons presented by Zipfel and for other reasons that will appear hereafter.

19. I am borrowing this expression from Greger Andersson in "Does an Application of Narratology in the Study of Fiction Generate Strange Interpretations?," a paper presented at the 2016 International Conference on Narrative in Amsterdam. It is taken up again in Andersson and Sandberg (2018, 251). Andersson and Sandberg also use the expression "disquieting interpretations," which is borrowed from Skalin (1991, 303).

20. The notion of "silly questions" is borrowed from Walton (1990, 174–83).

21. For a presentation of some of these theories, see my contribution in this volume (section "The History of the Question of the Narrator and Narrative Enunciation").

22. Quotations are from Margolin (2014).

References

Alward, Peter. 2007. "For the Ubiquity of Nonactual Fact-Telling Narrators." *Journal of Aesthetics and Art Criticism* 65 (4): 401–4.

Andersson, Greger, Per Klingberg, and Tommy Sandberg. 2019. "Introduction: Sameness and Difference in Narratology." *Frontiers of Narrative Studies* 5 (1): 11–16.

Andersson, Greger, and Tommy Sandberg. 2018. "Sameness versus Difference in Narratology: Two Approaches to Narrative Fiction." *Narrative* 26 (3): 241–61.

———. 2019. "A Reply to Mari Hatavara and Matti Hyvärinen." *Narrative* 27 (3): 378–81.

Bal, Mieke. (1978, 1985) 2017. *Narratology: Introduction to the Theory of Narrative*. Toronto: Toronto University Press.

Bally, Charles. (1912) 2018. "Le style indirect libre en français moderne." In *Le Style indirect libre. Naissance d'une catégorie (1894-1914)*, edited by Gilles Philippe and Joël Zufferey, 84–104. Limoges, France: Lambert-Lucas.

Banfield, Ann. (1983) 2019. "Linguistic Competence and Literary Theory." In *Describing the Unobserved and Other Essays: Unspeakable Sentences after "Unspeakable Sentences,"* edited by Sylvie Patron, 35–67. Newcastle upon Tyne, UK: Cambridge Scholars Publishing.

———. (2005) 2010. "No-Narrator Theory." In *Routledge Encyclopedia of Narrative Theory*, edited by David Herman, Manfred Jahn, and Marie-Laure Ryan, 396–97. London: Routledge.

Bareis, J. Alexander. 2020. "The Implied Fictional Narrator." *Journal of Literary Theory* 14(1): 120–38.

Barthes, Roland. (1966) 1975. "An Introduction to the Structural Analysis of Narrative." Translated by Lionel Duisit. *New Literary History* 6 (2): 237–72.

Birke, Dorothee, and Tilmann Köppe. 2015a. "Authors and Narrators: Problems in the Constitution and Interpretation of Fictional Narrative." In Birke and Köppe 2015b, 1–12.

———, eds. 2015b. *Author and Narrator: Transdisciplinary Contributions to a Narratological Debate*. Berlin: De Gruyter.

Bordwell, David. 1985. *Narration in the Fiction Film*. Madison: University of Wisconsin Press.

———. 2008. "Afterword: Narrators, Implied Authors, and Other Superfluities." In *Poetics of Cinema*, 121–33. London: Routledge.

Boyd, Brian. 2017. "Does Austen Need Narrators? Does Anyone?" *New Literary History* 48 (2): 285–308.

Brenkman, John. (2000) 2005. "On Voice." In *Essentials in the Theory of Fiction*, edited by Michael J. Hoffman and Patrick D. Murphy, 411–44. 3rd ed. Durham NC: Duke University Press.

Chatman, Seymour. 1990. *Coming to Terms: The Rhetoric of Narrative in Fiction and Film*. Ithaca NY: Cornell University Press.

Chomsky, Noam. 1975. *Reflections on Language*. New York: Pantheon Books.

Cohn, Dorrit. 1978. *Transparent Minds: Narrative Modes for Presenting Consciousness in Fiction*. Princeton: Princeton University Press.

———. 1999. *The Distinction of Fiction*. Baltimore: Johns Hopkins University Press.

Culler, Jonathan. (2004) 2006. "Omniscience." In *The Literary in Theory*, 183–201. Stanford: Stanford University Press.

Currie, Gregory. 2010. "Authors and Narrators." In *Narratives and Narrators*, 65–85. Oxford: Oxford University Press.

Davies, David. 2010. "Eluding Wilson's 'Elusive Narrators.'" *Philosophical Studies* 147 (3): 387–94.

Gammelgaard, Lasse, Simona Zetterberg Gjerlevsen, Louise Brix Jacobsen, Richard Walsh, James Phelan, Henrik Skov Nielsen, and Stefan Iversen, eds. Forthcoming. *Fictionality in Literature: Core Concepts Revisited*. Columbus: Ohio State University Press.

Gaut, Berys. 2004. "The Philosophy of the Movies: Cinematic Narration." In *The Blackwell Guide to Aesthetics*, edited by Peter Kivy, 230–53. Oxford, UK: Wiley-Blackwell.

Genette, Gérard. (1972) 1980. *Narrative Discourse: An Essay in Method*. Translated by Jane E. Lewin. Ithaca NY: Cornell University Press, 1980.

———. (1983) 1988. *Narrative Discourse Revisited*. Translated by Jane E. Lewin. Ithaca NY: Cornell University Press.

Hamburger, Käte. (1957, 1968) 1973, 1993. *The Logic of Literature*. Translated by Marilynn J. Rose. Bloomington: Indiana University Press.

Hersant, Marc. 2011. "Usages du discours direct chez Voltaire: Discours rapportés et discours créés dans les *Mémoires pour servir à la vie de M. de Voltaire, écrits par lui-même* et *Candide*." In *Histoire, histoires: Nouvelles approches de Saint-Simon et des récits des XVIIe et XVIIIe siècles*, edited by Marc Hersant, Marie-Paule de Weerdt-Pilorge, Catherine Ramond, and François Raviez, 203–20. Arras: Artois Presses Université.

———. 2015. *Voltaire: Écriture et vérité*. Leuven, Belgium: Peeters.

Hersant, Marc, and Catherine Ramond. 2015. "Introduction." In *La Représentation de la vie psychique dans les récits factuels et fictionnels de l'époque classique*, edited by Marc Hersant and Catherine Ramond, 5–18. Leiden, Netherlands: Brill/Rodopi.

Kania, Andrew. 2005. "Against the Ubiquity of Fictional Narrators." *Journal of Aesthetics and Art Criticism* 63 (1): 47–54.

———. 2007. "Against Them, Too: A Reply to Alward." *Journal of Aesthetics and Art Criticism* 65 (4): 404–8.

Köppe, Tilmann, and Jan Stühring. 2011. "Against Pan-Narrator Theories." *Journal of Literary Semantics* 40 (1): 59–80.

Kuroda, S.-Y. (1973) 2014. "Where Epistemology, Style, and Grammar Meet: A Case Study from Japanese." In Kuroda 2014, 38–59.

———. (1976) 2014. "Reflections on the Foundations of Narrative Theory, from a Linguistic Point of View." In Kuroda 2014, 71–101.

———. (1979) 2014. "Some Thoughts on the Foundations of the Theory of Language Use." In Kuroda 2014, 102–18.

———. (1980) 2014. "The Reformulated Theory of Speech Acts: Toward a Theory of Language Use." In Kuroda 2014, 119–32.

———. (1987) 2014. "A Study of the So-Called Topic *wa* in Passages from Tolstoi, Lawrence, and Faulkner (of course, in Japanese translation)." In Kuroda 2014, 133–50.

———. 2014. *Toward a Poetic Theory of Narration: Essays of S.-Y. Kuroda*, edited by Sylvie Patron. Berlin: De Gruyter.

Livingston, Paisley. (2001) 2013. "Narrative." In *The Routledge Companion to Aesthetics*, edited by Berys Gaut and Dominic McIver Lopes, 340–50. 3rd ed. New York: Routledge.

Lubbock, Percy. (1921) 1972. *The Craft of Fiction*. London: Jonathan Cape.

Margolin, Uri. 2014. "Narrator." In *Handbook of Narratology*, edited by Peter Hühn, Jan Christoph Meister, John Pier, and Wolf Schmid, 351–69. Berlin: De Gruyter, 2009. Reprinted in *The Living Handbook of Narratology*. http://www.lhn.uni-hamburg.de/article/narrator.

McHale, Brian. 1983. "Unspeakable Sentences, Unnatural Acts: Linguistics and Poetics Revisited." *Poetics Today* 4 (1): 17–45.

Patron, Sylvie. (2009) 2016. *Le Narrateur: Un problème de théorie narrative*. Limoges, France: Lambert-Lucas.

———. 2010. "The Death of the Narrator and the Interpretation of the Novel: The Example of *Pedro Páramo* by Juan Rulfo." Translated by Susan Nicholls. *Journal of Literary Theory* 4 (2): 253–72.

———. 2012. "Narrative Fiction Prior to 1850: Instances of Refutation for Poetic Theories of Narration?" Translated by Susan Nicholls. *Amsterdam International Electronic Journal for Cultural Narratology* (*AJCN*) 6, *Working with Stories: Selected Papers from the 2nd Conference of the European Narratology Network*. http://cf.hum.uva.nl/narratology/all_sylvie_patron.htm.

———. 2015. *La Mort du narrateur et autres essais*. Limoges, France: Lambert-Lucas.

———. 2019. *The Death of the Narrator and Other Essays*. Trier, Germany: Wissenschaftlicher Verlag Trier.

Pettersson, Anders. 1990. *A Theory of Literary Discourse*. Lund, Sweden: Lund University Press.

Pieper, Vincenz. 2015. "Author and Narrator: Observations on *Die Wahlverwandtschaften*." In Birke and Köppe 2015b, 81–97.

Prince, Gerald. (1982) 2012. *Narratology: The Form and Functioning of Narrative*. Berlin: De Gruyter.

Rimmon-Kenan, Shlomith. (1983) 2002. *Narrative Fiction: Contemporary Poetics*. London: Routledge.

Ryan, Marie-Laure. 2004a. "Introduction." In Ryan 2004c, 1–40.

———. 2004b. "Moving Pictures." In Ryan 2004c, 195–201.

———, ed. 2004c. *Narrative across Media: The Languages of Storytelling*. Lincoln: University of Nebraska Press.

———. 2005. "On the Theoretical Foundations of Transmedial Narratology." In *Narratology beyond Literary Criticism: Mediality, Disciplinarity*, edited by Jan Christoph Meister, 1–23. Berlin: De Gruyter.

———. 2006. *Avatars of Story*. Minneapolis: University of Minnesota Press, 2006.

———. 2010. "Fiction, Cognition, and Non-Verbal Media." In *Intermediality and Storytelling*, edited by Marina Grishakova and Marie-Laure Ryan, 8–26. Berlin: De Gruyter.

———. (2009) 2014a. "Narration in Various Media." In *Handbook of Narratology*, edited by Peter Hühn, John Pier, Wolf Schmid, and Jörg Schönert, 2nd ed., 1: 468–88. Berlin: De Gruyter. Reprinted in *The Living Handbook of Narratology*, https://www.lhn.uni-hamburg.de/node/53.html.

———. 2014b. "Story/Worlds/Media: Tuning the Instruments of a Media-Conscious Narratology." In *Storyworlds across Media: Toward a Media-Conscious Narratology*, edited by Marie-Laure Ryan and Jan-Noël Thon, 25–49. Lincoln: University of Nebraska Press.

Searle, John R. (1975) 1979. "The Logical Status of Fictional Discourse." In *Expression and Meaning: Studies in the Theory of Speech Acts*, 58–75. Cambridge: Cambridge University Press.

Segal, Erwin M. 1995. "Narrative Comprehension and the Role of Deictic Shift Theory." In *Deixis in Narrative: A Cognitive Science Perspective*, edited by Judith F. Duchan, Gail A. Bruder, and Lynne E. Hewitt, 3–17. Hillsdale NJ: Lawrence Erlbaum Associates.

Skalin, Lars-Åke. 1991. "Den vådlige seglatsen: *I havsbandets inledande episode*." In *Karaktär och perspektiv: Att tolka litterära gestalter i det mimetiska språkspelet*, Acta universitatis upsaliensis, Historia litterarum 17: 259–71 (summary in English, 303–9). Stockholm: Almqvist and Wiksell International.

Spearing, A. C. 2005. *Textual Subjectivity: The Encoding of Subjectivity in Medieval Narratives and Lyrics*. Oxford: Oxford University Press.

———. 2012. *Medieval Autographies: The "I" of the Text*. Notre Dame IN: University of Notre Dame Press.

———. 2015. "What Is a Narrator? Narrator Theory and Medieval Narratives." *Digital Philology* 4 (1): 59–105.

Stanzel, Franz K. (1979) 1984. *A Theory of Narrative*. Translated by Charlotte Goedsche. Cambridge: Cambridge University Press.

Thomson-Jones, Katherine. 2007. "The Literary Origins of the Cinematic Narrator." *British Journal of Aesthetics* 47 (1): 76–94.

———. 2009. "Cinematic Narrators." *Philosophy Compass* 4 (2): 296–311.

Thon, Jan-Noël. 2014. "Toward a Transmedial Narratology: On Narrators in Contemporary Graphic Novels, Feature Films, and Computer Games." In *Beyond Classical Narration: Transmedial and Unnatural Challenges*, edited by Jan Alber and Per Krogh Hansen, 25–56. Berlin: De Gruyter.

———. 2016. *Transmedial Narratology and Contemporary Media Culture*. Lincoln: University of Nebraska Press.

Walsh, Richard. (1997) 2007. "The Narrator and the Frame of Fiction." In *The Rhetoric of Fictionality: Narrative Theory and the Idea of Fiction*, 69–85. Columbus: Ohio State University Press.

———. 2007. *The Rhetoric of Fictionality: Narrative Theory and the Idea of Fiction*. Columbus: Ohio State University Press.

Walton, Kendall L. 1990. *Mimesis as Make-Believe: On the Foundations of the Representational Arts*. Cambridge MA: Harvard University Press.

Wilson, George W. 1997. "*Le Grand Imagier* Steps Out: The Primitive Basis of Film Narration." *Philosophical Topics* 25 (1): 295–318.

Wolff Lundholt, Marianne. 2008. *Telling without Tellers: The Linguistic Manifestation of Literary Communication in Narrative Fiction*. Copenhagen: Medusa.

Wolterstorff, Nicholas. 1980. *Works and Worlds of Art*. Oxford, UK: Clarendon Press.

Zipfel, Frank. 2015. "Narratorless Narration? Some Reflections on the Arguments for and against the Ubiquity of Narrators in Fictional Narration." In Birke and Köppe 2015b, 45–80.

PART 1 *Optional-Narrator Theory in Literary Studies*

1 Some Problems concerning Narrators of Novels and Speakers of Poems

JONATHAN CULLER

That every narrative has a narrator, explicit or implicit, separate from the author, has become an article of faith for narratology and even novel theory, and identifying narrators and their point of view has become a staple of literary education. In the case of poetry, we find a situation that seems analogous. Ever since the New Criticism, it has become widely accepted, in the Anglophone world at least, that every poem has a speaker other than the poet, and pedagogical handbooks tell students that the first question to ask when approaching a poem is who is speaking in what situation and to what end. Both of these theoretical assumptions, or methodological stipulations (I am inclined to call them articles of faith) seem to me contestable as general principles. That is to say, while there are definitely narratives with narrators and poems with speakers, it is scarcely evident that we must accept that every narrative necessarily has a narrator or that every poem has a speaker. But while I contest each of these principles or stipulations on its own, I am also interested in the relationship between these two cases, these two frameworks. What do they share and how do they differ? Do the two cases illuminate one another? Let me take up first the question of the narrator in prose fiction.

As Sylvie Patron has shown, the idea of a narrator distinct from the author seems to have been introduced at the beginning of the nineteenth century by Anna Laetitia Barbauld to describe first-person narratives where the narrating *character* is different from the author: for example, *Tristram Shandy* and *Moll Flanders* (Patron [2009] 2016, 15–18, 285–87; 2015, 13; 2019a, 4). In Barbauld's scheme, what we today call third-person narration is conceived as related or presented by the author, but the author can also create what she calls "an imaginary nar-

37

rator," a character, to recount his or her own story (Barbauld 1804, xxiv). The assumption that third-person narratives also have a narrator, and that in fact all narratives have a narrator separate from the author comes about only late in the twentieth century. Previously narratives not in the first person were said to be related or even narrated by the author. Even Anglo-American New Criticism, with its resistance to biographical criticism, initially treated fictional narratives without a first-person narrator as narrated by the author. Cleanth Brooks and Robert Penn Warren's classic textbook *Understanding Fiction* (1943) identifies four types of narration: *first-person participant or protagonist, first-person observer, author-observer, and omniscient author* (511). But an author who narrates is a narrator in a rather different sense from that of a character narrator: after all, the author creates the story, stipulates what happens, whereas a character narrator does not stipulate but reports the story as something that has already occurred. It was only with the work of Wolfgang Kayser in Germany and French structuralism that a model, now called "pan-narrator theory," was developed, in which every narrative had a narrator separate from the author, whether visible or invisible.[1]

In the case of poetry, the introduction of the ubiquitous speaker occurs earlier in Anglo-American criticism, as American New Criticism, in its desire to treat the poem as an artifact and dramatic structure rather than the discourse of the poet, made it a principle to distinguish the speaker of a poem from the poet. Already in 1938 John Crowe Ransom laid down the law: "The poet does not speak in his own but in an assumed character, not in the actual but in an assumed situation, and the first thing we do as readers of poetry is to determine precisely what character and what situation are assumed. In this examination lies the possibility of critical understanding and, at the same time, of the illusion and the enjoyment." From there it's only a small leap for Ransom to conclude that the poem "may be said to be a dramatic monologue. . . . Browning only literalized and made readier for the platform or the concert hall the thing that had always been the poem's lawful form" (1938, 254–55). As Randall Jarrell observed in 1953, the dramatic monologue, popularized by Robert Browning, with an identifiable speaker-character, went from being an exception in the realm of lyric poetry to being the norm (1953, 16). It takes a powerful ideology to imagine other forms of lyric as unlawful.[2]

In the Anglo-American world, this principle has become the foundation of pedagogy of the lyric. The classic textbook *Sound and Sense* tells students, "To aid us in understanding a poem we may ask ourselves a number of questions about it. Two of the most important are *Who is the speaker?* and *What is the occasion?*" After reminding students that "poems, like short stories, novels, and plays, belong to the world of fiction" and advising them to "assume always that the speaker is someone other than the poet," the textbook concludes: "We may well think of every poem, therefore, as in some degree dramatic—that it is the utterance not of the person who wrote it but of a fictional character in a particular situation that may be inferred" (Perrine [1956] 2013, 27).

Now in both cases, lyric and narrative fiction, there is a desire to deter biographical criticism, making the author not responsible for statements in the text, by separating author from narrator or speaker (though I think the concept of fiction itself ought to suffice to protect the author from being held responsible); but of course this move of attributing the discourse to a narrator or to a speaker does rather more than that: by turning attention away from the author, it deflects attention from the work of literature as something made, the product of artistic decisions, and it focuses attention on a supposed person, who except in special cases is not a writer and whose choices need therefore to be explained in other than artistic terms. This is especially evident when we consider the case of poetry. Many poems—not just shaped poems or poems impossible to read aloud, such as E. E. Cummings's "r-p-o-p-h-e-s-s-a-g-r"—have no speaker, and to try to imagine who speaks sets us on the wrong track. Consider, for instance, William Carlos Williams's "so much depends upon a red wheelbarrow":

so much depends
upon

a red wheel
barrow

glazed with rain
water

beside the white
chickens.

We could speculate about who is speaking—a gardener, a farmer, an aesthete?—and why, in what situation. But this is pointless, and it distracts us from the central question of why the poem is written in this way.³ Even if we did reach some hypothesis about a speaker, that would tell us nothing about the effect of the arrangement of words on the page, which is obviously the result of decisions by a poet, not of some alleged speaker. Or take a case where it is easier to imagine a speaker: Dylan Thomas's villanelle "Do not go gentle into that good night." The final stanza addresses "you, my father" ("And you, my father, there on the sad height, / Curse, bless me now with your fierce tears, I pray. / Do not go gentle into that good night"). This invites readers to imagine a speaker addressing his father, rather than a poet writing these lines; but if we posit a speaker, then irrelevant questions arise: why does he say the same thing over and over—is his father deaf? What is the significance of this hectoring behavior, which scarcely seems an acceptable bedside manner for the son of what we imagine is a dying father? The most striking features of this poem—its formal structures—are the work of a poet, not of a speaker. In fact, in the case of lyric poetry, we could venture a rule of thumb: that the greater the effects of aural patterning—alliteration, assonance, rhyme, rhythm—the less mimesis of voice (Culler 2015, 175–76, 247–48). In most of Gerard Manley Hopkins's poems, for instance, what we have is compelling verbal play but not a speaker. Here is the beginning of "Inversnaid":

> This darksome burn, horseback brown,
> His rollrock highroad roaring down,
> In coop and in comb the fleece of his foam
> Flutes and low to the lake falls home.
>
> A windpuff-bonnet of fawn-froth
> Turns and twindles over the broth
> Of a pool so pitchblack, fell-frowning,
> It rounds and rounds despair to drowning.

If we try to imagine a speaker here, we can conceive of someone looking at a mountain stream but it is hard to imagine someone who would choose these words (why would anyone but a poet select just these particular words?), and it is especially weird to suppose that the speaker chooses just these words but does not know that they are arranged in a rollicking tetrameter rhythm—a dolnik rhythm—and that every fourth beat rhymes. We could say that the speaker contemplates and celebrates the brook and expresses the hope that such wild natural beauty may be preserved. But it is scarcely clear what would be gained by imagining a speaker who is not a poet speaking these words with no appreciation of the intense aural play that we readers experience. Far better to say that the poet, rather than some speaker, has chosen these particular words, arranged this way, in order to create this experience, and that it is the poet who is celebrating the wild beauty here evoked with this harmonious exuberance. If we prefer, we can always say it is the implied author, but the fiction of a speaker serves no purpose, and introduces extraneous considerations if we were to take this fiction seriously and try to imagine what sort of pretentious person would choose to say "in coop and in comb the fleece of his foam."

But let me turn back to the example of narrative. The claim that every narrative must have a narrator is often presented without argument, as if the narrator were a logical entailment: by definition a narrative must have a narrator, as a story must have a storyteller. Many analysts take face-to-face narration as the norm or point of departure—somebody telling someone else that something happened—and extrapolate from there to build a general account of narrative (Phelan 2017, ix).[4] But in fact this is not a compelling argument and there is slippage in the move from storyteller to narrator. If a child asks me to tell her the story of Little Red Riding Hood, I am the storyteller, but suppose I say that she is old enough to read it herself and hand her the book; does this mean that suddenly the story acquires a narrator that it did not have before? As Nicholas Wolterstorff asks, "Why can't the novelist just straightforwardly tell us a tale of love and death . . . ? Why must it always be a tale of a narration of love and death . . . ?" (1980, 172). In fact, no one need be conceived as uttering the words of a story: they tell the story when read. And if pan-narrator proponents say that when I was telling the story I was really telling a story of a hidden narrator telling the story, then there is clearly a difference between the idea of a storyteller, who presents the story, and that of a narrator.

It was the structuralist attempt to devise a formal semiological account of narrative in general that led to the separating of the author from the narrator in third-person as well as first-person narratives and taking all narratives as communication between a narrator and narrative audience. But it is hard to defend this as a general model. When we consider nonfiction narratives, say a biography or a historical narrative, we don't claim that there must be a narrator separate from the author. We can distinguish different authorial attitudes or strategies: the author decides what sort of role to play, what sort of stance to adopt—distant, objective, or intimately acquainted with the thoughts of the actors, satirical, exuberant, reverent. So, for example, there is a considerable difference between the posture of Tom Wolfe's *The Right Stuff*, a celebration of the courage and dedication of the hotshot pilots who go on to become astronauts, and his snarky *Radical Chic*, which centers on a party given by Leonard Bernstein as a fundraiser for the Black Panthers. Both books have the lively writing that made the author famous but quite different attitudes toward their subjects, yet we do not feel any need to say that he invents two separate narrators to tell these two stories; he just writes them differently. Why, then, should the fact that a narrative is fictional, that it is imagined rather than researched, require an extra level of mediation?

In fact, many fictional narratives dispense with narrators and this creates no problems. Comic strips are an obvious case: they have a narrative but usually no narrator. No one ever asked who is the narrator of *Peanuts*: the thoughts, speech, and actions of the characters are simply represented.[5] Or again, think of film. Film narratives are created and presented; we can certainly say that this film "tells a story," but except very rarely, in films with voice-over narration, we would not say that films have a narrator who tells this story.[6] We have no sense that there is a person, a narrator, who observed or is observing the scenes represented and is showing them to us. We attribute the selection of what is being shown and of how it is shown to the director or to the entire production team. Even film theorists who want to defend the notion of fictional audiovisual narration balk at the notion that films have narrators.[7] Our natural attitude with respect to film is to experience what is shown in the same way as we look at the untold world: what we have is a fictional simulation of events. As Seymour Chatman notes, the structure of film is to present "a bare visual record of what happened 'out there.' . . . The whole movie may pass before us in pure visual objectivity" (1978, 159). "To give every film a narrator," writes David Bordwell, "is to indulge in an anthropomorphic fiction. . . . Narration is better understood as the organization of a set of cues for the construction of a story. This presupposes a perceiver, but not any sender, of a message. . . . But there is no point in positing communication as the fundamental process of all narrative films, only to grant that most films 'efface' or 'conceal' this process" (1985, 62). Film theorists explain the narrative process in different ways: a film cues viewers to imagine events or triggers for viewers the construction of a story, but the idea of a narrator for film narrative seems quite superfluous: the organizing agency that presents the film is the team that produced it; if there is no evidence of the existence of a narrator, there is no need to posit one. So we can reject the notion that fictional narratives necessarily require a narrator. Some have narrators and some do not.

A frequent argument for the ubiquitous narrator is that the author of a nonfictional narrative asserts what he knows, and that narrative fiction is a fictional imitation of a nonfictional narrative, an account of the world of the fiction by someone to whom that world is known. In fiction the narrator stands in for the author or teller of nonfictional narratives, as someone for whom this world is real, not imagined, and who thus can make assertions about this world and events in it. Here, there is an analogy with the case of the lyric, which some theorists treat as a fictional imitation of a real-world speech act—a view much less plausible, since large numbers of lyrics do not at all resemble real-world speech acts, and, as I have argued, to attempt to determine the situation of the speaker and the speech act he or she is fictionally performing often leads us astray. The analogy might at least make us wary of treating fictional narrative as a fictional imitation of real-world narrative. Certainly there are several problems with this model.

First, even in face-to-face storytelling, the storyteller is often not claiming *knowledge* of the events recounted: he or she may just be telling a story previously heard, because it is amusing, is strange, or offers a moral. The model of a speaker telling about events that he or she knows is already something of a fiction, a particular possibility, not a given that must be reproduced in the case of a fictional world. Second, if we take a novel as a fictional imitation of a real-world speech act, that immediately raises the question of what sort of act it could have been: the authors of extended nonfictional narratives, biographers or historians, write texts for readers to consult, but are we supposed to imagine the narrators of novels writing a text for an audience? This is occasionally the fiction, but usually critics speak as if narrators were "telling" the stories.[8] Is someone supposed to be speaking to an audience for hours on end? Of course, we characteristically ignore such questions, but to adopt a theoretical framework that requires us to ignore the questions it raises, as opposed to the simpler framework of an author offering us a written story, seems perverse, a violation of the principle of Occam's razor.

But if the pan-narrator model supplies a narrator in order to furnish for third-person narratives a person who knows this world, a further, third, problem immediately arises: when narrators are posited for third-person narratives, they characteristically do not behave like persons but, for instance, recount things that a person could not know: the thoughts of characters in the fiction or what happens on occasions where there is no observer present. These supposed narrators thus seem to be rather fantastical persons, yet, as Kendall Walton points out, in realist novels it is not fictionally true that the narrator has superpowers of omniscience: that is, the fictional world does not include such a person with powers of omniscience—that would make it a science fiction story (1990, 360). So bringing in a narrator to make what is told something known (and thus supposedly symmetrical with nonfictional narrative) creates a problem—precisely the problem it was supposed to solve.[9] In fact, to explain the presentation of thoughts of characters, happenings that no one observed, and so on, one needs to have recourse to the author, who stipulates these details.

Further, if a narrator is posited in order to make what is recounted into something known, a fourth problem emerges. If we suppose that there is a narrator who knows intimately this fictional world and the thoughts and doings of its characters, then the question arises of why the narrator tells us some things and not others. Every possible detail not recounted is something this supposed person has chosen not to relate. Since this narrator is specifically not the author, who would make these choices for artistic reasons, we must find other reasons for the narrator's choices: that he or she is obsessed with dress but indifferent to furnishings, for instance, and so gives detailed descriptions of what characters are wearing but not of the rooms they pass through; or that he or she is hostile to certain characters and does not report their thoughts but is sympathetic to others, whose thoughts are reported. If the narrator never tells us what color something is, perhaps he or she is color-blind. The novelist, of course, makes such choices to achieve particular artistic effects.

Here the analogy with lyric poetry is suggestive. In the case of a dramatic monologue, the convention is that the speaker—the Duke in "My Last Duchess" or Prufrock in "The Love Song of J. Alfred Prufrock"— chooses the words he uses but does not know he is speaking verse. The poet supplies the verse. A fortiori, when we imagine a speaker for lyrics that do not contain a first-person speaker, we confront a situation where the alleged speaker is deemed to select the words of the poem but not those properties of these words—rhythmical, phonological—that make them poetically effective. The reasons for the choices of words, therefore, are not supposed to be poetic ones (as I emphasized when discussing Hopkins's "Inversnaid" above). In fiction, pan-narrator theory gives us a similarly odd division of labor: the author is responsible for determining everything that happens in the novel, including what the characters think, wear, and so forth, but the narrator, overt or covert, is deemed to choose whether to reveal this information, whether to describe the clothes, thoughts, and so on, and exactly in which terms to do so. And the reasons for these choices are not supposed to be those of a novelist.

For instance, in Hemingway's "The Killers," if we posit a narrator and ask what this narrator knows, we might first say that he knows what a local observer sitting in the diner would know: he knows the names of George and Nick Adams, but he does not know the names of the two visitors who enter—until he hears them use each other's names. But an observer couldn't know what George sees back in the kitchen, where one of the killers has tied up Nick Adams and Sam, the cook, or what transpires in Ole Anderson's room when Nick later goes to warn him. To solve this problem, critics are sometimes led to see this as an omniscient narrator who just chooses not to tell us much. Barbara Olsen, argues, for instance, that though "The Killers" is often cited as the very model of a limited, camera-eye narrative, it "actually features Hemingway's omniscient narrator at his most reticent." This narrator *could* tell all but prefers not to: "He knows that 'Al' and 'Max' are only aliases for these intruders" (Olsen 1997, 42–43). With this strategy, the critic should find herself obliged to explain why the omniscient narrator declines to tell us all the relevant things he or she must know—including the real names and histories of Al and Max, the reason for their setting out to kill the Swede, and so on.

Imagining motivations for this refusal would yield strange contortions, because such choices are properly explained as choices made by the author, for artistic reasons, not as the psychologically motivated decisions of a narrator who is telling a story he or she knows. They are decisions about crafting the text, not selections of which bits of prior knowledge to relate. The artistic choices are obfuscated by being transformed into decisions of an imagined narrator to whose psychology we have no access and about which we can only speculate. Focusing on an author or implied author, on the other hand, we can imagine that he provides this narrowed vision to give us the experience of certain helplessness in a potentially sinister situation, along with information to allow us to understand the scope of what is happening.

This case, though extreme, perfectly illustrates how treating the story as something known to a narrator creates unnecessary problems: as soon as the knowledge exceeds that regularly accessible to persons, we solve the problem not by deciding that we shouldn't be thinking about what someone knows but by positing omniscience, and then the critic finds herself obliged to explain why the omniscient narrator declines to tell us all the relevant things he or she must know. Instead of Hemingway deciding whether to invent pasts for Al and Max, we have a scenario of an imagined narrator knowing all about them and deciding whether to reveal their pasts. Such a narrator would indeed be an oddity: functioning like an author but with no power over what happens or what characters said, thought, wore, but all power over what to reveal to us. Such an alleged narrator is like the alleged speaker of a poem who selects all the words but does not know that they fall into rhyming tetrameter quatrains. We do better to ask how the text is written rather than who speaks.

The theoretical trajectory of Seymour Chatman is instructive for thinking about this matter. In his classic narratological work *Story and Discourse: Narrative Structure in Fiction and Film*, he argued that the author "decides whether to have a narrator, and if so, how prominent he should be. . . . The 'narrator,' when he appears, is a demonstrable, recognizable entity immanent to the narrative itself. . . . A narrative that does not give a sense of this presence, one that has gone to noticeable lengths to efface it, may reasonably be called 'nonnarrated' or 'unnarrated'" (1978, 33–34). (The simplest example would be a story consisting purely of dialogue.) In this book Chatman devotes an entire chapter to "nonnarrated stories" before moving on to covert and overt narrators. This, then, is a version of what has come to be called "optional-narrator theory": there are narrators only when there are explicit manifestations of someone recounting the story. But in a later book, *Coming to Terms: The Rhetoric of Narrative in Fiction and Film*, Chatman recants this view, apparently to provide a general model that would apply equally to film and literary narrative: every narrative, he argues, is presented by a general narrator, who may tell the story or simply show the story, or some combination of the two (1990, 113). "Every narrative is by definition narrated—that is, narratively presented—and that narration, narrative presentation, entails an agent even when the agent bears no signs of human personality" (115). Even though this supposed narrative role may sometimes be "totally limited to showing," if we do not redefine narrator to include presenting "we have no way of accounting, in general narratological terms, for performed stories: movies, plays, mime shows, and the like" (115). That is to say, he takes it for granted that we need a general narratological model for all stories, and that this should include a narrator, even though what is then called narrator functions very differently in a play, much less a mime show, and in a novel with a first-person narration.

But the cost of reinstating a narrator for films as well as for stories with no overt narratorial presence is high and illustrates the difficulties of pan-narrator theory: the category of narrator itself becomes quite vacuous. In film and third-person narrative, what Chatman now calls the narrator is not someone telling a story, whose decisions about how to present it, what to say, we should examine. Rather, this "nonhuman narrative agency communicates all and only what the implied author provides" (130). What he here calls narrators in cases that were previously nonnarrated are purely formal agents who present details chosen by the author or implied author; there is no question of attributing to them human decisions about what to present or in what way to present it. And Chatman rightly objects to speaking about what a nonpersonified narrator "knows," since what this agent does is simply present the discourse, or transmit images and discourse, to the reader: it is a "discourse agent," whose "capacity to render this or that detail of the story depends not on 'knowledge' but on how much the implied author has delegated to him/her/it to present—as opposed to how much has been left to the reader to infer" (121). Such nonhuman narrators are stripped of the functions usually attributed to narrators: we are dealing with authorial choices, and we would not be tempted to work out ordinary human motivation for alleged choices. In fact this later version of his account ought to provide support for optional-narrator theory, since it actually identifies reasons for not treating such purely formal narrators in the way that we treat narrators in first-person narration. But it still promotes confusion by retaining in such cases the name of *narrator*, which Chatman admits could just as well be *presenter*: "For those who find 'narrator' awkward, 'presenter' is a good alternative" (113).

But why does pan-narrator theory still hold sway, given its disadvantages? There are, no doubt, several reasons. First, it absolves the author of responsibility for the statements, judgments, and so forth, of the narrative. But for statements about the characters and their doings, this result is accomplished by the notion of fiction: we don't need in addition to insert a narrator between the author and the text. The author invites readers to imagine these characters and events. For some statements, however—claims about our world and not specifically about the world of the novel—a narrator would not solve the problem, since the narrator's alleged knowledge is of the fictional world of the narrative, which for him is real. Statements such as "All happy families are alike; each unhappy family is unhappy in its own fashion" are observations about our world, not about the fictional world, and so must come from the author or implied author.[10] If we want to protect the author, we can always say that he or she is putting forward this claim to help connect the doings of the story he is creating to our world or positing that something might be true. Insertion of a narrator would not clarify this situation.

For some critics and theorists, the attraction of pan-narrator theory may be the desire for a comprehensive model that applies to all fictional narratives, but a more important reason for the success of the principle of the ubiquity of narrators is, no doubt, that it helps to distinguish sophisticated students and critics from ordinary readers, who take third-person narratives to be narrated by the author: this framework of the necessary narrator is thought to represent a cultural acquisition, knowledge of how literature actually functions, and we are, no doubt, loath to give up such special knowledge. While ordinary readers think that Jane Austen is telling the story of Elizabeth Bennet, those who have been taught to say "no, it's the narrator who tells this story" display what passes for superior understanding of how fiction works. Something similar is true in the case of poetry: you feel more sophisticated in saying "the speaker compares the foam of the rushing stream to a fleece" rather than "Hopkins compares the foam of the stream to a fleece," although the latter is certainly true.

But I think a related and more powerful factor is that pan-narrator theory has seemed pedagogically useful: it gives students something to do (whether this activity is worthwhile is a different question). We instruct students that they must overcome the idea that this is the discourse of Jane Austen or George Eliot and must work to identify the narrator: What does this covert narrator know? What are his or her values? If a novel tells us that "Mr. Bennet was so odd a mixture of quick parts, sarcastic humour, reserve, and caprice, that the experience of three and twenty years had been insufficient to make his wife understand his character," students can tell us that such an assertion implies a narrator with thorough knowledge of the characters and their history, not just their present affairs. Since identifying narrative perspective has become a staple of literary education, we are reluctant to renounce these skills, recently invented. But really this is make-work, as becomes obvious when we dispense with the necessity of a narrator.[11] Students take what the text affirms, what is stipulated by the author, and say this is what the narrator knows, and feel they have accomplished something. But this skill is actually pointless, misdirected. We don't have to ask what someone knows or doesn't know, much less how he or she comes to know it, because the supposed knowledge is just whatever the author wrote. In third-person narration the idea that there is someone who knows the facts of this story is a product of the theory that transforms what the author imagined into something a narrator knows. But, as I have probably stated too often, it is a simpler solution to observe that the text invites us to imagine this to be the situation of Mr. and Mrs. Bennet, rather than invent someone to assert it. Here the analogy with poetry is helpful: we do not need to invent a person to assert that "so much depends upon a red wheelbarrow."

In the case of both lyric poetry and narrative fiction, the assumption that we must explain assertions in literature by finding or inventing someone, not the author, who is responsible for them leads to a range of fruitless or inappropriate steps. Fortunately, better critics ignore in practice the implications of the theoretical frameworks they accept and allow themselves to discuss the artistic reasons for author's choices instead of speculating about what might have led fictional speakers or imaginary narrators to produce the sentences offered by the texts. But there is still considerable scope for optional-narrator theory to refine and improve the character of our engagement with and our teaching of literature.

Notes

1. For this history, see Patron ([2009] 2016), which distinguishes "communicational theories" of narrative, which treat narratives as a communication between a narrator and a narrative audience, from "poetic theories" of narrative, which treat them as the productions of an author that may or may not involve the invention of a narrator. See also Patron (2019b). Among the early proponents of poetic theories of narrative are the linguist S.-Y. Kuroda, the linguists and critics Ann Banfield and Mary Galbraith, and the critic Käte Hamburger.

2. For general discussion of the lyric and the problem of speakers, including the place of the dramatic monologue, see Culler (2015, especially 2–5, 18, 24, 76–77, 105–25, 271–75).

3. For discussion see Culler (2015, 31–32).

4. As Brian Richardson notes, narrative theory "is typically based on the mimesis of actual speech situations. If a narrative is, as commonly averred, someone relating a set of events to someone else, then this entire way of looking at narrative needs to be reconsidered in light of the numerous ways innovative authors problematize each term of this formula, especially the first one" (2006, 5).

5. Comic strips may have characters who narrate; and occasionally there are strips where theoreticians may posit a heterodiegetic, extradiegetic narrating instance who provides orienting information, such as a date or a place not presented as the thought of a character (Thon 2016, 185–87). In *Story and Discourse* Chatman analyzes a comic strip narrative in ten frames ("Short Ribs") without positing a narrator (1978, 37–41). On narration in comics, see Kai Mikkonen's contribution to this volume (editor's note).

6. And even in voice-over narration what we have is more like a character narrator, since the voice is generally not seen as controlling the images as well. Voice-over narrators seldom mediate every moment of the story (Kozloff 1988, 74). On narration in film, see Paisley Livingston's contribution to this volume (editor's note).

7. Some literary scholars may posit narrators, but the notion of a narrator, even a "non-represented narrating instance, to whom (or which) we can attribute the audio-visual narration in the fiction film is seldom found in narratological approaches developed within film studies itself" (Thon 2016, 142).

8. For example, in the article "Narrator" in *The Living Handbook of Narratology*, Uri Margolin explains, "Thus, in writing down his text, the flesh and blood author gives rise to a substitutionary *speaker* who performs the macro speech act of reporting and who is solely responsible for all claims, specific or general, made in this report" (2014, my italics).

9. For discussion of the problem of omniscience, which I argue is not a useful notion but lumps together a number of different kinds of effects, see Culler ([2004] 2006). Previously people spoke of "the omniscient author": the author is like God (Olsen 1997). But the author is omnipotent rather than omniscient: able to determine what happens.

10. The same is true for many lyrics, which are statements about this world, not some fictional world.

11. Margolin, in a comparison of arguments for and against the necessity of a narrator, maintains that "dispensing with the narrator's voice and the narratorial speech position as an essential constituent of the text model radically reduces our ability to appreciate and analyse the multi-faceted structure and dynamics of a narrative's stylistic and ideological system, thus depriving us of one major approach to and model of narrative, especially the novel" (2011, 52). But in fact, optional-narrator theory recommends dispensing with the narrator only where there is no explicit evidence that the author has created a narrator to tell the story. In these cases, choices that would be attributed to the narrator in pan-narrator theory are explained as choices made by the author or implied author, and aesthetic considerations come into play much more centrally. For an analysis showing that there is no loss to analysis when you do not posit a narrator for third-person narration, see Köppe and Stühring (2015).

References

Barbauld, Anna Laetitia. 1804. "Life of Samuel Richardson, with Remarks on his Writings." In *The Correspondence of Samuel Richardson*, 1: vii–ccxii. London: Lewis and Rodem, for R. Phillips. https://babel.hathitrust.org/cgi/pt?id=mdp.39015002712563;view=1up;seq=29.

Bordwell, David. 1985. *Narration in the Fiction Film*. Madison: University of Wisconsin Press.

Brooks, Cleanth, and Robert Penn Warren. (1943) 1979. *Understanding Fiction*. 3rd ed. Englewood Cliffs NJ: Prentice Hall.

Chatman, Seymour. 1978. *Story and Discourse: Narrative Structure in Fiction and Film*. Ithaca NY: Cornell University Press.

———. 1990. *Coming to Terms: The Rhetoric of Narrative in Fiction and Film*. Ithaca NY: Cornell University Press.

Culler, Jonathan. (2004) 2006. "Omniscience." In *The Literary in Theory*, 183–201. Stanford: Stanford University Press.

———. 2015. *Theory of the Lyric*. Cambridge: Harvard University Press.

Jarrell, Randall. 1953. *Poetry and the Age*. New York: Knopf.

Köppe, Tilmann, and Jan Stühring. 2015. "Against Pragmatic Arguments for Pan-Narrator Theories: The Case of Hawthorne's 'Rappacini's Daughter.'" In *Author and Narrator: Transdisciplinary Contributions to a Narratological Debate*, edited by Dorothee Birke and Tilmann Köppe, 13–43. Berlin: De Gruyter.

Kozloff, Sarah. 1988. *Invisible Storytellers: Voice-Over Narration in American Fiction Film*. Berkeley: University of California Press.

Margolin, Uri. 2011. "Necessarily a Narrator or Narrator If Necessary: A Short Note on a Long Subject." *Journal of Literary Semantics* 40 (1): 43–57.

———. (2012) 2014. "Narrator." In *The Living Handbook of Narratology*, edited by Peter Hühn, Jan Christoph Meister, John Pier, and Wolf Schmid. http://www.lhn.uni-hamburg.de/article/narrator.

Olsen, Barbara K. 1997. *Authorial Divinity in the Twentieth Century*. Lewisburg PA: Associated University Press.

Patron, Sylvie. (2009) 2016. *Le Narrateur: Introduction à la théorie narrative*. Limoges, France: Lambert-Lucas.

———. 2015. *La Mort du narrateur et autres essais*. Limoges, France: Lambert-Lucas.

———. 2019a. *The Death of the Narrator and Other Essays*. Trier, Germany: Wissenschaftlicher Verlag Trier.

———. 2019b. "No-Narrator Theories/Optional-Narrator Theories: Recent Proposals and Continuing Problems; Toward a History of Concepts in Narrative Theory." Translated by Melissa McMahon. In *The Death of the Narrator and Other Essays*, 153–68. Trier, Germany: Wissenschaftlicher Verlag Trier.

Perrine, Laurence. (1956) 2013. *Sound and Sense*, edited by Thomas R. Arp and Greg Johnson. 14th ed. New York: Cengage.

Phelan, James. 2017. *Somebody Telling Somebody Else: A Rhetorical Poetics of Narrative*. Columbus: Ohio State University Press.

Ransom, John Crowe. 1938. *The World's Body*. Baton Rouge: Louisiana State University Press.

Richardson, Brian. 2006. *Unnatural Voices: Extreme Narration in Modern and Contemporary Fiction*. Columbus: Ohio State University Press.

Thon, Jan-Noël. 2016. *Transmedial Narratology and Contemporary Culture*. Lincoln: University of Nebraska Press.

Walton, Kendall L. 1990. *Mimesis as Make-Believe*. Cambridge MA: Harvard University Press.

Wolterstorff, Nicholas. 1980. *Worlds and Works of Art*. Oxford: Clarendon Press.

2 Implied Authors and Imposed Narrators —or Actual Authors?

BRIAN BOYD

1

If I concoct a narrative joke, beginning, say, "A priest, a rabbi, and an imam walked into a bar," I present the joke to my audience when I tell it to listeners live or publish it on page or screen for later readers. As I spell out the joke I invite my audience to *imagine* these characters, for the pleasure ahead, but not to *believe* in them. I do not need to hand the joke to a presenter, a "narrator," since merely expressing the words before an audience, orally or in writing, is itself the act of presentation. And I do not, by the fact of being no longer around when the words are read, become merely the no-longer-relevant antecedent of the joke's "implied author." Of course, readers have to infer my intention from the joke's words, but so do listeners of a live presentation.

All we need to understand the central dynamics of storytelling are the terms *author, story, audience.* Many, indeed most, narrative theorists and academic literary critics and teachers insist otherwise, although what they insist on varies: we may or may not need an *implied author,* who may or may not be human; we at least need a *narrator* independent of the person telling the story, who also may or may not be human or even quasi-human, and who may in some sense inhabit and report from the story-world, or who may instead be only a function or feature of the discourse while yet a person—or not.[1]

Those who accept that narrators are optional rather than necessary accept that a storyteller may choose to *create* a narrator, as I would if, say, I chose to compound or rework the joke by inventing a Reverend Tippler or a Reverend Stickler to tell about the priest, the rabbi, and the imam. But even if I keep with the original version, my very words, "A priest, a

53

rabbi, and an imam walked into a bar," are supposed by many to establish automatically a narrator independent of me, even if I have no intention to create such a figure. For some, that will also generate a matching narratee independent of the actual audience.

Many—often conflicting—reasons have been given as to why there must always be a narrator independent of the author of a story, but none of them is *valid* (for critiques see Kania 2005; Walsh [1997] 2007; Wartenberg 2007; Bordwell 2008; Patron [2009] 2016; Currie 2010; Köppe and Stühring 2011; Livingston [2001] 2002; Birke and Köppe 2015a; Boyd 2017; and this volume, especially Culler and Livingston).

Why does choosing the words in the order in which they are in a story not itself automatically *tell* the story, without needing to add a narrator as presenter? Consider parallel cases. When someone uses words to describe a static scene without narrative elements, whether the scene be real or invented, is there necessarily a describer or descriptor independent of the person uttering these words, a descriptor who or which presents the description, perhaps to a descriptee different from the actual audience? When someone presents an argument in words, does there have to be an independent arguer presenting the argument, possibly to an arguee distinct from the actual audience?[2]

If unnecessary in these cases, why is an independent presenter, in this case an independent narrator, necessary for narrative? Of course, if an author invents one or more characters to tell the story, a Jane Eyre or a David Copperfield or the many correspondents of an epistolary novel or the many reminiscers in a Faulkner or Erdrich multivoice tale, these characters are indeed *character* narrators. But if an author does *not* invent characters to tell their story, why should anyone suppose there nevertheless is, indeed must be, a narrator independent of the author?

I have previously called the pan-narrator thesis, that a narrator independent of the author is always necessary in narrative, the Necessary Narrator principle (Boyd 2017) and now propose to call this postulated "necessary," nonoptional narrator also *the Imposed Narrator*. Why does it matter to remove this narrator—"he" or "she" in some formulations, according to the sex of the author, "he/she/it" in others (e.g., Chatman 1990, 121), only "it" in yet others (Bal [1978, 1985] 2017, 15)—from an account of how fiction works? Because this figure or function is only imposed, unnecessary, confused, and confusing to those who discuss narrative. And especially because it obscures much of the real pleasure of fiction, the relationships between authors as inventors, and the stories they invent, and the audiences who enjoy the inventions and their own role in engaging with both the inventions and their inventors.

2

Why was it ever thought necessary to propose implied authors in no way to be confused with real authors, and imposed narrators in no way to be confused with either real or implied authors?

The answer is partly, first, because of scepticism about what we can know of authors' whole lives or the complexities of their intentions (Beardsley [1959] 1981; Booth [1961] 1983; Genette [1972] 1980; Chatman 1990). But we have reason to be sceptical of what we can know even of those closest to us, which always requires inference and can offer no complete, transparent, certain knowledge. We may always discover unsuspected sides of people we think we know, but that does not require us to think of them as only "implied friends" or "inferred partners" (Boyd 2017, 288). So, too, when we try to understand a particular action or achievement, we simply bring together what we know of the person and the inferable purpose of the action in its context. We do not know all the details of Roger Federer's life, or all the calculations in his brain that have led to his scoring another brilliant point, but when we witness or retrospectively analyze the winning strokes, we need neither to abstain from focusing on Federer because we cannot know his mind in any detail nor to posit in his place an "implied tennis player": we simply select what's relevant in his action and ability and their outcome.[3] We do not know all the details of Jane Austen's life or all the minutiae of her physical and mental activity as she wrote and perhaps rewrote this or that line, but when we consider one of her fictions, we do not need to posit an "implied author": we simply focus on what's relevant to what we're interested in, such as the words Austen chose and the reasons for choosing them that we can infer from them and their context.

Implied authors and imposed narrators have been proposed partly, second, to deal with such things as authorial irony, or an author's diverse storytelling roles in different fictions, or the supposed contradiction between authorial assertion in telling fictional stories and the fictionality of the things asserted. But as Dan Sperber and Deirdre Wilson have convincingly shown (Sperber and Wilson [1986] 1995, 230–37, Wilson and Sperber 2012, 17–18, 86, 108), language in use has no default presupposition of literalness: we interpret language to make sense of it in its context, in terms of the relevance an utterance has in that context. If the context implies irony, or playful impersonation of an attitude or another person, or fiction, or metaphor, or in other ways something apart from the bare words, we are highly adept at interpreting utterances to infer the way the speaker or writer meant them in context. Adept, but not perfect: of course miscommunication occurs. That's no reason to set up a separate presenter who presents the words already in fact presented by the author in the very act of settling on them. Advocates for this *Passive Necessary Narrator* fail to show that the narrator has any cause, existence, or capacity, or any reason to report the author's words: the supposedly independent narrator is utterly dependent on, indeed only an imposed shadow of, the author's choosing the words that tell the story (Currie 2010, 65; Culler, 39, 45; Livingston, 270–71).

Imposed narrators have been proposed partly, third, because of confusion about fiction, a sense that to engage with fiction an audience must somehow believe it, must have a warrant for what happens in the world of the story (Martinez-Bonati 1981, 85; Genette [1983] 1988, 132–33; Schmid [2003] 2010, 32, 58, 65, 195). For many who argue for this *Active Necessary Narrator*, a narrator distinct from the inventor of the fiction is required to vouch for what happens in the storyworld—even if this leads to the absurd implications discussed at length by Kania, Köppe and Stühring, and others (Walsh [1997] 2007; Wartenberg 2007; Davies 2010; Pieper 2015; Boyd 2017). I will focus especially on this view of fiction, because rejecting it clarifies both the role of invention in every detail of a fiction (see Patron's "poetic" theory of fiction, [2009] 2016) and the role of audiences' engagement with authors.

3

I will argue—and readers outside literary studies are astonished that this even needs arguing—that real storytellers create fictional stories in their imaginations as they adjust the stories' details to prompt their audiences' imaginations, and that the stories are then re-created, partly similarly, partly differently, in the audiences' imaginations as they respond to those prompts. As part of their invention, authors have the option of inventing characters who narrate, for whom the world they report is real, even if, we can sometimes infer, they (Huck, Benjy, and Kinbote, for instance) do not report it undistorted. But if authors do not take the option to invent character narrators, then there is no reason to suppose the story has or needs a narrator: the storytellers themselves simply tell their story.

Unlike character-narrators, who report a story that is real to them and in which they feature more or less centrally as actors and witnesses, storytellers simply *offer* their story, inviting us to imagine it. This inviting to imagine is not unusual in the least. Nonfiction narrative also invites us to imagine individuals and events we (and even most authors of histories or biographies) have not witnessed, as Derek Matravers explains.

Indeed, almost all language, whenever it does not refer to the here and now, invites us to instruct our imaginations, as Daniel Dor shows in his *The Instruction of Imagination: Language as a Social Communication Technology* (2015). That is the unique characteristic of human language: referring to something beyond the direct experience of at least the receivers of the message, whether listeners or readers. To understand another's language, we have to use the words and sentences uttered as the prompts to construct an imagined equivalent to what we think the sender, whether speaker or writer, intends us to understand, by calling on all our own relevant experience, even though in infinitely many ways it won't coincide exactly with the sender's.

Tellers of fictional stories do not imply that anyone has witnessed what they present as immediate, even if past, experience (see Skalin's discussion of Hamburger on the "here and now" of the fictive past, 227–28). They know, and their audiences know, that we can imagine what is not the case and has never been the case, and that we like doing so if there is a promise of reward, if the fiction proves worth telling.

If Austen writes, "Emma Woodhouse, handsome, clever, and rich, with a comfortable home and happy disposition, seemed to unite some of the best blessings of existence; and had lived nearly twenty-one years in the world with very little to distress or vex her" (Austen [1815] 2003, 5), we not only understand the sentence meaning, this summary account of a person called Emma Woodhouse, but we infer the storyteller's meaning: "I have invented Emma Woodhouse as a fictional character, indeed, the heroine of this novel, *Emma*, that you are just starting to read. Her fate will prove interesting to you, even though she seems to face a life free of problems." "*Seemed* to unite some of the best blessings of existence": what is missing from Emma's life, or what will go wrong in it? How will her "blessings" work against her? Will there still be "very little to distress or vex her" as the story unfolds?

A storyteller tells stories because she expects them to be worth readers' or listeners' or viewers' time to engage with, to imagine, not because the story's events have happened but precisely because they have not: because the author has had the freedom to imagine and shape a story whose contours we will find fascinating as we imagine them under her prompting (Boyd 2018, 8–11). In Sperber and Wilson's relevance theory terms, language entails no presumption of literality. We infer from the context that "Emma Woodhouse, handsome, clever, and rich" is the opening of a fiction, and we will construe what follows in terms of its relevance to our expectation of a story, in fact of a novel, or, if we know more, of a romance novel in Austen's mode. As we focus on Emma's character and situation, her concerns will provide the relevance for us as we read. What matters to Emma, and what we infer matters to Austen in offering Emma's case to us, will determine what we feel as relevant.

In Dor's terms, Austen instructs our imaginations, as language naturally does, but instructs us here not to imagine a real existing person but only to imagine Emma as a fictional heroine, as the focus of a fictional story. To imagine her, as Dor explains, we will need to draw on our own remembered experience to understand the imagined people and situations Austen presents to us. Drawing on our own experience—in this case, for instance, of favoring people because their interest in us is flattering, of making mistakes through overconfidence, of embarrassment, of thoughtlessly hurting another, of being told that we were wrong by someone whose good opinion we cherish, and so on—will actively engage our memories and emotions.

As listeners or readers of a fiction, we do not suppose that the "world" of the story is real: that we could order a drink in the bar that the priest, the rabbi, and the imam walk into, or that we could visit Emma's Highbury and put flowers on her grave (Boyd 2017, 289; Walsh 2007). We actively respond to the elements of the story, as we do in the case of true stories we hear (or any other use of language), through trying to model it in our minds, by calling on our experience to instruct our imaginations. Fiction has the liberty of placing its characters in emotionally intense and volatile situations, and to imagine them we have to activate elements of our own memories of such situations, and therefore we feel a sense of being personally, intimately, emotionally engaged. But our engagement requires not belief but only imagining.

Let me contrast this with the utter confusion that the idea of a narrator independent of the author and inventor of a story can create. In *Story and Discourse*, the famous and influential flow chart "real author --> | implied author → (narrator) → (narratee) → implied reader | --> real reader" (1978, 151) brackets the narrator not because Chatman thinks there are cases where the author tells the story directly but because he sees cases of "nonnarration" or "unmediated narration." He proposes the quoting of documents like letters in a fiction as an example of "nonnarration," where the nonnarrator is no more than a collator of somehow preexisting documents (169). Direct dialogue is still almost "nonnarration": "the transcription of speech presupposes not only a collator but a stenographer" (173), as if fictional dialogue somehow preceded, in its storyworld, its rapid transcription into the discourse. The representation of a character's thought, Chatman thinks, "may also be unmediated" (181). "The most obvious and direct means of handling the thoughts of a character is to treat them as 'unspoken speech.' . . . '"Can this be Mr. Darcy!" thought she.' . . . To the function of stenographer has been added that of mind-reader. But no more than that. There is no interpretation. . . . The narrator is a bit more prominent by assuming this function, but only a bit" (182). For Chatman, the narrator remains present but tenuous here, playing no more than the role of a stenographer of thought, as if in the storyworld the character really does think these thoughts and the narrator-as-mere-stenographer, able to eavesdrop inside skulls, just happens to be inside the right skull at the right moment.

All this confusion begins with narratology's firmly separating story and discourse, giving story an independent reality and explaining discourse as dependent not on its actual author but on those who bring back verbal evidence from the storyworld: collators, stenographers, and narrators. It's as if we should envisage Elizabeth Bennet in the storyworld having thoughts a thought transcriber can then record in the discourse, rather than understand Austen telling Elizabeth's story by inventing her and her thoughts and the words in which she as author presents them to her audience.

Every detail and every angle within a worthwhile fiction have been included, and usually invented, to shape our response—our response not only to the characters and their fortunes but also to the creative intelligence of the author in inventing this story and its details to guide our response.

Such an account of fiction poses no ontological, epistemological, causal, or pedagogical problems. The story world does not exist (Lamarque and Olsen 1994, 94; Walsh 2007), except in the imaginations and memories of author and audience. Its events can be known to the author because she imagines them as she puts them into textual form, and to us in the audience because we imagine in response to the textual prompts she provides. The author invents the details and shapes their form—and revises them before allowing us access—precisely to prompt and guide our response (Phelan 2017). We therefore can enjoy not only the fiction but also our imaginative complicity with the author, our attempts to infer her intentions behind each choice (Boyd 2017).

Such an account of fiction has in its favor not only validity, clarity, and coherence but also agreement with age-old intuitions of all who participated in fiction until the pan-narrator or Necessary Narrator theory was proposed and soon turned sclerotic (see Patron [2009] 2016 for a historical account of the narrator and the recency of its extension beyond character-narrators). It squares with an evolutionary awareness of the role of play in higher animals and the swift bracketing-off of experience in the enjoyably intense testing ground that play offers (see Boyd 2018, 9–10, for an account of the origin of fiction in play).

For teachers, students, and other readers of literature, this account of fiction especially allows us to read texts more closely and with more pleasure and creative and critical engagement. It foregrounds the way we infer authors' reasons for making small-scale as well as large-scale choices in inventing a fiction. It highlights our appreciation of the close feedback between authors' inventions and their anticipation of effects on audiences, and it emphasizes the matching feedback between our comprehension, our imagining the scene, and our inferring authorial intentions behind the invention and presentation of fictional details (for feedback in narrative invention, see Phelan 2017, 6).

Such an account of fiction also allows us to trace the development of a storyteller's art from one work to another. The Necessary Narrator theory requires a different narrator for each fiction, each storyworld, so that differences in storytelling between *War and Peace* and *Anna Karenina*, say, can be attributed or misattributed to different narrators[4]—rather than to the development of the author's art and the changes in his or her purposes.

In *War and Peace* Tolstoy's singular penchant for analysis and his singular gifts of invention are both amply in evidence. He reflects analytically on the nature of causality, especially as manifest in Russia's encounters with France's armies in the Napoleonic wars, but at the same time his teeming imagination invents the multiple centers of causal force, at the intraindividual, individual, family, household, village, city, national, and international levels. His editorializing skew on the events he invents is readily, sometimes too readily, apparent, not least in the persistent irony that the French language and French aristocratic values had pervaded Russian life long before the French army invaded the Russian landscape.

The novel opens with a paragraph in French, deploring the emperor of the French, spoken in her St. Petersburg salon by Anna Pavlovna Scherer, maid of honor and intimate of the empress of Russia. Of course only Tolstoy the author could invent Anna Pavlovna's denunciation of Napoleon. A narrator—responsible, according to adherents of the Active Necessary Narrator, for the textual selections from what the author has invented—could have decided to open the novel with this speech and to choose to "record" Anna Pavlovna's anti-French and pro-war speech in French, as would naturally have been spoken in such a circle, rather than render it in the Russian that would have been more accessible to most of the novel's initial readers. But to make such a decision the narrator would first have had to have access to the storyworld in order to record the speech and other details of Anna Pavlovna's soirée. Moreover, Tolstoy's "large, loose, baggy monster" of a novel, to cite Henry James's famous phrase, could have started at many points in 1805. A narrator supposedly having the power to decide to open the novel precisely with Anna Pavlovna's speech rather than any other possibility would need to be capable of singling out one historically inconsequential moment from the much larger storyworld the Necessary Narrator theory most often requires. (If there is no larger storyworld, if there is only the text provided by the author, there would be nothing for a narrator to select, no need to invoke a narrator, and no space for the narrator to exist except as a presenter, an automatic playback mechanism—as, in effect, in Passive Necessary Narrator models.) Where would that larger storyworld exist? In some multiverse of fiction? Or only inside Tolstoy's imagination? If on the other hand we accept Tolstoy as the author, as simultaneously the inventor and the storyteller, his decision to begin his novel about Russia at war with France with a Russian's speech in French denouncing France's emperor requires him only to begin inventing Anna Pavlovna's words and penning what he stipulates she says.

The invention of Anna Pavlovna's opening sally can only be Tolstoy's. Even Necessary Narrator theorists accept that it is the author, not the narrator, who invents. But then Tolstoy also invents, in the second paragraph, that Anna Pavlovna has the flu. This has no consequence in the story beyond its first page, so it would be a detail unlikely for a narrator to single out from a wider storyworld. But the Tolstoy who opens his novel in French has a good reason for inventing that detail: so that he can write in the second paragraph, after identifying the speaker and her role in society: "Anna Pavlovna had been coughing for several days. She had the *grippe*, as she put it (*grippe* was a new word then, used only by rare people)" ([1869] 2007, 3). No mere narrator could invent her cough and her illness, but Tolstoy as author easily can, and for strategic purposes that invention, although without further consequence for the events of the story, fits perfectly with his opening gambit. The French word *grippe*, first used by members of the Russian élite like Anna Pavlovna, had become by the time Tolstoy wrote his novel a perfectly standard Russian loanword: another instance of an unstoppable cultural invasion from France. *Grippe* also means in French "dislike, aversion," like Anna Pavlovna's aversion for Napoleon. Anna Pavlovna's addressee, the first to arrive at her soirée, Prince Vassily Kuragin, responds to her speech: "*Dieu, quelle virulente sortie!*," translated, in the notes that Tolstoy provides for his non-French-speaking readers, as "Lord, what a virulent attack!" ([1869] 1973, 4:8).[5] Again, Tolstoy plays with peace and war, with French and Russian, with the artificial and safe world of a salon far from any battlefield but deploying warlike words in the language of the imminent enemy.

Tolstoy has an analytical largeness of vision that shapes the multiplicity of this novel and that will have untrammelled expression in his digressive reflections on cause and chance in history. But his broad analytical vision also meshes finely with the precision of his creation of characters and scenes. Prince Vassily, Tolstoy explains after the character's first utterance, "spoke that refined French *in which our grandparents not only spoke but thought*, and *with those quiet, patronizing intonations which are proper to a significant man who has grown old in society and at court.*" (3). Tolstoy generalizes (in the passages I italicize), with a broad confidence about human nature, but he individuates at the same time:

> Prince Vassily always spoke lazily, *the way an actor speaks a role in an old play*. Anna Pavlovna Scherer, on the contrary, despite her forty years, was brimming with animation and impulses.
>
> Being an enthusiast had become her social position, and she sometimes became enthusiastic even when she had no wish to, so as not to deceive the expectations of people who knew her. The restrained smile that constantly played on Anna Pavlovna's face, though it did not suit her outworn features, expressed, *as it does in spoiled children*, a constant awareness of her dear shortcoming, which she did not wish, could not, and found no need to correct. ([1869] 2007, 4)

The generalizations about an individual's character combine with generalizing similes about human life and an analytical penetration akin to that of the Tolstoy of the digressions on history and causality later in the novel and of the Tolstoy of his nonfiction. Tolstoy creates Anna Pavlovna's character partly by means of analyzing her: his invention and his presentation of her character are quite inextricable, quite uniquely Tolstoyan, and not to be attributed to any voice or agency but Tolstoy's alone.

6

In *Anna Karenina* Tolstoy's storytelling art has improved even beyond the high level of *War and Peace*. The generalizing and analyzing intelligence is still there, as in the famous opening sentence so much at odds with the concreteness of most of the novel: "All happy families are alike; each unhappy family is unhappy in its own way" ([1873–77] 2006, 1). But then, as the second paragraph begins, Tolstoy jumps to particulars: "All was confusion in the Oblonskys' house. The wife had found out that the husband was having an affair with their former French governess, and had announced to the husband that she could not live in the same house with him" (1).

Adherents of the Active Necessary Narrator principle hold that while the author invents the world of the story, a narrator somehow within the storyworld determines how and when its details are reported. Tolstoy invents the discovery of Stepan ("Stiva") Arkadyich Oblonsky's infidelity with the governess at the start of his novel presumably to trigger Stiva's sister Anna's coming to Moscow on a mission to rescue her brother's marriage, while at the same time her very arrival at the station prompts Vronsky to begin his campaign to lure her into infidelity. Tolstoy shows Anna Karenina first as a champion and a savior of marriage even as she inadvertently spurs Vronsky to draw her into betraying her own marriage. Features of the story this large, everybody agrees, must be the author's invention.

But the author invents not only large details; he also invents the small. He invents them because he knows just how he wants to tell the story, and how he wants to tell the story in turn prompts the details of the invention, in a close feedback cycle. Tolstoy wants to create a contrast between Stiva as naturally unfaithful and Anna as not at all unfaithful by inclination. Stiva has a deep love of pleasure, Anna a deep sense of responsibility. Here are the third and fourth paragraphs of the novel, introducing Stiva:

> On the third day after the quarrel, Prince Stepan Arkadyich Oblonsky—Stiva, as he was called in society—woke up at his usual hour, that is, at eight o'clock in the morning, not in his wife's bedroom but in his study, on a morocco sofa. He rolled his full, well-tended body over on the springs of the sofa, as if wishing to fall asleep again for a long time, tightly hugged the pillow from the other side and pressed his cheek to it; but suddenly he gave a start, sat up on the sofa and opened his eyes.
>
> "Yes, yes, how did it go?" he thought, recalling his dream. "How did it go? Yes! Alabin was giving a dinner in Darmstadt—no, not in Darmstadt but something American. Yes, but this Darmstadt was in America. Yes, Alabin was giving a dinner on glass tables, yes—and the tables were singing *Il mio tesoro*, only it wasn't *Il mio teso-*

ro but something better, and there were some little carafes, which were also women," he recalled. (1–2)

According to the Active Necessary Narrator thesis, the narrator selects and arranges and reports these details. But it is no absolutely requisite part of the story of *Anna Karenina* that Stiva should have this particular dream and wake up in this particular way. Only Tolstoy, as simultaneously inventor and storyteller, chooses to invent and present as the first concrete scene a household disrupted by adultery, as the occasion for Anna to come to restore family peace, and within that context to invent and present Stiva as a character in contrast to Anna (and, later in the story, as a natural link between Anna and Lyovin), and then to present Stiva first through the details of this retrieved dream.

Stiva wakes up "at his usual hour, that is, at eight o'clock in the morning." That's not a detail an independent narrator selects out of a solid storyworld that Tolstoy has invented, but a detail Tolstoy needs to characterize Stiva in the first sentence where he's introduced by name: despite the calamity of three days ago, the blithe Stiva has had a perfectly sound night of sleep. He wakes up "not in his wife's bedroom but in his study, on a morocco sofa," as Tolstoy invents, because Stiva can't sleep with Dolly after her appalled discovery. We can infer this at once, and we need it to be able to understand the shock to Stiva when he realizes where he has woken. Tolstoy, who has invented the move to the study, also drops this detail here to prepare us in advance for Stiva's shocked recognition, which he has also invented.

Stiva "rolled his full, well-tended body over on the springs of the sofa, as if wishing to fall asleep again for a long time, tightly hugged the pillow from the other side and pressed his cheek to it." This series of details Tolstoy as author invents, and discloses right here as storyteller, because he wants to give us a sense of Stiva as pleasure-loving, as indulgent, as wanting to prolong his pleasures, just as he would have prolonged his relationship with the governess had he not been found out. These minute details of the fiction are there not because they formed part of Tolstoy's invention of *Anna Karenina*'s world before he began putting the story into words, but because they serve to prepare our responses to the character, phrase by phrase: these small-scale inventions arrived in the process of telling the story.

But Stiva "gave a start, sat up on the sofa and opened his eyes": not because he has suddenly remembered the crisis in his marriage, as an alert reader might expect, but because he has remembered a sweet dream. Tolstoy as narrative strategist, as author and storyteller, devises and stipulates this detail. It might seem for a split second that Stiva has remembered the horrible situation, but no, this pleasure lover has only remembered a pleasure lover's dream. The dream is not something that exists as a given in some *Anna Karenina* storyworld; rather, it's a dream Tolstoy invents for Stiva precisely to characterize him in these few details: a dinner, a banquet, on fancy glass tables, on tables singing snatches of an opera (an art form Tolstoy abominated)—indeed a dream-improved version of the opera about the most famous of philanderers, *Don Giovanni*—and with carafes on it that were women, as if they existed only to pour out delight for men.

We have no reason whatever to suppose that this occurs as an independent dream somehow fixed in an *Anna Karenina* storyworld. Stiva need not have had this dream, and everything else in the story could have remained exactly as it is. But Tolstoy as author, as storyteller, concocts just these details to characterize Stiva even before he wakes up fully to the disaster in his household. He does not devise a complete dream and then select details from it: he invents just what he knows we need to imagine Stiva as Tolstoy wants us to imagine him. And he reports the details not from the outside but with Stiva groping for the fading fragments of the dream, and remembering the illogic of the dreamworld: a Darmstadt in America, singing tables, carafes that are women.

Tolstoy describes Stiva's position—sleeping, and not in his wife's bedroom—just enough for us to understand the situation; he describes his "full, well-tended body" just enough so that we do not imagine him lean or gaunt with worry; and then he invites us into Stiva by describing his last turn in bed, his last pressing of cheek to pillow, and his start awake. He invites us to imagine Stiva not by projecting him before our eyes—not by a Dickensian fixation on a striking external characteristic—but by inviting us to project ourselves into Stiva, by inviting us to trust what is common in human experience, and there are few things more intimately common than sleeping and waking with a dream on one's mind.[6] "Stepan Arkadyich's eyes glittered merrily, and he fell to thinking with a smile. 'Yes, it was nice, very nice. There were many other excellent things there, but one can't say it in words, or even put it into waking thoughts.'" Stiva's groping for the dream, a fragment at a time, his blurred sense of the delightful mood of the dream when he can't remember the details, like his turning over and hugging the pillow, give us a sense of instant identification with him: we have all loved the experience of waking in bed, wanting to sleep more, we have all groped for a dream on awakening. Tolstoy wants to invite us to experience with Stiva, not to look at him simply from the outside, so that the shock of his realizing where he is and why he is there will be something we feel *with* him.

Every detail of invention and every word and sequence of disclosure are there for their effects on us as readers. Tolstoy could arrive at these details of storytelling, of word and action, only through constant feedback between the world he was imagining and the effects he wanted to produce on his readers. There is no independent narrator, just Tolstoy at work as inventor and storyteller, a creator whose creative activity and strategy we can enjoy and engage with as rereaders, even more closely than we engage with Stiva, so long as we do not arbitrarily insert a narrator and perhaps an implied author between us and the author.

And we can also savor, as we read, Tolstoy's progress as a storyteller in *Anna Karenina* beyond even the art of *War and Peace*: his improved capacity to infect readers with his characters' emotions—as he would describe his aim himself ([1898] 1995)—through the particulars that allow us to imagine the characters. He can trigger our response in the later novel with much less authorial editorializing, simply by our engaging with the contrasting stories of Anna and Lyovin and the Stiva both know so well, and by our engaging with the author who made them live for us.

According to the Active Necessary Narrator thesis, by contrast, the differences in storytelling in Tolstoy's two major works of fiction would be ascribable to the two different narrators of the two stories. But the Necessary Narrators are not characters, by definition. There is no reason to suppose the narrator of one story older or more experienced as a narrator than the narrator of another. Each Active Necessary Narrator seems to be presupposed as unique to the storyworld it inhabits, and each storyworld as necessarily unique to its story. Each narrator also seems to report from this storyworld only once in its existence—that report being the story in question—acquiring its expertise in narrating without trial or revision, only by dint of being witness to the events of its storyworld.

Unlike real authors, Necessary Narrators seem to have no age and no development. Real authors on the other hand have individual styles that persist across their work, even if modified according to different contexts, but that also change gradually from period to period of their lives, in ways that match the storytelling in their fictions. The supposedly Necessary but actually superfluous Narrators keep in suspiciously, flawlessly close step with the development of their author's style—precisely because these Narrators-Not-Characters-or-Authors are an illusion.

7

Necessary Narrators have been invoked and imposed to explain how audiences have access to fictions—as if we no longer understood that, actually, fictions are inventions by real individuals.

Stories are not reports that supposed narrators make from supposed storyworlds that we are invited to believe must exist because entirely hypothetical narrators, not even envisaged by the storytellers, tell us about them. Stories are high-intensity games[7] that storytellers' imaginations unleash, move by move, play by play, to engage our imaginations and emotions with their characters at their most human, and with themselves at their most creative.

Notes

1. Implied author not human: e.g., Chatman (1978, 148, 158), Rimmon-Kenan ([1983] 2002, 89); narrator independent of the author: e.g., Barthes (1966, 19), Genette ([1972], 1980, 214), Ryan (1981, 517), Rimmon-Kenan ([1983] 2002, 89), Richardson (2011, 73); narrator not human: e.g., Bal ([1978, 1985] 2017, 15), Utell (2016, 27); narrator inhabiting and reporting from the storyworld: e.g., Genette ([1983] 1988, 132–33), Schmid ([2003] 2010, 32, 58, 65, 195); narrator only a function of the discourse: e.g., Chatman (1978; 1990, 85, 120–22), Margolin (2011, 44); narrator a person: e.g., Chatman (1990, 87, 114); narrator not a person: e.g., Chatman (1990, 115–22). Chatman equivocates on the necessity of a narrator (see, e.g., 1978, 33–34, 146–47, 151), generally accepting and even insisting on it (1990, 114), though sometimes arguing that reporting of direct speech, perception, or thought is unnarrated (even though reported!) (1978, 154, 184, 187), but he always maintains the distinction between author and narrator (147).
2. See Culler, p. 43, for a similar argument in the closer case of biographer or historian.

3. Herman (2012) and Phelan (2017, x) stress narration as an action. Bordwell (2008, 132) notes the similar absurdity of a reporter being an "implied recounter" and a trial witness an "implied testifier."

4. Pieper (2015) provides a detailed example of critics under the influence of pan-narrator theory inferring, and successively elaborating on and characterizing, a noncharacter "Necessary" Narrator whose role they increasingly deem central to the novel but whose presence would, as Patron shows, have been surprising news to Goethe.

5. "Gospodi, kakoe goryachee napadenie!" (Tolstoy [1869] 1973, 4:8). Pevear and Volokhonsky translate, "God, what a virulent outburst!" but Tolstoy's translation highlights the military sense of *sortie*.

6. This paragraph borrows from a longer discussion of Stiva's first scene in Boyd (2011, 233). Consciously considering Tolstoy as inventor and storyteller, examining the feedback between fictional detail and reader response, has here made my already close reading much closer.

7. See Skalin, pp. 235–36, for a discussion of fiction in terms of the rules of the game.

References

Austen, Jane. *Emma*. (1815) 2003. Edited by James Kinsley. Oxford: Oxford University Press.

Bal, Mieke. (1978, 1985) 2017. *Narratology: Introduction to the Theory of Narrative*. Toronto: University of Toronto.

Barthes, Roland. 1966. "Introduction à l'analyse structurale des récits." *Communications* 8: 1–27.

Beardsley, Monroe. (1959) 1981. *Aesthetics*. 2nd ed. Indianapolis: Hackett.

Birke, Dorothee, and Tilmann Köppe. 2015a. "Author and Narrator: Problems in the Constitution and Interpretation of Fictional Narrative." In Birke and Köppe 2015b, 1–12.

———, eds. 2015 b. *Author and Narrator: Transdisciplinary Contributions to a Narratological Debate*. Berlin: De Gruyter.

Booth, Wayne. (1961) 1983. *The Rhetoric of Fiction*. 2nd ed. Chicago: University of Chicago Press.

Bordwell, David. 2008. "Afterword: Narrators, Implied Authors, and Other Superfluities." In *Poetics of Cinema*, 121–33. London: Routledge.

Boyd, Brian. 2011. *Stalking Nabokov: Selected Essays*. New York: Columbia University Press.

———. 2017. "Does Austen Need Narrators? Does Anyone?" *New Literary History* 48 (2): 285–308.

———. 2018. "The Evolution of Stories: From Mimesis to Language, from Fact to Fiction." *Wiley Interdisciplinary Reviews Cognitive Science* 9 (January-February): 1–16. doi: 10.1002/wcs.1444.

Chatman, Seymour. 1978. *Story and Discourse: Narrative Structure in Fiction and Film*. Ithaca NY: Cornell University Press.

———. 1990. *Coming to Terms: The Rhetoric of Narrative in Fiction and Film*. Ithaca NY: Cornell University Press.

Currie, Gregory. 2010. *Narratives and Narrators: A Philosophy of Stories*. Oxford: Oxford University Press.

Davies, David. 2010. "Eluding Wilson's 'Elusive Narrators.'" *Philosophical Studies* 147 (3): 387–94.

Dor, Daniel. 2015. *The Instruction of Imagination: Language as a Social Communication Technology*. New York: Oxford University Press.

Genette, Gérard. (1972) 1980. *Narrative Discourse: An Essay in Method*. Translated by Jane E. Lewin. Ithaca NY: Cornell University Press.

———. (1983) 1988. *Narrative Discourse Revisited*. Translated by Jane E. Lewin. Ithaca NY: Cornell University Press.

Herman, David. 2012. "Authors, Narrators, Narration." In *Narrative Theory: Core Concepts and Critical Debates*, edited by David Herman, James Phelan, Peter J. Rabinowitz, Brian Richardson, and Robyn Warhol, 44–50. Columbus: Ohio State University Press.

Kania, Andrew. 2005. "Against the Ubiquity of Fictional Narrators." *Journal of Aesthetics and Art Criticism* 63: 47–54.

Köppe, Tilmann, and Jan Stühring. 2011. "Against Pan-Narrator Theories." *Journal of Literary Semantics* 40 (1): 59–80.

———. 2015. "Against Pragmatic Arguments for Pan-Narrator Theories: The Case of Hawthorne's 'Rappaccini's Daughter.'" In Birke and Köppe 2015b, 13–43.

Lamarque, Peter, and Stein Haugom Olsen. 1994. *Truth, Fiction and Literature: A Philosophical Perspective*. Oxford: Oxford University Press.

Livingston, Paisley. (2001) 2002. "Narrative." In *The Routledge Companion to Aesthetics*, edited by Berys Gaut and Dominic McIver Lopes, 275–84. 2nd ed. New York: Routledge.

Margolin, Uri. 2011. "Necessarily a Narrator or Narrator If Necessary: A Short Note on a Long Subject." *Journal of Literary Semantics* 40 (1): 43–57.

Martinez-Bonati, Felix. 1981. *Fictive Discourse and the Structures of Language*. Ithaca NY: Cornell University Press.

Matravers, Derek. 2014. *Fiction and Narrative*. Oxford: Oxford University Press.

Patron, Sylvie. (2009) 2016. *Le Narrateur: Un problème de théorie narrative*. Limoges, France: Lambert-Lucas.

———. 2011. "Discussion: 'Narrator.'" Translated by Susan Nicholls. In *The Living Handbook of Narratology*, edited by Peter Hühn, Jan Christoph Meister, John Pier, and Wolf Schmid. https://www.lhn.uni-hamburg.de/node /45.html.

Phelan, James. 2017. *Somebody Telling Somebody Else: A Rhetorical Poetics of Narrative*. Columbus: Ohio State University Press.

Pieper, Vincenz. 2015. "Author and Narrator: Observations on *Die Wahlverwandtschaften*." In Birke and Köppe 2015b, 81–97.

Richardson, Brian. 2011. "Nabokov's Experiments and the Nature of Fictionality." *StoryWorlds* 3: 73–92.

Rimmon-Kenan, Shlomith. (1983) 2002. *Narrative Fiction: Contemporary Poetics*. 2nd ed. London: Routledge.

Ryan, Marie-Laure. 1981. "The Pragmatics of Personal and Impersonal Fiction." *Poetics* 10 (6): 517–39.

Schmid, Wolf. (2003) 2010. *Narratology: An Introduction*. Berlin: De Gruyter.

Sperber, Dan, and Deirdre Wilson. (1986) 1995. *Relevance: Communication and Cognition*. 2nd ed. Malden MA: Wiley-Blackwell.

Tolstoy, Leo. (1869) 1973. *Sobranie sochineniy v 12 tomakh*. Moscow: Khudozhestvennaya Literatura.

———. (1869) 2007. *War and Peace*. Translated by Richard Pevear and Larissa Volokhonsky. London: Vintage.

———. (1873–77) 2006. *Anna Karenina*. Translated by Richard Pevear and Larissa Volokhonsky. London: Vintage.

———. (1898) 1995. *What Is Art?* Translated by Richard Pevear and Larissa Volokhonsky. London: Penguin.

Utell, Janine. 2016. *Engagements with Narrative*. London: Routledge.

Walsh, Richard. (1997) 2007. "The Narrator and the Frame of Fiction." In Walsh 2007, 69–85.

———. 2007. *The Rhetoric of Fictionality: Narrative Theory and the Idea of Fiction*. Columbus: Ohio State University Press.

Wartenberg, Thomas E. 2007. "Need There Be Implicit Narrators of Literary Fictions?" *Philosophical Studies* 135 (1): 89–94.

Wilson, Deirdre, and Dan Sperber. 2012. *Meaning and Relevance*. Cambridge: Cambridge University Press.

3   Real Authors, Real Narrators, and the Rhetoric of Fiction

VINCENZ PIEPER

Introduction

Narrative theory in its traditional forms is troubled by a misleading picture: Theorists are inclined to think of the literary work as a piece of language detached from its author, as a sequence of signs correlated to meanings. They accept a Cartesian conception of the author's mind, which they think of as a private realm. This picture suggests that the *real* author's ideas and intentions are inaccessible to the reader, which then leads to the idea that literary scholars must posit an *implied* author to account for the work's composition. The idea that the author is located outside the text gives plausibility to the claim that every work of narrative fiction has an internal narrator. If one accepts uncritically this a priori stipulation, it seems no longer possible to appreciate a great narrative artist such as Thomas Mann as poet *and* narrator. While the narrator is usually understood to be an agent who reports the events, the (implied) author is commonly thought to be a voiceless and silent agent who produces the text. It is considered impossible for one and the same agent to conduct the narration *and* produce the narrative text. In this essay, I will present an alternative approach to narrative fiction that emerges from a poststructuralist or enactivist conception of language. According to this view, the only narrative that can be meaningfully analyzed is the author's *written* narrative. In defending this idea, I will develop Sylvie Patron's "noncommunicative" or "poetic" theory of narration that focuses not on the misleading question "Who speaks?" but rather on the author's practice of writing ([2009] 2016, 227).

Real Acts of Narration

The view I would like to explain and defend is an optional-narrator theory, which leaves open whether the author introduces a fictional narrator or presents the story in his own person. My main thesis is that the only narrative that we can really understand and explain is constituted by the use of language, which we bring to life when reading the author's text. The narrative that a literary scholar tries to explain is a higher-order achievement that emerges from the lower-level use of linguistic expressions. In some cases the narration is transferred to a character; but this character's behavior can be analyzed only to a very limited extent. Even if there is an internal narrator responsible for a fictional narrative, we can always make it clear to ourselves that the real narrative is shaped by the author. Following Wilhelm Scherer, who suggests a tripartite classification in his *Poetik* (1977, 161–62), I will distinguish three modes of presentation:

1. Poets do not really assert anything about the life and opinions of fictional persons. But this does not mean that they introduce a separate narrator. That they speak in their own person is compatible with the fact that they pretend that the events are taking place. Disregarding this mode of presentation leads to serious errors. The pseudo-orality of a real narrator who recounts a fictional sequence of events by using written words is all too often misconstrued as the presence of a narrative voice. Dorrit Cohn, for example, assumes that we hear a "disincarnated, nameless and faceless" narrator "perorating loudly and volubly in Mann's . . . third-person novels" (1999, 132). She assumes that Mann employs an unreliable narrator who merely reports the events but does not create them. It is important to realize, however, that the narrator who talks about Aschenbach is also the "real" author who puts words in the character's mouth, guides the course of events, and carefully sets up his demise.

2. Sometimes poets introduce themselves as another person. In *The Holy Sinner*, Thomas Mann presents himself as "the spirit of story-telling" and claims that he is embodied in Clemens the Irishman. Some critics credit Clemens with an "uninhibited language-mixing . . . parallel to Mann's practice in this book" and even with a "theory of language" (Hatfield 1979, 138–39). We should distinguish, however, between Mann's playful self-presentation and the authentic self-presentation of a separate speaker. Neither the spirit of storytelling, whose work is humor-

ously associated with the work of God, nor Clemens solidify into separate objects of representation. What we are dealing with is a "masked author" who gives descriptions of himself that are philosophically interesting and brilliantly incoherent at the same time (Detering 2012, 161). They are not representations of a character; rather, they prompt the reader to imagine that he, the narrative poet, is a ghostlike being and a monk. The appeal of this technique derives from the recognition that the supposed monk who reports the outrageous events with apparent piety is in fact the narrating author. The role he assumes results in a peculiar mixture of alleged saintliness and blatant insolence.

3. Often poets unambiguously introduce a narrator who is a separate character. Mann's *Confessions of Felix Krull* would be a clear example of this mode of presentation. The narrator-as-character mode can be explained in only a limited sense, however. While it is always possible to understand why the author *makes* the invented narrator say this rather than that, it is usually pointless to ask questions about this narrator's reasons for doing something. A character does not have any purposes or interests unless the author decides for the character to have them. If we think of *Felix Krull* as a work of narrative fiction, we have to analyze the "real" narrator's use of linguistic expressions. The author is, of course, the real narrator even if he does not speak in his own person. Some critics have noticed this fact, albeit in a confused manner: "While Felix is . . . the narrator of these confessions, at times a more practiced hand pushes his aside" (Hatfield 1979, 150). The only "hand" whose narrative decisions we can understand is that of the narrating author. In this context, it would be useful to revive notions like "epic technique" (Heinze [1903] 1993).

In all three cases, the object of literary scholarship is "real acts of narration," not the speech acts of fictional narrators (Culler 1984, 11). Real acts of narration, like word choice, syntax, metrical composition, and plot construction, are aspects of the author's use of language, which can be meaningfully analyzed. The fictional narrator that resides within the work, if there is such an entity, cannot be the primary subject matter of narrative theory. Apart from the fact that narrating authors are not to be confused with fictional narrators, this way of thinking about narrative fiction allows one to better appreciate the written nature of narration, the relationship between narrative techniques and other literary procedures, and the relationship between narration and authorial self-stylization. The aim of literary scholarship is to understand what the author is doing in writing his or her text. It is an open question whether the author represents fictional events by creating a separate narrator, or represents these events by speaking in his or her own person.

The Structuralist Conception of the Literary Work

Some theorists reject the tripartite classification of narrative modes for purely conceptual reasons. In a recent article, Frank Zipfel objects that "it is not legitimate to use 'narrator' as a term for an author performing a fictional narration" (2015, 59–60). In response to the suggestion that the writer can also be the narrator, he insists that "the question of what the author does while composing his work is of no importance whatsoever and belongs to the realm of psychological speculation" (60). Zipfel sympathizes with Peter Alward's idea that "the relation between authors and readers is better modeled on the relation between sculptors and appreciators than on the relation between speakers and listeners" (Alward 2010, 392). What makes Alward's word-sculpture theory so appealing to Zipfel is that it "blocks speculations about what speech acts authors of fictional narrations perform when writing particular sentences" (Zipfel 2015, 59). These considerations indicate that Zipfel is under the spell of a misleading model of the literary work and of the author's mind. This model leads him to assume, for example, that statements about the text itself can be distinguished from statements about the use of the constituent words. And it prompts him to think that sentences that include words like "thought" or "intention" are psychological speculations. I would propose that this unexamined picture accounts for Zipfel's strenuous adherence to the claim that every work of fiction has a fictional narrator. In defending this conception, he reaffirms the traditional tenets of structuralism.

It is, of course, not uncommon to compare literary works to structures like organisms or monuments. But it was not until the twentieth century that critics began to take these analogies literally. Roman Ingarden's *The Literary Work of Art* (1931) may be the first systematic attempt to define works of literature as products detached from their authors. For

Ingarden, the work is a "many-layered structure" that needs to be distinguished from the author's psychological states but also from the process of writing ([1931] 1973, 8). The finished work is an independent sequence of signs correlated to a sequence of meanings that are reconstituted in the process of reading. For Ingarden, the author "remains completely outside the literary work" (22). While there may be important connections between the work and the author's psychology, he insists that "the author and his work constitute two heterogeneous objects" (22). Notably, Ingarden is one of the first critics to introduce a more rigid distinction between "the lyrical subject and the real poet" (265). The word "real" has a peculiar meaning here. It is used to distinguish the person who says or does something in the text from the author who in fact produced it.

Ingarden's book was not widely read in the English-speaking world, yet it was nonetheless an important inspiration for René Wellek and Austin Warren. Their highly influential *Theory of Literature* popularized Ingarden's "ingenious, highly technical analysis of the literary work of art" (1949, 152). The famous distinction between extrinsic and intrinsic approaches to the study of literature presupposes Ingarden's picture of the work as "a whole system of signs, or structure of signs" (141). While Wellek and Warren do not exclude the possibility of narrating poets, Monroe Beardsley and William Wimsatt insist on a logical separation between writer and speaker, similar to the separation we find in Ingarden. They, too, compare the poem to an autonomous structure. In their famous article "The Intentional Fallacy," they describe writing as the production of linguistic expressions that are separated from the author's intentions. The poem, they say, "is detached from the author at birth and goes about the world beyond his power to intend about it or control it" (1954, 5). They conceive of the author's mind as an inner place. Accordingly, the author's intention is defined as "the design or plan in the author's mind" (4). Even Jacques Derrida clings to this misleading picture of writing. "To write," says Derrida, "is to produce a mark that will constitute a sort of machine which is productive in turn, and which my future disappearance will not, in principle, hinder in its functioning" ([1971] 1988, 8). Derrida's thought is remarkably close to Beardsley and Wimsatt's. At least in one passage, they use the very same analogy: "Judging a poem," they write, "is like judging a . . . machine" (1954, 4).

The philosophical intuition that the text is a self-existing product separated from the author's linguistic activities generates a reconciliation problem: If one were to acknowledge that the expressions that constitute the literary work are used to express the author's attitudes, the distinction between the use of words and the finished work cannot be maintained. The following statement by Beardsley and Wimsatt may be an attempt to solve this conflict: "We ought to impute the thoughts and attitudes of the poem immediately to the dramatic *speaker*, and if to the author at all, only by a biographical act of inference" (1952, 5). Notice that the idea of authors never speaking in their own person is different from the empirical claim that authors *sometimes* introduce a dramatic speaker. It is not a generalization but a stipulation that derives its appeal from a simplistic picture, which is never put into question, at least not by Beardsley and Wimsatt. What I tentatively call "structuralist" narratology is shaped by the same preconceived conception of literary texts that is presupposed by Ingarden, Wellek, and Beardsley and Wimsatt.

Chatman's Structuralist Narratology

In calling his own approach "structuralist" (1978, 9), Seymour Chatman means, among other things, that the literary work is a linguistic product that can be explained by reference to a system of conventions without reference to the author's practice of writing. His first narratological analysis, "New Ways of Analyzing Narrative Structure," (1969) is a detailed examination of James Joyce's *Eveline* in which he applies Roland Barthes's methods of analysis from his renowned "Introduction à l'analyse structurale du récit" (1966). In explaining his approach Chatman points out that Barthes's account of narration rejects "the traditional concepts" of literary scholarship, especially the idea of narrating authors (1969, 33). Chatman was persuaded that the intrinsic approach to works of literature must be correct: Barthes's reasoning, he argues, "is immanent, as he carefully avoids Wimsatt and Beardsley's Intentional and Affective fallacies" (33).[1] Like Beardsley and Wimsatt, Chatman is convinced that the text is detached from the author. The intuition that the linguistic product and its author are distinct objects leads him to question the validity of statements that refer to the author's activities and attitudes.

In his later contributions Chatman feels no need to revise his structuralist convictions. In *Story and Discourse* he still quotes approvingly from Beardsley's *Aesthetics*: "The speaker of a literary work cannot be identified with the author" (1958, 240). Likewise, Chatman does not characterize the author as the "narrator" because the narrator is an entity "immanent to the narrative itself" (1978, 33), while the author is "extrinsic . . . to the narrative" (150).[2] In *Coming to Terms*, Chatman insists that Beardsley's work remains "the best discussion of literary intention" (1990b, 78). For Chatman, Beardsley's philosophy is an embodiment of realism and common sense that can be invoked against the vague threat of poststructuralist conceptions of language: "The anti-intentionalist position . . . has not been successfully refuted. In an era when skepticism prevails about the very possibility of knowledge, communication, and interpretation, it seems worthwhile to recall the sensible views of philosophers such as Beardsley" (1990b, 80).

One of the skeptics against whom Chatman wants to defend his position is Barbara Herrnstein Smith. In her article "Narrative Versions, Narrative Theories," she points out that narratology, as it is presented by Chatman, remains "tied to dualistic models of language and confined to the examination of decontextualized structures" (1981, 186). What she finds objectionable is not that Chatman ignores linguistic norms, literary traditions, or the broader cultural context but that he views the work as a product separated from the author's agency. When Smith denies that the work is a "detached and decontextualized entity" (183), what she really means is that the linguistic signs that constitute the text are integrated with "verbal behavior" (182). Her poststructuralist approach to the study of narrative is based on the observation that narration is a form of social behavior: "An alternative to the current narratological model would be one in which narratives were regarded not only as *structures* but also as *acts*" (182). Her proposal is to make the behavior of *real* narrators the primary subject matter of narrative theory.

Chatman observes that Smith's criticism "strikes at the heart of the theory and beyond at basic tenets of linguistics and semiotics as we know them" (1981, 802). It is interesting to see how he rejects her approach that, as he continues to acknowledge in later articles, "diverges sharply from structuralist narratology" (1990a, 309). His main reservation is that Smith's theory "is less concerned with the definition of a narrative text as such and more with the conditions of production of narratives" (1981, 806). To discredit her "alternative to the structuralist model" (806), Chatman argues that the inquiry into the methods and techniques, into the beliefs, intentions, and interests of real narrators, should be called "'narrative pragmatics' rather than 'narratology'" (806–7). Smith's theory is allegedly "irrelevant" to classical narratology, for it deals with the behavior of authors who are external to the narrative (807). In *Coming to Terms*, similar arguments are employed to dissociate the study of literary works from the study of verbal behavior: "Real authorial behavior" Chatman claims, "is a subject for literary biography, not text theory" (1990, 80). Cohn, too, describes Smith's article as an "antinarratological polemic" (1999, 111), which does not warrant serious consideration by narrative theorists.

Chatman's Problems

It is quite remarkable that Chatman's idea of narratology is also threatened by Wayne Booth's conception of rhetoric *and* by the French poststructuralist concept of *écriture*: "Thus, my position lies halfway between that of some poststructuralists, who would deny the existence of *any* agent—who would acknowledge only our encounter with *écriture*—and that of Booth, who has spoken of the implied author as 'friend and guide.' For me the implied author is neither. It is nothing other than the text itself in its inventional aspect" (1990b, 86). It is worth dwelling briefly on this passage and discussing the conflicting positions. Chatman is probably alluding to Roland Barthes, whose work after 1966 is often characterized as "poststructuralist." His famous article "The Death of the Author" (1968) is usually read as an unambiguous refutation of every notion of authorial agency—at least according to the standard interpretation. In a recent polemical article on Barthes, Joshua Landy argues, "It isn't always entirely clear what Barthes is trying to say in his essay, but one thing is certain: he wants us to stop thinking of writers when we talk about literary texts" (2017, 465). This is not an accurate construal of what Barthes is trying to do.

It is important to consider the evolution of Barthes's ideas. Raymond Picard offers a powerful critique of Barthes's work on Racine. In his forceful polemic *Nouvelle Critique ou Nouvelle Imposture*, Picard accuses Barthes of disregarding the work's dramaturgical structures (1965, 119–21). Less well known is the challenge posed to Barthes by Pierre Macherey, whose brilliant article "Literary Analysis: Tomb of Structures" was published in a structuralism issue of Jean-Paul Sartre's *Les Temps Modernes* in 1966 and appeared in the same year as a chapter in *Pour une théorie de la production littéraire*. In this essay, Macherey makes fun of Barthes's empty rhetoric and ridicules his idealized conception of structures ([1966] 1978, 136–56). He argues that the author is not a *creator* but a *writer* who operates with linguistic and ideological materials. He rejects the idea that the text is a mere product, distinct from the writer's use of language. This position was taken up by Jean-Louis Baudry (1968), Jean-Louis Houdebine (1968), and other writers who gathered around the avant-garde literary magazine *Tel Quel*. They deny that language is a vehicle of meaning, yet they nonetheless acknowledge the connection between the text and the author's artistic agency. In line with Paul Valéry's *Monsieur Teste*, they want to retain the idea of art while eliminating the mythology of artistic creation ([1934] 1947, 83).[3]

In response to the challenge posed by Picard, Macherey, Baudry, and others, Barthes gradually modified his position. In "The Death of the Author" he reaffirms his objection to intentionalism, yet while giving up the immanent approach to the study of literature. His reference to "Oxford philosophy," the conception of linguistic analysis advanced by Wittgenstein and J. L. Austin, indicates his new way of thinking about literature (1977, 145). In a later interview, Barthes acknowledges that the movement that led to French poststructuralism was initiated by Wittgenstein and Austin: "Le mouvement est parti certainement de la philosophie oxfordienne, des philosophes anglais qui ont réfléchi sur le langage, à savoir Wittgenstein et Austin" (1979, 435). Even though Wittgenstein worked in Cambridge, it is clear that leading figures of postwar Oxford philosophy were influenced by his ideas. Wittgenstein and Austin no longer consider language an outward sign of the invisible traffic of ideas or as a vehicle of meaning. They believe that a verbal utterance is more than mere words but not that there is a meaning or content that exists in addition to the words. Language conveys itself to us, and the reader's task is not to supplement words with the right meanings but to reconstruct and clarify their use. Similarly, Barthes rejects the idea that the author is a source of meaning, yet invokes the concept of a writer and considers the practice of writing the central concern of literary scholarship. For Barthes, the reader is a "scripteur virtuel" who takes up the author's words, reenacts their use, appreciates their emergent structures, and tries to explain them to others (see Zanetti and Mareuge 2018).

Chatman's objection to Booth's idea of rhetoric is noteworthy. Booth's distinction between real and implied author seems to be a concession to structuralism. But his decision to treat the work not as a self-sufficient thing but as a display of the author's rhetoric is clearly a movement away from the structuralist conception advocated by Ronald Crane, who had repeatedly emphasized the separation between the finished product and the author's agency: "Our task," he says, "is not to explain the writer's activity but the result thereof; our problem is not psychological but artistic; and hence the causes that centrally concern us are the internal causes of which the only sufficient evidence is the work itself as a completed product" (1953, 166). Like Crane, Booth does not want to return to a mentalistic conception of literary criticism. In contrast to Crane, however, he wants to examine the beliefs, purposes, and interests manifested in the author's verbal behavior. He is looking for a general concept such as "technique" or "rhetoric" that covers everything the author is doing with words: "We can be satisfied only with a term that is as broad as the work itself but still capable of calling attention to that work as the product of a choosing, evaluating person rather than as a self-existing thing" ([1961] 1983, 74).

There is an interesting similarity between Booth's insistence on the author's rhetoric and the French poststructuralists' notions of "textual production" and "scriptural practice." Critics such as Jean-Louis Baudry and Jean-Louis Houdebine would call into question Booth's idea of rhetoric as communication. But they, too, are looking for terms that describe the text as a locus of the author's artistic inventiveness: "In scriptural practice," says Baudry, "textual production is written legible in its product" (1968, 362). Françoise Van Rossum-Guyon is a poststructuralist who has seriously studied Booth's *The Rhetoric of Fiction*. She discusses his turn to the author's rhetoric with great sympathy (1972a, 222; see Van Rossum-Guyon 1970, 482–94). Booth's approach to narrative fiction lends support to her conviction that the text itself can no longer be meaningfully contrasted with the author's use of language. The ideas explored in *The Rhetoric of Fiction* are closer to her views than are Michel Riffaterre's, who revives "structuralisme" with its inappropriate preference for "lectures immanentes" and its dubious assumption of the "autonomie . . . du texte" (Van Rossum-Guyon 1972b, 253). Chatman's response to Booth's conception of authorial agency is strikingly different from Van Rossum-

Guyon's: "I stick by the anti-intentionalist view that a published text *is* in fact a self-existing thing" (1990b, 81). Again, he wrongly supposes that there is a necessary connection between intentionalism and the idea that words are embedded in behavior.

Chatman's main objection to Booth, Barthes, and Smith is that they confuse the process of writing with the finished product. He simply reiterates the distinction that is called into question. Moreover, one can easily show that Chatman, too, uses concepts that refer both to the author's linguistic activities and to the literary work itself. He seems to recognize this but is unable to acknowledge that a work of literature is constituted by the author's use of words (see 1993, 90). To reinterpret the sentences that apparently refer to the author's agency, he introduces the notion of an implied author: "Positing an implied author inhibits the overhasty assumption that the reader has direct access through the fictional text to the real author's intentions and ideology" (1990b, 76). He offers various definitions, none of them satisfying. In some places, Chatman equates the "implied author" with the literary work: "The text is itself the implied author" (1990b, 81). This statement is clearly absurd, for linguistic activities such as choosing words, constructing sentences, and describing fictional events must be attributed to an agent who is distinct from the text. In other passages, Chatman suggests that the "implied author" is a hypothetical reconstruction of the author's artistic inventiveness by the literary scholar: "The implied author is not a historical human being, but rather the agent through whom we re-create the fiction" (1993, 95). This is an obvious confusion of the hypothetical *conception* of the author developed by the literary scholar in the process of reading with what it is a conception *of*. In contrast to Booth and Smith, Chatman refuses to acknowledge that the written word is intertwined with the author's behavior. While he presents himself as a defender of common sense against poststructuralism, the poststructuralist notion of writing is far more promising than his incomprehensible claim that the implied author is the text itself or an "imaginary person" (1993, 24n1).

Not entirely unfounded, admittedly, is the fear that by including "real" authors, one reinvokes an intentionalism that uses the text to speculate about the author's mental states. In his recent article "Does Austen Need Narrators? Does Anyone?," Brian Boyd combines the idea of narrating authors with the commitment to an "inferential model of lan-

guage" (2017, 291). According to Boyd, we have "no direct access to authors' minds" (288). We make sense of their works by hypothesizing and
re-creating the hidden mental processes behind their overt linguistic behavior: "In order to fathom and predict others' behavior, we need and
want to infer and model the beliefs, desires, and intentions behind their
actions" (302). At best, this is a metaphorical description of literary interpretation. Beardsley was surely right that it is not the critic's task to infer what the author had in mind when writing the text. It does not imply,
however, that we can avoid talking about the author when studying literary works. The analysis of the author's practice of writing is to be distinguished from traditional forms of literary criticism that conceive of
the author's mind as the source of meaning. Progress in narrative theory can be achieved by questioning the assumptions shared by intentionalists such as Boyd and structuralists such as Chatman.

Toward a Poststructuralist or Enactivist Theory of Narrative Fiction

A more promising conception of narrative theory emerges from a "poststructuralist or naturalist" account of language, advanced by Barbara
Herrnstein Smith (1997). Smith's general conception of mind and language is compelling. I would like to restate the position as follows:
Poststructuralism or enactivism is the attempt to develop a conception
of mind and language that rejects both the misleading picture of the mind
as an inaccessible place populated by thoughts *and* the equally misleading picture of the text as a structure separated from the author's use of
language. In this way, it challenges both structuralism and intentionalism. On the one hand, it claims that an engagement with the text is an
engagement with a practice of writing. On the other hand, it attempts
to "depsychologize psychology" (Cavell 1976, 91). "Having" a meaning is
not to be understood as a relation between a word and its meaning but
rather in terms of having a purpose or value in the context of verbal behavior. Similarly, "having a mind" is defined no longer as a relation between a person and an inner place where ideas are located, but rather as
the possession of a behavioral repertoire that is manifested in, among
other things, reading and writing.

The most important challenge facing an enactivist theory of narrative
is to formulate a coherent theory of reading. Enactivists must reconcile

the idea that one can perceive the author's "real" acts of narration with the idea that the author is not present while we as readers try to make sense of the author's text. Now one of the guiding principles of an enactivist approach to narrative is that language is not a vehicle of meaning. When we read a narrative text, we form ideas about what the author is doing in writing. But to form ideas about what the author is doing, we ourselves need to be able to use the words. After all, one grasps their purpose not simply by paying attention to them, nor by reproducing their intended meaning or even producing a new meaning in one's own mind. Rather, one understands what the author is doing by producing a correct reconstruction of a pattern of behavior. In other words, it is not enough simply to *describe* the text; it must be brought to life. To do this, a reader must develop a certain degree of narrative competence. What Gilbert Ryle has established for intelligent behavior in general applies in particular to the appreciation of narratives: "Roughly, execution and understanding are merely different exercises of knowledge of the tricks of the same trade" (2009, 42).

Just as understanding linguistic expressions can be freed from the myth of meanings, understanding the author's thoughts can be separated from the myth of mental processes. Here we can draw on the conception of empathy outlined by Willard Quine (2013, 200–201) and further developed by Howard Wettstein (2004). According to their theory, statements that refer to the author's thoughts, beliefs, feelings, or intentions do not attempt to describe mental states in the way that structuralists such as Chatman and intentionalists such as Boyd suppose. The phrase "The narrator thinks that . . ." is followed by what Quine called a "dramatic act" (2013, 200), which identifies the readiness to manifest a pattern of behavior by imitating this pattern in our own behavioral repertoire. Empathy is conceived here not as an attempt to reproduce an unobservable mental experience but as the deployment of one's behavioral repertoire to identify a behavioral disposition. The characterization of patterns of behavior can take many forms, such as recitation, paraphrase, indirect speech, propositional attitude report, and rehearsal of a complex argument. Every perception of the author's practice of writing involves the activation of one's own linguistic abilities. Of course, this enactivist conception of empathy should be spelled out in much more detail. With these considerations I merely intend to establish the viability of the idea that reading a text is neither a production of meanings nor an inference to unobservable intentions but an attempt to reconstruct and explain the writer's patterns of behavior. This idea that we integrate the author's words into our own repertoire helps us to see how we can engage with authors even though they are not present when we read their texts.

Conclusion

As soon as one overcomes the separation between the work itself and the author's verbal behavior, there is no longer any reason to hold on to the rigid assumption of a fictional narrator inherent in the work. The thesis I have defended in this article, however, is a more fundamental one. I have argued that real narrators are the only narrators whose methods and interests are the proper object of literary studies. What is needed is an epistemology of literary studies that is based on a sophisticated theory of reading that avoids the pitfalls of intentionalism and structuralism. One principle of such a theory has been proposed in this article: We take up the words that constitute the text and deploy our behavioral repertoire to bring "real" acts of narration to life. With our own linguistic abilities, we tentatively reenact what the "real" narrator tries to do. Our hypotheses may prove to be wrong, but they reconstruct the author's use of language.

Notes

1. This lends support to Gérard Genette's observation that "structural analysis," "close reading," and "immanent analysis" are roughly equivalent: "In a way, the notion of structural analysis can be regarded as a simple equivalent of what Americans call 'close reading' and which would be called in Europe, following Spitzer, the 'immanent study of works'" (Genette [1966] 1986, 69).
2. Following Chatman, Dorrit Cohn favors a "formalist-structuralist approach to narrative" (1999, 110), which is essentially an "intratextual approach" (148). It requires the postulation of an internal narrator, even for Mann's *Death in Venice*.
3. "One of Teste's pet notions, and not his least fanciful, was wanting to keep art—*Ars*—and yet do away with the artist's or author's illusions" ([1934] 1947, 83).

References

Alward, Peter. 2010. "Word-Sculpture, Speech Acts, and Fictionality." *Journal of Aesthetics and Art Criticism* 68 (4): 389–99.

Barthes, Roland. 1966. "Introduction à l'analyse structurale du récit." *Communications* 8: 1–27.

———. (1968) 1977. "The Death of the Author." In *Image-Music-Text*, essays selected and translated by Stephen Heath, 142–54. London: Fontana Press.

———. 1979. "Rencontre avec Roland Barthes." *French Review* 52 (3): 432–39.

Baudry, Jean-Louis. 1968. "Linguistique et production textuelle." In *Théorie d'ensemble*, 351–64. Paris: Le Seuil.

Beardsley, Monroe C. 1958. *Aesthetics: Problems in the Philosophy of Criticism.* New York: Harcourt.

Beardsley, Monroe C., and William K. Wimsatt. 1954. "The Intentional Fallacy." In Wimsatt, *The Verbal Icon: Studies in the Meaning of Poetry*, 3–18. Lexington: University Press of Kentucky.

Booth, Wayne. (1961) 1983. *The Rhetoric of Fiction.* 2nd ed. Chicago: University of Chicago Press.

Boyd, Brian. 2017. "Does Austen Need Narrators? Does Anyone?" *New Literary History* 48 (2): 285–308.

Cavell, Stanley. 1976. "Aesthetic Problems of Modern Philosophy." In *Must We Mean What We Say: A Book of Essays*, 73–96. Cambridge: Cambridge University Press.

Chatman, Seymour. 1969. "New Ways of Analyzing Narrative Structure." *Language and Style* 2: 3–36.

———. 1978. *Story and Discourse: Narrative Structure in Fiction and Film.* Ithaca NY: Cornell University Press.

———. 1981. "Reply to Barbara Herrnstein Smith." *Critical Inquiry* 7 (4): 802–9.

———. 1990a. "What Can We Learn from a Contextualist Narratology?" *Poetics Today* 11 (2): 309–28.

———. 1990b. *Coming to Terms: The Rhetoric of Narrative in Fiction and Film.* Ithaca NY: Cornell University Press.

———. 1993. *Reading Narrative Fiction.* New York: Macmillan.

Cohn, Dorrit. 1999. *The Distinction of Fiction.* Baltimore: Johns Hopkins University Press.

Crane, Ronald. 1953. *The Languages of Criticism and the Structure of Poetry.* Toronto: University of Toronto Press.

Culler, Jonathan. 1984. "Problems in the Theory of Fiction." *Diacritics* 14 (1): 2–11.

Derrida, Jacques. (1971) 1988. "Signature Event Context." In *Limited Inc.* Evanston IL: Northwestern University Press.

Detering, Heinrich. 2012. "Das Werk und die Gnade. Zu Religion und Kunstreligion in der Poetik Thomas Manns." In *Der ungläubige Thomas. Zur*

Religion in Thomas Manns Romanen, edited by Niklaus Peter and Thomas Sprecher, 149–69. Frankfurt am Main: Klostermann.

Genette, Gérard. (1966) 1986. "Structuralism and Literary Criticism." In *Modern Criticism and Theory: A Reader*, edited by David Lodge, 62–78. London: Longman.

Hatfield, Henry. 1979. *From "The Magic Mountain": Mann's Later Masterpieces*. Ithaca NY: Cornell University Press.

Heinze, Richard. (1903) 1993. *Virgil's Epic Technique*. Translated by Hazel Harvey, David Harvey, and Fred Robertson. Berkeley: University of California Press.

Houdebine, Jean-Louis. 1968. "Première approche de la notion de texte." In *Théorie d'ensemble*, 257–72. Paris: Le Seuil.

Ingarden, Roman. (1931) 1973. *The Literary Work of Art*. Translated by George Grabowicz. Evanston IL: Northwestern University Press.

Landy, Joshua. 2017. "The Most Overrated Article of All Time?" *Philosophy and Literature* 41 (2): 465–70.

Macherey, Pierre. (1966) 1978. *A Theory of Literary Production*. Translated by Geoffrey Wall. London: Routledge.

Patron, Sylvie. (2009) 2016. *Le Narrateur: Un problème de théorie narrative*. Paris: Lambert-Lucas.

Picard, Raymond. 1965. *Nouvelle critique ou nouvelle imposture*. Paris: Jean-Jacques Pauvert.

Quine, Willard. 2013. *Word and Object*, edited by Dagfinn Føllesdal. Cambridge MA: Harvard University Press.

Ricardou, Jean, and Françoise Van Rossum-Guyon, eds. 1972. *Nouveau Roman: Hier, aujourd'hui*. Paris: Union Générale d'Édition.

Ryle, Gilbert. 2009. *The Concept of Mind*, edited by Julia Tanney. London: Routledge.

Scherer, Wilhelm. 1977. *Poetik*, edited by Gunter Reiss. Tübingen: Niemeyer.

Smith, Barbara Herrnstein. 1981. "Narrative Versions, Narrative Theories." In *American Criticism in the Poststructuralist Age*, edited by Jonathan Culler and Ira Konigsberg, 162–86. Ann Arbor: University of Michigan Press.

———. 1997. "Doing without Meaning." In *Belief and Resistance: Dynamics of Contemporary Intellectual Controversy*, 52–72. Cambridge MA: Harvard University Press.

Valéry, Paul. (1934) 1947. *Monsieur Teste*. Translated by Jackson Mathews. New York: Alfred A. Knopf.

Van Rossum-Guyon, Françoise. 1970. "Point de vue ou perspective narrative. Théories et concepts critiques." *Poétique* 4: 476–95.

———. 1972a. "Discussion." In Ricardou and Van Rossum-Guyon 1972, 230–54.

———. 1972b. "Le Nouveau Roman comme critique du roman." In Ricardou and Van Rossum-Guyon 1972, 215–29.

Wellek, René, and Austin Warren. 1949. *Theory of Literature*. London: Jonathan Cape.

Wettstein, Howard. 2004. *The Magic Prism. An Essay in the Philosophy of Language.* Oxford: Oxford University Press.

Zanetti, Sandro, and Agathe Mareuge. 2018. "Roland Barthes im Gespräch mit Georges Charbonnier: Über eine mögliche Theorie der Lektüre (1967)." *Sprache und Literatur* 47 (1): 97–109.

Zipfel, Frank. 2015. "Narratorless Narration? Some Reflections on the Arguments for and against the Ubiquity of Narrators in Fictional Narration." In *Author and Narrator: Transdisciplinary Contributions to a Narratological Debate*, edited by Dorothee Birke and Tilmann Köppe, 45–80. Berlin: De Gruyter.

4   Voice and Time

JOHN BRENKMAN

Novel theory greets narratology as an insightful but overconfident and often dogmatic friend. The narratologist proposes formulas of vast scope and seeks to generalize, ideally to the point of universal validity, the nature and techniques of storytelling across all narrative genres, forms, and media. The novel theorist is more likely preoccupied with the historical specificities and artistic singularities of novelistic practice and works from the premise that the rise of the novel—as it has occurred, and continues to occur, in various societies, among various groups, and at different historical moments—requires particular social, educational, technological, and economic conditions. The novel is at once a literary form, a particular cultural phenomenon and social practice, and a unique commodity (the book) that unites artwork and manufactured object. All of which is why the novel's survival is often seen as inevitably or already precarious.

What narratology and novel theory undoubtedly do share is the fuzzy category of *narrator*. Is the narrator a subject? a rhetorical construct? a fiction? a simulacrum? a readerly illusion? Is the narrator a purely linguistic effect? Is it neuropsychologically grounded? Is it an evolutionarily acquired cognitive capacity—if so, is it essential or superfluous to our species survival?

The invitation from Sylvie Patron to contribute an essay to a discussion and debate regarding the concept of narrator and, in particular, its validity in the analysis of third-person narrations brought to my attention the narratological controversy over what are called optional-narrator and pan-narrator theories. Patron's own work brought me back to the differences between narrative theory and novel theory, which are sometimes productively in tension and sometimes in irreconcilable conflict.

How do those tensions, productive and antagonistic, play out when it comes to the category of *narrator*?

Perhaps the most basic and hence scarcely noticed convention of fictional storytelling, a convention pilfered from factual storytelling, is that events are being *recounted*. When I pick up a novel, I know full well that the events making up the story I will read are invented, fictive, did not happen. But the moment I begin reading, I fully accept that these events are being recounted. Invention and recounting. Roland Barthes's *Writing Degree Zero*, an essay as provocative and enigmatic today as it must have been in 1953, cast a suspicious eye on the novelistic tradition's use of the *passé simple*—the preterit—that is, the verb tense in French that places the story's events in a past that is absolutely cut off from the present. A chasm separates the past of the story from the present of the narration, the deeds of the *énoncé* from the act of the *énonciation*, the past of the narrated events from the present of the speech event. It is as though, as Barthes sees it, the very act of writing tried to detach itself from *l'histoire*—that is, from the story it tells and from history itself ([1953] 1968, 29–41). That sense that events in a novel are being recounted gives rise to a consequent question, obvious and yet, as a somewhat later Barthesian provocation demonstrates, enigmatic: Who is speaking? It is then that the concept of "narrator" can be said to arise—as a too easy and easily unexamined answer to *Qui parle?* The narrator problematic is a question of voice and a question of time and a question of the linkages of voice and time.

Theoretical models of the narrator in impersonal third-person narratives—from Wayne Booth's distinction between author, implied author, and narrator through the various narratological models placing a narrator and a narratee within an imaginary space that brackets out the empirical writer and reader—arose, I suspect, as a kind of back-formation from aspects of certain first-person narratives. I argue elsewhere that Edgar Allan Poe in an uncanny story like "The Black Cat" organizes the relation of the *I*-storyteller to the discourse as a whole in such a way that the moral dread expressed by the narrator is encased within an aesthetic fascination with that dread. Poe achieves his ideal of "unity of effect" through the simultaneity and differentiation of the two attitudes. In my hypothesis, such an artful joining-differentiating of narrator and discourse contributed to establishing "the conventions of the imaginary space of narration" in prose fiction, a space that will be theorized via the narrator/narratee relation or the distinction of narrator and implied author and projected as a valid account of all narrational practices.[1]

If, however, we refuse to use narrator and narratee to bracket out writer and reader and if we resist the postulate of an implied author, which sets up the ungraspable triplet of subjects—[writer (implied author [narrator])]—text—[([narratee] implied reader) reader]—a different question imposes itself. How does the writer write the telling of the story? The *writing*-of-the-*telling* is the act and process whose nature, procedures, and techniques ought to be the theoretical focus. For there is only one actual subject in prose fiction, namely, the writer. It is more than a little weird that narrative theory works so hard to keep the writer and writing out of bounds.

Structuralism's distinction between the *énoncé* and *énonciation* and delineation of "shifters" as those linguistic features that establish links between *énoncé* and *énonciation* remain helpful terms because they bear predominantly on, precisely, subjectivity and temporality. To modify the terms a bit, they bear on the relation between a discourse's articulated temporality and its articulating subject, including the convention of recounting that is so basic to fictional narration as to be considered a norm. The norm, however, is hardly fixed. The entwining of articulating subject and articulated time has turned out to be marvelously malleable, paradoxical, and fluid in novelistic discourse. Novelists exploit an intrinsic capacity of language to volatilize subject and temporality in the *énonciation/énoncé* relation. Shifters determine where the speaker is situated in time and space relative to the events spoken about. I will illustrate language's volatilizing capacity with a nonliterary—or at least nonnovelistic—example. One day, setting out to jog down the esplanade along the East River in New York, I caught sight of graffiti that had been written on the back of a street sign. It exploits the paradoxes of subjectivity and temporality in the relation of *énoncé* and *énonciation* in but nine syllables:

> We were so in love
> when I wrote this

Logically, the shifter has missed a gear. If these lines were those that a poet inscribed in a copy of his or her latest book of poems given to a former lover, the voice/time relation would seamlessly make sense; *this* would refer to the book of poems in which the message is inscribed. In the graffiti, by contrast, *this* refers to the utterance itself and so loops the *énonciation* through the *énoncé* to paradoxical effect. Yet rhetorically and poetically the sentence does make sense. Its playful violation of discourse-and-time logic evokes a variety of possible intentions, moods, tonalities: a cheeky sense of love's fleetingness, anticipatory melancholy, fatalistic self-doubt, self-defeating fatalism.

In the novel the very difference between invention and recounting, the separation of writing and telling, the time of the story and the time of the discourse, can be volatilized. It is the marvel of narrative art. There are innumerable, still unexhausted ways of crossing those boundaries back and forth, over and over, in order to weave a narrative discourse. In Toni Morrison's *Jazz*, to summarize an example I discuss in the earlier essay, the first-person narrator is not given a precise identity. She—and there is reason to assume the narrator is a woman—is ostensibly a neighbor of the protagonists in 1920s Harlem, who are known to her through incidental contact and neighborhood gossip. But her knowledge of Joe and Violet continually exceeds what a gossipy neighbor could actually know; in a kind of inversion of free indirect discourse, the neighborly narrator starts blending into her discourse the sort of inventing and shaping act that belongs to the writer, culminating at the end in a crisis in which events outstrip the story's very moral design: "It never occurred to me that they [Joe and Violet] were . . . putting their lives together. . . . They danced and walked all over me." At that crux the *me* is indistinguishably the *I*-narrator and the writer.

A number of other novelists in recent decades have also treated the inner life or history of characters as a matter of *conjecture*. And, indeed, a writer's relation to the characters he or she creates is closer to conjecture than to knowledge, and readers, it turns out, slide—shift gears—rather effortlessly between the recounted and the invented. In *American Pastoral*, Philip Roth's narrator and alter ego, the novelist Nathan Zuckerman, now sixty, tells the story of Swede Levov, the older brother of his boyhood friend Jerry; what he is able to piece together from a brief meeting with the elderly businessman and the startling revelations he learns from Jerry after Swede's death leave Zuckerman with unanswerable questions, so he meshes the facts he has into an invented interiority and conjectural history of Swede's life. The narrator in Tim O'Brien's *In the Lake of the Woods* is a blend of an investigative journalist and a novelist, meticulously assembling facts and going through archives to solve the mystery of the disappearance of a disgraced politician shortly after the suspicious disappearance of his wife and, on the other hand, conjecturing and inventing the protagonist's inner life, childhood, and Vietnam-era secrets, all the while drawing on memories of his own (see Brenkman 2018). O'Brien's John Wade and Roth's Swede Levov, like Morrison's Joe and Violet, are no less compelling as characters, no less engaging of the reader's imagination and empathy, for being in narratives that shuttle back and forth between recounting and invention.

The art of the novel, whether the narrative is first-person or third-, is not essentially a matter of knowing or watching. The epistemic metaphor—the omniscient narrator, limited omniscience, partial omniscience—like the visual metaphors—point of view, perspective, focalization—eclipses the *discourse* nature of the novel in favor of categories separated from language though often, to be sure, evoked and sustained by it. For Morrison, Roth, and O'Brien the limits of knowledge, specifically the pitfalls, blind spots, and illusions endemic to knowing another person, become part of the thematic texture as well as narrational techniques of *Jazz, American Pastoral,* and *In the Lake of the Woods.* For these authors, omniscience with regard to a character is an absurdity. They are not mind readers. To use a little Heideggerian terminology, these novelists bring out that every bit of discourse disclosing a character leaves something undisclosed; the oscillations of deconcealing and concealing, of the undeconcealed and the simulated, constitute the very *movement* of novelistic prose, a movement that eludes the epistemic and visual metaphorics of narrative theory.

How far ought we question the epistemic metaphor when it comes to novelistic discourse and the conception of the narrator? The viability of the concept of omniscience for narrative analysis is carefully taken apart and refuted by Jonathan Culler. He seeks to liberate narrative theory from this notion that owes its coherence to a theological and monotheistic idea. He opens an alternative account of the various narrative "effects that people have sought to describe through the dubious notion of omniscience," including, principally, "the performative authoritativeness of many narrative declarations"; "the reporting of innermost thoughts and feelings"; and "the synoptic impersonal narration of the realist tradition" (Culler [2004] 2006, 190). Commenting on the opening sentence of Jane Austen's *Emma*, Culler writes, "Critics are inclined to say that the narrator knows these things. Since we cannot dispute them, arguing that probably Emma was really older and not handsome at all, we might think that we are dealing with special, superhuman knowledge. But in fact it is not a question of knowledge. You could know this about a friend—it would be a permissible sort of generalization—but in the novel the claim has a different status: by convention we accept the statement as a given of the narrative world" (190).

Novelists in the nineteenth century encountered two phenomena that elicited contrary artistic possibilities. Newly radicalized individual possibility, at once a promise and an ideology, fostered aspirations and ideals, especially in the life histories of young men, including writers and artists themselves, which social conditions seldom allowed to be fulfilled. On the other hand, the rise of the positive sciences postulated the idea and ideal of truth as the adequation of a discourse to reality. The novelistic exploration of lost illusions found artistic means in the power to expose and debunk that originated in Cervantes. Thus Balzac, Stendhal, Flaubert. The notion that the adequation of discourse and reality produce truth inspires the kind of realism associated with the British novel, backed by the tradition of empiricism in Anglophone philosophy.

Outside the theological register of divine omniscience, the positive sciences developed a concept of truth that undoubtedly guided novelists' rhetorical, stylistic, and narrational strategies. According to this conception, truth is attained when *discourse* is "adequate to" *reality*. The adequation of discourse and reality produces truth. Whereas the theorists of omniscience covertly employ a quasi-theological idea of knowledge, as Culler decisively demonstrates, the novelists whose works came to exemplify narrative omniscience may have adapted, rather, the contemporary scientific understanding of knowledge. By the same token, of course, the scientific aspiration to total knowledge resonates with the antecedent of divine omniscience.

How to break open the sense of *discourse* deployed in the adequation theory of truth and measure it against the nature of *novelistic* discourse? When Heidegger questions the adequation theory of truth—as he puts it, "the agreement or conformity of knowledge with fact" (1971, 51)—he does not reject it out of hand but rather argues that for entities to appear *as* beings to which discourse *can* conform, that is, to appear *as* facts, there must be an unacknowledged interpretation of being that allows them to appear as just that in the first place. Heidegger calls this unacknowledged interpretation of being the forgetting of being and blames it on the Cartesian modernity of rationalism and science. In a rejoinder, Milan Kundera says that the literary form that Cervantes's modernity inaugurated "is nothing other than the investigation of this forgotten being" (Kundera [1986] 1988, 4). It is, I've tried to suggest, in the movements and oscillations of novelistic invention and recounting, writing and telling, time of the story and time of the discourse, subjectivity and temporality, that that novelistic investigation of being occurs.

There is a pitch-perfect passage of third-person narration in *The Great Gatsby*, oscillating gently between commentary and observation, between social behaviors and a character's interiority (just short of free indirect discourse). It touches on the moment, four years before the main events of the novel, when Daisy, in the face of Gatsby's absence and delayed return from the Great War, decides to marry Tom Buchanan:

> For Daisy was young and her artificial world was redolent of orchids and pleasant, cheerful snobbery and orchestras which set the rhythm of the year, summing up the sadness and suggestiveness of life in new tunes. All night the saxophones wailed the hopeless comment of the *Beale Street Blues* while a hundred pairs of golden and silver slippers shuffled the shining dust. At the gray tea hour there were always rooms that throbbed incessantly with this low, sweet fever, while fresh faces drifted here and there like rose petals blown by the sad horns around the floor.
>
> Through this twilight universe Daisy began to move again with the season; suddenly she was again keeping half a dozen dates a day with half a dozen men, and drowsing asleep at dawn with the beads and chiffon of an evening dress tangled among dying orchids on the floor beside her bed. And all the time something within her was crying for a decision. She wanted her life shaped now, immediately— and the decision must be made by some force—of love, of money, of unquestionable practicality—that was close at hand.

That force took shape in the middle of spring with the arrival of Tom Buchanan. There was a wholesome bulkiness about his person and position, and Daisy was flattered. Doubtless there was a certain struggle and a certain relief. The letter reached Gatsby while he was still at Oxford. (Fitzgerald [1925] 2004, 151)

The passage is readily classifiable as third-person "partial omniscience." So, what makes it remarkable other than its eloquence and tact? Simply that this novel is not a third-person narration at all but first-person. The narrator, Nick Carraway, is Daisy's cousin—"second cousin once removed" (5)—and while he is presumably told of Daisy's letter by Gatsby, he witnesses none of the other events, social or psychic, detailed in the passage. If one were not a literary theorist tasked with rethinking the very idea of the third-person narrator this passage would almost certainly be read through without the least sense of disjunction or irregularity. In style, tone, and attitude it is on a par with several moments where Nick's aesthetic, moral, and psychological inflections of the narrative intensify, usually for no more than a few sentences or a paragraph. The passage does, though, break the epistemic decorum scrupulously maintained on every other page of the novel. Yet it seems wrong to call it a lapse. How then to understand this event within the narrative discourse?

It could be taken as Nick's suddenly freer exercise of his imaginative powers—or Fitzgerald's exercise of *his*, a brief foray to test out the voice of third-person narration. The passage is at once fully consonant with Nick's voice and yet, as is clear when it is set off by itself, capable of sustained narration unattached to Nick or any other particular entity within the story. The overlap and the difference throw light on the theoretical controversy posed by those who question the validity of attributing third-person narration to a "narrator." Stylization and individuating inflections imbue the prose of a third-person narration, even a staunchly "impersonal" third-person narration, with a sensibility. The more at once complex and coherent, fluid and formative the sensibility the better. In this instance, the stylization, inflections, and sensibility are derived from, or associated with, the first-person narration attributed to Nick Carraway and firmly established by this late point in the novel. The passage allows a complex and coherent, fluid and formative third-person voice to emerge from Fitzgerald's creation of Nick's first-person narration. This overlap underscores that the novelist's task of creating voice requires much the same elements for first-person and third-person narration. What then of the difference? Prevailing narratological categories could define the difference as that between "homodiegetic" and "heterodiegetic" narrators, Nick being in the story and the ostensible narrator of the third-person passage outside the story.

That distinction would overlook the fact that here the difference is at the same time a relation *within* the text. *The Great Gatsby* is by no means "metafiction" as the term has been applied to a number of later twentieth-century novels, and yet a reflection on the art of the novel is here embedded within its own narrative procedures. The passage I have been discussing is the culminating instance, intentional or not, of that self-reflection; it amounts to a transmutation within the narrative discourse itself. The other instances are explicit, but they too loop the *énonciation* through the *énoncé*, the discourse through the story, and the writing through the telling to effect a paradox, a paradox that we readily accept. The first chapter opens with a short preamble that identifies the narrative to follow as the book Nick Carraway writes, casting it as recollection, unshakeable fascination, and self-reflection, all of which is tinged with irony and ambivalence: "When I came back from the East last autumn I felt that I wanted the world to be in uniform and at a sort of moral attention forever; I wanted no more riotous excursions with privileged glimpses into the human heart. Only Gatsby, the man who gives his name to this book, was exempt from my reaction—Gatsby, who represented everything for which I have an unaffected scorn" (2). Nick's act of writing is referred to in one other moment early on: "Reading over what I have written so far, I see I have given the impression that the events of three nights several weeks apart were all that absorbed me. On the contrary, they were merely casual events in a crowded summer." (55).

Nick's narration is granted the status of writing, as though Fitzgerald's own endeavor of creating voice is doubled by Nick's effort to recount events and personages that profoundly affected him. Fitzgerald writes Nick writing. When that relation folds back on itself in the momentary slide from first- to third-person, Nick's sensibility mutates into the sensibility of impersonal third-person narration. How to imbue a third-person narration with sharply etched attitudes, values, and inner turmoil at the same time as acute powers of disinterested observation, empathy, and incisive social commentary—is that not perhaps the artistic problem Fitzgerald tacitly poses for himself in this hinge passage? Looked at the other way around, the passage reveals that Fitzgerald's path to discovering the full potential of third-person narration was to write a novel in first-person.

The artistic problem requires more than a grammatical solution. Fitzgerald's solution is to create a first-person narrator who is at once fully implicated in all the other characters' actions and relations and at the same time removed from their field of action. The remove has to do with romance and sexuality. Beyond the premise, stated in the preamble, that Nick attracts people's confidences and is "inclined to reserve all judgment" (1), it is his aversion to, perhaps incapacity or disdain for, romance that sets him apart, most sharply and distinctly of course from Gatsby, whose fascination for Nick lies in his having "some heightened sensitivity to the promises of life . . . an extraordinary gift for hope, a romantic readiness" (2). Nick listens to everyone, rides along on their adventures, facilitates their clandestine rendezvous, while his own romantic attachments arise in vagueness and end by evaporation. He comes to escape "a girl out West" (19) and rumors they are engaged; he has "a short affair with a girl who . . . worked in the accounting department" until her brother signals disapproval, "so when she went on vacation in July I let it quietly blow away" (56); his affair with Jordan Baker follows—"I wasn't actually in love, but I felt a kind of tender curiosity" (57)—until it ends in an aimless phone call the day after the hit-and-run: "I don't know which of us hung up with a sharp click, but I know I didn't care" (155). Nick's passionless attachments and drift toward disaffection are what make him an apt, complex, and unobtrusive narrator. His sensibility suffuses the novel's prose, but he initiates none of its action. That harbingers the brief transmutation to third-person. He even has "partial omniscience" thanks to circumstances, that is, thanks to Fitzgerald's artfully woven storyline as it makes him the only character who knows everyone's relation to everyone else.

A parallel in another novel of the mid-1920s jolted the course of American fiction. It too is a first-person narration; it too involves a small circle of acquaintances whose relations with one another seethe with potential violence; and its narrator too has a crippled relation to romance and sexuality. Unlike Nick Carraway, though, Jake Barnes is filled with yearning and deep attachment. In love with the free-spirited, ever fragile Brett Ashley and wrapped up in all her adventures and misadventures, Jake has no future with her because of the unspecified injury to his genitals suffered during the war. Like *The Great Gatsby* (1925), *The Sun Also Rises* (1926) is told by a narrator who is implicated in everything and initiates nothing. His attitudes, values, and inner turmoil inform his acute powers of disinterested observation, empathy, and social commentary. Hemingway mostly deployed third-person in the short fiction he wrote before he took on the project of this, his first novel, and faced the task of sustaining a narrative voice over multiple episodes and characters. Short stories easily eschew duration, whereas novels require it. It would be mere speculation to argue, as I just have with Fitzgerald, quite speculatively, that Hemingway needed to explore the *novelistic* possibilities of third-person via first-person narration in order to achieve a stylistic synthesis of sensibility and impersonality—would be mere speculation were it not for the fact that he tried to transform his first draft of *The Sun Also Rises* from first-person to third- and abandoned the effort after a chapter and a half.

The hopelessness of Jake's desire gives the story its shape, not because he strives and fails but because he cannot strive at all. No future unwinds from his desire. The narrative of *The Sun Also Rises* is relentlessly in the present. Structurally, the chronology of the story and the order of its presentation match. There are no movements in time backward or forward. The present is not thereby full, however. The sheer movement of time passing carries the story and the characters along as they go from café to café, bar to bar, bar to dance hall, fishing to bullfights, resort to festival, Paris to Pamplona, San Sebastián to Pamplona, Paris to San Sebastián, Paris to Madrid, and Brett from lover to lover. The past does not give the present meaning or form; the present finds no orientation to the future. The ever-passing present is empty, an unmasterable flow.

The future is foreclosed in *The Great Gatsby* as well, but with a different theme and structure. The thematic of time charges the novel's final sentence: "So we beat on, boats against the current, borne back ceaselessly into the past" (180). It became the epitaph on the Fitzgeralds' tomb. In the novel it captures something essential in the experience of both the romantic protagonist and the disaffected narrator. The framing of the narration as Nick's writing marks out the events of the story from

two years earlier as something he tries to flee and is drawn back to because of the force of his fascination with Gatsby the romantic. The past
pulls on Gatsby himself in the sense that everything he has done for four
years has been in search of lost love, a prodigious effort through crim-
inal activity to remake himself and become rich enough to be worthy
of Daisy's love and seduce her out of her marriage. But the novel does
not structure itself on his quest. James Gatz might plausibly have been
the protagonist of an ironic bildungsroman patterned after Julien Sorel
or Frédéric Moreau, but Fitzgerald does not center the narrative on his
striving. Rather the story in effect begins with the fulfillment of Gatsby's
dream and its nearly simultaneous unraveling. The future goes dark at
the very instant of its brightest promise, as Daisy unveils her love for
Gatsby while at the same time refusing to deny her love for her husband
Tom. All the combustible materials are meticulously gathered together,
and they ignite in a stuffy room at the Plaza on a scorching August afternoon and explode on the highway back to Long Island Sound. All the
characters pass through the scene of the crime: Myrtle run down and
her husband a witness; Daisy behind the wheel and Gatsby beside her;
Jordan, Nick, and Tom arriving to see Myrtle's body laid out on a work-
bench in the gas station garage. Error and deception do the rest and carry the story to the end.

The car accident is at once an event and an emblem of the power of the
accidental, which dissolves quest, meaning, identity, and responsibility
into absurdity. Myrtle is run down while trying to flag down the yellow
station wagon she believes contains, as it had earlier in the day, Tom and
Jordan, her lover and the woman she mistakenly assumes is his wife. The
car is in fact driven by Daisy, Tom's actual wife, who hits Myrtle unin-
tentionally and without knowing she is Tom's lover; her act is drained of
even the meaning of jealous rage and revenge. Wilson knows that Myrtle
has been unfaithful but is unaware of who her lover is; he sees the car
that kills her but not the driver. Seeking revenge, he assumes it was a
man. Tom directs him to Gatsby as the owner of the station wagon, and
Wilson kills Gatsby and then himself. Tom's is the only meaning-laden
act in the story!—a murderous revenge against his wife's lover carried
out by proxy by his own lover's unsuspecting husband. Tom and Daisy
pack up and slip away unscathed. Such is the last of Nick's "privileged
glimpses into the human heart"; he leaves New York shortly after en-

countering Tom, who has returned to New York, and learning his role in Gatsby's death. Returned to the Midwest, two years after the accident and the murder, Nick is pulled back into the troubled realm of the human heart and writes "this book."

"This book" exists on two planes at once: Nick's writing recounts and Fitzgerald's writing invents Nick's recounting and all that he recounts. On the face of it this kind of doubling is peculiar to first-person narration, whether the *I* dwells in the imaginary space of storytelling or more rarely, as here, in an imagined space of writing. Third-person would seem to forgo such doubling, and yet the voice of third-person narration has a distinctive air of artifice about it—it is a literary voice—and manifests a concrete sensibility, though not a personality, and it sustains the paradoxical difference-within-identity of recounting and invention. The brief passage slipping into third-person in *The Great Gatsby* brings to light all these features of the impersonal third-person novelistic voice. It is my view that a conception like implied author attempts to take account of just such a voice but does so by postulating a questionable hypothetical subject and casting this postulated subject in the exaggerated role of knowledge and judgment vis-à-vis events and characters. However engrained and habitual our tendency to call the voice of third-person narration a narrator, that conception too is open to question and doubt.

In the debates in narrative theory between so-called optional-narrator and pan-narrator theories, optional-narrator theorists take a strong stance in such questioning and doubting. Patron states the stakes of the debate by drawing on Käte Hamburger's conception of fictional narrative:

> The prototypical narrative is the third person narrative traditionally referred to as omniscient. What Hamburger says is that the supposed dissociation between the author and the narrator in this type of narrative could more be aptly described as the absence of a narrator. The author is not a narrator: he does not "recount" in the usual sense; he uses the narrative function to constitute a fictive world, with fictive characters and events (his role is closer to that of a film maker than to that of an historian). Nor does he delegate the narrative to a fictive representative. Käte Hamburger's definition has the merit of clearing away the epistemological haze that surrounds the notion of the fictive narrator: "[. . .] only in cases where the narra-

tive poet actually does 'create' a narrator, namely the first-person narrator of the first-person narrative, can one speak of the latter as a (fictive) narrator." (Patron 2006, 123)

I share the critical thrust of the argument against taking the cogent definition of "narrator" in first-person narration and simply transposing it to third-person, and I assume that what Hamburger and Patron are questioning in asserting that the novelist writing in third-person "does not delegate the narrative to a fictive representative" are notions like implied author or narrator in the narrator-narratee model. I do, however, see two related problems in the position described. It is not possible, first of all, simply to slough off the idea of recounting, since it is precisely the dynamic and paradoxical entwining of invention and recounting that is at stake in novelistic narration. Second, the only way that it can be so neatly resolved is by construing the inventedness of character and action as a "fictive world," but that simply displaces the problem since it begs the question of the relation of the fictive world to the historical and social world in which the novel itself exists and reference to which the reader never wholly abandons even as one "enters" the "world" of the fictional narrative.[2]

Optional-narrator theory and the theory of novelistic voice I am pursuing most fully overlap in rejecting narratology's narrator-narratee model. Patron identifies a crucial ambiguity in Gérard Genette's handling of the relation of factual and fictional narrative. In factual narrative, according to Genette, there is an absolute identity between author and narrator: "'the author assumes full responsibility for the assertions of his narrative,'" whereas "'their dissociation . . . defines fiction'" ([1991] 1993, 121). Patron notes how these definitions overlook the specificity of fictional narrative. If factual narrative is defined as the identity of author and narrator, then it follows for Genette that fictional narrative rests upon the difference of author and narrator and so, without further investigation, third-person narratives must have a narrator. The presence of a "narrator" is presupposed everywhere: in factual narrative where the narrator is identical to the author and in fictional narrative where they are different. This move, Patron points out, "allows narratology to examine the fictional narrative 'as narrative' and not 'as fiction,' in other words according to the same narratological and pragmatic modalities as factual narratives" (2006, 121). The notion that the author does not assume responsibility for the assertions of a fictional narrative is trivial if it simply refers to the fact that the author does not claim that the fictional events of the story are real, while on the other hand it ignores that in another register the novelist takes full responsibility for the novel he or she produces. The fact that such a question lies outside the purview of narratology confirms that the very nature and specificity of the novel elude narratology.

Let me therefore sharpen once again the difference between novel theory and narratology. In anchoring narrative on the relation *narrator—text—narratee*, narratology postulates two nonexistent subjects. The *narrator* is not the one who writes the novel, and the *narratee* is not the one who reads it. By means of this distillation and abstraction, narrative is deemed a communication in the sense of a sender's message to a receiver. Setting aside for the sake of argument whether the message received in everyday communication between subjects is identical to the message sent, a novel is not a communication in that sense. Like all artworks, a novel is ventured into a public context and historical process that open it to varying interpretations. In any particular moment, interpretations are contested. And over time the interpretations and contestations change. More accurately perhaps, novels like all artworks open the very space for such multiplicity and contestation. They endure as art because their reception and meaning change.

The particular way in which novels open themselves to varying interpretation can in fact be approached through structuralist and narratological categories themselves. According to those categories, the operation of language selects elements from the language's paradigm and concatenates them along the syntagmatic plane into a specific utterance. In narrative the end of the metonymical concatenation yields a "whole," that is, a metaphorical substitution disclosing the story's meaning. There's a catch, however. Consider, despite a common theoretical prejudice, how difficult plot summary is. And it is difficult because it is consequential. How a plot is summarized shapes how meaning is grasped, and how meaning is sought shapes plot summary. The metonym/metaphor conception at once orders narrative and exposes its volatility. No reading *first* lets all the elements of the syntagm unfold one by one and *only then* assembles them into a paradigm, nor can any paradigm order the syntagm in advance of its unfolding. The temporality of reading is neither linear nor simultaneous. The hermeneutical circle spirals within spirals. When interpretation cuts off at some moment, *punctuating* the syntagmatic-paradigmatic spiraling of plot and meaning, it is neither arbitrary nor definitive. The process I've just described is not that of a narratee supposedly receiving a message. Rather, it is the activity of the reader whose process of understanding is ineluctably caught up in temporality, finitude, and fluidity.

Let's come back to the question of voice. The concept of voice that I have been exploring concerns a voice that is neither the author's nor the narrator's, whether first-person or third-, nor an implied author's. I find an antecedent in a neglected essay from one of the past half-century's most provocative and influential collections, *The Languages of Criticism and the Sciences of Man: The Structuralist Controversy* (1970), which brought together the papers and discussions of a 1966 conference at Johns Hopkins University that in effect introduced structuralism and poststructuralism to America as surely, if not as publicly or immediately shockingly, as the Armory Show introduced modern art in 1913:

> Among all the voices to be heard in the literary work, there is one which sets itself apart by its singularity: it seems to be independent of both the representations and the masks of the work, so that even if it reaches us as if through a veil, even if it is only a refracted voice, it is not necessarily indefinable. This voice is not that of the protagonists of the narrative, nor that of the author, nor is it the voice of the "narrator."
>
> Can we define more precisely and go beyond these purely negative characteristics? (Rosolato 1970, 201–2)

The citation is from Guy Rosolato's essay "The Voice and the Literary Myth." I cannot do justice to its density and its movement among literature, religion, and myth, all within a psychoanalytic framework; I will merely enlist its help in tying a central thread of my own argument. Rosolato calls this singular voice a *relative voice* vis-à-vis the identifiable voices in a text, an *anonymous voice*. The operations of literary discourse render the voice in the literary work distinct from the person of the author as well as from any of the personages that may or may not take up the pronoun *I*. For Rosolato, at that moment in 1966, the key categories of discourse are *énonciation* and *énoncé*, shifters, and metonymy and metaphor. It is for that reason, along with the fact that those categories and their avatars have shaped narrative theory and narratology, that I have deployed them here. In my account, the looping of the *énonciation* through the *énoncé* is intrinsic to novelistic discourse (and fictional narrative more generally), and it is that looping that creates a voice that is not identical to the actual subject who produces the narrative (the writer), whether first-person or third-, since the doubling of writing and telling, inventing and recounting, cannot be *voiced* by any actual or imaginary entity. The attempt to encase this voice in a simulated subject, whether the implied author or the narrator of the narrator-narratee pair, misses what makes voice novelistic, literary, aesthetic.

Notes

1. See Brenkman (2000). "As in the E. T. A. Hoffman tale Freud analyzes, Poe here produces the uncanny by projecting a set of symbolic equivalences and doublings onto the plane of the character's reality. The symbolic happens as the real, not in the mode of a symbolically rich universe realizing itself in events as is the case with myth, fairy tale, or providential history, but in the disenchanted world of 'natural causes and effects,' the 'chain of facts,' 'a series of mere household events.' The uncanny requires the 'homely narrative' as its base" (295). The essay is reprinted in Hoffman and Murphy (2005, 411–42).

2. I leave the problem of world and fictional worlds aside as lying beyond the scope of this essay. In an essay on the centenary of *The Theory of the Novel* (Brenkman 2016), I explored the idea that the dynamic Lukács developed between the *problematic individual* and *contingent reality* with regard to the protagonist has a corollary for the novelist. The act of writing ventures his or her subjectivity, talents, intellect, powers of expression, and so on, by exposing them to the contingencies and uncertainties of the public realm. The risk is not only one of money and reputation; it is also the risk of being misunderstood.

References

Barthes, Roland. (1953) 1968. *Writing Degree Zero*. Translated by Annette Lavers and Colin Smith. New York: Hill and Wang.

Brenkman, John. 2000. "On Voice." *Novel: A Forum on Fiction* 33 (3): 281–306.

———. 2016. "World and Novel." *Narrative* 24 (1): 13–26.

———. 2018. "My Lai at 50." *American Interest*, May-June, 45–47.

Culler, Jonathan. (2004) 2006. "Omniscience." In *The Literary in Theory*, 183–201. Stanford: Stanford University Press.

Fitzgerald, F. Scott. (1925) 2004. *The Great Gatsby*. New York: Scribner.

Genette, Gérard. (1991) 1993. *Fiction and Diction*. Translated by Catherine Porter. Ithaca NY: Cornell University Press.

Hamburger, Käte. (1957, 1968) 1973, 1993. *The Logic of Literature*. Translated by Marilynn J. Rose. 2nd ed. Indianapolis: Indiana University Press.

Heidegger, Martin. 1971. "The Origin of the Work of Art." In *Poetry, Language, Thoughts*, translated by Albert Hofstadter, New York: Harper and Row.

Hemingway, Ernest. 1926. *The Sun Also Rises*. New York: Scribner.

Hoffman, Michael J., and Patrick D. Murphy, eds. 2005. *Essentials of the Theory of Fiction*. 3rd ed. Durham NC: Duke University Press.

Kundera, Milan. (1986) 1988. *The Art of the Novel*. Translated by Linda Asher. New York: Harper Collins.

Patron, Sylvie. 2006. "On the Epistemology of Narrative Theory: Narratology and Other Theories of Fictional Narrative." Translated by Anne Marsella. In *The Traveling Concept of Narrative, COLLEGIUM: Studies across Disciplines in the Humanities and Social Sciences*, edited by Matti Hyvärinen, Anu Korhonen, and Juri Mykkänen, 118–33. http://www.helsinki.fi/collegium/journal/volumes/volume_1/.

Rosolato, Guy. 1970. "The Voice and the Literary Myth." In *The Languages of Criticism and the Sciences of Man: The Structuralist Controversy*, edited by Richard Macksey and Eugenio Donato, 201–17. Baltimore: Johns Hopkins University Press.

5 The Narrator
A Historical and Epistemological Approach to Narrative Theory

SYLVIE PATRON

> *A large part of what we believe to be true (and this applies even to our final conclusions) with a persistence equaled only by our sincerity, springs from an original misconception of our premises.*
>
> —MARCEL PROUST, *The Sweet Cheat Gone* (translated by C. K. Scott Moncrieff)

This chapter is located within the sphere of the history of linguistic theories as it is understood by the so-called French school: as something more closely related to epistemology than to pure historiography.[1] It also belongs to a discipline or field of research that does not yet exist in literary disciplines as a whole: the history and epistemology of literary theories. The two disciplines share a common plight, which is that recent theories are often vulnerable to being overlooked in the same way that very old theories are, and not necessarily because they have been falsified or absorbed into a more general theory. There is in addition, in the case of recent theories, the phenomenon of voluntary ignorance or "valorization" in the Bachelardian sense of the term—the attribution of value to certain theories or hypotheses on the basis of nonscientific interests.

In this chapter, two narrator theories (*pan-narrator theory* and *optional-narrator theory*) will be placed within the broader framework of the history of literary theories and the complex relationship that history maintains with linguistics. The first section will offer a brief chronology of the issue of the narrator and narrative enunciation in the modern era, which will then be discussed in more detail in subsequent sections. The aim is to lift the veil on a certain number of received ideas—for example, the idea that narrative theory achieved scientific status (under the name of narratology) with the recognition of the existence of a fictional narrator in all fictional narratives. We will show on the contrary the confusions and errors that narratologists fall into when they present the concept of the narrator, or related and associated concepts. We will also comment on the general presentism of narrative theory. The fact, for example, that there was a coherent theory of narration (of the narrator and narrative enunciation) already available in 1804 is of hardly any interest to classical and current narratologists, no more than to current proponents of optional-narrator theory.

Overall, this chapter aims to show two things: first, that incorrect or incomplete historical interpretations, or simple ignorance, can have a domino effect on research and distort its orientation, and second, that reversibility is always possible. Thus we will see that past, overlooked, or even voluntarily ignored states of the discipline can regain their pertinence within a current context.

The History of the Question of the Narrator and Narrative Enunciation

The notion of modes of narration is inherited from Greek antiquity. For a long time its content has remained what can be found in book 3 of Plato's *Republic*, without always having a real linguistic consistency. It is based on an opposition between the author (more precisely "the poet," *poietes*), who is the sole enunciator in the case of "simple narrative," and the character or characters, who are the fictional enunciators in the case of "narrative by way of imitation." This opposition accounts for the fictional narratives of the Classical era, which frequently make use of embedded narratives (a character's narrative embedded in the authorial narrative). In this context, there is no need for a concept of the narrator distinct from the author.[2]

In the modern era, we can break down the history of the treatment of the narrator and narrative enunciation into five major stages.[3]

The Emergence of the Concept of the Narrator over the Course of the Eighteenth Century

The concept of the narrator (meaning the narrator as a concept, as opposed to nonconceptual uses in which "narrator" simply means, as its suffix implies, "the one who narrates") was introduced to account for the distinctive character of memoir-novels or first-person novels in the original sense of the term.[4] The essential component of the definition of this concept is *the distinction between the author and the narrator*, which can also be expressed as: *the author is real; the narrator is fictional.*

Use of the concept of the narrator can be seen in the writings of Anna Laetitia Barbauld, a poet, essayist, and editor of Samuel Richardson's correspondence (1804).[5] Barbauld's reflections concern narrative prose fiction in the eighteenth century. She states that there are "three modes of carrying on a story." The first is "the narrative or epic," in which "the author relates himself the whole adventure" ("The author . . . is supposed to know everything," "He can be concise, or diffuse," "He can indulge . . . in digressions"). This is the mode used by Cervantes in *Don Quixote* and Fielding in *Tom Jones*; according to Barbauld, it is the most common mode—or the dominant prototype. The second is that used in fictional memoirs, where "the subject of the adventures relates his own story." Barbauld cites *The Adventures of Roderick Random* by Smollett, *The Vicar of Wakefield* by Goldsmith, and *La Vie de Marianne* by Marivaux. The third mode is that of the epistolary novel ("*epistolary correspondence*, carried on between the characters of the novel"), illustrated by Richardson and Rousseau. The term "narrator" appears in the description of the second mode, which corresponds to the prototype of fictional memoirs: "it confines the author's stile, which should be suited, though it is not always, to the supposed talents and capacity of the imaginary narrator" ([1804] 1977, 258). Barbauld also highlights some of the difficulties faced by authors in this mode:

> But what the hero cannot say, the author cannot tell, nor can it be rendered probable, that a very circumstantial narrative should be given by a person, perhaps at the close of a long life, of conversations that have happened at the beginning of it. The author has all along two characters to support, for he has to consider how his hero felt at the time of the events to be related, and how it is natural he should feel them at the time he is relating them. (259)

This is the archeology of the division between the narrator as hero or heroine and the narrator proper, which Leo Spitzer (1928) calls, respectively, the *erlebendes Ich* (experiencing I) and the *erzählendes Ich* (narrating I).

We can note that the focus is always on the work of the author who creates the existence and verisimilitude of the fictional narrator ("what the hero cannot say, the author cannot tell," "the author has all along two characters to support," "he has to consider," etc.).

I will return in the following sections to the problems posed by the persistence of the original concept of the narrator in more recent narrative theories.

The German Controversy over Author-Intrusions
at the End of the Nineteenth Century

This controversy in itself had little international impact, although it had precedents and parallels in France, England, and the United States. It opposed, on the one side, Friedrich Spielhagen, novelist and theorist of the novel, who supported "objectivity" or "dramatization," which is to say the dissimulation of the author in the novel, and on the other, Käte Friedemann, student of Oskar Walzel and author of *Die Rolle des Erzählers in der Epik* (The role of the narrator in epics, 1910), who on the contrary advocated the traditional mode of narration, even making the presence of a narrator who is more or less clearly distinguished from the author the essential characteristic of epic narrative as opposed to drama. It should be noted that condemning the personal presence of the author in the novel meant condemning the works of the great English novelists—and this was so in Spielhagen's case in relation to Fielding, Thackeray, and above all George Eliot. Spielhagen and Friedemann each had their supporters: Heinrich and Julius Hart, Jakob Wassermann, and the earlier Alfred Döblin on the one side; Oskar Walzel, Robert Petsch, Thomas Mann, and the later Döblin on the other.[6] The controversy continued into the 1950s in the works of Wolfgang Kayser, Franz K. Stanzel, and Käte Hamburger, whole sections of which can only be understood against this historicotheoretical backdrop.

In the works of contemporary narratologists, Friedemann is often presented as the originator of the concept of the narrator: the narrator "invented as a separate figure by K. Friedemann and Wolfgang Kayser" (Fludernik 2005, 42). But this claim is incorrect: the concept of the narrator, inseparable from the distinction between the author and the narrator, is much older than Friedemann's work. It is, however, correct to say that several of Friedemann's formulations prefigure some of Kayser's famous ones, in particular that "the narrator, in all narrative art, is never the known or as yet unknown author, but a role that the author invents and takes on" (Kayser [1957] 2000, 125; my translation). What can also be seen in Friedemann's work is a recurrent confusion, which will later be perpetuated by the narratologists, between the original concept of the narrator, meaning the character with the status of narrator in first-person novels, and the new concept of the narrator that comes from the controversy over author-intrusions and Friedemann's attempt to define the epic narrative as structurally distinct from drama.

There is an intellectual genealogy that links Friedemann, Kayser, and Stanzel (and, through Stanzel, Monika Fludernik). In 1979 Stanzel writes that the "recognition of the fictionality of the first-person narrator preceded the recognition of the fictionality of the third-person narrator" and that the latter "was not generally recognized until the mid-1950s" ([1979] 1984, 81), clearly alluding to Kayser's article. His formulation, however, conceals the fact that this "recognition" is not a discovery but a *stipulation*. It is far removed from Spielhagen's conceptions, for example. It also deliberately ignores the challenge to the proposition "the narrator of the third-person narrative is a fictional narrator" in Hamburger's narrative theory. As Hamburger asserts at a very early stage of this affair, "only in cases where the narrative poet actually does 'create' a narrator, namely the first-person narrator of the first-person narrative, can one speak of the latter as a (fictive) narrator" ([1957, 1968] 1993, 140).

Hamburger's theory, where we can find a descriptive and linguistic translation of Spielhagen's prescriptive propositions (even though Hamburger makes very little reference to Spielhagen), moving beyond the controversy over author-intrusions, is the starting point for another genealogy, the one that connects Hamburger, Kuroda, and Banfield, which we will come back to later.

Gérard Genette's Coup de Force

This chapter is partly concerned with the close relationship between narratology and the theory of the existence of a fictional narrator in all fictional narratives, henceforth *pan-narrator theory*. The definitive form of the relationship is found in Genette's *Discours du récit: Essai de méthode* (1972).[7] Genette posits that all fictional narratives can be divided into two categories that are mutually and necessarily opposed: "homodiegetic" narratives, which are told by a narrator who is a character in the story, and "heterodiegetic" narratives, which are told by a narrator outside the story (Genette, unlike Kayser, does not go so far as to speak of a character in this case). Even though Genette's examples of heterodiegetic narrators are potentially misleading ("Homer in the *Iliad*, and Flaubert in *L'Éducation sentimentale*"—in other words, authors; [1972] 1980, 244–45), the opposition between homo- and heterodiegetic narratives must be seen for what it is: a theoretical and ideological *coup de force* which is part of a movement that aims to impose a new conception of fictional narrative and justify a fundamental shift in the way its analysis and interpretation are conceived.

In another passage in this work, Genette attributes the property of being fictional to the narrator of the third-person narrative, or the heterodiegetic narrator, in his own terminology:

> The references in *Tristram Shandy* to the situation of writing speak to the (fictive) act of Tristram and not the (real) one of Sterne; but in a more subtle and also more radical way, the narrator of *Père Goriot* "is" not Balzac, even if here and there he expresses Balzac's opinions, for this author-narrator is someone who "knows" the Vauquer boardinghouse, its landlady and its lodgers, whereas all Balzac himself does is imagine them. (214)

The argument he puts forward is very close to the one already found in Kayser, in support of the proposition that "the narrator is never the known or as yet unknown author, but a role that the author invents and takes on": "To him, Werther, Don Quixote and Madame Bovary do exist; he is associated with the poetic world" (Kayser [1957] 2000, 125; my translation). It quickly became a commonplace of literary theory and criticism. The argument, however, can be turned around. If fictional narrative refers to nonexistent entities (characters, places, etc.) as though these entities really existed, this essential given of fiction can be seen as independent of whether there is a fictional narrator for whom these entities "really" (i.e., fictionally) exist—except in cases where there is effectively a fictional narrator, namely the narrator of the first-person narrative.[8]

Linguistic Discussions in the 1970s and 1980s

Two American linguists, S.-Y. Kuroda and Ann Banfield, significantly advanced the question of the narrator and narrative enunciation thanks to the methods of transformational generative grammar. They showed that the theories they call "communicational," based on the concepts of real or fictional narrators and narratees, could only account for a subcategory of fictional narratives, namely first-person narratives, or indeed an even narrower subcategory where the first-person narrative is explicitly marked as communicational with a fictional "I" addressing a fictional "you." With their work, narrative theory took on an openly affirmed optionalist orientation. It led to the position that there are fictional narratives with a narrator and fictional narratives without a narrator—which means not that nobody has produced them but simply that they contain no linguistic marker indicating a real or fictional subject and situation of enunciation. We can speak of the *enunciative effacement* or *disappearance* of the author of fictional narrative: for Banfield, the author "is not directly embodied in a first person, as a speaker in his speech," "he does not speak. . . . He writes, rather, and in writing disappears" ([1991] 2019, 138). We should rather speak of the *absence of a narrator* (and not the enunciative effacement of the narrator or, as it is more often described, an "effaced narrator") when the narrative does not contain any linguistic marker indicating a fictional subject and situation of enunciation. Sentences in the free indirect style in the third person and the past tense, in English or in French, represent a particular case that falsifies the hypothesis of the implicit or effaced narrator.[9]

This conception is very close to the disappearance of the author as the point of origin for referential values and deictic markers (real "I-Origo") conceptualized by Hamburger. Kuroda and Banfield did in fact read Hamburger early on (in Kuroda's case, before its translation into English in 1973), much earlier than the narratologists, the French narratologists in particular.[10]

Banfield also draws on the opposition between *telling* and *showing* that was proposed by Percy Lubbock in 1921, where *showing* can in her view be interpreted in linguistic terms as the use of sentences in free indirect style in the third person and the past tense over long passages in the novel. A parallel can be drawn between the German controversy over author-intrusions and the thoughts of Henry James and his disciple Lubbock on the writing of the novel.[11]

Kuroda's work has been ignored in narratological circles, as can be seen from most bibliographies. Banfield's has received reactions that are often as vehement as they are inadequate (see McHale 1983; Genette [1983] 1988, 99–102; see also an answer to McHale in Galbraith 1995, 35–46, 50–51). The considerable growth of contemporary narrative research (conferences, publications, narrative studies societies and research networks, projects funded by universities and research centers) has sanctioned the domination of pan-narrator theory on the international level. Just as Genettian narratology was conceived only within the cultural paradigm of "generalized structuralism," so the current domination of pan-narrator theory is part of a new paradigm, which could be called the "paradigm of naturalization" of narrative research, symbolized by Fludernik's "natural" narratology or David Herman's cognitive narratology, for which "natural"—meaning oral—narratives are the archetypal form of all narratives, including fictional ones. The result is a banalization of the term "narrator" and the effacement of the difference between the conceptual and ordinary usage of the term in the case of fictional narratives.[12]

The Original Narrator and the Necessary Narrator: An Irresolvable Duality

The first two stages in the history of the question of the narrator and narrative enunciation, briefly presented above, introduce not *one* but *two* concepts of the narrator into narrative theory. I draw here on Jean-Claude Milner's observation that "concepts with the same name may in fact be totally different, because they encapsulate different sets of issues," just as "concepts with different names may be strictly equivalent because it becomes clear that the issues they encapsulate are in fact the same" ([1989] 1995, 17–18; my translation).

The issues encapsulated in the original concept of the narrator are the following:

- an "I" who is not the author but a character in the fiction (which can also be expressed, as we have seen, as: *the author is real; the narrator is fictional*; or: *there is a fictional narrator created by the author*);

- a factuality pact inside the fiction: the narrator is supposed to provide a factual narrative, specifically the narrative of his or her life (which could be expressed as: *the author invents the fictional facts; the narrator fictionally reports nonfictional facts, originally consisting of autobiographical facts*);
- a restriction of the narrative information to what the narrator can know but also what he or she can plausibly recall (especially in the case of reported dialogue);
- a more or less marked opposition between the experiencing "I" and the narrating "I," to use Spitzer's terminology.

There are numerous examples in writers' metatexts—prefaces, for example—of statements which say that despite the use of "I," the author must not be confused with the narrator (see, for example, Balzac in the preface to *The Lily of the Valley*, which also highlights the ontological difference between the author who is real and the narrator who is fictional). The possibility of what is called the "unreliable narrator" also forms part of the core of the definition of the concept.[13]

There are also issues that, without being really encapsulated in the concept of the narrator, are regularly associated with its use in theoretical and critical discourses. This is the case with what we can call "formal mimetics" (Głowiński [1973] 1977, 106), which is to say the imitation, by means of a given form, of other types of literary, paraliterary, and extraliterary discourses, as well as everyday language. The practice is mostly regarded favorably: people refer to the "truth effect" specific to the first-person novel, and praise the successful imitation of vernacular modes of speech. Authors and commentators also regularly return to the subject of the limits of this narrative mode: the restriction of narrative information to what the narrator can know and plausibly recall, but also the tendency to analysis and introspection that can contradict certain personality traits or social characteristics of the narrator. Finally, an important issue raised by the essayist Charles Lamb, for example, is that of the elimination of the presence of the author. In first-person narrative, the author completely disappears through the use of the narrator, and this disappearance is again regarded favorably. Lamb, for example, expresses at the same time his aversion to personal intrusions by the author (quoted in Patterson 1952, 379–80).

The original concept of the narrator goes hand in hand with a *dualist* or *differentialist* conception of fictional narrative that considers first-person fictional narrative to be *a specific case of fictional narrative*. In other words, the narrator in the original conception is an option that authors can choose to use or not.

I move now to the second concept of the narrator, the one that arises from the controversy over author-intrusions. First of all, the narrator is not distinguished from the author by Spielhagen or any of the other writers involved in this controversy. The distinction does, however, appear in Friedemann, even if not always in a clear or systematic way—a point I will return to. Secondly, the fictional narratives under consideration are third-person narratives, even if we also find references in Friedemann's work to first-person narratives (she also occasionally refers to the epistolary novel and the diary-novel, which she presents as belonging to the same narrative type). A new element is introduced with the reference to drama. Drama is held up as a model for the novel by Spielhagen and other defenders of the "objectivity" or "dramatization" of the novel, but without being considered from a structural point of view. In contrast, drama is structurally opposed to the novel in Friedemann: drama being associated with the absence of a narrator, and the novel with the structurally necessary presence of a narrator.[14]

I maintain that this concept is homonymous to but completely different from the original concept of the narrator. It in effect encapsulates different issues:

- while it is true that there can be an "I" in third-person narratives with author-intrusions, this "I" is precisely not that of a character within the fiction. This is quite explicit in Spielhagen and even in Friedemann: Friedemann's narrator is derived from the oral storyteller of the epic poem, who is an intermediary between the story and the readers and by definition not part of the fiction;
- there is no "I" in the type of third-person narrative without intrusions that is advocated by Spielhagen and also enters into Friedemann's considerations;
- no issues are raised about restrictions regarding narrative information and plausibility, no more than they are raised about the opposition between the experiencing "I" and the narrating "I";

- Friedemann makes the presence of a narrator who is more or less clearly distinguished from the author the essential feature of fictional narrative in relation to drama (she also speaks of the "indirect character of narration").

It should be emphasized here that in the original conception, the narrator is not and cannot be an essential feature of fictional narrative in relation to drama, since the presence of a narrator only characterizes a certain type of fictional narrative, namely first-person narrative, which is neither the easiest to practice nor the most commonly used by authors. On the contrary, the narrator is not an option in Friedemann but *a theoretical necessity* that precedes and eliminates the question of the author's choice.

Friedemann, unlike Spielhagen, makes no basic distinction between first- and third-person narratives. In other words, she makes the effective, empirical difference between first- and third-person narratives a secondary consideration within a *monist* theory of fictional narrative.

Friedemann insists on the independence of the work of art from its creator, which is why she distinguishes the author and the narrator. This distinction therefore does not mark a separation between, as in Barbauld and in the original conception, a real being and a fictional being. Friedemann's distinction is internal to the author him- or herself: it separates the personal existence of the author from his or her aesthetic existence. The narrator, according to Friedemann, represents an aestheticized form of the author. Even where the narrator, whose presence is revealed by an intrusion, bears the name of the author (as in the works of Jean Paul or E. T. A. Hoffmann), Friedemann considers it to be a pretense, a feigned personality. (She does not, however, refer to it as a character.) The narrator, as the aestheticized form of the author, is an organic part of the narrative work and, as such, may freely intervene in the work without compromising its unity.

Friedemann's distinction between the author's personal identity and the aestheticized form of the author is not always clear. At times, she uses the word *Dichter* where it must be assumed that she means the aesthetic identity of the author, which is to say, the narrator (*Erzähler*). It is possible to quote passages containing contradictory statements from this point of view.

Friedemann's distinction between the author and the narrator was not immediately adopted by later critics (we can cite, for example, Emil Ermatinger, Ernst Hirt, and Rafael Koskimies). Robert Petsch made a similar distinction between the real and the "epic" identity of the author (in German, *reales Ich, episches Ich*). It is the latter who is supposed to be narrating—intrusions included. It is also the latter who selects and arranges and assembles the work of art. The "epic I," then, is the creative force of the author, not only the narrator. Finally, Kayser conceived of the narrator not as a form of the author but as a purely fictional figure, or even a character created by the author to tell the story.

To conclude this section, the opposition between the two concepts of the narrator, the original concept and the new one that arose from the controversy over author-intrusions, cannot be resolved. The original concept of the narrator refers to a concrete empirical object that distinguishes the prototype of the first-person narrative from the other narrative prototypes available in a given period. The second concept of the narrator refers to a theoretical object, an abstraction or construction, and not an empirical given, even if in Friedemann it is revealed empirically in the passages called author-intrusions. This second concept has imposed itself as a pillar of narrative theory; it is the source of the narrator being considered a theoretical necessity by proponents of current pan-narrator theory, with all the obscurities and even contradictions that implies. In contrast, the original concept of the narrator corresponds to an effective, empirical reality: the narrator of the first-person narrative, which pan-narrator theory is obliged to integrate. We can see, however, that this integration always introduces a theoretical disequilibrium or disparity, as when Genette or Stanzel draws a parallel between the obvious fictionality of the narrator of the first-person fictional narrative, and the much more problematic fictionality, or the supposed fictionality, of the narrator of the third-person narrative.

Even in the case of third-person narratives with intrusions, it may seem erroneous to confuse the creation of a character, which is to say a fictional person who belongs to the same fictional world as the other characters, and the construction of a *persona* or a feigned personality of the author, which rather calls for the rhetorical notion of ethos. As we have seen, none of the theorists before Friedemann confused these, and many theorists after Friedemann are still able to avoid doing so.

Some Historical Errors of Genette's

Even a quick reading of the passages devoted to the narrator in Genette's work shows that Genette does not know, or does not acknowledge, the existence of an original concept of the narrator that goes hand in hand with the dualist conception of fictional narrative, which considers first-person narrative to be a specific case of fictional narrative. He also makes many errors in this discussion, as when he opens the "Person" section:

> Readers may have noticed that until now we have used the terms "first-person—or third-person—narrative" only when paired with quotation marks of protest. Indeed, these common locutions seem to me inadequate, in that they stress variation in the element of the narrative situation that is in fact invariant—to wit, the presence (explicit or implicit) of the "person" of the narrator. This presence is invariant because the narrator can be in his narrative (like every subject of enunciation in his enunciated statement) *only* in the "first person." ([1972] 1980, 243–44)

The problem is that in the traditional definition of the terms "first-person narrative" and "third-person narrative" (more precisely, "first-person novel" and "third-person novel"), the focus is not on the narrator but on the hero:

- first-person fictional narrative (novel) = narrative in which the hero is the narrator;
- third-person fictional narrative (novel) = narrative in which the hero is a third person whose story we are told by the author.

In the language of art, we call a novel in which the hero appears as being himself the narrator of his fate a first person novel, in opposition to other novels, where the hero is a third person whose adventures we are told by the poet. (Spielhagen [1883] 1969, 66; my translation)[15]

There is thus nothing inadequate in these common locutions. They stress variation in an element effectively subject to variation—not of the "narrative situation" in Genette's sense but of the poetics of fictional narrative. The same comment can be made regarding the "unfitness" of the term "first-person narrative":

The presence of first-person verbs in a narrative text can therefore refer to two very different situations which grammar renders identical but which narrative analysis must distinguish: the narrator's own designation of himself as such, as when Virgil writes "I sing the arms and the man," or else the identity of person between the narrator and one of the characters in the story, as when Crusoe writes "I was born in the year 1632, in the city of York." The term "first-person narrative" refers, quite obviously, only to the second of these situations, and this dissymmetry confirms its unfitness. (Genette [1972] 1980, 244)

There is nothing unfit in the term "first-person narrative," if we refer again to the definition of this term in Spielhagen and his followers, as well as the history of the concept or rather of the two concepts of the narrator, which Genette conflates here.

These cases of ignorance and errors have had significant consequences in the history of narrative theory, which I will not elaborate on here. Suffice it to say that it meant narratologists were unable to correctly read and understand John R. Searle's "The Logical Status of Fictional Discourse," for example, based as it is on the original concept of the narrator that goes hand in hand with the dualist conception of fictional narrative, which considers first-person narrative to be a specific case of fictional narrative.[16]

The Denial of Falsification

Another point that needs elucidating is the relationship between contemporary research and the marginalization of results obtained by linguists. Some of the several possible explanations are narratologists' lack of familiarity with linguistic reasoning; the influence of Genette, even in those aspects where he is the most vulnerable to criticism; skepticism regarding the possibility of falsification in the domain of narrative theory; and misinterpretation of the term "communication" as it is used by linguists.

The lack of familiarity with linguistic reasoning among narratologists is clearly apparent in their accounts of Banfield's work. Brian McHale acknowledges it himself at the beginning of a 1983 article (17, 18). With regard to Genette, the widespread myth that "structuralist" narratology is a linguistic approach to narrative needs to be dispelled. Genette well represents a "literary structuralism" that has always privileged a typological and classificatory approach over a conceptualization of the linguistic discourse or performance that narrative represents, and over the goal of characterizing this discourse by specific linguistic markers. Genette refers periodically to enunciative linguistics and pragmatics, which provide him with maxims, and arguments from authority (see, for example, [1972] 1980, 244; [1983] 1988, 99). His reading of Émile Benveniste's famous article "The Correlations of Tense in the French Verb" ([1959, 1966] 1971), however, devoted in part to narrative enunciation, is a typical example of distorting assimilation.[17]

Genette's proposition, "Insofar as the narrator can at any instant intervene *as such* in the narrative, every narrating is, by definition, . . . [virtually] in the first person" ([1972] 1980, 244; translation slightly modified), should have been discredited within the narratologist community, and justifiably so, as we will see. This discrediting did not happen, however. On the contrary, the proposition was reiterated in *Narrative Discourse Revisited*—"in my view every narrative is, explicitly or not, 'in the first-person' since at any moment its narrator may use that pronoun to designate himself" ([1983] 1988, 97)—and has been repeated by numerous narratologists. We can explain this state of affairs by the influence of Genette, which was founded on the success of *Narrative Discourse*, especially once it was translated into English. The reiteration of this proposition in *Narrative Discourse Revisited* deliberately ignores Banfield's falsification of its presupposition: "the narrator can at any instant intervene *as such* in the narrative." It should be highlighted here that the whole section of *Narrative Discourse Revisited* dedicated to Banfield's narrative theory (see Genette [1983] 1988, 99–102) is characterized by the use of very questionable modes of argumentation (untruths, misinterpretations of certain terms, generalizations and conflations, plays on words, quotations taken out of context) and, more generally, the use of ridicule in place of genuine arguments.

Banfield's demonstration rests on the characterization of certain sentences of free indirect discourse (*represented speech and thought*, in her own terminology) in linguistic terms. Genette is right to point out the link between the first linguistic descriptions of the free indirect style in Charles Bally and Marguerite Lips, and the systematization proposed by Banfield in the context of transformational generative grammar, even if for him it is an object of ridicule (see Genette [1983] 1988, 53). He also pays insufficient attention to the conceptualization of expressive elements and constructions—exclamations, for example. Banfield's theory is difficult and demands a lot from its readers. I will just mention here the crucial test, which I have elsewhere called "the Banfield test" and which is as much a discovery as the theory being tested. If we define the sentence of free indirect discourse in the third person and the past tense as a sentence in which expressive elements and constructions are attributed to the referent of a third-person pronoun, for example,

> n'importe! elle n'était pas heureuse, ne l'avait jamais été (Gustave Flaubert, *Madame Bovary*)

> No matter! She was not happy—she never had been (translated by Eleanor Marx-Aveling)

we realize that, with the addition of a pronoun or other forms of the first person ("mon" and "my" in the following examples), the sentence loses all of its original characteristics:

> N'importe! elle n'était pas heureuse, ne l'avait jamais été, à mon avis.

> No matter! She was not happy—she never had been, to my mind.

In the modified sentence, it is no longer possible to attribute the expressive elements and constructions (in this case, the exclamations) to any subject other than the referent of the "I" contained in "my." In other words, *it is no longer possible to consider the sentences as sentences of free indirect discourse.* This test, to my knowledge, has never been refuted. The general difficulty of the theory, however, in addition to the skepticism regarding the possibility of applying the criterion of falsifiability to narrative theory, has meant that Banfield's theory has been marginalized by narratologists and its results disregarded by a rhetoric of minimization.

The term "communication" as it is used by linguists has given rise to numerous misinterpretations (see again Genette [1983] 1988, 101–2, but more recently Walsh [1997] 2007, 174n1, for example). Briefly put, "communication" for Kuroda and Banfield refers to the use of a particular type of sentence (early Kuroda, Banfield) or speech act (later Kuroda) that is characterized by an explicit or implicit "I-you" structure, or as having an intended hearer, one intentionally designated by the speaker as the addressee of the speech act, as opposed to unintended hearers or bystanders. Banfield and Kuroda's work establishes that certain sentences commonly found in third-person fictional narratives in English, French, and Japanese do not conform to the communication model. But Kuroda and Banfield do not deny the existence of communication in another sense between the author and reader of the fictional narrative, which can be variously called "co-intentionality" (Kuroda), "inferential communication" (Walsh), and so on. This other sense of communication does not seem incompatible with the transmedial considerations of the type proposed by Richard Walsh.

The Presentism of the Contemporary Era

The domination of pan-narrator theory in current narrative research on the international level has not prevented the emergence of criticisms that have sometimes developed into genuine alternative theories (henceforth, *optional-narrator theories*). These dispute the relevance of the concept of the narrator treated as a theoretical necessity by proponents of current pan-narrator theory. On the other hand, they seem no more aware than Genette, for example, of the existence of an original concept of the narrator that is older than and different from the previous one.[18]

These criticisms focus in particular on the internal inconsistency of the concept of the narrator in pan-narrator theory and its fuzzy relationship with the concept of character. We can quote for example this pertinent comment of Walsh's on Genette's typology: "Such narrators [extradiegetic homodiegetic narrators], because they are represented, *are* characters, exactly as intradiegetic narrators are. . . . But of course, it is the fourth class of narration, the extradiegetic heterodiegetic, that constitutes the real issue" (Walsh [1997] 2007, 72).

On the other hand, none of the current optional-narrator theories seem able to develop a constructive dialogue with the theories that came before them. Walsh ([1997] 2007, 174n1) refers to the theories of Hamburger, Kuroda, and Banfield but at the same time excludes them from the proposed discussion. Tilmann Köppe and Jan Stühring (2011, 75n3) dilute them in a sea of uncategorized and unranked references, none of which are included the field of copresence and discussion. In such circumstances, there is nothing surprising in the fact that certain propositions of the optional-narrator theorists

- unknowingly repeat some of Banfield's propositions, for example, the criticism of the inverted hierarchy between the fictional narrator and the language of fiction: "to treat a represented instance of narration as ontologically prior to the language doing the representing is to press the logic of representation beyond representation itself and to make the subordinate term superordinate—that is, to assert a paradox in the name of logic" (Walsh [1997] 2007, 80); and
- appear regressive in relation to some of Hamburger's, Kuroda's, and Banfield's stronger propositions, such as when the role of the author of the fictional narrative is simply assimilated to that of the narrator—"The answer I am proposing to my original question, 'Who is the narrator?' is this: the narrator is always either a character who narrates, or the author" (Walsh [1997] 2007, 78); "we can say that Watson is the *internal* author/narrator and Doyle the *external* author/narrator" (Currie 2010, 67).

These propositions forget or sidestep the fact that *the author of a fictional narrative does not narrate in the same way as a narrator narrates (more precisely, fictionally narrates, or is created as narrating) about characters, places, and so on, that exist independently of and prior to his or her act of narration.* This opposition is at the core of Hamburger's theory of fictionality, but it is also found in Searle and perhaps, in another way, in Walsh, despite his misleading use of the term "narrator."

Reversibility

History and historical comparisons necessarily lead to relativism. I will mention again a few of the results this inquiry has produced. Narrative theory has not always been the pan-narrator theory with which it is predominantly and most commonly identified today. It has posited an older concept of the narrator that is different from the one considered a theoretical necessity by proponents of current pan-narrator theory. It is not obvious that the representatives of this other narrative theory were in the wrong and the proponents of current pan-narrator theory are in the right. The proof of this statement is that some of the proponents of current optional-narrator theory have reconnected—most of the time unknowingly, but sometimes knowingly—with some of the propositions of the older theories ("the narrator is always either a character who narrates, or the author"). The inquiry has also shown that there is nothing inevitable and natural in conceiving all fictional narrative, which narrates a fictional story, as something enunciated by a fictional narrator whose story is for him or her made up of real facts. Note that this is the description the older theory reserved for first-person fictional narrative, considered as a specific case of fictional narrative.

Some theorists also reconnect with the original concept of the narrator, for example, Nicholas Wolterstorff's concept of the *narrating character* (see 1980, 163–79), which is picked up—apparently unknowingly—by Roger Edholm (2018). Another example is Jan-Noël Thon, from the perspective of a study of fictional narratives across different media (see 2016, 138–52, on the opposition between narrating characters and "narrating instances"). We can also quote this observation made by Lucien Dällenbach in 1977, right in the middle of the period of Genettian influence; it is perfectly consistent with the usage of the original concept of the narrator:

> It goes without saying that I do not use this term ["author"] in its biographical, but rather in its *poetic* sense. By "author"—or, in Booth's more precise terminology, "implicit author" . . .—I mean the donor of the book, the organizer and the *real* enunciating subject of the narrative. The "narrator," despite common usage, is merely the fictive enunciating subject. . . . In line with this bipartite division, which tends to rehabilitate the function of the author, I would say that a third-person narrative is a narratorless narrative. (Dällenbach [1977] 1989, 198n5; translation slightly modified)

The relativism of historical description must, however, be qualified by considering how adequate the clusters of theorization, concepts, and theories are to the phenomena. It is clear that theoretical propositions like "the narrator is always either a character who narrates, or the author," and "Watson is the *internal* author/narrator and Doyle the *external* author/narrator" suffer from underconceptualization. This deficit concerns the specificity of the act of narrating a fictional narrative in relation to the act of narrating a factual narrative. In Hamburger's terms, "the narrative poet is not a statement subject. He does not narrate about persons and things, but rather he narrates these persons and things. . . . *Between the narrating and the narrated there exists not a subject-object relation, i.e., a statement structure, but rather a functional correspondence"* ([1957, 1968], 1993, 136; Hamburger's italics). The propositions quoted above also say nothing about the act of "creating" or "bringing into existence" a fictional narrator, which is nevertheless an interesting object of study.

*

Narrative theory has undergone a dogmatic phase with the generalization of pan-narrator theory. The concept of the narrator today brings together questions from a critical phase in the evolution of both narrative theory and the theory of fictionality. It is reasonable to assume that a better knowledge of the history of concepts, clusters of theorization, or fully formed theories constitutes the foundation for critical thought to address, examine, and correct errors and inadequacies, and in so doing be able to grow and develop.

Translated by Melissa McMahon with
the collaboration of Sylvie Patron

Notes

1. See the work of the Laboratoire d'Histoire des Théories Linguistiques (http://htl.linguist.univ-paris-diderot.fr) and Colombat, Fournier, and Puech (2010, esp. 32–33). See also Patron ([2012] 2014; 2019, chap. 10; 2020).
2. See Esmein-Sarrazin (2008, 437; my translation): "In the theoretical and critical texts [of the seventeenth century], . . . the explicit distinction between these two agencies never appears." The situation in England seems to have been identical.
3. This part concerns only the United States and Western Europe, limited to England, France, and Germany. For a more developed version of sections "Gérard Genette's *Coup de Force*" and "Linguistic Discussions in the 1970s and 1980s," see Patron ([2009] 2016, chaps. 1, 8, and 9).
4. Unless they use the fiction of the "found manuscript," memoir-novels do not have an embedding structure, which means that we do not necessarily know who the character speaking is, nor even that it is a character speaking, when we first encounter the pronoun "I."
5. According to Rothschild (1990, 22–23), it is "the first explicit discussion of the concept of the narrator in a work originally written in English." For my own part, I have not found earlier mentions in either English or French.

6. For an English account of the controversy, see Frey (1948).

7. Without being able to go into more detail here, I maintain that there are still elements of openness, indeterminacy, and hesitation in prior works, even in Chatman (1978), who is nevertheless strongly inspired by Genette.

8. Or a fictional editor, as in the preamble of *Werther*, for example. In *Don Quixote*, the case is more complex.

9. Regarding the expression "free indirect style," see my introduction (9), and for an explanation of the procedure of falsification, see section "The Denial of Falsification."

10. It was not until 1986 that *Die Logik der Dichtung* was translated into French. The translation distorts and in some places mutilates the text; a new translation is due.

11. See Gerber (1968, appendix: "Friedrich Spielhagen and Henry James").

12. In this context, it is intriguing to find this salutary clarification in the work of a specialist of everyday oral narrative: "[I] want to make clear that the concept [of the narrator], in its narratological meaning, has nothing to do with everyday oral narration." "If the word 'narrator' is used in social research, it is only a term, a name for the person who is telling, and has no connection whatsoever to the narratological distinction between author and narrator" (Hyvärinen 2019, 63–64).

13. I will not elaborate on this concept, which is well known to narratologists and other narrative theorists, but will simply indicate the origin of the term "unreliable narrator" in Booth ([1961] 1983, 158–59). I will also mention Mander (1999), which contains a historicization of the concept of the unreliable narrator in the French domain.

14. For an exposition of Friedemann's theoretical background, borrowed from the poetics of Goethe and Schiller, I refer English-speaking readers again to Gerber (1968).

15. I recall here the traditional definition of the term "first-person novel," setting aside the case that appeared quite quickly in the history of the genre, of the first-person novel where the narrator is not the hero but a secondary character and a witness to the story of the main character (e.g., the narrator in Balzac's *Louis Lambert*).

16. For a more detailed development of this topic, see Patron ([2009] 2016, chap. 5).

17. This is amply demonstrated in Kuroda ([1976] 2014, 79–80, 89), and Patron (2019, chap. 2).

18. For a more detailed development of this point, see Patron (2019, chap. 8), and Patron in Gammelgaard et al. (forthcoming).

References

Banfield, Ann. (1982) 2014. *Unspeakable Sentences: Narration and Representation in the Language of Fiction*. London: Routledge Revivals.

———. (1987) 2019. "Describing the Unobserved: Events Grouped around an Empty Center." In Banfield 2019, 105–27.

———. (1991) 2019. "L'Écriture et le Non-Dit." In Banfield 2019, 128–42.

———. 2019. *Describing the Unobserved and Other Essays: Unspeakable Sentences after "Unspeakable Sentences,"* edited by Sylvie Patron. Newcastle upon Tyne, UK: Cambridge Scholars Publishing.

Barbauld, Anna Laetitia. (1804) 1959, 1977. "Three Ways of Telling a Story?" In *Novelists on the Novel*, edited by Miriam Allott, 258–60. 2nd ed. London: Routledge and Kegan Paul, 1959.

Benveniste, Émile. (1959, 1966) 1971. "The Correlations of Tense in the French Verb." Translated by Mary E. Meek. In *Problems in General Linguistics*, 205–15. Coral Gables FL: Miami University Press.

Booth, Wayne C. (1961) 1983. *The Rhetoric of Fiction*. 2nd rev. ed. Chicago: University of Chicago Press.

Chatman, Seymour. 1978. *Story and Discourse: Narrative Structure in Fiction and Film*. Ithaca NY: Cornell University Press.

Colombat, Bernard, Jean-Marie Fournier, and Christian Puech. 2010. *Histoire des idées sur le langage et les langues*. Paris: Klincksieck.

Currie, Gregory. 2010. *Narratives and Narrators*. Oxford: Oxford University Press.

Dällenbach, Lucien. (1977) 1989. *The Mirror in the Text*. Translated by Jeremy Whiteley and Emma Hughes. Chicago: University of Chicago Press.

Edholm, Roger. 2018. "The Narrator Who Wasn't There: Philip Roth's *The Human Stain* and the Discontinuity of Narrating Characters." *Narrative* 26 (1): 17–38.

Esmein-Sarrazin, Camille. 2008. *L'Essor du roman: Discours théorique et constitution d'un genre littéraire au XVIIe siècle*. Paris: Honoré Champion.

Fludernik, Monika. 2005. "Histories of Narrative Theory (II): From Structuralism to the Present." In *A Companion to Narrative Theory*, edited by James Phelan and Peter J. Rabinowitz, 36–59. Malden MA: Blackwell Publishing.

Frey, John R. 1948. "Author-Intrusion in the Narrative: German Theory and Some Modern Examples." *Germanic Review* 23 (4): 274–89.

Friedemann, Käte. (1910) 1969. *Die Rolle des Erzählers in der Epik*. Darmstadt, Germany: Wissenschaftliche Buchgesellschaft. http://www.literature.at/webinterface/library/alo-book_v01?objid=1071.

Galbraith, Mary. 1995. "Deictic Shift Theory and the Poetics of Involvement in Narrative." In *Deixis in Narrative: A Cognitive Science Perspective*, edited by

Judith F. Duchan, Gail A. Bruder, and Lynne E. Hewitt, 19–59. Hillsdale NJ: Lawrence Erlbaum Associates.

Genette, Gérard. (1972) 1980. *Narrative Discourse: An Essay in Method.* Translated by Jane E. Lewin. Ithaca NY: Cornell University Press.

———. (1983) 1988. *Narrative Discourse Revisited.* Translated by Jane E. Lewin. Ithaca NY: Cornell University Press.

Gerber, Margy Jean. 1968. "The Concept of the Narrator in German Literary Criticism." PhD diss., Stanford University.

Głowiński, Michał. (1973) 1977. "On the First-Person Novel." Translated by Rochelle Stone. *New Literary History* 9 (1): 103–14.

Hamburger, Käte. (1957) 1968. *Die Logik der Dichtung.* 2nd rev. ed. Stuttgart: Ernst Klett Verlag.

———. (1957, 1968) 1973, 1993. *The Logic of Literature.* 2nd ed. Translated by Marilynn J. Rose. Bloomington IN: Indiana University Press.

———. (1957, 1968) 1986. *La Logique des genres littéraires.* Translated by Pierre Cadiot. Paris: Le Seuil.

Hyvärinen, Matti. 2019. "Sameness, Difference, or Continuity." *Frontiers of Narrative Studies* 5 (1): 57–75.

Kayser, Wolfgang. (1957) 2000. "Wer erzählt den Roman?" In *Texte zur Theorie der Autorschaft*, edited by Fotis Jannidis, Gerhard Lauer, Matías Martínez, and Sabine Winko, 124–37. Stuttgart: Reclam.

Köppe, Tilmann, and Jan Stühring. 2011. "Against Pan-Narrator Theories." *Journal of Literary Semantics* 40 (1): 59–80.

Kuroda, S.-Y. (1976) 2014. "Reflections on the Foundations of Narrative Theory, from a Linguistic Point of View." In Kuroda 2014, 71–101.

———. 2014. *Toward a Poetic Theory of Narration: Essays of S.-Y. Kuroda*, edited by Sylvie Patron. Berlin: De Gruyter.

Lubbock, Percy. (1921) 1972. *The Craft of Fiction.* London: Jonathan Cape.

Mander, Jenny. 1999. *Circles of Learning: Narratology and the Eighteenth-Century French Novel.* Oxford: Voltaire Foundation.

McHale, Brian. 1983. "Unspeakable Sentences, Unnatural Acts: Linguistics and Poetics Revisited." *Poetics Today* 4 (1): 17–45.

Milner, Jean-Claude. (1989) 1995. *Introduction à une science du langage.* Paris: Le Seuil.

Patron, Sylvie. (2009) 2016. *Le Narrateur: Un problème de théorie narrative.* Limoges, France: Lambert-Lucas.

———. (2012) 2014. "Introduction." Translated by Susan Nicholls. In Kuroda 2014, 1–36.

———. 2019. *The Death of the Narrator and Other Essays.* Trier, Germany: Wissenschaftlicher Verlag Trier.

————. 2020. "No-Narrator Theories/Optional-Narrator Theories: Recent Proposals and Continuing Problems; Toward a History of Concepts in Narrative Theory." Translated by Melissa McMahon. In *Contemporary French and Francophone Narratology*, edited by John Pier, 31–53. Columbus: Ohio State University Press.

————. Forthcoming. "Narrator." Translated by Melissa McMahon. In *Fictionality in Literature: Core Concepts Revisited*, edited by Lasse Gammelgaard, Simona Zetterberg Gjerlevsen, Louise Brix Jacobsen, Richard Walsh, James Phelan, Henrik Skov Nielsen, and Stefan Iversen. Columbus: Ohio State University Press.

Patterson, Charles I. 1952. "Charles Lamb's Insight into the Nature of the Novel." *Publications of the Modern Language Association of America* 67 (4): 375–82.

Rothschild, Jeffrey M. 1990. "Renaissance Voices Echoed: The Emergence of the Narrator in English Prose." *College English* 52 (1): 21–35.

Searle, John R. (1975) 1979. "The Logical Status of Fictional Discourse." In *Expression and Meaning: Studies in the Theory of Speech Acts*, 58–75. Cambridge: Cambridge University Press.

Spielhagen, Friedrich. (1883) 1969. "Der Ich-Roman." In *Zur Poetik des Romans*, edited by Volker Klotz, 66–161. Darmstadt, Germany: Wissenschaftliche Buchgesellschaft.

Spitzer, Leo. (1928) 1961. "Zum Stil Marcel Prousts." In *Stilstudien, Zweiter Teil: Stilsprachen*, 2: 465–97. 2nd ed. Munich: Max Hueber.

Stanzel, Franz K. (1979) 1984. *A Theory of Narrative*. Translated by Charlotte Goedsche. Cambridge: Cambridge University Press.

Thon, Jan-Noël. 2016. *Transmedial Narratology and Contemporary Media Culture*. Lincoln: University of Nebraska Press.

Walsh, Richard. (1997) 2007. "The Narrator and the Frame of Fiction." In *The Rhetoric of Fictionality: Narrative Theory and the Idea of Fiction*, 69–85, 174–75. Columbus: Ohio State University Press.

Wolterstorff, Nicholas. 1980. *Works and Worlds of Art*. Oxford: Clarendon Press.

6   Biblical Narrative and the Death of the Narrator

ROBERT S. KAWASHIMA

For untold millennia language was coterminous with speech. There simply was no instantiation of language that was not spoken out loud, so that all narratives during this prehistorical period were necessarily told by actual flesh-and-blood narrators, namely, a storyteller. Several millennia ago, the invention of writing created new linguistic possibilities, possibilities that would eventually reveal that language need not be limited to speech, which revelation would ultimately have momentous consequences for narrative. Writing, to be sure, originally sought (and often still seeks) to transcribe speech—from Homer to *Huck Finn*.[1] Written narratives, in this case, are conceived of as being spoken by a narrator, whether this literary figure is implicit or heterodiegetic (external to the narrative world), or explicit or homodiegetic (internal to the narrative world)—more on which below. Writing, however, would subsequently make possible linguistic constructions that cannot be understood as belonging to the spoken language. In doing so, it made possible the existence of narratives without a narrator, narratives that are, grammatically speaking, "unspeakable" (Banfield [1982] 2014). This isn't to say that this linguistic possibility was realized right away. Indeed, it wasn't until the invention or discovery of literary prose in ancient Israel, as I will argue, that writing was finally freed from the task of transcribing the spoken word.

Nearly three millennia more had to pass before scholars in the second half of the previous century came to perceive this distinction between writing and speech. Käte Hamburger ([1957, 1968] 1973, 1993) and Émile Benveniste ([1959, 1966] 1971), and later S.-Y. Kuroda ([1973] 2014; [1976] 2014) and Ann Banfield (1973; [1982] 2014), proposed several related hypotheses, based on compelling empirical argumentation, according to which writing had made possible narratives that cannot be attributed to an act of speaking. The expression "no-narrator theory" came to be used to characterize this notion of a narratorless narrative. As Sylvie Patron has observed, however, this designation is "inadequate" and "leads to confusion" (2019, 154). For it can lead, and in fact has led, some to misunderstand this position as a universal denial of the existence of the narrator in all cases, when in fact it merely denies the existence of a narrator in some cases. The expression "optional-narrator theory" is thus meant to make clear that a typology is being established that divides the set of all narratives into two classes, those with and those without a narrator.

Properly evaluating this theory, which entails understanding scholarly resistance to it, requires us to make explicit an axiomatic decision that all must make regarding the logical status of the concept of the narrator. Namely, one must decide whether the proposition "All narratives have a narrator" is analytic or synthetic. Does the existence of the narrator simply go without saying (analytic)? Or is its merely possible existence an empirical question (synthetic)? All too often, those who believe in the "pan-narrator theory" implicitly conceive of the narrator as an integral part of the definition of narrative as such. Those who take the trouble to argue against it would do well to take this fact into consideration. If this proposition is thought to be analytic, all argumentation regarding the narrator's existence will be seen as nonsensical and superfluous. It is no doubt for this reason that denying the existence of the narrator, as Ann Banfield likes to attest from personal experience, is often received with the same sense of pious dismay as denying the existence of God. *Belief* in the narrator, that is, is all too often an unfalsifiable hypothesis. If, on the other hand, this proposition is thought to be synthetic, then one must search for empirical evidence, whether to corroborate it or to falsify it. In this chapter, I will argue for the optional-narrator theory based on the tense system governing Classical Biblical Hebrew (CBH) prose narrative—namely, Genesis through Kings, less the Book of Ruth[2]—synthesizing arguments I have presented on various occasions (Kawashima 2004, 2010, 2011, 2013).

Hans Reichenbach provides the standard formal account of tense (1947, 287–98). He defines tense value as a complex of three "time points": E (point of the event), R (point of reference), S (point of speech). Tense proper is defined in terms of the relation between S and R: past (R–S), present (R, S), future (S–R).[3] These three basic tense values are each further specified in terms of the relation between E and R: anterior (E–R), simple (E, R), posterior (R–E). Reichenbach thus posits nine basic tense values corresponding to the nine possible combinations of past, present, or future, and anterior, simple, or posterior. According to his notation, then, the simple past is transcribed as E, R–S; the anterior past or pluperfect as E–R–S. One peculiarity of CBH is that it makes do with only three primary tense forms: the "perfect," *qatal* (E–R); the "predicative participle," *qotel* (E, R); and the "imperfect," *yiqtol* (R–E).[4] Reichenbach would characterize these forms as anterior, simple, and posterior, respectively. In CBH, tense proper—the relation of R to S—depends on syntactic context. Thus, *qatal* (E–R), to take merely one example, can have the tense value of the anterior past (E–R–S), the anterior present (E–R, S), or the anterior future (S–E–R).

More generally, in fact, a tense form in any given language might have more than one tense value. Consider the following two uses of the English present tense: "It is (now) raining"; "One plus one is (*now) equal to two." The first is the true present tense, for which reason the adverbial "now," cotemporal with S, can co-occur with it. The second is the generic present or present of definition. It does not refer to an event (which as such would occupy a particular location in time), and so the adverbial "now" cannot co-occur with it—hence the asterisk, which marks it as an unacceptable construction. Finally, one should carefully note that in Reichenbach's account, each and every tense value entails S by definition. Insofar as the narrator is he who speaks the narrative, the location of the narrator must be identified with S. Reichenbach's tense system applied to narrative, then, amounts to a pan-narrator theory.

It was Benveniste's great achievement in his celebrated essay "The Correlations of Tense in the French Verb" to revise, in effect, Reichenbach's account of tense—apparently without being aware of it—by demonstrating that S is *optional* to tense. His 1959 essay was republished in *Problems in General Linguistics* as part of a series of chapters under the heading "Man and Language" (*L'homme dans la langue*): "Here it is the mark of man upon language defined by the linguistic forms of 'subjectivity' and the categories of person, pronouns, and tense" (Benveniste 1971, viii). In particular, he posits, based on the distribution of tense in French, the existence of "two systems which are distinct and complementary . . . two different planes of utterance" (206), which he refers to as "discourse" (*discours*) and "narration" (*histoire*). Discourse consists of a communication uttered by a speaker (I) located in the speaker's present. Thus, the French perfect (*passé composé*) "creates a living connection between the past event and the present in which its evocation takes place. . . . Like the present, the perfect belongs to the linguistic system of discourse, for the temporal location of the perfect is the moment of the discourse" (210). Discourse, in other words, is grounded in temporal deixis. In Reichenbach's terms, it locates an event (E) in relation to a moment of speech (S). Narration, in stark contrast, consists of a non-deictic account of events made possible by the medium of writing: "The historical utterance, today reserved to the written language, characterizes the narration of past events. These three terms, 'narration,' 'event,' and 'past,' are of equal importance. Events that took place at a certain moment of time are presented without any intervention of the speaker in the narration" (Benveniste [1959, 1966] 1971, 206); "As a matter of fact, there is then no longer even a narrator. The events are set forth chronologically, as they occurred. No one speaks here; the events seem to narrate themselves. The fundamental tense is the aorist, which is the tense of the event outside the person of a narrator" (208). In other words, narration—the aorist (*passé simple*), in particular—locates E without reference to S, to a narrator. Banfield, taking up Benveniste's arguments within the research program of generative grammar (Chomskyan linguistics), noted that native French speakers judge the *passé simple* to be "unacceptable" in the spoken language, and thus pronounced the sentence of pure narration (that employing the *passé simple*) "unspeakable" (Banfield [1982] 2014, 141–71).[5] Not coincidentally, Benveniste attributes three primary tenses to narration: the pluperfect, aorist, and prospective tenses, which Reichenbach refers to, respectively, as the anterior (E–R–S), simple (E, R–S), and posterior (R–E–S) past tenses.[6] But once it is revealed that the *passé simple* is a nondeictic preterite making no reference to the intervention of a speaker (S), merely locating the event at "a certain moment of time" (E, R), the anterior (E–R) and posterior (R–E) past tenses in narration likewise fall into place, simply by removing S. Transcribing Benveniste's concept of narration with Reichenbach's notation thus makes clear that the narrator is literally (*à la lettre*) optional.

CBH, like French, deploys two distinct tense systems, discourse and narration (Kawashima 2004, 35–76). The three primary tense forms I mentioned earlier—*qatal, qotel, yiqtol*—function, in discourse, more or less, as the anterior present (E–S, R), simple present (E, S, R), and posterior present (S, R–E) tenses, respectively – anterior (E–), simple (E,), and posterior (–E), that is, in relation to the present tense (S, R). *Qatal*, in particular, then, is equivalent to the French *passé composé*. And in fact, the perfect occurs in CBH narrative primarily, if not exclusively, in direct discourse, that is, in the quoted speech of characters, Benveniste's *discours*. Now, in order to describe CBH narration, I must draw attention to the existence of an additional tense, the so-called "converted imperfect," *wayyiqtol*.[7] Here, the prefixal conjunction *wa-* (and)—sometimes called the "conversive" *waw*[8]—"converts" the future tense, *yiqtol*, into a preterite. And in fact, the converted imperfect occurs primarily, if not exclusively, in narration, Benveniste's *histoire*.[9] The converted imperfect is equivalent, I maintain, to the French *passé simple*.

Let me begin by presenting paired examples of narration and discourse, which will enable us to observe directly the complementary distribution of *qatal* and *wayyiqtol* in CBH narrative. (My awkward English translations generally attempt to reflect the word order of the Hebrew, since certain syntactic constraints will prove relevant to the distinction between narration and discourse in CBH.)

And sighed (*wayye'an^eḥu*) the children of Israel from their labour and cried out (*wayyiz'aqu*). And rose up (*watta'al*) their groaning to God from their servitude. And heard (*wayyišma'*) God their clamour, and remembered (*wayyizkor*) God his covenant with Abraham, with Isaac, and with Jacob. And looked (*wayyar'*) God upon the children of Israel, and understood (*wayyeda'*) God. (Exodus 2:23–25)

I have *certainly* seen (*ra'oh ra'iti*) the misery of my people who are in Egypt, and their outcry I have heard (*šama'ti*) because of their taskmasters. How well (*ki*) do I know (*yada'ti*) their sufferings. . . . And now (*w^e'attah*), look (*hinneh*),[10] the outcry of the children of Israel has come (*ba'ah*) to me, and indeed (*w^egam*), I have seen (*ra'iti*) the oppression which Egypt inflicts on them. (Exodus 3:7, 9)

And went (*wayyelek*) Balaam with the leaders of Balak. (Numbers 22:35)

Look (*hinneh*), I have come (*ba'ti*) to you now (*'attah*). (Numbers 22:38)

And committed (*wayyim'alu*) the Israelites a trespass against the devoted things. And took (*wayyiqqaḥ*) Achan . . . from the devoted things. And burned (*wayyiḥar*) the anger of the Lord against the Israelites. (Joshua 7:1)

Sinned has (*ḥaṭa'*) Israel. And indeed (*wᵉgam*), they have transgressed (*'aberu*) my covenant, which I had enjoined upon them. And indeed (*wᵉgam*), they have taken (*laqeḥu*) from the devoted things, and indeed (*wᵉgam*), they have stolen (*ganᵉbu*), and indeed (*wᵉgam*), they have acted (*kiḥašu*) falsely, and indeed (*wᵉgam*), they have put (*śamu*) it amongst their own things. (Joshua 7:11)

And fought (*wayyillaḥamu*) the Philistines, and defeated was (*wayyinnagep*) Israel, and they fled (*wayyanusu*), each man to his tent, and was (*wattᵉhi*) the slaughter very great. And fell (*wayippol*) from amongst Israel thirty thousand foot soldiers. (1 Samuel 4:10, 11)

Fled has (*nas*) Israel before the Philistines. And indeed (*wᵉgam*), a great slaughter has come about (*hayᵉta*) among the people. (1 Samuel 4:17)

And fought (*wayyillaḥem*) Joab against Rabbah of the sons of Ammon, and captured (*wayyilkod*) the royal city. (2 Samuel 12:26)

I have fought (*nilḥamti*) against Rabbah. Indeed (*gam*), I have captured (*lakadti*) the City of Waters. (2 Samuel 12:27)

And conspired (*wayyiqšor*) against him [king Elah of Israel] his servant Zimri, chief of half the chariots. . . . And came (*wayyabo'*) Zimri and struck (*wayyakkehu*) him and killed (*waymitehu*) him. (1 Kings 16:9, 10)

Conspired (*qašar*) has Zimri, and indeed (*wᵉgam*), he has struck (*hikkah*) the king. (1 Kings 16:16)

In each pair of examples, the first is narration, the second discourse. In each case, narration employs *wayyiqtol* (translated as the simple past, mostly with verb-subject word order), while discourse employs *qatal* (translated as the present perfect). Crucially, the temporal deictic "now" (*'attah*) co-occurs with *qatal*, never with *wayyiqtol*. Equally important are constructions such as "indeed" (*gam*), "how well" (*ki*), and "*certainly* seen" (*ra'oh ra'iti*),[11] which are found in discourse, not in narration. These are examples of what Banfield has named "expressive" constructions, namely, subjective linguistic forms whose full interpretation requires reference to a speaker ([1982] 2014, see index). Their presence in discourse demonstrates the presence of a narrator (S); their absence in narration helps indicate his absence.

The distribution of *wayyiqtol* observable in CBH narrative—the fact that it is uncharacteristic of discourse—and the corresponding distribution of deictics and expressive constructions raise the historical possibility that the converted imperfect, like the French *passé simple*, was a strictly (or primarily) literary or written tense. One should carefully consider the burden imposed by the syntactic constraints entailed by the converted imperfect: it may appear only in sentence-initial position; by definition, then, it requires verb-subject word order; and the form itself requires a marked (archaic) form of the conjunction "and"—*wa* as opposed to *wᵉ*. It is unlikely that such syntactic constraints could function in the extemporaneous flow of speech (Kawashima 2013, 648). Consider the following examples, which I take to be more or less representative (mimetic) of colloquial speech.

> [Isaac speaking to Esau]: Look (*hinneh*), please. I am old (*zaqan-ti*). Not know I (*lo' yada'ti*) the day of my death.[12] (Genesis 27:2).

> [Saul's servant speaking to Saul]: Look (*hinneh*), please. A man of God is in this city, and the man is honored. All that he says *certainly* comes to pass (*bo' yabo'*). Now (*'attah*), let us go there. Perhaps he will tell us about our way, by which we have gone. (1 Samuel 9:6f)

Note again the occurrence of deictic and expressive constructions typical of discourse: "look"; "*certainly*"; "now." Not coincidentally, the syntactic constraints typical of narration do not hold here. These two examples suggest that word order in discourse is much more flexible, as one would expect of the spoken language. It might begin with the grammatical subject ("A man of God is . . . and the man is") or an adverbial

("Now") or the negative particle ("not know" [*lo' yada'ti*]) or the direct object of an embedded verb phrase ("All that he says"). Finally, while the reader may already have begun to notice from the examples given so far that the sentence-initial conjunction "and" is ubiquitous in narration—due largely but not entirely to *wayyiqtol*—what these two examples already suggest is that this "and" is not ubiquitous in the spoken language. Presumably, these two sequences of asyndetic (conjunction-less) declarative sentences mimic a syntactic pattern of actual speech, in which, one easily imagines, sentences did not have to begin with "and," never mind a marked form thereof.

So ubiquitous is this sentence-initial "and" in narration that its mere absence suffices to signal some sort of syntactic disruption.

> And she called (*wattiqra'*) the name of Yahweh, who was speaking to her. . . . *Therefore* ('al ken) *the well is called Beer Lahai Roi. There it is* (hinneh), *between Kadesh and Bered.* (Genesis 16:13–14)

> And went up and encamped (*wayya'alu wayyaḥanu*) [some men from the tribe of Dan] at Kiryat Ye'arim in Judah. *Therefore* ('al ken) *they have called this place Mahaneh Dan until this day* (hayyom hazzeh). *There it is* (hinneh), *beyond* ('aḥarey) *Kiryat Ye'arim.* (Judges 18:12)

> And sent (*wayšallaḥ*) Yahweh against him. . . . *Surely* ('ak) *by the mouth of Yahweh this came about in Judah, to remove them from his presence for the sins of Manasseh.* (2 Kings 24:2–3)

As these examples demonstrate, the absence of sentence-initial "and" in narration indicates the sudden intervention of discourse (*italicized* in the examples just above). These contain deictic and expressive constructions typical of discourse: "there it is"; "surely"; "this day"; "beyond." And yet, they are not introduced by verbs of speech, for they are not directly quoted speech. They are, rather, authorial intrusions. It is an author/editor, then, external to the narrative world, and not some supposed narrator, who comments on the name Beer Lahai Roi, who comments on the name Mahaneh Dan, who comments on God's punishment of the northern tribes—all in the "real" world. It is the position of this writer in the external world, not some putative narrator within the narrative world, that defines S. That is, it is in relation to a point in the "real" world, not some virtual point inside the narrative world, that "this day" and "beyond" are located. And as the designation "intrusion" suggests, this fleeting authorial discourse is perceived as being foreign to narration proper.

To summarize, then, there are various syntactic features that distinguish between narration and discourse: the distribution of tense forms, of deictics, of expressive constructions, not to mention constraints on word order. All of these factors argue against the intervention of a narrator. In other words, CBH narration should not be conceived of as transcribed speech. Having established these basic features of narration and discourse in CBH, we are now in a position to consider additional syntactic evidence in support of the optional-narrator theory.

Related to the converted imperfect, *wayyiqtol*, is a derivative syntactic phenomenon I have elsewhere named "orphaned converted tense forms," in particular, *'az yiqtol* (2010). This well-attested construction, combining the temporal adverbial *'az* (then) with the imperfect *yiqtol*, has a past-tense value, rather than the future-tense value expected of *yiqtol*. Hebraists have generally accounted for this anomalous tense value with a diachronic explanation: it preserves the archaic preterite **yaqtul* (see note 7). As linguists know, however, grammar is a purely synchronic affair, diachronic explanations being largely irrelevant. I have therefore offered a synchronic explanation instead: the conversive *waw* has been replaced by the adverbial *'az*; the now self-standing *yiqtol* is still a converted imperfect, but it has been "orphaned," bereft of its conversive *waw*. True, *wayyiqtol* is written in CBH as a single "word," but as the presence of the conjunction indicates, it should actually be analyzed as a verbal phrase, not a mere verb. In which case it stands to reason that it might undergo syntactic manipulations. The equivalence of *'az yiqtol* and *wayyiqtol* is evident in the following set of parallel examples.

And sang (*wattašar*) Deborah, and Barak son of Abinoam, on that day (*bayyom hahu'*). (Judges 5:1)

Then sang (*'az yašir*) Moses, and the Israelites, this song to the Lord. (Exodus 15:1)

Then sang (*'az yašir*) Israel this song. (Numbers 21:17)

As a type of thought experiment, let us compare these examples synchronically. Syntactically speaking, "then" in Exodus 15:1 and Numbers

21:17 has replaced the conversive *waw* in Judges 5:1. Semantically speaking, "then" has replaced the prepositional phrase, "on that day." That is, both "then" and "on that day" refer anaphorically to a certain moment in time (R), an unspecified albeit specific date established earlier in the narrative—rather than referring to a moment defined deictically in relation to S.

What is more, there is, one should carefully consider, a scribal quality to these occurrences of *'az yiqtol*, in that the narrative function of this verbal phrase seems to be to insert a secondary independent "historical" event at a particular moment in the plot arc of the primary narrative.

> Then consecrated (*'az yabdil*) Moses three cities beyond the Jordan in the east. (Deuteronomy 4:41)

> Then built (*'az yibneh*) Joshua an altar to Yahweh the God of Israel on Mount Ebal, just as had commanded Moses, the servant of Yahweh, the children of Israel, as it is written in the book of the law of Moses. (Joshua 8:30–31)

> Then spoke (*'az yᵉdabber*) Joshua to Yahweh . . . and said (*wayyoʾmer*) . . . "Sun, at Gibeon stand still . . ." And stood still (*wayiddom*) the sun (Joshua 10:12–13)

> Then gave (*'az yitten*) Solomon the king to Hiram twenty cities in the land of Galilee. (1 Kings 9:11)

> Then built (*'az yibneh*) Solomon a high place for Chemosh. (1 Kings 11:7)

> Then went up (*'az yaʿaleh*) Hazael king of Syria and fought (*wayyillahem*) against Gath and took it (*wayyilkᵉdah*). (2 Kings 12:18)

Regarding such examples in the Book of Kings, James Montgomery goes so far as to hypothesize that these were extracted from an actual archival source: "This stylistic adverb appears to replace some definite date or circumstance in the original record" (1934, 49). (Note his intuition that the adverb "then" replaces, is equivalent to, a "date" or "circumstance.") Regardless of whether an actual archival source stands behind all of these examples, in each case, a writer used the adverbial *'az* to correlate a secondary well-known or significant event with a specific juncture (date) in the primary narrative sequence, that is, with a previously established circumstance to which "then" anaphorically refers. Consider, for example, Joshua 8. The source referred to by the editor—"the book of the law of Moses" (8:31)—is Deuteronomy, where Moses commands Israel to build an altar at Mount Ebal "on the day that you cross the Jordan" (27:2–5). The writer chose to insert Israel's fulfillment of this command, a discrete event having no clearly defined place in the narrative arc of Joshua, just after Joshua's defeat of Ai—thus, not literally "on the day" they crossed the Jordan. What is interesting both here and in other related examples is that, synchronically speaking, the writer understood *wayyiqtol* to be a converted imperfect, as evidenced by his chosen substitute, *'az yiqtol*—a glimpse into his "linguistic competence," in the Chomskyan sense of the term. And if there is any lingering doubt as to the tense value of *'az yiqtol*, one should note how it can be seamlessly continued by a narrative sequence using *wayyiqtol*, as in Joshua 10:12–13 and 2 Kings 12:18 above.

Part of the evidence for the distinction between narration and discourse is the distribution of *qatal* (discourse) and *wayyiqtol* (narration). And yet, I admitted that this distribution isn't absolute in CBH, as it is in French. It is noteworthy, then, that *'az yiqtol* always has a past-tense value in narration, and always has a future-tense value in discourse. The complementary distribution of these two uses of *'az yiqtol* is as absolute as the distribution of the perfect and the aorist in French. Synchronically speaking, *'az yiqtol* in narration is a transmutation of the converted imperfect, in discourse, an occurrence of the regular imperfect.

> [Abraham speaking to his servant]: Then you will be free (*'az tinnaqeh*) from my oath, when you will come (*ki tabo'*) to my relatives, and if (*we'im*) they will not give (*yitnu*) her to you, and [then] you will be (*wᵉhayita*) free from my oath. (Genesis 24:41)

> [God speaking to Moses]: Then will enjoy (*'az tirṣeh*) the land its sabbaths . . . (Leviticus 26:34)

> [Jonathan speaking to David]: When I will probe (*ki 'eḥqor*) my father . . . tomorrow or the day after, and look, if it is good for David, will I not then send (*'az yišlaḥ*) to you . . . ? (1 Samuel 20:12)

Relatedly, *'az qatal* in discourse—including in biblical poetry (e.g., Exodus 15), which is conceived of, and presented in narrative, as quoted speech—always retains the expected past-tense value of *qatal*.[13]

[Moses speaking to God]: And since [lit. "from then"] I have come (*ume'az ba'ti*) to Pharaoh . . . (Exodus 5:23)

Then were dismayed (*'az nibhalu*) the chiefs of Edom. (Exodus 15:15)

[Phineas speaking to the Reubenites et al.]: Now [lit. "then"] you have rescued (*'az hiṣṣaltem*) the children of Israel from the hand of Yahweh. (Joshua 22:31)

As these examples of discourse demonstrate, *'az* converts only the imperfect (not the perfect), only in narration (not in discourse).

CBH narrative was apparently preceded by an ancient tradition of oral poetry (Kawashima 2004, 17–34). Not coincidentally, the oldest texts in the Bible are "archaic poems," such as Exodus 15 and Judges 5, which conserve traces of oral traditions analogous to those thought to have produced Homer's epics (Parry 1971; Lord 1960). Such a historical development fits into a broadly attested cross-cultural phenomenon in which (oral) poetry precedes prose (Godzich and Kittay 1987). The question thus arises whether oral epics have a narrator. As I have already suggested, they do. While I cannot address this question in detail, I will briefly sketch a few grammatical traces left by the epic narrator.

Consider Homer. Both of his epics begin with an invocation of the Muse: "Sing, goddess, the anger of Peleus' son Achilleus / and its devastation, which put pains thousandfold upon the Achaians" (*Iliad* 1.1–2); "Tell me, Muse, of the man of many ways, who was driven / far journeys, after he had sacked Troy's sacred citadel" (*Odysseus* 1.1–2).[14] Both the imperative verbs—"sing" (*aeide*), "tell" (*ennepe*)—and the vocative addressees—"goddess" (*thea*), "Muse" (*mousa*)—make grammatically explicit the presence of a second person, a "you," which as Benveniste observed, logically presupposes an "I" ([1946, 1966] 1971, 197). *Gilgamesh* similarly begins with a first-person declaration: "[Of him who] found out all things, I [shall te]ll the land, / [Of him who] experienced everything, [I shall tea]ch the whole" (Dalley [1989] 2000, 50). Such a narrator—namely, the epic singer or rhapsode—may be heterodiegetic, external to the story proper, but his presence is nonetheless assured by linguistic signs. Indeed, in both Mesopotamia and Greece, epic was conceived of as a story performed for and addressed to a listening audience—implied, for example, by the intention to "tell" and "teach" Gilgamesh's exploits.

Here we should recall that according to Banfield's definition of narration ([1982] 2014, 171), what is excluded from narration is not a first-person "SPEAKER" (I), but an "ADDRESSEE/HEARER," typically, but not necessarily referred to explicitly as "you."[15] Proust's so-called narrator, then, insofar as he does not, linguistically speaking, address an audience (Banfield [1982] 2014, 149, 171–80, 247), is not a true narrator. The homodiegetic narrator of *The Adventures of Huckleberry Finn*, on the other hand, is. It is not just that Huck addresses an explicit "you." For Mark Twain's written imitation of English as it is spoken—what the Russian formalists referred to as *skaz*—effectively transcribes Huck's telling of his story, and thus suffices to establish the presence of an audience who hears his story's telling. Similarly, the oral-traditional language of *Gilgamesh* and of Homer—but not Virgil—effectively represents the live performance of an epic singer, and thus suffices to establish the presence of an audience who hears the singer tell his tale.

No surprise, then, that Homer's epics do not instantiate the linguistic dualism of narration and discourse. Citing Plato, I would say, rather, that Homer alternates between *diēgēsis*—when, speaking in his own voice, he narrates events in the third person—and *mimēsis*—when, imitating one of his characters, he speaks in his or her place in the first person (Kawashima 2011, 358–65). In both cases, Homer *speaks*. His epics, again, are transcriptions, are placed, as it were, within quotation marks. In contrast to CBH narrative—and much modern fiction—Homer's language thus constitutes a type of linguistic monism. Thus, in stark contrast to French and CBH, Homer employs only one primary past-tense form, the aorist. But this is negative evidence.

We find compelling positive evidence for the voice of Homer-as-narrator in the presence of "expressive" constructions in *diēgēsis* as well as *mimēsis*. Consider Homeric examples of what Banfield calls "evaluative adjectives" (1973), that is, adjectives that express the subjective evaluation of the speaker.

> You foolish countrymen (*nēpioi agroiōtai*), who never think of tomorrow, / poor wretches (*deilō*), why are you streaming tears, and troubling the lady. (*Odyssey* 21.85–86)

Here, Antinoös, speaking in the first person (*mimēsis*), expresses his contempt for his countrymen, whom he addresses in the vocative case.

Crucially, Homer uses this evaluative adjective in third-person narrative (*diēgēsis*) as well.

> He [Agamemnon] wished . . . to soften Athene's deadly anger, poor fool (*nēpios*) / who had no thought in his mind that she would not listen to him. (*Odyssey* 3.143–46)

> For he [Agamemnon] thought that on that very day he would take Priam's city; / fool (*nēpios*), who knew nothing of all the things Zeus planned to accomplish. (*Iliad* 2.37–38)

These examples are not authorial intrusions; they form rather a seamless part of Homer's *diēgēsis*. Such evaluative adjectives thus positively reveal the presence of a narrator who evaluates his characters using the same language as his characters: *diēgēsis* and *mimēsis* are linguistically one, monologic to borrow Mikhail Bakhtin's term ([1975] 1981). There is, then, neither Homeric *histoire*—Homer speaks—nor Homeric *discours*—no one ever spoke Homer's *Kunstsprache*. In order to capture the distinctive quality of epic poetry, I thus propose a third term, *mémoire*, insofar as the function of the epic narrator is precisely that of Memory, albeit in the third person, hence his invocation of the Muse.

As I have already suggested, the typology of narratives with and without a narrator has a diachronic dimension. The death of the narrator constitutes an event in the history of narrative. Consider Barthes's annunciation of "the Death of the Author." Contrary to popular opinion, it does not represent an atheistic stance toward the author in general; rather, it posits a historical thesis regarding the evolution of narrative: "As soon as a fact is *narrated* (raconté) no longer with a view to acting directly on reality but intransitively . . . the voice loses its origin, the author enters into his own death, writing (*l'écriture*) begins. The sense of this phenomenon, however, has varied" (Barthes [1968] 1978, 142). In broad strokes, he discerns three discrete stages in the history of narrative, which he identifies in relation to three emblematic figures: the reciter, the author, and the scriptor. Here we need only consider the first two. First comes the "reciter": "In ethnographic societies the responsibility for a narrative (*récit*) is never assumed by a person but by a mediator, shaman, or reciter (*récitant*) whose 'performance'–the mastery of the narrative code—may possibly be admired but never his 'genius'" (142). Next comes the "Author":

"The Author (*L'auteur*) is a modern figure, a product of our society insofar as . . . it discovered the prestige of the individual, of . . . the 'human person'" (142–43); "The Author . . . is always conceived of as the past of his own book" (145). The primitive form of narrative, in other words, is an oral story performed by a reciter. Just as every speaking being learns to speak before—if ever—he learns to write, so too all cultures learned to recite stories before—if ever—they learned to author them. Literary or written narratives—whether fictional or historical—are thus a derived form, one that presupposes both logically and chronologically the prior existence of oral stories.

Barthes's literary-historical schema can be read in part as a diachronic illustration of the concept of the "optional" narrator. For the ethnographic performance of the reciter originates in the voice of a speaking being, an "I." Thus, Barthes glosses the reciter as the "*I sing* of very ancient poets" (146). Indeed, Barthes's evocation of the reciter and his "mastery of the narrative code" would seem to allude to the Parry-Lord hypothesis in Homer studies (Parry 1971; Lord 1960), which hypothesis is based on ethnographic fieldwork undertaken in Yugoslavia in the 1930s.[16] This singer of tales is a flesh-and-blood narrator standing before an actual audience. With the ascendance of the author, conversely, emerges the "work" (*œuvre*) or "book" (*livre*). As we know from Barthes's related historical thesis in *Writing Degree Zero*, regarding the evolution of the novel, novelistic writing (*l'écriture*) entails various "Signs of Literature," among which is the *passé simple*: "Obsolete in spoken French, the preterite, which is the cornerstone of Narration, always signifies the presence of Art. . . . Its function is no longer that of a tense. The part it plays is to reduce reality to a point of time, and to abstract, from the depth of a multiplicity of experiences, a pure verbal act, freed from the existential roots of knowledge, and directed towards a logical link with other acts, other processes, a general movement of the world" ([1953] 1968, 30). The present and present perfect, in a telling contrast, are "more full-blooded and nearer to speech" (32). Writing, in other words, and the preterite in particular, signify nothing less than the death of the reciter and the birth of the author.[17]

As I have argued here, an analogous "death" took place already in ancient Israel. First comes the archaic singer or rhapsode of ancient Near Eastern epics, for example, *Gilgamesh*. Next, we find the CBH author of biblical prose narrative. As I have argued elsewhere at greater length (Kawashima 2004), the advent of the prose writer in ancient Israel signals the death of the epic narrator.

Notes

1. Or it presents a text as if it had been spoken—letter writing, for example, in epistolary novels. Even if these lack a proper narrator who tells the story as a whole, they are still presented as collections of quasi-spoken texts.
2. The first nine books of the Jewish Bible—the Law (Torah) or Pentateuch (Genesis-Deuteronomy) and the Former Prophets (Joshua, Judges, Samuel, Kings)—were essentially written before the Babylonian Exile in 586 BCE, and in this sense are "classical." The Book of Ruth is post-exilic, for which reason it does not follow Judges in the Jewish Bible, as it does in the Christian Bible.
3. The notation "R–S" indicates that R precedes S; the notation "R, S" indicates that these two points coincide.
4. According to a long-standing convention, the Hebrew tense forms are designated by the third-person masculine singular forms of the verb *q-t-l*, the consonants of which are not susceptible to morphological irregularities.
5. Banfield further revised Benveniste's definition of narration to include fiction as well as history, and first-person as well as third-person narratives, more on which below.
6. I leave to the side the "present of definition" and the imperfect (Benveniste [1959, 1966] 1971, 207), which do not concern us here.
7. Readers familiar with CBH will know that, diachronically speaking, the converted imperfect (*wayyiqtol*) isn't actually "converted." Rather, it constitutes a kind of linguistic fossil: namely, the archaic form of the conjunction "and" (*wa-*) prefixed to the archaic preterite **yaqtul*, as opposed to the archaic imperfect **yaqtulu*. Hebraists are thus generally embarrassed by the traditional-grammatical idea of tense "conversion," wrongly thinking that it is an obsolete concept, replaced by more recent diachronic analysis. But as Ronald Hendel (1996) has correctly observed, *wayyiqtol* is indeed, synchronically speaking, a "converted" tense; that is, *wa* + **yaqtul* has been "synchronically reinterpreted" as the converted imperfect.
8. *Waw* is the name of the Hebrew letter transliterated as *w*.
9. The exceptional occurrences of *qatal* in narration and *wayyiqtol* in discourse that I have mentioned do not undermine my overall thesis. Due to syntactic constraints on the use of *wayyiqtol* as well as the fact that it contains the conjunction "and," it cannot begin the narration of a sequence of events; it can only continue it. For this reason, *wayyiqtol* is often referred to

as the *waw*-consecutive. *Qatal* thus regularly appears in narration in order to initiate a narrative sequence. Even if *wayyiqtol* is not as grammatically constrained as the *passé simple*, there are still good reasons to think that it was generally confined to writing in ancient Israel. Its not infrequent use in direct discourse, then, actually points to the fact that CBH narrative does not present a naturalistic imitation (*mimēsis*) of the language as it was actually spoken; it is, rather, stylized, slightly tainted as it were by the elevated (literary) syntax of CBH. Finally, the same tense form can take different tense values: for example, the present tense and the present of definition mentioned earlier. In discourse, *wayyiqtol* is linked via *qatal* to S; in narration, *qatal* is located at a certain moment of time, without connection to any S.

10. Often translated as "look" or "behold," the presentative *hinneh* is similar to French *voici/voilà*.

11. In this emphatic construction, the infinitive absolute of a verb (here, *ra'oh*) co-occurs with a finite form of the same verb (*ra'iti*), creating something like *contrastive stress*. A hyperliteral translation would be "seeing I have seen."

12. For stative verbs—to be old, to know, and so on—*qatal* is best translated as the present tense: I am old; I do not know.

13. On a few occasions, *'az qatal* with past-tense value occurs in narration. Montgomery (1934, 49) already described these occurrences as "ungrammatical."

14. All translations of Homer are by Richard Lattimore (see Homer 1951 and 1967).

15. Roland Barthes relatedly notes that "literary discourse" is apparently "a discourse without *you*" ([1967] 1989, 131).

16. Milman Parry undertook his doctoral studies at the University of Paris under the celebrated linguist Antoine Meillet, for whom he wrote two theses on Homer in French. Meillet, in turn, taught Benveniste, mentor, in turn, of Barthes.

17. One should recall here Walter Benjamin's related historical thesis regarding the "rise of the novel," that it is a "symptom" of the "decline of storytelling" ([1936–37] 1968, 87).

References

Bakhtin, Mikhail. (1975) 1981. "Discourse in the Novel." In *The Dialogic Imagination: Four Essays*, edited by Michael Holquist, 259–422. Austin: University of Texas Press.

Banfield, Ann. 1973. "Narrative Style and the Grammar of Direct and Indirect Speech." *Foundations of Language* 10 (1): 1–39.

———. (1982) 2014. *Unspeakable Sentences: Narration and Representation in the Language of Fiction*. London: Routledge Revivals.

Barthes, Roland. (1953) 1968. *Writing Degree Zero*. Translated by Annette
Lavers and Colin Smith. New York: Hill and Wang.

———. (1967) 1989. "The Discourse of History." In *The Rustle of Language*, 127–
40. Translated by Richard Howard. Berkeley: University of California Press.

———. (1968) 1978. "The Death of the Author." In *Image—Music—Text*, 142–
48. Translated by Stephen Heath. New York: Hill and Wang.

Benjamin, Walter. (1936–37) 1968. "The Storyteller." In *Illuminations*, 83–109.
Translated by Harry Zohn. New York: Schocken Books.

Benveniste, Émile. (1946, 1966) 1971. "Relationships of Person in the Verb." In
Benveniste, 1971, 195–204.

———. (1959, 1966) 1971. "The Correlations of Tense in the French Verb." In
Benveniste 1971, 205–15.

———. 1971. *Problems in General Linguistics*. Translated by Mary E. Meek.
Coral Gables FL: Miami University Press.

Dalley, Stephanie. [1989] 2000. *Myths from Mesopotamia: Creation, The Flood,
Gilgamesh, and Others*. Oxford: Oxford University Press.

Godzich, Wlad, and Jeffrey Kittay. 1987. *The Emergence of Prose: An Essay in
Prosaics*. Minneapolis: University of Minnesota Press.

Hamburger, Käte. [1957, 1968] 1973, 1993. *The Logic of Literature*. Translated by
Marilynn J. Rose. 2nd ed. Bloomington: Indiana University Press, 1973.

Hendel, Ronald S. 1996. "In the Margins of the Hebrew Verbal System:
Situation, Tense, Aspect, Mood." *Zeitschrift für Althebräistik* 9: 152–81.

Homer. *The Iliad of Homer*. 1951. Translated by Richmond Lattimore. Chicago:
University of Chicago Press.

———. 1967. *The Odyssey of Homer*. New York: Harper and Row.

Kawashima, Robert S. 2004. *Biblical Narrative and the Death of the Rhapsode*.
Bloomington: Indiana University Press.

———. 2010. "'Orphaned' Converted Tense Forms in Classical Biblical Hebrew
Prose." *Journal of Semitic Studies* 55 (1): 11–35.

———. 2011. "The Syntax of Narrative Forms." In *Narratives of Egypt and the
Ancient Near East: Literary and Linguistic Approaches*, edited by Frederik
Hagen, John Johnston, Wendy Monkhouse, Kathryn Piquette, John Tait, and
Martin Worthington, 341–69. Leuven, Belgium: Peeters.

———. 2013. "Stylistics (Biblical Hebrew)." In *Encyclopaedia of the Hebrew
Language and Linguistics*, edited by Geoffrey Khan, 3: 643–50. Leiden,
Netherlands: Brill.

Kuroda, S.-Y. (1973) 2014. "Where Epistemology, Style, and Grammar Meet: A
Case Study from Japanese." In Kuroda 2014, 38–59.

———. (1976) 2014. "Reflections on the Foundations of Narrative Theory, from
a Linguistic Point of View." In Kuroda 2014, 71–101.

———. 2014. *Toward a Poetic Theory of Narration: Essays of S.-Y. Kuroda*, edited by Sylvie Patron. Berlin: De Gruyter.

Lord, Albert B. 1960. *The Singer of Tales*. Cambridge MA: Harvard University Press.

Montgomery, James A. 1934. "Archival Data in the Book of Kings." *Journal of Biblical Literature* 53(1): 46–52.

Parry, Milman. 1971. *The Making of Homeric Verse: The Collected Papers of Milman Parry*, edited by Adam Parry. Oxford: Oxford University Press.

Patron, Sylvie. 2019. *The Death of the Narrator and Other Essays*. Trier, Germany: Wissenschaftlicher Verlag Trier.

Reichenbach, Hans. 1947. *Elements of Symbolic Logic*. New York: MacMillan.

7 The Narrator in Biblical Narratives

GREGER ANDERSSON

Introduction

The subject of this chapter is the debate about the obligatory narrator of standard narratology. To be more specific, I discuss the narrator as a logical and pragmatic concept (Greve 2019) from the perspective of biblical studies.

A central issue in the debate is whether all narratives belong to the same system—the obligatory narrator is regarded as an essential part of that system—or if there are different narrative "language-games" (I will use the term "frames") that adhere to different rule systems. Theoreticians who advocate the latter alternative do not accept the obligatory narrator and propose instead that the narrator is optional, referring to character narrators or to voice effects. According to the latter distinction, there are character narrators without voice effects—that is, as a kind of style or empty form—as well as heterodiegetic narratives with voice effects (for example, *skaz*).

The debate primarily concerns literary fiction; for example, Lars-Åke Skalin criticizes the thesis of the generality of narrative as a phenomenon or concept as defined by the theory of narratology and argues that literary art (literary fiction) as a consequence has been included as just a species into an overarching genus that is narrative in a wide sense. Fiction and nonfiction are hence not regarded as distinct "language-games" (e.g., Skalin 2004, 2008, 2011a, 2011b) and "rule systems" (e.g., 2008, 2011b). A similar critique has been voiced by Richard Walsh (2007) and Sylvie Patron (2006, 2013). Readers, according to critics of the standard theory, relate to fiction "with another attitude than the one they assume for non-fiction, which is to say that they know that the text is constructed by an author with the specific intent to create something that cannot be grasped as non-fiction" (Andersson and Sandberg 2018).

The obligatory narrator holds a central position in the critique of the standard theory, since it is said to "establish a representational frame," which means that fiction is not viewed as invention (Walsh 2007, 69), and to imply a "communicational theory" according to which narratology can "examine the fictional narrative 'as narrative' and not 'as fiction'" (Patron 2006, 121).

It is not always totally clear what terms like "fiction" and "nonfiction" denote in this discussion. At times the terms seem to imply that something is made up or not, while at other times they refer to the generic status of a narrative. The distinction could also be taken—mistakenly, I believe—to imply a simple dichotomy between two distinct categories. But I will not consider these issues here.

What is important for my reasoning is instead the suggestions that there are different narrative frames, that the term "narrator" can have different denotations, and that there are narratives in relation to which the concept of a narrator, as it is commonly used in the standard theory, becomes irrelevant because these narratives are not appreciated as belonging to a "representational frame." I will refer to such narratives as "storytelling" (I use this term instead of "fiction," since "fiction" connotes something made up). The questions I address are therefore whether the Bible contains different kinds of "narratives" and, if so, whether some of them can be described as "narratorless storytelling." Moreover, I am interested in how the frame issue is handled by scholars who take on a literary or narratological approach in the study of the Bible and apply the concept of the narrator.

In the first part of this chapter, I refer to Uri Margolin's entry "Narrator" in *The Living Handbook of Narratology*, especially a section about "alternative models" and his distinction between different versions of the critique of the standard position. My biblical example in this part is Jesus's parable of the Good Samaritan. My aim with this section is to elucidate different positions in the debate. I then turn to the topic of the teller of Old Testament (Hebrew Bible) narratives. I discuss the application of the concept of the narrator in the study of these texts as well as the frame issue and the suggestion that some narratives might be "narratorless." Finally, I suggest some conclusions.

Obligatory versus Optional Narrator and
Jesus's Parable of the Good Samaritan

Margolin begins his section "Alternative Models" by explaining that the theory of the narrator in standard narratology is based on three assumptions:

> (a) there exists a specifiable inner-textual, highest-level speech or communication position functioning as the point of origin of the current discourse. In other words, all narrative fiction is communication. . . . (b) There is always an individual figure or agency occupying this speech position and thus backing the assertions contained in the narrative discourse or presenting the fictional world to us. . . . (c) This individual figure or agency exists on a strictly fictional level, and is a distinct entity within the fictional universe projected by the text. ([2012] 2014, 26–28)

Together with previous parts of Margolin's article, these points imply to me that all narratives are communication and consist of assertions by a teller. In fiction these assertions are made by a fictional figure of whom readers might make an image in their minds. This figure may be naturalized (anthropomorphized) and analyzed regardless of whether she or he is an inscribed narrator character or not, and regardless of her or his overtness.

Theoreticians who call into question the obligatory narrator can, according to Margolin, reject assumption (c); assumptions (b) and (c); or all three assumptions. To not accept (c) would, to my mind, mean that one does not accept the assumptions that there must be a fictional narrator in fictional narratives and that readers imagine such a teller; the narrative is instead produced and transmitted by an author. To not accept (b) and (c) means, for example, that the concept of the narrator is meaningless in relation to many heterodiegetic narratives. More radical critics even discard (a). This rejection must be taken to imply they do not accept that fictional narratives consist of someone's assertions about events in a fictional world.

There are hence some possible positions in the discussion about the narrator: we can support the traditional view (an obligatory narrator); we can argue that the idea that there always is a narrator-figure in fictional narratives is mistaken and that it is only meaningful to talk about a narrator when there is a narrator-motif (a character) or when there are voice-effects; we can finally dismiss the assumption that fiction belongs to the referential frame and argue that some or all fictional narratives are narratorless, if the narrator is taken in the sense of standard narratology (that is, even the existence of a narrator-motif or voice-effects should not be taken to imply an individual fictional figure or agency backing the assertions).

I will try to concretize the assumptions of the standard theory and possible objections to this theory by means of Jesus's parable of the Good Samaritan, since Jesus's narrative obviously is regarded as fictional (in the sense of "made up"). The tenth chapter of the gospel of Luke relates how a lawyer tests Jesus with the question "What must I do to inherit eternal life?" Jesus replies, "What is written in the law?" The lawyer then quotes the most important commandments: "You shall love the Lord your God with all your heart, and with all your soul, and with all your strength, and with all your mind; and your neighbor as yourself." To this Jesus replies, "You have given the right answer; do this, and you will live." At this point the discussion seems to be over, but the lawyer is not content with this development, and "to justify himself" he asks, "And who is my neighbor?" Jesus answers with the parable of the Good Samaritan:

> A man was going down from Jerusalem to Jericho, when he was attacked by robbers. They stripped him of his clothes, beat him and went away, leaving him half dead. A priest happened to be going down the same road, and when he saw the man, he passed by on the other side. So too, a Levite, when he came to the place and saw him, passed by on the other side. But a Samaritan, as he traveled, came where the man was; and when he saw him, he took pity on him. He went to him and bandaged his wounds, pouring on oil and wine. Then he put the man on his own donkey, brought him to an inn and took care of him. The next day he took out two denarii[e] and gave them to the innkeeper. "Look after him," he said, "and when I return, I will reimburse you for any extra expense you may have." (Luke 10:30–35)[1]

Since Jesus is telling a story there must be, according to Margolin, "an individual figure or agency . . . backing the assertions contained in the narrative discourse or presenting the fictional world to us." This narrator cannot be Jesus, but "exists on a strictly fictional level, and is a distinct entity within the fictional universe projected by the text." Accordingly, even though Jesus tells the story in the text, the assertions are actually made by a fictional narrator in the fictional world of Jesus's story. The speech act this narrator performs to a narratee (who is not Jesus's audience) is a report about certain events on the road to Jericho. Now, if we do not agree with this reasoning but still accept the basic assumptions of standard narratology we could, according to Margolin, take on a "minimalist position," which holds that "the occupant of the highest-level speech position in a work of narrative fiction is always the actual author but in a ludic or make-believe guise, feigning the making of true assertions, and sometimes also pretending to be someone else" ([2012] 2014, 30). If we were to take on this position, we would not need to assume a fictional teller in Jesus's parable. We could instead hold that the teller is Jesus but that he pretends to make assertions, playing a game of make-believe and at times imitating the voice of, for example, the Samaritan. The suggestion that all narratives belong to a common category would hence still be valid. This, I think, points to the watershed between standard theory and its critics. The critics would say that Jesus neither makes assertions nor pretends to do so. He is presenting (performing) a parable! There is hence no fictional narrator, no game of make-believe, no willing suspension of disbelief, no pretense, and the lines of entities such as the Samaritan are not to be naturalized as the voice of a person. They are rather the expression of an ideological position—the voice of goodness—that relates to the theme and message of the parable. There would thus be a kind of frame, which should be distinguished from the frame of representations, assertions, et cetera, that determines the meaning and function of the forms (see Skalin 2004, 2008). Accordingly, it would be both counterintuitive and meaningless to attempt to analyze a putative fictional narrator in Jesus's story. I am not claiming that narratologists in their praxis would assume a fictional narrator in Jesus's story; I am just saying that the theory, as presented by Margolin and others, says that whenever someone tells a fictional story there must be a fictional narrator in the fictional universe backing the assertions.

The Narrator as an Image of the Teller of Biblical Narratives

Meir Sternberg says in *The Poetics of Biblical Narrative* that although neither storyteller nor audiences are identified in the Bible, the "product can hardly be understood apart from the communicative situation that produced it." He therefore suggests that readers ask, "Who is the teller? To whom does he tell? Why does he tell? Whence his authority for telling what and as he does?" (1987, 58). These questions are, Sternberg says, "newfangled," which might appear surprising since biblical scholars always have posed questions about the authors and tried to identify the actual voices behind different segments of texts as well as the purpose and context of these voices. But the "new" aspect is that the questions now concern a teller constructed from the text. Sternberg's reasoning appears thus to comply with standard narratology, as described by Margolin, since he assumes that we pose the same kind of questions about the "teller" to all narratives. Since Sternberg does not accept that the biblical narratives are fictive, however, but holds that they aspire to be historical, it is not totally clear how his "teller" relates to Margolin's fictional "narrator."

We could, if we relate to the debate about the obligatory narrator and Sternberg's suggested questions, raise at least two theoretical issues about, for example, the introduction to the story of David and Bathsheba:

> In the spring, at the time when kings go off to war, David sent Joab out with the king's men and the whole Israelite army. They destroyed the Ammonites and besieged Rabbah. But David remained in Jerusalem.
>
> One evening David got up from his bed and walked around on the roof of the palace. From the roof he saw a woman bathing. The woman was very beautiful, and David sent someone to find out about her. The man said, "She is Bathsheba, the daughter of Eliam and the wife of Uriah the Hittite." Then David sent messengers to get her. She came to him, and he slept with her. (Now she was purifying herself from her monthly uncleanness.) Then she went back home. The woman conceived and sent word to David, saying, "I am pregnant." (2 Sam. 11:1–5)

The first question is whether readers can be assumed to ask Sternberg's questions about this text. Sternberg and advocates of standard narratology would probably argue that they would, while critics of his position who hold that we must distinguish between different narrative "language-games" would say that it depends on readers' apprehension of the frame.

Readers could, for example, appreciate this text as a kind of storytelling, in relation to which questions about the teller are irrelevant. The second issue is this: If we were to accept that readers ask the suggested questions, would they then search for historical answers or would they direct these questions to a teller constructed from the text?

If these questions were posed to so-called biblical literary scholars (other than Sternberg), they would, regardless of whether they hold that the biblical texts are fictive or not, probably not even consider the first query and would answer the second one, saying that their task is to study the teller that can be constructed from the text, often referring to this teller as the narrator of narratology.

An important outcome of such an approach is that individual narratives as well as larger sections such as books or collections of books, which, according to biblical exegesis, are conglomerates, can now be regarded as coherent narratives, since all the historical authors, editors, and interpolators have used the same narrator mask or persona (Sternberg 1987:73–74). Large parts of the Bible hence become a single narrative or a compilation of narratives by the same "teller."

The "Teller," the "Narrator," and the "Implied Author"

The construction of a narrator in the biblical texts, however, generates interesting issues. One such issue relates to the fact that the teller is omniscient; that is, he knows things no one can know and does not provide any explanation for this knowledge. Some scholars, like Jan P. Fokkelman, simply say, "The narrator knows because he knows, and he knows because he says it, and maybe he only knows when he says it; it is not necessary to consider such a statement 'historically reliable' and assume a prior phone call from the Holy Ghost to the writer" (1999, 56). Yet since Sternberg does not regard biblical narratives as fiction, he suggests that these texts are written by authors whose omniscience is (implicitly) explained by the fact that they were inspired by God. This means, to my mind, that we are supposed to regard the texts as assertions, and that the authors take responsibility for them even when they assert things they cannot know. The assumption that omniscience signals fiction would hence not be valid in this context. A common way to handle this issue and similar ones is to suggest that although these texts are not fictive they are still not history writing in a modern sense, but rather a kind of "traditional history" (see Person 2016; Linafelt 2016). This latter explanation relates to the frame issue, since "traditional history" is supposed to belong to a rule system different from that for both fiction and modern history.

The story of David and Bathsheba takes a new turn, after David has solved the problem of Bathsheba's pregnancy by having her husband killed, signaled with this line: "But the thing David had done displeased the Lord" (2 Sam. 11:27). I will compare this text with two other texts, with my first example from Nehemiah:[2]

> They were all trying to frighten us, thinking, "Their hands will get too weak for the work, and it will not be completed." But I prayed, "Now strengthen my hands."
>
> One day I went to the house of Shemaiah. . . . He said, "Let us meet in the house of God, inside the temple, and let us close the temple doors, because men are coming to kill you—by night they are coming to kill you." But I said, "Should a man like me run away? Or should someone like me go into the temple to save his life? I will not go!" I realized that God had not sent him, but that he had prophesied against me because Tobiah and Sanballat had hired him. He had been hired to intimidate me so that I would commit a sin by doing this, and then they would give me a bad name to discredit me. (Nehemiah 6:9–13)

When Ralph W. Klein discusses passages like these from Nehemiah he uses phrases like "omniscient author" (1999, 783) and "omniscient narrator" (1987, 787). Yet I think that readers, if they come across passages like these in nonfiction texts, do not regard this as omniscience, but as an author's speculations. They simply add, in their minds, a phrase like "I assume" before the statements; for example: "[I assume] [t]hey were all trying to frighten us." Omniscience is hence not a fictional signpost in this context, and it does not affect our global appreciation of the text, since the frame determines the meaning of the forms. But consider 2 Sam. 11:27, "But the thing David had done displeased the Lord," or this example from Genesis:

> The Lord saw how great the wickedness of the human race had become on the earth, and that every inclination of the thoughts of the human heart was only evil all the time. The Lord regretted that

he had made human beings on the earth, and his heart was deeply troubled. (Genesis 6:5–6)

Do we read these texts as speculations, adding an "I assume" before the statements? Or do we take this as something that cannot be called into question? And if the answer to the second question is yes, does that, as such, indicate that we read this as inspired talk (the author makes these assertions as inspired by God), as fiction (the author does not assert anything, but a fictional narrator does), or as a kind of storytelling (these are not someone's assertions but motifs in a meaningful literary composition such as traditional history)? This last question is not easily answered. But I think it can be argued that many readers assume the last option, which would imply a kind of narratorless, nonfictional frame.

A second issue that relates to the assumed teller of biblical texts goes something like this: If we presume that narratives, biblical books, or larger works consisting of several books are told by the same teller, how can we then handle the tensions, ambiguities, and inconsistencies that once gave rise to traditional source criticism? Some biblical literary scholars tend to talk about such features as literary devices regardless of whether they were intended to be so or not. They can hence, for example, discuss which voice holds "the inner-textual (textually encoded) highest-level speech position" (see Margolin's suggested assumptions). Robert Polzin suggests that the Deuteronomistic History (part of Deuteronomy to 2 Kings) is a dialogical work in which different voices representing various ideological positions are heard (see Polzin 1993; Andersson 2009, 28–39, 219–22). Lillian Klein, who reads the book of Judges as a coherent work rather than as a collection of stories, claims that the book is ironic (Klein 1988; Andersson 2001; Anderson 2009, 39–45, 217–19). David M. Gunn even argues that if we assume Deuteronomistic History is told by the same teller, this teller cannot be omniscient and completely reliable, since he, for instance, says that David killed Goliath in 1 Samuel 17, while in 2 Samuel 21:19 he says that it was Elhanan who killed him (Gunn 1990; Andersson 2009, 222–25).[3] Sternberg, however, asserts that it is meaningless to distinguish between the narrator and the implied author in the biblical texts because there is, he says, no ironic distance that separates "these figures of the maker and the teller" (1987, 75). Even though Sternberg constructs the teller from the text and regards the texts as history writing, he seems thus still to distinguish between intended effects and unintended coincidences (see his reasoning about gap filling, 1987, 186–229). While, for example, Gunn does not seem, when he questions Sternberg's assertion that the teller is omniscient and reliable, to distinguish between, for example, unintended mistakes by an author and unreliability as an intended device.

The problems I have pointed to in this section and in the section about Jesus's parable relate to the frame issue as well as to the application of narratology in the analyses of texts. I have suggested that the meaning and function of forms are determined by the frame. It is thus not possible to discuss, for example, the teller, the narrator, the implied author, omniscience, irony, et cetera without considering the frame. This observation can be considered as a critique of narratology taken as a description of a rule system that is supposed to be valid for all narratives. I hold, however, that narratologists, although their theory can be taken to open the door to an application according to which all narratives function in the same way, and forms always have the same function, seldom make this mistake in their praxis. This apparent contradiction can be explained by the fact that they generally apply narratology as a method or a heuristic device rather than as a theory or a kind of universal rule system (see Andersson 2012; Andersson and Sandberg 2018). Like Sternberg, they thus tend to base their interpretations on their intuitions as good readers, and then relate these interpretations to the theory.

Narratives without a Narrator

I have suggested that the narrative about David and Bathsheba could be regarded as assertions about certain historical events by a writer using the mask of an omniscient teller, as fiction with a fictional omniscient narrator, or as narratorless storytelling. The last option is not accepted in standard narratology, since according to Margolin, "good reasons, stemming from text linguistics, philosophy, narratology and common sense, can be adduced for the necessity or at least advisability of granting the narrator category as defined above a central place in the description and interpretation, both informal and professional, of literary narratives." This is so since "a narrative consists of someone telling someone else that something happened, and no such act can be imagined without a sendernarrator position" ([2012] 2014, 3). This narrator is "the single, unified, stable, distinct human-like voice who produces the whole narrative discourse we are reading" (5). Readers would or should hence relate to and analyze the narrator regardless of whether they read Nehemiah's memoirs, the flood narrative in Genesis, the parable of the Good Samaritan, or the story about David and Bathsheba. But they should realize, as I have noted, that the narrator in fictional narratives is a fictional figure. I have instead argued that different kinds of narrative frames exist, and that this variation affects the reader's attitude and interpretive process even when it comes to the narrator or teller.

Consider this text from 2 Samuel 1:

> After the death of Saul, David returned from striking down the Amalekites and stayed in Ziklag two days. On the third day a man arrived from Saul's camp with his clothes torn and dust on his head. When he came to David, he fell to the ground to pay him honor.
>
> "Where have you come from?" David asked him.
>
> He answered, "I have escaped from the Israelite camp."
>
> "What happened?" David asked. "Tell me."
>
> "The men fled from the battle," he replied. "Many of them fell and died. And Saul and his son Jonathan are dead."
>
> Then David said to the young man who brought him the report, "How do you know that Saul and his son Jonathan are dead?"
>
> "I happened to be on Mount Gilboa," the young man said, "and there was Saul, leaning on his spear, with the chariots and their drivers in hot pursuit. When he turned around and saw me, he called out to me, and I said, 'What can I do?'
>
> "He asked me, 'Who are you?'
>
> "'An Amalekite,' I answered.
>
> "Then he said to me, 'Stand here by me and kill me! I'm in the throes of death, but I'm still alive.'
>
> "So I stood beside him and killed him, because I knew that after he had fallen he could not survive. And I took the crown that was on his head and the band on his arm and have brought them here to my lord."

The narrative then recounts how David and his men kill the Amalekite because he has dared to lift his hand against the king. Now what I want to discuss is this: Even though the diegetic and the intradiegetic narratives on a surface level appear very similar—someone reports about how an Amalekite comes to David's camp, quotes a long dialogue, and recounts a killing, while the Amalekite reports about how he came across Saul, quotes a dialogue, and recounts a killing—it is natural, that is, in accordance with the communicational agreement, that David poses questions about the narrator's identity, authority, knowledge, and so on at the same time as it is not natural for us to ask these questions of the teller of 2 Samuel 1. I would suggest that this must either indicate that both men are reporting, but that the teller of 2 Samuel 1 for some reason has an authority that cannot be called into question, or that these narratives do not belong to the same frame; that is, that the author of 2 Samuel 1 performs a different narrative act than the Amalekite in the narrative. If the text is taken as propaganda (see Halpern 2001) its character becomes an ethical problem, since this propaganda then is presented in the guise of storytelling, which means that it is not presented as a version that can be called into question. This is an interesting reasoning that presumes the distinction between different frames that I have tried to point out, that is, that the parable of the Good Samaritan, the story of Nehemiah, the flood narrative in Genesis, the story of David and Bathsheba, the Amalekite's report, and the narrative about this report adhere to different rule systems and that it would be a mistake to naturalize a narrative from one frame in terms of another frame assuming, for example, a similar kind of narrator or even that there needs to be a narrator at all.

Some Concluding Remarks

The main claim in this chapter is that our apprehension of the frame of a narrative will affect our analysis of it. This assertion might seem trivial, but it poses a challenge both to the "universality" of narratology including the assumed obligatory narrator, to the common distinction between fact and fiction, and to the application of narratological concepts in the study of texts (see Margolin [2012] 2014, 30).

Referring to the Good Samaritan, I called into question Margolin's suggested assumptions (b) and (c): "(b) There is always an individual figure or agency occupying this speech position and thus backing the assertions contained in the narrative discourse or presenting the fictional world to us. . . . (c) This individual figure or agency exists on a strictly fictional level, and is a distinct entity within the fictional universe projected by the text." I view these assumptions as a theoretical reasoning that tends to lead to a naturalization paradigm in which we end up with suggesting readings that do not go well with either our own or other readers' intuitions. This conflict implies that the described rule system is not congruent with the actual rule system we apply when reading fiction.

What, then, about assumption (a), "all narrative fiction is communication"? To me, the problem with this assumption is not the concept of communication, taken in a wide sense, but the implied assumed "representational frame" (Walsh 2007, 69), according to which narratology can "examine the fictional narrative 'as narrative' and not 'as fiction'" (Patron 2006, 121) or as art (Skalin 2008). Considering assumptions (a), (b), and (c) together, I would suggest that readers do not always ask the questions about the teller or narrator that Margolin and Sternberg suggest. It seems thus, for instance, meaningless and counterintuitive to assume that such questions would be relevant to direct to a putative fictional narrator in Jesus's parables; on the other hand it seems obvious that this kind of question is posed about the many reporters who appear in the Books of Samuel, such as the Amalekite in 2 Samuel 1; in addition, which is perhaps most remarkable, some texts in the Bible appear to exemplify a kind of narratorless storytelling about which we do not direct, at least not spontaneously, the suggested questions (see Genesis 6 and 2 Samuel 11–12). The author, whoever she, he, or they were, does not, if my intuitions are correct, hence present a report about David's affair with Bathsheba but has transformed this presumably historical tradition into a story that, so to speak, is played up for us almost like a drama or a film.

I have also pointed out problems with the application of the concept of the narrator as a tool in the analysis of biblical texts. This application is problematic, first, because the term "narrator" is used to denote different features, like a construction of the author from the text ("the teller"), an obligatory fictional figure, narrator-characters, and voice effects. It would probably be better to have different terms for these phenomena, since they are not easily combined; for instance, if there is always a narrator in the texts, how shall we then distinguish between texts with no overt narrator and texts with a narrator-character or voice effects? Secondly, I have argued that the meaning and function of forms are determined by the frame; as such, it is necessary to distinguish between an analysis based on the assumption that narratological concepts like the narrator, omniscience, et cetera denote devices with an intended function in a composition, and an analysis in which they have a quite different meaning.

Notes

1. Quotations from the Bible are from the New International Version.
2. I discuss this text and the excerpt from Genesis in "Narrating Selves and the Literary in the Bible," 2019.
3. The books of Chronicles assert that Elhanan killed Goliath's brother (1 Chronicles 20:5).

References

Andersson, Greger. 2001. *The Book and Its Narratives: A Critical Examination of Some Synchronic Studies of the Book of Judges*. Örebro, Sweden: Universitetsbiblioteket.

———. 2009. *Untamable Texts: Literary Studies and Narrative Theory in the Books of Samuel*. London: T. & T. Clark.

———. 2012. "Is There a Narrative Method of Text Analysis and Interpretation?" In *Disputable Core Concepts of Narrative Theory*, edited by Göran Rossholm and Christer Johansson, 279–305. Bern: Peter Lang.

———. 2019. "Narrating Selves and the Literary in the Bible." *Partial Answers* 17 (1): 87–105.

Andersson, Greger, and Tommy Sandberg. 2018. "Sameness versus Difference in Narratology: Two Approaches to Narrative Fiction." *Narrative* 26 (3): 241–61.

Fokkelman, Jan P. 1999. *Reading Biblical Narrative: An Introductory Guide*. Louisville KY: Westminster John Knox.

Greve, Anniken. 2019. "'I'll Teach You Differences': A Meta-Theoretical Approach to Narrative Theory." In *Sameness and Difference in Narratology*, edited by Greger Andersson, Per Klingberg, and Tommy Sandberg. *Frontiers of Narrative Studies* 5 (1): 147–66.

Gunn, David M. 1990. "Reading Right: Reliable and Omniscient Narrator, Omniscient God, and Foolproof Composition in the Hebrew Bible." In *The Bible in Three Dimensions: Essays in Celebration of Forty Years of Biblical Studies in the University of Sheffield*, edited by David J. A. Clines, Stephen E. Fowl, and Stanley E. Porter, 53–64. Sheffield, UK: JSOT Press.

Halpern, Baruch. 2001. *David's Secret Demons: Messiah, Murderer, Traitor, King*. Grand Rapids MI: Eerdmans.

Klein, Lillian R. 1988. *The Triumph of Irony in the Book of Judges*. Sheffield, UK: Almond.

Klein, Ralph W. 1999. "The Books of Ezra and Nehemiah?" In *The New Interpreter's Bible: General Articles & Introduction, Commentary, & Reflections for Each Book of the Bible Including the Apocryphal/ Deuterocanonical Books*. Vol. 3, *The First and Second Books of Kings; The First and Second Books of Chronicles; The Book of Ezra; The Book of Nehemiah; The Book of Esther; Additions to Esther; The Book of Tobit; The Book of Judith*. Nashville: Abingdon Press.

Linafelt, Tod. 2016. "Poetry and Biblical Narrative." In *The Oxford Handbook of Biblical Narrative*, edited by Danna Nolan Fewell, 84–94. Oxford: Oxford University Press.

Margolin, Uri. (2012) 2014. "Narrator." In *The Living Handbook of Narratology*, edited by Peter Hühn, Jan Christoph Meister, John Pier, and Wolf Schmid. http://www.lhn.uni-hamburg.de/article/narrator. Hardcover edition published 2009 as *Handbook of Narratology*, edited by Huhn et al., Berlin: De Gruyter.

Patron, Sylvie. 2006. "On the Epistemology of Narrative Theory: Narratology and Other Theories of Fictional Narrative." Translated by Anne Marsella. In *The Traveling Concept of Narrative, COLLeGIUM: Studies across Disciplines in the Humanities and Social Sciences*, edited by Matti Hyvärinen, Anu Korhonen, and Juri Mykkänen, 118–33. http://www.helsinki.fi/collegium/ journal/volumes/volume_1/.

———. 2013. "Unspeakable Sentences: Narration and Representation in Benedetti's 'Five Years of Life.'" Translated by Susan Nicholls. *Narrative* 21 (2): 243–62.

Person, Raymond F., Jr. 2016. "Biblical Historiography as Traditional History." In *The Oxford Handbook of Biblical Narrative*, edited by Danna Nolan Fewell, 73–83. Oxford: Oxford University Press.

Polzin, Robert. (1980) 1993. *Moses and the Deuteronomist: A Literary Study of the Deuteronomic History*. Part 1. *Deuteronomy, Joshua, Judges*. Bloomington: Indiana University Press.

———. (1989) 1993. *Samuel and the Deuteronomist: A Literary Study of the Deuteronomic History*. Part 2. *1 Samuel*. Bloomington: Indiana University Press, 1993.

———. 1993. *David and the Deuteronomist: A Literary Study of the Deuteronomic History*. Part 3. *2 Samuel*. Bloomington: Indiana University Press.

Skalin, Lars-Åke. 1991. *Karaktär och perspektiv: Att tolka litterära gestalter i det mimetiska språkspelet*. Uppsala, Sweden: Uppsala University Press.

———. 2004. "Vad är en historia?" *Tidskrift för litteraturvetenskap* 33 (3–4): 4–21.

———. 2008. "'Telling a Story': Reflections on Fictional and Non-Fictional Narratives." In *Narrativity, Fictionality, and Literariness: The Narrative Turn and the Study of Literary Fiction*, edited by Lars-Åke Skalin, 201–60. Örebro, Sweden: Örebro University Press.

———. 2011a. "How Strange Are the 'Strange Voices' of Fiction?" In *Strange Voices in Narrative Fiction*, edited by Per Krogh Hansen, Stefan Iversen, Henrik Skov Nielsen, and Rolf Reitan, 101–26. Berlin: De Gruyter.

———. 2011b. "Start with Theory—Then Enter the Literary Pedagogy! Or Should the Process Go the Other Way Around?" Paper presented at the international conference organized by the Nordic Network of Narrative Studies, Tampere, Finland, May 2011.

Sternberg, Meir. 1987. *The Poetics of Biblical Narrative*. Bloomington: Indiana University Press.

Walsh, Richard. 207. *The Rhetoric of Fictionality: Narrative Theory and the Idea of Fiction*. Columbus: Ohio State University Press.

8   Narrator Theory and Medieval English Narratives

A. C. SPEARING

To begin autobiographically, with an *I* that refers not to a fictional being but to the actual writer of this chapter, I was trained as a medievalist
and for many years taught and wrote about medieval English literature.
Initially I gave little thought to narrative theory, and was content to follow the prevailing habit among literary scholars in the second half of the
twentieth century of referring to all narratives as having narrators. What
enabled that habit was a gradual, unnoticed shift from an earlier neutral
sense of the term "narrator," referring merely to an author's storytelling
function, toward a more loaded sense as a fictional person whose consciousness might differ from the author's and who was therefore always
potentially unreliable (Spearing 2015). The narrator approach seemed
particularly appropriate to the most famous work of England's most famous medieval poet, Chaucer's *Canterbury Tales*, where the frame identifies a teller for every tale; and, since Chaucer also wrote several first-
person narratives, and nearly all his works contain traces of a storytelling
I, it was in due course extended to them all. I accepted the extension un-
questioningly, and once gave it crude expression by writing that over
Chaucer's career, "The idiot-dreamer of *The Book of the Duchess* develops into the idiot-historian of *Troilus and Criseyde* and the idiot-pilgrim
of *The Canterbury Tales*" (Spearing 1965, 121). That assertion by the idiot-
scholar who was myself dates from 1965; only later did a growing sense
of the distortions produced by seeing every Chaucerian narrative as the
expression of a fictional teller's limited consciousness, along with a recognition that some medieval narratives had no overt narrator at all, led
me to doubt the validity of this approach. So I embarked on theoretical
reading, and learned that what had seemed natural was based on a theory, "the narrator theory of narration" (Kuroda [1976] 2014, 75), and that

it was not the only possible theory. My work then took a different turn, and in later publications I have focused on the distinctive ways in which medieval poets told stories and the ways of reading most appropriate to those ways of telling (Spearing 2005, 2012, 2015, 2019).

I begin like this to make clear that my concern is less with narrative theory as such than with its practical implications for the reading of specific medieval narratives.[1] Monika Fludernik, one of the few narratologists interested in medieval narratives, has noted the "general failure of classical narratology to engage with narratives before the early eighteenth century" (2011, 69; 2003a; Contzen 2014), and there has been little attempt to remedy that failure. In a recent 172-page theoretical study of (un)reliable narration, purportedly comprehensive, the only pre-1700 examples are the Hebrew Bible, Homer, and Cervantes, and no medieval narrative is mentioned (Sternberg and Yacobi 2015). Even a scholar arguing against the narrator theory can in one sentence define his field as "literary narratives" and in the next explain that he is investigating "whether or not novels invariably have narrators," as if "literary narratives" *meant* novels (Kania 2005, 47).[2] Narrative theory is not a purely logical construct: how you theorize narrative depends on what narratives you theorize; and a theory derived from medieval narratives would have a conceptual framework different from that of current narratology. That difference will emerge, I hope, from my discussion of two Middle English narratives.

Two Middle English Narratives

Apart from being of similar length and composed in short rhyming couplets, the two Middle English narratives I have chosen to discuss differ greatly from each other as well as from the narratives on which most narrative theory is based. One, the thirteenth-century *King Horn*, belongs to the fuzzy genre known as "popular romance." This consists of third-person verse tales of the lives and adventures of persons of noble birth, generally with fundamental family relationships as their underlying theme. In theorizing such works, basic and supposedly universal concepts such as "author," "fiction," and even "text" become questionable. The romances are generally anonymous and often survive in several widely differing manuscript versions: there is no fixed text, and still less any fixed paratextual frame such as title page, date, publisher, and so forth. Coming from a culture that placed authority higher than originality, they are *retellings* of stories evidently perceived as possessing an autonomous preexistence, not created by any identifiable author, and it is hard to name the composite human agency behind any such retelling. (Here I reluctantly settle for "poet.") Moreover, popular romances were not apparently seen as belonging to a different category from history. A distinction between *historia* and *fabula* was available to the learned, and is drawn by Chaucer when he asserts of a narrative said to derive from Livy, "this is no fable, / But knowen for historial thyng notable" (this isn't a legend, but is acknowledged as noteworthy historical material),[3] but for romances that distinction was blurred. Romance and chronicle existed side by side in manuscript miscellanies, and the division between them was permeable.[4] To think in familiar and apparently universal terms is tempting, but when a medievalist writes that "popular romance flaunts its status as fiction" (McDonald 2004, 14),[5] she is being misleadingly anachronistic. The relevant medieval concept is neither fiction nor history but simply "story"—stories envisaged as always already existing, prior to any individual telling. Medieval Latin treatises on literary composition, the *artes poeticae*, assume the preexistence of stories (and arguments), and teach how to present them; their writers would have been surprised by the narratological assertion that "story is only an effect of discourse" (Dawson 2012, 100). When the poet of *Emaré*, another popular romance, writes "Forsothe, as Y say the" (in truth, as I tell you) he means, as he writes a few lines later, "As the story telles" (Mills 1973, 48–49)[6]: the truth *is* what the story tells.

My other example, Chaucer's *Book of the Duchess* (1368 or later) is a first-person narrative whose *I* tells of suffering from melancholic insomnia, reading a book, falling asleep, and having a dream in which he converses with a knight in mourning; but he then appears not to know what he has already told us; and he is also the composer of the poem itself, "I, that made this book" (Chaucer, 96). The *Book* belongs to another fuzzy genre, one established in French as the *dit* but new to English: writing that creates the illusion of first-person speech while calling attention to its own textuality, a form of free composition (often the rearrangement of discontinuous fragments in a kind of mosaic or montage) that perhaps developed in reaction against the retelling of existing stories (Cerquiglini 1980; Spearing 2012, chaps. 2, 4). Here, a century after *King Horn*, and in a courtly Anglo-French context, we come somewhat closer to the expectations of modern narratology. There is an identifiable author and at least the possibility of reconstructing an authorial text from early witnesses; and the narrated events, within and outside the dream, are fictional in a now familiar sense ("made up," imagined, we aren't meant to believe they really happened), though they allude to a real-life event, the death of John of Gaunt's first wife. But, as I shall argue, the *I* has been wrongly understood by modern readers as what I called "the idiot-dreamer," a fictional, fallible narrator, of the same type as, say, the butler Stevens in Ishiguro's *The Remains of the Day*. With this kind of narrative, discussion in terms of an author/narrator binary produces distortion, and we need to think differently.

King Horn

King Horn may be the earliest romance in English. The three manuscripts all tell the same story, one also found in twelfth-century Anglo-Norman and later English versions, but differ so widely in wording as to suggest many stages of memorial and scribal transmission: author and authorial text can only be hypotheses. Its rhyming couplets vary between three and four beats, and its style is highly formulaic, with identical phrases frequently repeated—hence the variation among the manuscript versions: a scribe, or a performer chanting the poem aloud, perhaps from memory, could substitute one formula for another without changing the meaning significantly, and the absence of stanzaic form and fixed line length meant that there was little to hold any specific wording in place. The story is briefly this: Horn, son of the king of Suddene, is driven into exile by Saracen pirates who kill his father and usurp his kingdom. (The "Saracens" appear to be a fanciful fusion of Vikings and Muslims.) Accompanied by two friends, the faithful Athulf and the false Fikenhild, he crosses the sea to Westernesse, where King Aylmar's daughter Rymenhild falls in love with him, but Aylmar is deceived into exiling him. There follows a complicated series of adventures, separated by sea voyages, at the end of which Horn is accepted by Aylmar, kills Fikenhild, reclaims his kingdom of Suddene, and marries Rymenhild. It is a male coming-of-age story of a type common in Middle English romances: a boy of royal birth suffers deprivation, finds his identity and proves his manhood and virtue through a series of dangerous adventures, gains a wife, and ends as the king his father was.

King Horn is a strikingly economical narrative; its language is plain and bare, suggesting a world of scarcity, very different from the lavish descriptions of expensive clothing and delicious feasts found in many other romances, including the Anglo-Norman *Romance of Horn*. Its narrative method has more in common with classic cinema than with the classic novel.[7] It proceeds by elliptical cutting, with short pieces of event joined together in series, often without such basic syntactical links as *and* or *but*, while its commonest stylistic figure is synecdoche, corresponding to cinematic close-up (Spearing 1987, 28–43). Thus when a messenger from Rymenhild crosses the sea to inform Horn that she is being forced to marry, Horn sends him back to say that he will return shortly, and the messenger

> . . . highede aghen blive.
> The se bigan to throwe
> Under hire wowe.
> The knave there gan adrinke.
> Rymenhild hit might ofthinke.
> The see him con ded throwe
> Under hire chambre wowe.
> Rymenhild undude the durepin
> Of the hus ther heo was in,
> To loke with hire ighe
> If heo oght of Horn isighe.
> Tho fond heo the knave adrent
> That heo hadde for Horn isent,
> And that scholde Horn bringe;
> Hire fingres heo gan wringe.[8]

. . . hurried back quickly. The sea began to toss beneath [Rymenhild's] wall. The servant was drowned there. Rymenhild might well regret that. The sea cast him up dead beneath her chamber wall. Rymenhild unfastened the door-bolt of the house where she was dwelling, to look with her eyes whether she could see anything of Horn. Then she found the servant drowned whom she had sent for Horn and who was to bring him [back]. She began to wring her fingers.

Here synecdochic "close-ups" of the stormy sea, the corpse cast up beneath Rymenhild's chamber wall, her hand unbolting the door, her eyes peering out and seeing the drowned messenger, her fingers twisting in anguish, are enough to convey significance without any narratorial commentary. And indeed a further similarity to cinematic narrative is that here and almost throughout the poem there is no narrator, no narrating *I*: the story simply unfolds before us, apparently of its own accord.

The only exceptions are at the opening and the close. An *I* as singer appears in the opening lines—"Happiness to all who listen to my song! I shall sing you a song about King Murray [Horn's father]" (1–4)—and reappears briefly in an asseveration at line 32: "As I can tell you." After that the narrating *I* vanishes completely until it reemerges fifteen hundred lines later at the poem's conclusion as part of a plural *we* embracing singer and audience: "Here ends the tale of Horn, who was beautiful and not ugly. Let us continually rejoice, for that is how the song of Horn ends. May Jesus, the king of heaven, give us all his sweet blessing. Amen" (1539–44). Such opening announcements and closing prayers were common in Middle English romances; so were references to singing and listeners, which might indicate the reality of performance for a household but could also offer the illusion of community to private readers. The *I* of these brief framing passages is a grammatical space to be filled by a real or imagined performer; and apart from these passages, there is no narrator in *King Horn*. To refer to "the involvement of the narrator with the story and its protagonists" (Fludernik 1996, 115) is misleading. There are statements of the characters' inner experience, and also occasional metanarrative comments, as in "Rymenhild hit might ofthinke" (980), quoted above—a line implying that future events will show what reason she has to regret the messenger's death. (In a film, the narratorless effect of foreboding might be produced by ominous music.) But in the absence of any *I* in the body of the narrative as the origin of such statements, to refer to *King Horn* as having a narrator in the modern sense of a fictional person can only hinder understanding of how it works. Any such narrator would have to be described as omniscient, but the concept "omniscient narrator," itself of doubtful coherence (Culler [2004] 2006), was unknown to the audience of popular romances, because for them it was simply the case that, as in the Bible or folktales, or in modern jokes and other nonliterary narratives, storytelling about third persons could include statements about their inner lives, with no question raised as to how that could be possible.

Storytelling, then, was essentially different from real-life reporting, in which the question of the limits of the reporter's knowledge could arise; and indeed this difference emerges strikingly from certain passages in *King Horn* itself. Among speeches by the poem's characters are three first-person reports in which a human speaker tells of what he has experienced, reporting only what he knows. The first (951–66) occurs when Horn is in exile. A man he meets by chance while out hunting proves to be a messenger from Rymenhild—the messenger whose death is narrated in the passage above. He says he has searched in vain for Horn, and concludes by lamenting Rymenhild's situation. Horn reveals who he is, and orders the messenger to return, promising that he is himself on his way back to Westernesse. The narrative content of the messenger's speech is confined to what he could know in real-world terms, and also to what we already know from the story: but now we see it from a specific, humanly limited point of view.

The second speech (1275–1300) is by Horn after he has reached Westernesse, and is delivered to Aylmar and his court. Horn identifies himself and explains that he does not blame Aylmar for his exile, for Aylmar was deceived into believing that he wished to seduce Rymenhild. He declares that he will not make Rymenhild his until he has avenged his father and recovered Suddene from the Saracens; then Rymenhild shall "Ligge bi the kinge" (1300: lie beside the king). Horn begins this speech by promising that it will be "A tale mid the beste" (1276: a tale among the best), but he tells it not as a narratorless tale like the poem, but with the restricted consciousness that belongs to first-person reporting: he tells only what in real-life terms could be part of his own experience. Again, we already know what he reveals to Aylmar, but from it we gain a fuller sense of the shape and significance of the story to them both.

The third speech (1329–60) occurs shortly after, when Horn, accompanied by Athulf, arrives in Suddene. He finds a knight asleep under a shield bearing a cross, wakes him, and requires him to explain how a Christian can live there under Saracen rule. The knight explains that he serves the Saracens unwillingly: they made him outwardly renounce Christianity and appointed him as coastguard to warn them if Horn, "that is of age"

(1338) but dwells elsewhere, should return. The Saracens slew the king of Suddene and many more, and it is a marvel that Horn has not returned to fight them—may the wind blow him back! They killed King Murray and drove out Horn with twelve companions, among them Athulf, "Min owene child, my leve fode" (1354: my own child, my dear son); and he knows, he says, that if Athulf is unwounded and Horn is alive he is still Horn's faithful protector. If only he could see Horn and Athulf again, he would die of joy! Horn then reveals that he and Athulf stand before him. Once again, there is a speaker who tells only what he has himself experienced; and this time the new perspective opened by his speech is especially revealing, because it has probably never before occurred to us to think of Athulf as having a father. Athulf has appeared only as Horn's *fidus Achates*; now his father's first-person narrative sets him in a new light as a son, and also brings home in a particular case the human suffering caused by the Saracen occupation of Suddene—the father's need to conceal his true faith and loyalty to the extent of collaboration with the enemy, his inability to understand why Horn has not returned to expel the occupiers, and his longing to see his son and the true ruler of Suddene. This third instance of first-person narrative, even more than the previous two, by giving a restricted and concentrated view, enriches our emotional response to the narratorless narrative enclosing it.

These three speeches underline an important general truth: for a medieval audience the retelling of a third-person story was narration of a different kind from the report of events by a human character possessing an individual consciousness. The latter was envisaged, as it would be now, as a form of communication—"somebody telling somebody else on some occasion and for some purpose(s) that something happened"[9]—but the former was not, and must therefore be interpreted in distinct, noncommunicational terms. That difference has generally been disregarded by modern narratology and also by medievalists, unknowingly under its influence, who read popular romances as having narrators in the same sense as many novels.

The Book of the Duchess

The Book of the Duchess may be Chaucer's earliest surviving poem. John of Gaunt, a son of Edward III, was one of the richest and most powerful men in England; his first wife, Blanche of Lancaster, who brought him his dukedom and much of his wealth, died in 1368. Wordplay near the end identifies the knight in black, met in a dream, as John, while the beloved lady called "White," whose death, it emerges, the knight is mourning, plainly represents Blanche. Chaucer elsewhere refers to the poem as "the Deeth of Blaunche the Duchesse,"[10] and its purpose must surely be commemorative and consolatory, but the occasion is approached indirectly, through a rambling first-person narrative, much of which seems to have little to do with Blanche's death or John's mourning.

The *I* (henceforward "Chaucer") begins in the present tense by announcing that he is suffering from melancholic insomnia, the cause of which he cannot reveal. One recent night he passed the time by reading a book of pagan legends containing the story of Ceyx and Alcyone, which he repeats. Unknown to his wife Alcyone, King Ceyx died at sea; she lamented his absence, prayed to Juno to reveal his fate in a dream, swooned, and fell asleep. Juno ordered Morpheus, the god of sleep, to enter Ceyx's corpse and make it tell Alcyone what had happened. Morpheus did so, and Alcyone died of grief. This Ovidian story gives Chaucer the idea of praying to Morpheus to send *him* to sleep; he sleeps, and he in turn has a dream. He dreams that, lying in bed, he hears the noises of a hunt. Following it, he comes upon "a man in blak" (445), a young knight, who speaks a lyric lamenting the death of his lady. Chaucer begs him to reveal the cause of his grief, for "Paraunter hyt may ese youre herte" (556: perhaps it may comfort your heart). The knight explains that he is inconsolable because, in a game of chess with Fortune, he lost his queen. Chaucer apparently fails to understand the metaphor, but urges him to go on, and the knight speaks at length of how in youth, dedicated to love, he fell in love with a beautiful lady, approached her and was first rejected but then accepted, "And thus we lyved ful many a yere" (1295). "Where is she now?" (1298), asks Chaucer; the knight answers that she is dead, and Chaucer can say no more than "Is that youre los! Be God, hyt ys routhe!" (1310: Is that your loss? By God, it is a pity!). At that the hunt comes to an end, and Chaucer wakes with the book in his hand and plans to turn his dream into a poem.

The *Book* is a more complex and subtle narrative than *King Horn*, and to convey its effect in summary is hard. It is a montage of distinct segments, borrowed from various sources, sometimes tenuously linked, but intricately interrelated by parallels and inversions: Chaucer's melancholy and that of the knight; Ceyx's death revealed in Alcyone's dream and the revelation in Chaucer's dream of White's death; the "hert-huntyng" (1313: hunt for the hart) and the dialogue it frames in which Chaucer aims to "ese youre herte"; the black knight/white lady and the game of chess with Fortune; the omission from the Ceyx story of its Ovidian conclusion with metamorphosis and reunion and the omission of religious consolation from Chaucer's dream; the stark factuality of death in both cases—"For certes, swete, I am but ded" (204: for certainly, sweetheart, I am nothing but dead) says the dream-Ceyx, and "She ys ded!" (1309) is all the dream-knight can finally tell Chaucer. The only possible remedy is human pity, of which the poem is full: "such pittee and suche rowthe" (97: such compassion and such pity); "The moste pitee, the moste rowthe" (465); "Is that youre los? Be God, hyt ys routhe!" (1310). Scholars have noted these and other internal relationships in the *Book of the Duchess*, and it seems likely that Chaucer envisaged the plural *yow*[11] occasionally addressed by its *I* as a coterie of sophisticated readers, familiar with the French *dits* that lie behind it, who would to some extent shape their own poem from the materials he had assembled. (Later poets did so, as witnessed by Lydgate's *Complaint of the Black Knight* in the fifteenth century and Spenser's *Daphnaïda* in the sixteenth.)

For narrative theory, the *Book of the Duchess* presents greater problems than *King Horn*. It starts with *I*, "for the first time in an English love narrative," but in a line translated from the first line of a poem by Froissart, so the *I* was originally his (Butterfield 2009, 269–72); and parts of it are intensely first-personal, as in the opening lines with their cluster of first-person pronouns:

I have gret wonder, be this lyght,
How that **I** lyve, for day ne nyght
I may nat slepe wel nygh noght;
I have so many an ydel thoght
Purely for defaute of slep
That, by **my** trouthe, **I** tak no kep
Of nothyng, how hyt cometh or gooth,
Ne **me** nys nothyng leef nor looth.
Al is ylyche good to **me** . . . (1–9)

I am greatly puzzled, by heaven, at how I remain alive, for I
can hardly sleep at all by day or night; I have so many empty

thoughts, simply for lack of sleep, that, I swear, I pay no attention to anything, how it comes or goes, and nothing is either pleasing or displeasing to me—to me everything is the same . . .

Until the dialogue with the knight begins, the poem remains intermittently and sometimes emphatically first-personal, with repeated use of passive forms that convey a kind of subjection to experience: *me thoghte* (it seemed to me) at lines 61, 233, 291, 345, 453, and 535, and *me mette* (literally, "it dreamed to me," a regular Middle English construction) at lines 276, 293, 298, and 442. These forms reappear once the dialogue is over, *me thoghte* at 1314 and *me mette* at 1320 and 1321, and the poem concludes with another cluster of first-person pronouns:

> Therwyth **I** awook **myselve**
> And fond **me** lyinge in **my** bed;
> And the book that **I** hadde red,
> Of Alcione and Seys the kyng,
> And of the goddes of slepyng,
> **I** fond hyt in **myn** hond ful even.
> Thoghte **I**, "Thys ys so queynt a sweven
> That **I** wol, be processe of tyme,
> Fonde to put this sweven in ryme
> As **I** kan best, and that anoon."
> This was **my** sweven; now hit ys doon. (1324–34)

With that I woke myself up and found myself lying in my bed; and the book that I'd been reading, about Alcyone and King Ceyx and the gods of sleep, I found right in my hand. I thought, "This is such a curious dream that, in the course of time, I'll try as best I can to turn it into a poem, and promptly too." This was my dream; now it's over.

Yet in the poem's mosaic structure there are large segments with no trace of a narrating first person. In the dream-dialogue, conveyed in *oratio recta*, by far the larger part is played by the knight's account of his life. Here the *I* is his, not Chaucer's, and as in the three embedded speeches in *King Horn*, but at much greater length—nearly half the poem—he reports only what he could himself have experienced. He repeatedly applies superlative, even transcendent, terms to his love and his loss, and these are doubtless to be taken seriously, as appropriate to the high social status of John of Gaunt; but that they represent his individual experience and perception is underlined at a point where he praises White in extreme terms and Chaucer agrees only that

> **Yow thoghte** that she was the beste
> And to beholde the alderfayreste,
> Whoso had loked hir with **your eyen**. (1049–51)

> It seemed to you that she was the best and the fairest of all to behold, if one had seen her through your eyes.

In nearly all modern criticism, the *I* is referred to as "the narrator" or "the dreamer," terms that distinguish him as a fictional being from the real author of the poem. That approach originated a century ago with the eminent Chaucer scholar George Lyman Kittredge, who wrote: "The Dreamer speaks in the first person. One might infer, therefore, that he is Geoffrey Chaucer, but that would be an error: he is a purely imaginary figure, to whom certain purely imaginary things happen, in a purely imaginary dream. He is . . . a part of the fiction of the Book of the Duchess" (1915, 48). With this view there is an obvious difficulty, well recognized but brushed aside by critics who refer to "the narrator," since the *I* is also "I, that made this book," the creator of the *Book of the Duchess*, Geoffrey Chaucer. An imaginary narrator can only be the author of an imaginary book, not of the *Book* we actually have, and this leads into an infinite regress.

There is a more specific problem with narrator readings of the *Book of the Duchess*, one much discussed with no agreed solution.[12] As mentioned above, when Chaucer encounters the knight in his dream, he overhears him speaking a lyric lamenting that "my lady bright . . . Is fro me ded and ys agoon" (477–79: my fair lady is dead and is taken from me). And yet, after all the knight's speeches describing his love and the loss of his lady, Chaucer asks him, "Where is she now?" (1298), and is astonished to be informed that she is dead. As a perceptive critic has recently put it, "it is possible to imagine a very satisfying reading of the poem as a work that deliberately postpones the revelation of a terrible truth, and in doing so makes a number of narrative feints to imply a range of possibilities that are then frustrated in the starkest terms"—yet the inclusion of the knight's lyric makes this reading impossible (Knox 2018, 148). Why? Those who see the *I* as a fictional character have proposed various explanations. One is that he is indeed an "idiot-dreamer," too stupid or inattentive to remember the lyric. Another is that he's confused by its elegant courtly language and mistakenly takes its reference to death to be metaphorical (perhaps as he later takes the knight's chess metaphor to be literal). A third is that he fails to grasp that the lyric concerns the knight's own situation. (Though courtly doctrine held that love lyrics must be made out of personal experience—"of sentement" as Chaucer puts it in the *Legend of Good Women* ["Prologue," F 69]—anyone reciting a love lyric must adopt its *I*. The resultant uncertainty emerges in *Troilus and Criseyde* when a lady recites a first-person love lyric, apparently expressing her own experience but, asked "Who made this song?" [2:878], explains that it was composed by someone else.) An alternative explanation is that the "narrator" is not stupid but tactful. He pretends not to know what he has overheard, to give the knight an excuse to give his grief full expression; for polite inattention to something accidentally overheard was a recognized element in medieval courtesy (Burrow 2006).

This last explanation may seem opposed to the others, but what they all have in common is that they try to solve a problem seen as peculiar to a specific first-person narrative by speculation about the character or intentions of that narrative's "narrator." In fact, though, similar problems arise with other medieval first-person narratives. I will mention two examples. In the first part of the most widely read of medieval dream-poems, the *Roman de la Rose* (here quoted from the English version attributed to Chaucer), the dreaming *I* explores the garden of Myrthe, and the God of Love follows him, bow at the ready:

Now God, that sittith in mageste,
Fro deedly woundes he kepe me,
If so be that he hadde me shette!
For if I with his arowe mette,
It hadde me greved sore, iwys.
But I, that nothyng wist of this,
Wente up and doun ful many a wey,
And he me folwed fast alwey . . .[13]

Now may God enthroned in majesty protect me from being mortally wounded, if [the God of Love] had happened to shoot at me! For if I encountered his arrow, it would indeed have hurt me severely. But I, who knew nothing of this, went up and down in many directions, and he always followed me closely.

Here the *I* narrates what he does not know (and what we could not know unless he narrated it), that he is being secretly pursued by Cupid and is in serious danger. The second example is from Chaucer's *Legend of Good Women*. In the revised version of the prologue the dreaming *I* sees the God of Love accompanied by a beautiful lady, and tells us that "Hire name was Alceste" (G 179); yet later when the God asks who he thinks she is, and reminds him of the story of Alcestis, the *I* exclaims in astonishment, "And is this goode Alceste?" (G 506)—he does not know what he has previously narrated.

It seems clear from these examples that the *I* of medieval first-person narrative cannot be assumed to be a narrator in the sense of a fictional reporter of (fictional) events; the *I* is not a consistent self who must know all that he has reported and who cannot report what in real life he could not know. I suggest that medieval first-person narrative, as much as narratorless narrative, was a form of storytelling in which epistemological questions did not arise. Another way of putting this, as is suggested by Chaucer's opening adoption of Froissart's *I*, is to say that the storytelling *I* did not necessarily function as a pronoun referring to a specific person but was rather a proximal deictic, the purpose of which was to produce a certain literary effect, one that is hard to define except as "*I*-ness"—the sense of being a centre of experience and perception, I-here-now, and appealing intimately as such to the poem's audience. I call the *I* of the *Book of the Duchess* "Chaucer," because that is less misleading than "the narrator" and less clumsy than "the *I*," but he is not a character, a fictionalized version of the real Chaucer. He is rather, perhaps, the Chaucer of Chaucer's dreams; as Fludernik has observed, in English verse of this period "first-person narratives only occurred in dream poems" (2003b, 252n6). When I dream, the events in which I am involved are fictional events, but that does not make me a fictional character, "the dreamer." The *I* of the *Book of the Duchess* may be involved with "purely imaginary things," but that does not make him "a purely imaginary person." I remain *I*, never more so than when dreaming. And when I wake from a dream I retain the same "*I*-ness" that pervaded it, which is why dreams have a power to affect the waking mind with longing or fear or shame. The consistency of the *I* of these first-person narratives, as of dreams, lies not in any pronominal reference to a represented character (whether "narrator" or "poet"), but simply in its floating *I*-ness, its proximality and experientiality (which includes the intimacy of its appeal to an equally floating *yow*); and that means that it cannot be adequately conceptualized in the terms of current narratology.

There are of course other types of medieval narrative besides the two samples I have been discussing, but in my view the concept of the narrator as envisaged by current narratology can almost never be usefully applied to medieval storytelling. I do not know of any word in medieval English (or French) that corresponded to that concept, and to apply it to medieval narratives, treating it as a natural and universal phenomenon, is unhistorical and repeatedly leads to misinterpretation. We are a long way from arriving at any theory that would fruitfully encompass the various ways in which medieval narratives work, but I am convinced that to move in that direction will require questioning much that narratology now takes for granted.

Notes

1. Hence I do not engage with purely theoretical discussions such as Zipfel (2015). Zipfel's argument, like many in narrative theory, is presented as universally valid but in fact emerges from a historical situation in which the model for narrative is the novel.

2. Similarly, it isn't possible to apply directly to medieval narratives Brian Boyd's cogent argument about Jane Austen when he writes, "We engage with authors of fiction knowing they are story *inventors* inseparably from their being *storytellers*" (2017, 286).

3. Chaucer quotations are from Benson; line numbers given in text, here *Canterbury Tales* VI,155–56. Translations from Middle English, and emphases, are mine.

4. In the Auchinleck manuscript, containing many popular romances, a chronicle includes "a lengthy account of Richard I drawn directly from the romance *King Richard*" (Purdie 2008, 96–97). At a higher cultural level, the scribe of a manuscript of Wace's *Brut*, an Anglo-Norman verse chronicle based on Geoffrey of Monmouth's *Historia Regum Britanniae*, inserted

Chrétien's romances to fill a gap of twelve peaceful years in Arthur's supposedly historical reign (Putter 1994, 5–6).

5. Medieval notions of what might happen in real life differed from those of
   modern academics; see recent studies of "unnatural narrative" such as Alber and the critique of this concept's application to medieval narratives in
   Contzen (2017).

6. The presence of a narrating *I* is more common in popular romance than its
   absence, as in *King Horn*.

7. On narration in films, see Paisley Livingston's contribution in this volume
   (editor's note).

8. *King Horn* quotations from Herzman, Drake, and Salisbury (1999) but with
   changes in punctuation; line numbers in text, here 976–87. Allen (1984), a
   scholarly attempt to reconstruct the original behind the manuscripts, involves heroic conjectural emendation.

9. This often repeated rhetorical definition of narrative is taken here from
   Phelan (2007, 203).

10. *Legend of Good Women* F 418, G 406.

11. Lines 16, 189, 216, 218, 226, 271, 1321. *I* and *yow* are conjoined in the plural
    first person at lines 41, 43, and 283.

12. For a brief survey of the extensive controversy, see Fumo (2015, 53–55).

13. *Romaunt* 1339–46, in Benson (1987).

References

Alber, Jan. 2016. *Unnatural Narratives: Impossible Worlds in Fiction and Drama.*
   Lincoln: University of Nebraska Press.

Allen, Rosamund, ed. 1984. *King Horn.* New York: Garland.

Benson, Larry D., ed. 1987. *The Riverside Chaucer.* 3rd ed. Boston: Houghton
   Mifflin.

Boyd, Brian. 2017. "Does Austen Need Narrators? Does Anyone?" *New Literary
   History* 48: 285–308.

Burrow, J. A. 2006. "Politeness and Privacy: Chaucer's *Book of the Duchess.*"
   In *Studies in Late Medieval and Early Modern Texts in Honour of John
   Scattergood*, edited by Anne Marie D'Arcy and Alan J. Fletcher, 65–74.
   Dublin: Four Courts Press.

Butterfield, Ardis. 2009. *The Familiar Enemy: Chaucer, Language, and Nation in
   the Hundred Years War.* Oxford: Oxford University Press.

Cerquiglini, Jacqueline. 1980. "Le Clerc et l'écriture: Le *Voir Dit* de Machaut
   et la définition du *dit.*" In *Literatur in der Gesellschaft des Spätmittelalters*,
   edited by Hans Ulrich Gumbrecht, 151–68. Heidelberg: Carl Winter.

Contzen, Eva von. 2014. "Why We Need a Medieval Narratology: A Manifesto." *Diegesis* 3 (2): 1–21.

———. 2017. "Unnatural Narratology and Premodern Narratives: Historicizing a Form." *Journal of Literary Semantics* 46 (1): 1–23.

Culler, Jonathan. (2004) 2006. "Omniscience." In *The Literary in Theory*, 183–201. Stanford: Stanford University Press, 2006.

Dawson, Paul. 2012. "'Real Authors and Real Readers': Omniscient Narration and a Discursive Approach to the Narrative Communication Model." *JNT: Journal of Narrative Theory* 42 (1): 91–116.

Fludernik, Monika. 1996. *Towards a "Natural" Narratology*. London: Routledge.

———. 2003a. "The Diachronization of Narratology." *Narrative* 11 (3): 331–48.

———. 2003b. "Natural Narratology and Cognitive Parameters." In *Narrative Theory and the Cognitive Sciences*, edited by David Herman, 243–67. Stanford: Stanford University Press.

———. 2011. "Through a Glass Darkly; or, the Emergence of Mind in Medieval Narrative." In *The Emergence of Mind: Representations of Consciousness in Narrative Discourse in English*, edited by David Herman, 69–100. Lincoln: University of Nebraska Press.

Fumo, Jamie C. 2015. *Making Chaucer's Book of the Duchess: Textuality and Reception*. Cardiff: University of Wales Press.

Herzman, Ronald B., Graham Drake, and Eve Salisbury, eds. 1999. *Four Romances of England*. Kalamazoo: Medieval Institute Publications (TEAMS).

Kania, Andrew. 2005. "Against the Ubiquity of Fictional Narrators." *Journal of Aesthetics and Art Criticism* 63 (1): 47–54.

Kittredge, George Lyman. 1915. *Chaucer and His Poetry*. Cambridge: Harvard University Press.

Knox, Philip. 2018. "'Hyt am I': Voicing Selves in the *Book of the Duchess*, the *Roman de la Rose*, and the *Fonteinne Amoureuse*." In *Chaucer's Book of the Duchess: Contexts and Interpretations*, edited by Jamie C. Fumo, 135–56. Cambridge, UK: D. S. Brewer.

Kuroda, S.-Y. (1976) 2014. "Reflections on the Foundations of Narrative Theory, from a Linguistic Point of View." In *Toward a Poetic Theory of Narration*, edited by Sylvie Patron: 71–101. Berlin: De Gruyter.

McDonald, Nicola. 2004. "A Polemical Introduction." In *Pulp Fictions of Medieval England: Essays in Popular Romance*, edited by Nicola McDonald, 1–21. Manchester, UK: Manchester University Press.

Mills, Madwyn, ed. 1973. *Six Middle English Romances*. London: Dent.

Phelan, James. 2007. "Rhetoric/Ethics." In *The Cambridge Companion to Narrative*, edited by David Herman, 203–16. Cambridge: Cambridge University Press.

Purdie, Rhiannon. 2008. *Anglicising Romance: Tail-Rhyme and Genre in Medieval English Literature*. Cambridge, UK: D. S. Brewer.

Putter, Ad. 1994. "Finding Time for Romance: Mediaeval Arthurian Literary History." *Medium Ævum* 63 (1): 1–16.

Spearing, A. C. 1965. "Chaucer the Writer." In *An Introduction to Chaucer*, edited by Maurice Hussey, A. C. Spearing, and James Winny, 115–52. Cambridge: Cambridge University Press.

———. 1987. *Readings in Medieval Poetry*. Cambridge: Cambridge University Press.

———. 2005. *Textual Subjectivity: The Encoding of Subjectivity in Medieval Narratives and Lyrics*. Oxford: Oxford University Press.

———. 2012. *Medieval Autographies: The "I" of the Text*. Notre Dame: University of Notre Dame Press, 2012.

———. 2015. "What Is a Narrator? Narrator Theory and Medieval Narratives." *Digital Philology* 4 (1): 59–105.

———. 2019. "Narration in Two Versions of 'Virginius and Virginia.'" *Chaucer Review* 54 (1): 1–34.

Sternberg, Meir, and Tamar Yacobi. 2015. "(Un)Reliability in Narrative Discourse: A Comprehensive Overview." *Poetics Today* 36 (4): 327–498.

Zipfel, Frank. 2015. "Narratorless Narration? Some Reflections on the Arguments for and against the Ubiquity of Narrators in Fictional Narratives." In *Author and Narrator: Transdisciplinary Contributions to a Narratological Debate*, edited by Dorothee Birke and Tilmann Köppe, 45–80. Berlin: De Gruyter.

9 Marquis de Sade's Narrative Despotism
The Mystified Magistrate and *The Misfortunes of Virtue*

MARC HERSANT

Literary theory has often tended to take its examples from recent literature.[1] A particular case is the confrontation between the proponents of a "communicative" conception of fictional narrative and a "poetic" one, which has mostly neglected an issue from literary history that nevertheless directly engages with the questions it raises. I have in mind the progressive emergence of first-person fictional narratives in European literature—a canonical form of which is the eighteenth-century French and English memoir-novel (see Démoris 1975)—and the possible relationship between these first-person fictional narratives and the third-person fictional genres (historical novella, tragic story, heroic romance, fairy tale, "philosophical" tale, etc.) that initially dominated the fiction produced during the Ancien Régime. Sade's work in particular, which has attracted so much theoretical attention for other reasons, has been little examined from the perspective of the mechanisms of fictional creation. In its own way, it offers a sort of late synthesis of the main narrative problems raised by eighteenth-century writers, offering rich avenues for theoretical interrogation, in particular concerning the existence or nonexistence of a "narrator" in the third-person fictional narrative, which has become one of the main points of tension in literary theory in recent decades.

Sade wrote many works of short[2] fiction in prison, specifically during his years at the Bastille. His creative peak from this point of view was 1787, when the two main texts I am going to comment on were written.[3] Some of these, written in a dark and tragic vein, at times almost gothic, were later grouped together by the writer in his 1800 collection *Les Crimes de l'amour* (*The Crimes of Love*). Many other lighter or openly comic pieces were published only in the twentieth century, under various titles such as

Historiettes, contes et fabliaux ("Little Stories, Tales and Fables"), in the more or less complete editions of Sade's works by Gilbert Lely or Jean-Jacques Pauvert, and *Contes étranges* ("Strange Tales"), in the edition by Michel Delon.[4] As Stéphanie Genand notes,[5] Sade seems to have hesitated, depending on the period, between collections with a strong aesthetic unity and collections showcasing the fundamentally heterogeneous nature of his fictional output in prison: zany little erotic narratives—some in the light style of a bawdy skit, others more disturbing and perverse—mingled with tense tales that are dark but don't have the crude elements of the 1800 collection. It is of course a continuum, and the opposition is not clear-cut, but we can make a general distinction between pieces written in a risqué or farcical vein and darker pieces, each of which produced its own small masterpiece: *Le Magistrat mystifié* (*The Mystified Magistrate*), the centerpiece of Sade's comic work, and *Les Infortunes de la vertu* (*The Misfortunes of Virtue*), later developed separately into an independent novel, are the crown jewels of this set of short fictional narratives. These two stories are, moreover, written *in the third person*: from beginning to end in the case of *The Mystified Magistrate*, and with a very large embedded section in the first person that makes up the bulk of the text in the case of *The Misfortunes*.[6] Structurally, these are therefore "fictions" in the sense Käte Hamburger gives the term in *The Logic of Literature* (chap. 3). In her view, the dominant person (in this case the third person, even in the second of the two texts) governs the narrative as a whole and determines its status.

Eighteenth-century narrative fiction is largely dominated by first-person narratives: the "enunciative realism"[7] of the memoir-novel and epistolary novel, governed by a complex and ambiguous fictional "I." Alongside this is the hypervisible metafictionality of third-person tales like Voltaire's, which refuse any attempt at realism and flaunt their fabricated nature,[8] whose characters are by contrast schematic and psychologically impoverished (see Hersant 2015). Not all works can be neatly categorized in this simple way, of course,[9] but the opposition is nonetheless relevant for understanding what is essentially at issue in narratives at the time of the Enlightenment. Regarding the texts by Sade that will be the focus here, they are more "tales" than "novels," if we take the distinction outlined above as our guideline. It is, however, necessary to add an existential element in this case to the questions of genre and type of utterance, namely the *conditions* of their production. These texts are the works of a man who stewed for years[10] in his hatred of and frustration with his situation as prisoner. They display the author's vengeful will to reign over a fictional world that he creates at his own pleasure and to subjugate it to the law of his own whims and desires. The author who reigns supreme over the fictional worlds of his own invention is not only a "theoretical" instance that could be contrasted with the purely formal function often attributed to a useless and reassuring "narrator." The man Sade languishing in his cell is unquestionably the person responsible for the fictions he invents, as well as their principal, and perhaps even sole, recipient. On all levels, the idea that a "narrator" would have the responsibility for Sade's tales, even those written in the third person, is therefore a delusion.

For the sake of convenience, and in reverse chronological order, I will first consider *The Mystified Magistrate* and then examine *The Misfortunes of Virtue*, which will be my main focus, as it has a much more complex enunciative structure and offers a more profound exploration of the topical issues around novelistic creation in the eighteenth century. Both tales, however, have obvious commonalities, the most important being their principle of composition as a series of episodes that come one after the other and in a certain way are always the same. In the case of *The Mystified Magistrate*, each episode shows the humiliation of the main character—and through him his whole class, the Nobility of the Robe (*noblesse de robe*)—and the narrative is nothing more than the production of brilliant variations on the same basic formula. The magistrate, who wants to consummate his marriage with his wife, is drawn into a succession of traps by her accomplices, which each time prevent the consummation from taking place, and mechanically ensnare the magistrate in grotesque and carnivalesque situations where his virility is cruelly mocked. He is spared nothing, from bathing with pigs to having his buttocks taped to a commode stool. The repetitive mechanism of *The Misfortunes of Virtue* is much more famous but deserves a brief mention in the context of this analysis: poor Justine suffers a parody of fate whereby all her virtuous acts are punished with infernal regularity. A symmetrical law, with equally few exceptions, rewards and raises to the highest social positions the criminals who have persecuted her.

Even if the first work is more obviously comic, both are based on the tireless repetition of the same scene that can potentially be replicated to infinity (as the extended versions of *Justine* will show), with endless variations. The fact that new episodes can always be added to the existing ones from one version to the next already demonstrates on an initial level that the story is not what has been "remembered" by a narrator (who would recount *what happened* in the fictional world to which he or she belongs) but what has been invented by an author, who is always able to thread another pearl onto his "narrative necklace," and does so freely and with obvious and wanton glee.[11] This playfulness erupts in hilarious recapitulations, copied from those of the Old Woman or Cunégonde in Voltaire's *Candide*, where the magistrate and Justine go back over all of the misfortunes that have befallen them with appalling regularity, indignant at being the victims of a kind of "negative Providence," which we know is nothing but the pleasure of the author at work, the only "finger of fate"[12] (*MM*, 170/23) in action in these two stories. I will come back to this point at more length in relation to *Justine* by itself.

The Mystified Magistrate is a standard third-person fictional narrative with no large-scale embedded first-person narratives. No "character," strictly speaking, assumes a narrative function which has any place in the narrative, even that of simple witness. And yet there is an enunciative voice that constantly intrudes in judgment of the characters—the main character in particular—as though it had a *real relationship* with them. The key to this mystery is not really very difficult to find, but we must first illustrate what kind of sometimes untimely intervention we are referring to. The old magistrate of the Parliament of Aix is brutally presented as "one of the most dreadful creatures who has ever existed on the face of the earth" (*MM*, 150/1), a "grumpy spouse" (*MM*, 152/1), a "slightly grotesque combination of a physical Ostrogoth and Justinian morality" (*MM*, 153/4), an "extraordinary creature" (*MM*, 153/5), an "old satyr" (*MM*, 167/20), an "abominable person" (*MM*, 215/71), and so on. There are many displays of contempt and even *hatred* for the central character by the storyteller, and this could naturally give the impression of a "narrator" who has a *personal* grievance against someone he knows. Other details suggest a humorous imitation of a "historical" narrative, in the technical sense:[13] the narrator notes occasional flaws in his story due to the fact that some details "have not been brought to our attention" (*MM*, 154/5), and he makes references to real and known figures in Aix en Provence (*MM*, 153–54/5–6) that would be understood by the reader. But these instances are very scattered and in no way enough to place the narrative function *inside* the fictional field in any serious and credible way: it is clearly external to it, and its role is not to *report* events, but to *create* them, subjugating them to an inflexible law. Paradoxically, the thing that highlights the artificiality of the story and emphasizes its quality as a pure invention emanating from a sovereign creative author is precisely this insistent score settling and constant introduction of real feelings and facts into his fictional creation.

The magistrate is thus nothing other than the fictional projection of Sade's hatred for the *noblesse de robe* and its role in his current situation as a prisoner. Working in the Parliament of Aix, the magistrate is imagined as one of those "persecutors" who sentenced Sade to death following the Marseille affair. As a husband belonging to the Nobility of the Robe forced onto a young aristocratic girl, he is a projection of Madame de Sade, whom Sade—imbued with his own Nobility of the Sword—married with hatred in his heart, as he expresses with frightening clarity in a letter to his uncle the Abbé de Sade.[14] As a petty and authoritarian *robin* (a pejorative term for a magistrate) abusing his influence and power, the magistrate is even more clearly a sort of male transvestite of Sade's main real-life enemy, his mother-in-law, the *présidente* of Montreuil. All the imaginary fictional punishments inflicted by Sade on this male magistrate are carried out, in the manner of a voodoo doll, on the *présidente* herself, whom Sade dreams of torturing in many of the letters he wrote to his wife (and thus the daughter of the person in question). Sade is so little concerned with concealing his personal investment in the story that he constantly multiplies allusions to the affairs that earned him his infamy and incarceration, reducing them (as he often does in his correspondence) to simple orgies with prostitutes. Thus, the magistrate boasts of having persuaded his "learned colleagues into exiling from the province for a period of ten years—and thereby ruining forever—a nobleman who had already served his king faithfully and well. And all that over a party of females"[15] (*MM*, 163/15). Sade is obviously the model for this "nobleman" (and obviously proud of being so) persecuted by essentially despicable and inferior *robins*. The count of Elbene, the lover of the magistrate's wife disguised as a valet under the name of La Brie, mentions in a discussion with his grotesque rival a judge "who had become so mad that nary a young libertine from the region could have a bit of fun with a girl without this rascal straightway accusing him and bringing him to trial" (*MM*, 175/28). The libertine is obviously yet another embodiment of Sade who has "invited" himself into his own fiction.

Later in the story, the situation becomes increasingly clear, and the Marquis d'Olincourt, when Sade's pet punching bag is suffering from colic, makes a transparent allusion to the Marseille affair, mocking the judges who thought that "a few whores who were suffering from colic were *poisoned*" (*MM*, 186/40). The author's voice immediately echoes the sentiment by presenting the story's main character as "one of the most rabid judges in the case . . . that had heaped shame on the whole judicial body of Provence forever." It would be difficult to make the fictional character a clearer "crystallization" of Sade's real hatreds. In the comic episode of a fake haunted castle where the magistrate is terrorized, he recalls, in a hilarious monologue, one of the cases with which he was associated, referring to "a thirteen-year-old valet we bribed" to tell the judges "that this poor fellow was murdering whores in his château" (*MM*, 197/52). This is a clear allusion to the so-called Little Girls affair, the darkest cloud over the libertine life of Sade, who in the "great letter" of 1781, already cited, tries to prove that all the women he used for his pleasure at Lacoste *are still alive* (an argument that shows he was suspected of murder), and to discredit the overwhelming testimony that had accused him of the worst in this case. Furthermore, in an obviously and absurdly improbable gesture, the author places words in the mouth of the magistrate, who openly displays his cruelty and his pleasure in making "innocents" (or so they claimed) suffer—innocents like Sade, who considers himself a victim. I will give just one example.

In reply to the marquise, who tries to speak "reason" to him, the magistrate says, "As far as we judges are concerned, reason is the one thing in the world we manage to do without most easily: we banish it from our tribunals as we do from our heads; we make a sport of riding roughshod over it. This is what makes our decrees such masterpieces, for, although they are completely devoid of common sense, we carry them out as resolutely as though we knew precisely what they meant" (*MM*, 162–63/15). The device, borrowed from Voltaire, who makes frequent use of it (see Hersant 2015, 209–30), is to attribute to the enemy words that condense the "unspoken" elements of what he actually says, which, it goes without saying, is a boast about the rational foundation of his injustice. Such an utterance can in no way be "reported" by a narrator. It can only be created by an author who makes his characters not only say but also think what their real models are accused of. The whole of *The Mystified Magistrate* is the logical result of this process, where Sade counters an unbearable reality with a visibly "fabricated" fiction, so that he can take revenge on the imaginary puppet figures of his real enemies. If we refer to the key point of Hamburger's theory of fiction, the tenses in the narrative mean not "this is what happened" but "this is what I would like to see happen if the world matched my desires." These past tenses do not serve to *relate* anything; they *invent*, and this invention is rooted in Sade's hatred and frustration that is unleashed on his enemies—his "persecutors"— as in a dream.

We move now to *The Misfortunes of Virtue*, the text of which is presented, unlike the previous one, as the articulation of two distinct narrative utterances. The first is a narrative "in the third person," where Justine appears as one of the story's characters, especially on the first and the last pages, but the greater part is an embedded narrative in the first person, where Justine tells her sorry adventures to characters she has just met, among whom, unbeknownst to her, is her sister Juliette. According to dominant views such as Genette's and all of the communicative theories of fictional narrative, a first-level "narrator" delegates his role (for more than three quarters of the text) to a second-level narrator (Justine herself). From the perspective of a "poetic" conception of fictional narrative, there is on one side of the main narrative an "author" who freely creates his narrations, and on the other a "narrator" proper, who more or less imitates what Hamburger calls a "statement of reality" (except of course that we are not dealing here with a structurally pure "memoir-novel").

Sade's text, however, which is experimental without the author giving any thought to its theoretical implications, blatantly undermines the autonomy and coherence of Justine's second-level narrative voice by regularly attributing statements to her that are radically incompatible with the image of her that is built up over the course of the story: that of a poor guileless girl, naive and virtuous. Another voice undermines the credibility of Justine's voice from within, acidly corroding everything in it that might suggest the fictional voices manufactured by Marivaux, Prévost, and Crébillon in the heroic period of the first-person novel. Those are voices endowed with verisimilitude, depth, and complexity, which are as utterly lacking in Justine's character as a character in a fairy tale or a fable.[16] To attribute this corrosive effect to a "narrator" created by the author makes absolutely no sense, and it is obviously the author who is engaged in this shadowy game of deconstruction of the fictional utterance. What is in play here is what I call in my book on Voltaire "co-narration" (Hersant 2015, 416–18), a phenomenon that consists precisely in creating a collision between the author's and the narrator's voices by attributing to the fictional narrator incongruous formulations that obviously emanate from another voice—that of the author. The author plays a little narrative duet with the narrator that eats away at the fictional regime of make-believe from within, emphasizing its manufactured character and constantly revealing the figure of the creator in the background. Whereas the first-person novel tries in principle to conceal the manufactured nature of the voices, Sade, on the contrary, like Voltaire—particularly the Voltaire of the *History of the Travels of Scarmentado* and the embedded narratives in *Candide*—emphasizes it with sardonic complacency.

The Voltaire-Sade filiation is clear,[17] because the Sadean tale imitates devices inherited from Voltaire's, which show a similar desire to undermine the fictional voices that narrate the story, mock their authority, and put on display the only real voice, that of the author, which in principle is hidden behind them, revealing with much amusement that they are only "speech puppets."[18] Sade even helps us understand Voltaire retroactively, because he places such dramatic emphasis on the practice and with such glee that its mechanism is fully exposed in the plain light of day. In the first two versions of *Justine*, as I have already mentioned, the narration is essentially performed by Justine herself, who recounts her successive misfortunes to her sister Juliette. A framing narrative briefly provides the circumstances, and it is from the point of view of the virtuous victim that we then discover her series of ordeals. And at the end of the story, in an obvious allusion to Voltaire, Justine presents an extraordinary summary of her misfortunes, just as Candide, the Old Woman, and Cunégonde did before her, and which, as in their cases, highlights the perfect implausibility of such a perfect run of bad luck.

And yet arising on a regular basis is the suspicion that elements of Justine's voice cannot in fact be completely attributed to her and thus have another origin. For example, the scene where she sees Bressac sodomize his valet (in the first version only, because in the two later versions the roles are reversed and Bressac discovers the joys of sexual passivity) should arouse only horror in her, and yet she feels a strange need to praise the manly charms of the valet, which we gather had actually excited Sade in the depths of his prison when writing the work, and he "places" his own lustful point of view here without giving any thought to the coherence of the fictional utterance that he stages:

> One of these men, the one who dominated the other, was twenty-four years of age; he was neatly dressed in a green overcoat so that one assumes he was of fine birth; the other appeared to be a young servant of his house, about seventeen to eighteen years old, and *very shapely*.[19] The scene was long and scandalous, and that lapse of time seemed all the more cruel to me, as I dared not move for fear of being seen.[20]

At other times, Justine refers to the crude sexual realities she faces in a veiled way but one that is so contrived and so clearly playful that it is hard to see how the poor girl could be capable of such virtuosity. A good example at the beginning of the story concerns the trader Dubourg, an old satyr who greets Justine as he just comes "out of bed wrapped in a floating robe that barely hid his disorder" (*IV*, 13). This way of conveying the fact that the libertine is in a threatening state of erection allows Justine to avoid the crudeness of explicitly pornographic language, but she does so with a suspicious refinement and skill that obviously derive from another source. The collision of the two voices creates a discursive cacophony, the real voice of Sade "piercing" the fictional voice of Justine and at the same time highlighting the fragility of its purely verbal existence. We could multiply the examples, because Sade never gives Justine's voice true autonomy, but the apex of this kind of discourse is indisputably the episode of the Sainte-Marie-Des-Bois convent, when Justine loses her virginity with a fourth monk after the first three performed their assaults on parts of her body that had left her conventional virginity intact.

Sodomy, forced fellatio, and sadistic violence can be discerned in turn through the veiled language with which Justine conveys what happened to her. The linguistic pleasure that governs this passage, which rivals the best passages of Crébillon in the genre, is dazzling, but most significant here is the absolute impossibility of attributing such extraordinary virtuosity to Justine herself. How could she engage, with such humor, in the almost Oulipo-like game of periphrasis here? The Sadean laughter in this case comes not only from the veil that allows the nature of the acts described to be glimpsed behind the stylistic fireworks but also from the glaring inconsistency between the playful intoxication that takes over the writing and the poor virtuous creature to whom the words are attributed:

> And this dishonest man, placing me on a sofa in a position suitable to his hateful pleasures, having Antonin and Clément constrain me . . . Raphaël, the depraved Italian monk, satisfies his desires upon me in the most outrageous fashion, yet does not compromise my virginity. Oh pinnacle of debauchery! One would have thought that each of these villainous men had made it a point of honor to ignore the statutes of nature in the choice of his unworthy pleasures. Clément comes forward, piqued by the vision of his superior's infamies and even more so by the actions he has undertaken while watching them. He professes that he will be just as innocuous as his superior and that the place where he will lodge his offering will equally safeguard my virtue. He has me kneel and clutches me to him in this position; his perfidious passions exert themselves in such a way that I am prohibited, during the sacrifice, from complaining in any way of his unorthodoxy. Jérôme follows him, his temple was identical to Raphaël's but he was unable to reach the sanctuary; content to observe the parvis, moved by primitive episodes whose obscenity cannot be depicted, he was incapable of attaining the completion of his desires except by the barbaric means which you nearly saw me fall victim to at Dubourg's, and which I suffered completely at the hands of Bressac. (*IV*, 61–62)

A good example of what strikes me as poetically remarkable in this text is the passage on the fellatio that "prohibited" Justine "during the sacrifice, from complaining in any way of [the] unorthodoxy" of Clement. We understand that Justine cannot speak because her mouth is full, but she conveys this with a strange and provocative humor that is completely foreign to her and comes directly from the perverse wit of Sade, who entertains himself alone in his cell with this euphemistic fantasy. So there is a "play," in the sense of a floating and unstable disjunction, between two "voices" here, but it is essential to remember that only one of these voices is real and that it can therefore impose itself on the other one, a simple cardboard cutout, however it wishes. The "poetic" dimension (in the sense of pure creation) of the text as a whole is thus retroactively emphasized.

On the other hand, this story is based on the relentless reiteration of a logic of misfortune that befalls the virtuous Justine like a negative Providence that automatically produces the worst scenarios and is essentially diabolical. The only god who orchestrates this infernal mechanism, however, is obviously not a narrator, omniscient or otherwise, who would want to demonstrate some kind of general law (that virtue is always punished), and use this rhetorical logic to convince some "narratee" of this equation. It is an *author* who, profoundly indifferent to any persuasive logic (and who, in particular, does not care whether his very hypothetical reader supports the law that presides over this story), makes the sovereign decision out of his own "good pleasure" as a prisoner that each good action by Justine will be rewarded with torture, rape, and humiliation. Governed by the law of his desires as an imprisoned writer, Sadean fiction is thus the ideal illustration of the creation of an author who alone reigns over his narration and produces his fiction without any mediation.

The author, who is alone responsible for the third-person narrative that forms the basis of Justine's story, is also the only one responsible for the narrative statements he attributes to his character, and finally the only one responsible for the enunciative "gaps" that constantly emphasize the artificiality and structural fragility of this voice. Voltaire's model is essential here because it is obviously his characters—Scarmentado, the Old Woman, and Cunégonde, as deprived of real psychological depth and complexity as they are—who inspire Sade to take his poor paper creation on a journey to the extremes of horror, guided by what Sade's text regularly and sardonically calls "Providence." The word occurs about thirty times in the text, which shows Sade's insistence on having fun with this notion, and Providence is presented as the main subject of the story in the preface. The author sets himself the task, and at least officially the ideal, of deciphering the mysterious will of Providence, an operation that would, according to the preface and its different versions, be the "triumph" (*IV*, 3) or the "masterpiece" (*IV*, 131) of philosophy. This idea persists from one version to another, even if the idea of Providence, already singularly abused in the 1787 text, is increasingly mocked by the enunciator. In the version of *The New Justine* in particular, it is carelessly mixed in with competing notions that are all the targets of his sarcasm ("Destiny, God, Providence, Fate, Chance, all denominations as vicious, as devoid of common sense as each other, and which bring to the mind only vague and purely subjective ideas") (*IV*, 395).

In the story, the question of Providence occupies a central place both as an object of the characters' preoccupations and as a structuring element of the narrative itself. In the foreground, Justine's relationship to Providence wavers between two equally stereotyped attitudes, both of which have their novelistic models in the eighteenth century, as Paul Pelckmans has shown in his book *Le Problème de l'incroyance au XVIIIe siècle*. First of all there is submission to an impenetrable will that mistreats people in a cruelly systematic way but whose "mysteries" are nevertheless respected. In her discussions with La Dubois in prison, Justine elaborates on her little system of submission and hope with a certain energy: "There are in me," she says, "ideas of religion which thanks to heaven will never abandon me; if Providence makes life's path painful to me, it is to compensate me more fully in afterlife" (*IV*, 21). A little later, and after the Bressac episode, she throws herself on the ground and thanks the heavens for the ordeals it inflicts on her, for which she hopes to be rewarded one day. Meeting La Dubois again at the end of her journey, she still finds the heart to threaten her with a "Providence that is always ultimately right" (*IV*, 100), even if in her own case she is still suffering in wait for this justice which is so slow to manifest itself. There are many times when the poor creature doubts this Providence in which she has put all her hopes and finds herself tempted by a form of revolt against God, sometimes even by the idea that this God could be wholly cruel and truly "sadistic." Sometimes she has barely formed this idea before it causes her immediate remorse, and she prostrates herself again in a fit of repentance. After the Bressac episode, for example, Justine initially doubts heavenly justice, then repents and apologizes to God for what she herself calls a blasphemy against Providence. But in other passages, and especially at the end of the great recapitulation of her misfortunes, Justine directly challenges Providence, doubts its justice, and does not recant. The idea of a negative Providence that is devoted to causing her misfortune emerges more than once, and poor Justine cannot guess that the only Providence tormenting her is in reality the will of the novelist who, in virtue of his supreme liberty as creator of fiction, chooses to make her fictional existence a pitiless series of ordeals.

If we turn now to the first-level statements (in other words, those of the author, since we do not believe in the necessary mediation of a "narrator" here), they take to an absurd extreme the gap between the discursive moments that mimic submission to Providence and faith in its justice, and a narrative that resolutely contradicts what it is supposed to prove. In the preface, the storyteller claims, for example, that he portrays evil for a moral purpose, and thinks that the result of reading Justine's story will be "submission to the commands of Providence, part of the unfolding of its most secret mysteries and the fateful warning that it is often in order to bring us back to our duties that its hand strikes us" (*IV*, 4). This phony moral pact is reiterated in the last lines of the work, where the reader is invited to be persuaded, after reading this edifying tale, that "true happiness lies only in virtue and that if God allows it to be persecuted on earth, it is to prepare a more sublime reward for it in Heaven." The story, in addition, which is firmly on the side of the libertines and always rules in their favor, is entirely guided by an implacable principle that is its most famous feature—the misfortunes of virtue and the prosperity of vice—and strives with icy black humor to make the poor creature on paper the scapegoat and martyr of a negative Providence.

This principle is also borrowed from Voltaire and *Candide*, but with the difference that Sade seems to turn the evil world that terrified Voltaire into an object of perverse desire. In Sade's case, the sole source of the negative Providence at work in the story is the writer's poetic freedom. This negative pseudotranscendence is only a simulacrum, because the only authority that gives meaning to Justine's human adventure is no other god than the author himself, who decided that in the fictional world in which he placed his creature all virtue would be flouted and all vice triumphant. The creator, all-powerful over his creation, is therefore the only Providence at work in this story, and is properly "poetic" in the sense given to this term by Sylvie Patron, as opposed to a "communicational" conception of fictional narrative ([2009] 2016). This leads us back to another question: does Sade really want to convince the reader that this is how things happen in the real world, and that virtue is always punished and vice rewarded? I don't think so. This communicative and rhetorical perspective is completely foreign to Sade. For him it is not a matter of proving anything about the real world but rather one of creating a fictitious world where things happen the way they do to satisfy the fantasy life of the creator, and him alone. In the two narratives I have analyzed, the magical lantern of victims and persecutors is a spectacle that the poet-novelist projects for himself, and in a certain way for himself alone, in the solitude of his cell. To inject a "narrator" into this creative process would be to completely overlook the kind of despotic violence with which the writer fabricates his fiction.

> *Translation by Melissa McMahon*
> *based on a first version by*
> *Agnès Bouvier, Delphine Mouquin, and*
> *Malina Stefanovska*

Notes

1. The same reproach could be made to Dorrit Cohn and Gérard Genette.
2. "Short" is a very elastic term here, since the shortest stories are no longer than one page, while *The Misfortunes of Virtue* is over a hundred, and *The Mystified Magistrate* about half that.
3. There is a note on the manuscript of *The Misfortunes of Virtue*: "Completed after fifteen days on the 8th of July 1787," and on *The Mystified Magistrate*'s: "Finished this tale on the 16th of July at 10 pm." One tale has been written immediately after the other, and they can therefore be said, at least from a chronological point of view, to form a diptych, even though they have very seldom appeared in the same volume.
4. For *Le Magistrat mystifié*, I refer to the edition by Michel Delon (see Sade 2014a). The page numbers are given in parentheses within the text (*MM*, page), followed by the English page number from the English version translated by Richard Seaver (see Sade 2000).
5. In her preface to what she calls *Contes libertins* (Sade 2014b). Delon's and Genand's volumes are not duplicates of each either, as the texts chosen are not always the same, and the choices influence the way they are read in interesting ways.
6. Sade keeps this structure in the 1791 version, *Justine, or The Misfortunes of Virtue*, but presents the overall narrative in the third person for *The New Justine*. But *The Story of Juliet*, his longest novel—even when detached from *The New Justine* and considered on its own account—takes the form of a memoir-novel.

7. Not related in any way, of course, to nineteenth century "realism."

8. I refer the reader on this point, if I may, to the third part of my work: *Voltaire: Criture et vérité* (Hersant 2015). There are many arguments in favor of treating memoir-novels and epistolary novels as metafictions (as Jan Herman or Jean-Paul Sermain do, for instance) but doing so tends, in my view, to minimize the opposition between them and these more explicit metafictions.

9. And many critics have tried to show the metafictional dimension of first-person fictions by Marivaux, Prévost, or Crébillon.

10. His long period of detention begins in 1777 and, after a brief escape, continues with no interruption between 1778 and 1790. When he writes the tales examined here, he has therefore been a prisoner for ten years.

11. This observation is only historically true of course for *The Misfortunes of Virtue*, but *The Mystified Magistrate* has the same sort of potential, which was not, however, exploited. To return to the question of the successive versions of her story, it is obviously not the case that Justine has "forgotten," in the 1787 version, to relate the adventures that are added in the two later expanded versions. The tension between "invention" and "relation" is obvious here. The narrator only relates what the author has decided to invent.

12. According to an expression in *The Mystified Magistrate*.

13. Paul Ricoeur's, for instance, or Hamburger's "reality statement."

14. In a 1765 letter (see Sade 1991, 246–47). These parallels with Sade's life and his letters from prison aren't based in a naïve confusion between life and work but on the contemporaneity of the epistolary and fictional forms of his writing while in prison, and the obvious dialogue between the two domains, which is only perceptible to someone who reads Sade's letters and then picks up his dossier of "tales" or "novels." The incursion of "lived experience" into the fiction is moreover even more spectacular in Sade's great epistolary novel: see my forthcoming work, *Genèse de l'Impur: L'Écriture carcérale du marquis de Sade*.

15. In a letter to his wife dated February 21, 1781, which is nothing more than a pleading for the defense in narrative form, Sade claims he is just being punished for "a party with girls, no different to the kind of which there are eighty every day in Paris" (Sade 2007, 45). The phrase "party with girls" (*partie de filles*, translated "party of females" in the Leaver translation) occurs frequently in Sade's prison letters as a way of referring to the "affairs."

16. Like the characters in Voltaire's tales.

17. It is confirmed by many expressions of admiration for Voltaire in Sade's letters and in his preface to *The Crimes of Love*, "An Essay on Novels."

18. In Voltaire's case, this has to do with an aversion, not shared by Sade, to memoir-novels and epistolary novels, which Voltaire sees as the products of a whining psychologism.

19. The emphasis is mine.
20. All quotes from *Les Infortunes de la vertu* are from Michel Delon's precious edition, whose second volume brings together the three versions of Justine's story (Sade 1995), henceforth referred to only as *IV* followed by the page number, in this case, 26. Quotes of Sade's from this volume have been translated by Kelly Crelier and Malina Stefanovska.

References

Cohn, Dorrit. 1999. *The Distinction of Fiction*. Baltimore: Johns Hopkins University Press.

Démoris, René. 1975. *Le Roman à la première personne*. Paris: Armand Colin.

Genette, Gérard. 1972. *Figures III*. Paris: Le Seuil.

Hamburger, Käte. (1957, 1968) 1973, 1993. *The Logic of Literature*. 2nd ed. Translated by Marilynn J. Rose. Indianapolis: Indiana University Press

Herman, Jan, Mladenà Kozul, and Nathalie Kremer. 2008. *Le Roman veritable: Stratégies préfacielles au XVIIIe siècle*. Oxford, UK: Studies on Voltaire and the Eighteenth Century.

Hersant, Marc. 2015. *Voltaire: Écriture et vérité*. Leuven, Belgium: Peeters.

———. Forthcoming. *Genèse de l'Impur: L'Écriture carcérale du marquis de Sade.*

Patron, Sylvie. (2009) 2016. *Le Narrateur: Introduction à la théorie narrative*. Paris: Armand Colin. Reprinted as *Le Narrateur: Un problème de théorie narrative*. Limoges, France: Lambert-Lucas.

Pelckmans, Paul. 2010. *Le Problème de l'incroyance au XVIIIe siècle*. Quebec: Presses de l'Université Laval.

Ricoeur, Paul. 1983–85. *Temps et récit*. 3 vols. Paris: Le Seuil.

Sade, Donatien Alphonse François de. 1991. *Correspondance du marquis de Sade et de ses proches*, vol. 3. Edited by Alice Laborde. Paris: Champion-Slatkine.

———. 1995. *Œuvres*, vol. 2. Edited by Michel Delon. Paris: Gallimard.

———. 2000. *The Mystified Magistrate and Other Tales*. Translated by Richard Seaver. New York: Arcade Publishing.

———. 2007. *Correspondance du marquis de Sade et de ses proches*, vol. 16. Edited by Alice Laborde. Paris: Champion-Slatkine.

———. 2014a. *Contes étranges*. Edited by Michel Delon. Paris: Gallimard.

———. 2014b. *Contes libertins*. Edited by Stéphanie Genand. Paris: Flammarion.

Sermain, Jean-Paul. 2002. *Métafictions (1670–1730). La Réflexivité dans la littérature d'imagination*. Paris: Honoré Champion.

PART 2   *Optional-Narrator Theory before and beyond Literature*

10 Silent Self and the Deictic Imaginary
Hamburger's Radical Insight

MARY GALBRAITH

Introduction: Language and Genesis

Käte Hamburger's *Logic of Literature* argues that fictional narration is an act of genesis distinct from statemental language. This insight entails a radical elevation of fiction's status in the taxonomy of language, as Gérard Genette observed in his preface to the 1993 edition: "What to my mind speaks most forcefully in favor of [Hamburger's] argument is its quite evident and entirely explicit promotion of narrative fiction to the rank of what naturalistic classifications call a *type*, as opposed to a *species*" (Genette [1986] 1993, 112–13).

When Ann Banfield and S.-Y. Kuroda took up Hamburger's thesis in the 1970s, influential narrative theorists persistently evaluated their work by focusing on two subarguments: Hamburger's rejection of first-person narrative as fiction and Banfield's rejection of dual voice. These arguments threaten foundational principles of classical narratology, so it is not surprising that they were given first attention, but the most radical implications of the Hamburger-Banfield-Kuroda thesis were missed. Here I will explore some of these radical implications, using supporting arguments from disciplines not in my area of expertise but accessible enough to my reading understanding that I feel able to use them heuristically—subject, of course, to modification.

The first part of this essay attempts a highly schematic and interdisciplinary inquiry into the origins of fictivity as a human evolutionary adaptation that incorporates older animal ways of experiencing as it moves into language. This broad line of reasoning supports Hamburger's radical notion that fiction, far from being parasitic on the statemental function of language, is coemergent with or even ontologically prior to it. At its most stripped down, fiction potentiates a narrative space with no fictional narrator, address, enunciation, message, or narratee. At the same time, this space is collaboratively created and maintained by means of real authors, materialized linguistic artifacts, and real readers.

The section titled "Methods: A Process Model of the Literary Transaction and a Critical Agenda" briefly outlines a methodological "process model" (Gendlin 2018) responsive to the nuances and distinctions of the literary transaction, and an agenda for a narrative theory and practice beyond enunciative narratology (see Patron 2011).

The section titled "Application" offers a brief application of this process model and agenda to two passages from nineteenth-century short stories representing nonverbal childhood subjectivity: Hans Christian Andersen's "The Little Match Girl" (1845) and "The Girl Who Trod on a Loaf" (1859).

Theory: Semiosis and the Deictic Imaginary

Although language is intergenerationally transmitted, it is not genetically determined. No one is born speaking a particular language. Instead, native language is acquired through bodily interaction between child and parent, and thus is epigenetically existential and chiasmic. Long before they point intentionally, babies engage in dyadic improvisational exchanges with caregivers (Merleau-Ponty [1945] 1986, Trevarthen 2015). The establishment of joint attention is the first step toward intentional communication, and children's first intentional communicative acts are nonverbally enactive and deictic. And before they speak in sentences, babies use objects as imaginary devices (see Rakoczy, Tomasello, and Striano 2017). This behavior suggests that the fictional or creative mind begins as a bodily, chiasmic "haptic interaction" with other people and the world before the development of statemental mind.

In the evolution of language as shared mind, language's affordance of representing events that are not present is seen as crucial (Donald 1993, Brandt 2013, Zlatev 2005). The first evolutionary step to representing the not-present is *bodily mimesis*, which is the preverbal "capacity to use our bodies as resonance boxes, so to speak, in feeling the emotions of others, understanding their intentions, and eventually for understanding and expressing communicative intentions" (Zlatev 2012, 124). Early humans, by this account, acted out events in mimetic gestures including dance and music that involved mutual understanding through performance: events of great significance ritually created rather than given.

According to the speculative but empirically sensitive account of language evolution advanced by Merlin Donald, Daniel Dor, and Zlatev, the move from whole-body mimesis to semiosis using arbitrary signs afforded the further capacity to signal and differentiate multiple epistemic modalities. This capacity gave humans the ability to evolve culturally as well as genetically.

Of particular relevance here, two distinct epistemic modalities made possible by semiosis are statements about absent events and fictive creation of imaginary events. These two modalities are covered by the same semiotic category in Bühler's taxonomy: *deixis am phantasma*. Cognitive semiotician Donna E. West notes that Bühler's umbrella term *deixis am phantasma* requires further articulation to bring out the critical distinction between constructed (i.e., fictive) realities and "static remembered ones" (West 2013, 39). This distinction is the cornerstone of Hamburger's argument about fiction: "When Bühler speaks of the 'deixis in [*sic*] phantasma', he has in mind the broader Greek meaning of mental representation in general, irrespective of whether it is the representation of real data or that of imagined constructs. . . . It is in the domain of fiction that the theory of displacement breaks down" (Hamburger [1957, 1968] 1973, 1993, 128). To keep this distinction between imaginary and displaced deixis in what follows, I adopt the term *deictic imaginary* to refer strictly to the imaginary sense of *deixis am phantasma* and to Hamburger's fictive deixis.

The deictic imaginary disengages language not only from its anchorage in a speaker's *origo* but also from all the trappings of the speech situation: address, enunciation, discourse, and social rules, thus potentiating in literature a freedom to show what cannot be said in engaged social interaction.

In addition to epistemic modality, which is not always coded grammatically but must be signaled somehow in order to be operative, language enables the grammatical coding of ontic relations between nouns and verbs. The Greek term for this is *diathesis*, usually translated as grammatical "voice"—categorized as active, passive, or middle. English no longer has a middle voice in its surface morphology, but it still signals this relation through a fossilized lexicon and certain deep-structure usages (Weiner n.d., Lamont 2005). The middle voice designates the ontic relation of noun to verb as recursive and creative, as in the common example *the bread bakes*: the bread comes into being as bread by being baked. This middle voice relation has been identified by a number of twentieth-century writers and theorists (e.g., Roland Barthes, Hayden White, Martin Jay, J. M. Coetzee) as capturing the enigmatic, intransitive sense of the verb *to write*, and this is the relation Hamburger describes as adhering between writer and fiction: "*Between the narrating and the narrated there exists not a subject-object relation, . . . but rather a functional correspondence*" ([1957, 1968] 1973, 1993, 136, emphasis original).

Whereas *deixis ad oculos* is anchored in the enunciative instance of speech, the deictic imaginary is anchored in the experience field of a third-person character (Bühler [1934] 2011, Hamburger [1957, 1068] 1973, 1993, Banfield [1982] 2014). The shift to a deictic imaginary, then, is a shift not only from real to fictional but from first to third person and from speaking to being. A mimesis of speech can be created as an embedded frame within fiction, but this evocation is local and must be continually refreshed to remain active (Galbraith 1989, Patron 2011)—the default plane is existential rather than enunciative. Authors and readers collaborate as producers and inhabitors of the existential field of the deictic imaginary, and their joint effort of production is necessary to the enterprise. Rather than addressing the reader, the author, in Jean-Paul Sartre's words, "appeals to the reader's freedom to collaborate in the production of his work" ([1947] 2008, 54). In this sense the literary transaction is language in the middle voice for both author and reader. In writing and reading, we create and are created through our participation in the literary act.

Counterintuitively, it is only by withdrawing from the speech model of communication that this literary collaborative transaction is made possible. The epistemic modality of fiction *disengages* statemental reference and makes space for the modality of creation. In A. J. Greimas and Joseph Courtès's usage of Roman Jakobson's deictic concept *shifter*, the shifter is conceived as a gearbox in a car engine: "What these theorists have done is to divide Jakobson's concept of the shifter into two operations, *débrayage* and *embrayage*, which may be translated as shifting-out and shifting-in. For them, shifting-out is the prior operation by means of which a not I/not now/not here is disconnected from the I/now/here anchored to the speaker's utterance" (Moorjani 1990, 23). This version of *débrayage* connects to Ludwig Wittgenstein's notion of the "dynamic idling" of language: "In Wittgenstein's conception . . . language in this [grammatical display] condition is 'idling,' though one would want to add here that when the revolutions per minute get as high as they can in some literary expressions, 'idling' is no longer the right word for verbal forms whose inertia . . . is enormous but whose activities within themselves— in the integral and complex play of their exposed possibilities—is very quick indeed" (Guetti 1993, 12–13).

As conceived by the ancient Greeks, disengagement from ordinary social calculus is a necessary preliminary to works of the imagination; this is Plato's reasoning for including *poiesis* in the category of "divine madness" alongside prophesy and erotic passion. A crucial variable of success in artistic genesis is its creator's ability to bracket social calculus and invite the Muses to take over. Literary creation might thus be compared to Perseus's shield—a deflective instrument that allows a proximity to truth that would otherwise dazzle and transfix those who approach.

The deictic imaginary not only *creates* imaginary beings but *appears* them. The Greeks called this luminous appearing *enargeia*, a word originally used to describe the luminescence of encountering a god: "[ἐνάργεια is] a central 'criterion of truth' in [archaic Greek] epistemology. From the first use of the adjective ἐναργής, -ές in Homer, a sublime context is present, as the term usually refers to the powerful lucidity of divinities in an epiphanic setting. For instance, Hera remarks that Achilles 'will be struck with fear if ever a god meets him face to face in the midst of battle. For gods are hard to bear when they appear distinctly . . .' (20.130– 131). The association of the adjective *enarges* with indescribably vivid moments of sensation persists in later uses of the term" (Hedrick 2018, abstract). Paradoxically, imaginary creation allows an approach "with one's face averted" to this unbearable power.[1]

Methods: A Process Model of the Literary Transaction and a Critical Agenda

All poetry is of the nature of soliloquy. . . . What we have said to ourselves we may tell to others afterwards; what we have said or done in solitude we may voluntarily reproduce when we know that other eyes are upon us. But no trace of consciousness that any eyes are upon us must be visible in the work itself.

—JOHN STUART MILL

Authors' own phenomenological descriptions of the writing process are a valuable—even if not conclusive—source of evidence about the middle voice of poiesis. Here is James Baldwin, for example: "When you're writing, you're trying to find out something which you don't know. The whole language of writing for me is finding out what you don't want to know, what you don't want to find out. But something forces you to anyway" (Elgrably and Plimpton 1984).

Authors are also readers, and they write evocatively about the experiential intimacy of reading: "Because book-writing, by which I mean literary writing, is the best means by which we express what is innermost, and because book-reading leaves the entire act of interpretation to the reader's inner self, we not only come intimately closer to the consciousness of another person than is possible in any other way but are also engaged with our own consciousness more intricately and more actively than by any other means. This is why we so often feel when we have read a great book, a book that matters to us, that we have grown, that we are more aware of some aspect of our self, of other people, of life itself, than we were before" (Chambers 2001, 27).

Stated in less personal language, the literary *epoché* allows a "figural breakthrough": "The figural introduces in aesthetics a sense of cultivating those moments of intensity that resist and escape all regulating power, be it linguistic discourse or the order of the conscious or political constraints" (Ionescu 2013, 144).

The figural breakthrough afforded by fiction is not a mimesis of speaking or of the situation of verbal communication. Instead, it is for the author a verbal *ekphrasis* of felt sense, verbalization that emerges from direct reference to nonverbal phenomena (Gendlin 1997), and for the reader a mimetic or "following" performance of the author's words into an imaginary *origo*, that is, a new direct presence created by language (Kuzmičová 2013).

Literature's ontogenesis in bodily mimesis and imaginative creation entails a critical project of noticing what literary language does through its distinct grammatical display of language. In my own attempt to conceptualize this project, I have found Eugene Gendlin's "process model" and his taxonomy of language acts in *Experiencing and the Creation of Meaning* useful for focusing on the steps of the literary transaction:

a) Person 1 (the writer) disengages from statemental reference and address to allow fictional genesis to happen (invoking the muse, in classical parlance)
b) Person 1 experiences a deictic imaginary as felt sense or phantasm in the middle voice ("it comes" rather than "I create")
c) Person 1 captures this deictic imaginary in writing that ekphrastically performs or enacts the felt sense as a palpable enargeic *origo*
d) In collaboration with Person 2 (publishers and editors), Person 1 edits this writing in light of accessibility to readers
e) The work is published and becomes materially available
f) Person 3 (the reader) reads the work, which requires . . .
g) following its instructions for the genesis and performance of a deictic imaginary and
h) becoming progressively immersed in the work
i) The reading experience of Person 3 is related to the felt sense of Person 1 at step (b), not as a copy but as a complex and profound collaborative performance, reversing the direction of fit—that is, proceeding from language to presence rather than vice versa
j) Result: Person 3 is, in a labyrinthine, mysterious, but grammatically materialized way, intimately touched by the actual felt sense that inspired Person 1 to write.

This process model fits well with the agenda Sylvie Patron proposes for a literary practice beyond enunciative narratology:

- [Moving beyond the limits of enunciative narratology] involves making the author the arch-enunciator, as in theatre, or more simply the narrative's real subject of enunciation. Rethinking the enunciative analysis of narratives from the position of the author would allow us:
- To reflect on the author's enunciative dis-inscription (*désinscription énonciative*) in fictional narratives. . . .
- To think consequently about the author's inscription of a fictive or fictional narrator in certain narratives. . . .
- To also think about the vocation of certain narratives or certain passages of narratives so as to suspend the question of the enunciative source. . . .

The reanalysis I am proposing would further enable us to perform the following tasks:

- To reexamine the question of the author's or narrator's intrusions . . . from a "discontinuist" perspective. . . .
- To think, more generally, about montage or the narrative's local, rather than global, enunciative coherence. (Patron 2011, 330–31)

To this list I propose adding (as suggested by recent discussion among contributors to this volume):

- Observing, explicating, and theorizing the functioning of words in specific fictional passages, replacing the limiting question "Who speaks?" with "What is the language doing?"

Application

Here are brief readings—under the *aegis* of Patron's agenda and my adaptation of Gendlin's process model—of two short passages that create "phantasms of childhood solitude and silence" from Hans Christian Andersen, focusing on how language works to create a montage of deictic imaginary levels of being. My intention is simply to demonstrate how this concept of fiction can function in a literary close reading.[2]

"The Little Match Girl": It Would Be Better to Die

I consider Hans Christian Andersen to be the first author of children's literature, defined as the authentic creation of a fictional child self, in book form, embraced by child readers. Andersen's best narratives use the scaffolding of folktales as a springboard to dialogical, modernist, figural prose. "The Little Match Girl" and "The Girl Who Trod on a Loaf" are dominated by phantasms that appear to doomed child characters. Unlike the child figures of William Blake, who dwell in untouchable purity even in the face of diabolical adults, Andersen's most memorable child selves (the match girl, the girl who trod on a loaf, the ugly duckling, Karen in "The Red Shoes") are pinned and tortured bodily by others' judgments before they ultimately rise above them.

"The Little Match Girl" began as an *ekphrasis* in the traditional sense of the term: an enargeic meditation written on an image created by some-

Fig. 1. Johan Thomas Lundbye and Hans Christian Henneberg, "Den Lille Pige Med Svovlstikkerne," *Dansk Folkekalender* no. 184, December 1845. Courtesy Lars Bjørnsten.

one else. The image used by Andersen was a lithograph sent to him in 1845 with a specific request that he write a story based on it (Andersen and Tatar 2008, Lassen 2006).

According to Henrik Lassen, Andersen wrote the first draft of "The Little Match Girl" in a single afternoon. The story consists of only 866 words, and yet it is one of the best-known narratives in world literature. In many ways the tale belongs to the familiar *topos* of dying children described in Gillian Avery and Kimberley Reynolds's *Representations of Childhood Death*. But several properties of the story take it out of the realm of genre expectations and in the direction of Blakean "radical innocence" (Haven)—its frank critique of an abusive father and the blindness of conventional adults (unseen in carriages that "rattled by"), in the unorthodox personal details of the girl's visions, and most important, in the weight it gives to the girl's unselfconscious experience. The primal impact of the story comes from the girl's fulfillment of desire through phantasm and her chiasmic reunion with her grandmother, while its ontological irony, comedy, and bitterness come from a juxtaposition of adult obliviousness and childhood anguish.

The tale's narrative refraction, in Mikhail Bakhtin's sense, reveals several ideologies and perspectives contending through juxtaposition—especially the misery of a life uncared-for and the bliss of a caring death, but the touchstone of the tale's power is its successful evocation of the child's suffering and encounter with death in presences created by her own phantasmic vision. The words of narration are ekphrastic—the verbal materialization of a nonverbal phenomenon—rather than a part of the fictional world. The girl does not "benefit" from these words, but the words are not merely transparent; like the wall in the story, they materialize her figural experience without being part of it. The match girl's own production of presence is exactly this combination of suffering, vulnerability, and creativity:

> She struck another match against the wall. It burned brightly, and when the light fell upon the wall it became transparent like a thin veil, and she could see through it into a room. On the table a snow-white cloth was spread, and on it stood a shining dinner service. The roast goose steamed gloriously, stuffed with apples and prunes. And what was still better, the goose jumped down from the dish and waddled along the floor with a knife and fork in its breast, right over to the little girl. Then the match went out, and she could see only the thick, cold wall. (http://www.andersen.sdu.dk/vaerk/hersholt/TheLittleMatchGirl_e.html)

Only in Andersen's universe would a steaming roast goose jump off its dish and waddle towards you with a knife and fork in its breast. My first reflective thought about this incongruous image—no ecclesiastical overtones here!—is followed by a bizarre second thought: What a reenactment of the Last Supper! an alive-dead animal offers itself to be eaten but at the same time to be encountered as a fellow being. And then the match goes out.

This passage from "The Little Match Girl" enacts in its own grammatical ontic relations the very heart of what it does as a visionary narrative. The girl as self figure creates a vision through the instrument of the match, which gives life and light to the girl's own hunger and creative spirit, but the match is not itself a part of the vision. The child self is complexly creator of and subject to rather than master of the match. In epistemic terms, the vision of the match enacts—through its brevity—the limitations of its own wish-granting power. The dramatic irony of "Someone is dying" resonates not only with the girl's lack of realization of who is dying but also to our own.

After this passage comes the sublime moment of full I-Thou presence: "Grandmother had never been so grand and beautiful." The end of the story grants the child's appeal for human care in effect by allowing her to die; however, we as readers are left behind among the living, for now. Adults in the story see her dead body and—too late—feel pity. They don't know about her visions, and thus don't know what she experienced as she died. Readers know much more: we do know what she experienced as she died. We do not know, however, what happened to her next.

"The Girl Who Trod on a Loaf": The Journey from Judgment to Instress

"The Girl Who Trod on a Loaf" is a much less familiar narrative than "The Little Match Girl," and its treatment of the child self, Inger, far more dissonant, at least at first. The tale is in fact recounted three times in the course of the story. The first iteration employs standard cautionary-tale plot logic: a little girl bespoils a loaf of bread (a gift meant for her impoverished mother) by using it as a stepping-stone in order to keep her shoes clean while crossing a marsh, and she is pulled down to hell as punishment. The second iteration provides further damning backstory, but also exculpatory subtext. Inger also likes to pull the wings off insects and use them as puppets in a tiny theater. She seems an irredeemably cruel child, but we begin to see cracks in the modality of her creation; her "puppets" become expressive stand-ins for herself. Finally, the third iteration follows a Frankenstein logic, shifting our identification from judgmental creator to suffering creature—ultimately, a modernist figural narrative emerges. A story that begins in seeming affirmation of the commandment to honor one's parents turns inside out, like the Book of Job, into a questioning of creation itself. In its overall impact the story puts us in uneasy relation to the power of divine judgment, and in prolonged identification with the child's predicament. Between its judgmental beginning and martyred ending is a decades-long sojourn in a solitary hell full of bodily misery and paralysis.

In "The Impromptu That Trod on a Loaf," musical narratologist Susan McClary offers a penetrating narrative interpretation of Schubert's Impromptu, op. 90, no. 2 in E-flat major (1827) by reading it in musical parallel to "The Girl Who Trod on a Loaf." "This [musical] fable of minimal infraction answered by incommensurate brutality brings to mind one of Hans Christian Anders[e]n's cruelest stories, "The Little Girl Who Trod on a Loaf." . . . As she treads on the loaf, it sinks down with her into hell where she is tortured by slimy creatures for the span of several lifetimes—and justly so, the narrator of this dour Protestant tale implies" (McClary 1997, 20). McClary surmises that ordinary narrative theory would not qualify instrumental music as narrative (precisely because of its requirement for a mediating narrator), but her own interpretation shows how revelatory and applicable such a parallel can be. Here I will argue similarly but in the other direction, using musical concepts such as counterpoint and harmonics and a logic of serially self-destructing ideology to interpret Andersen's tale "The Girl Who Trod on a Loaf" as a tale of direct presence akin to music—and to Wittgenstein's enigmatic method of argumentation. This reading sees the tale as a mounting rejection of "dour Protestant" plot logic through the thundering counterforce of its deictic imaginary.

In "Wittgenstein's Deictic Metaphysics," Ignace Verhack summarizes Wittgenstein's enigmatic method of philosophical argument as manifesting and performing itself through its own narrative logic. One must build on fallacious or simplified premises that are gradually transcended at each step—a style of argument also called, significantly, "lie-to-children." In fact, Wittgenstein wraps up his Tractatus thus: "He must so to speak throw away the ladder, after he has climbed up on it" (90). "The Girl Who Trod on a Loaf" employs this perverse presentational logic—a child leads adults to truth by refusing adults' judgmental pedagogy. The adult judgment in the first sentences of the story is presented as self-evident: here is a girl who sinned, and here are the consequences, which you children should dread and avoid. The story is then retold in more depth, providing details about the girl's behavior: she sadistically pulls wings off flies and sticks pins in bugs to turn them into characters in the plays she devises. In this second telling, the girl is unlikable but—in my case—close to home (I too pulled the wings off insects as a child). Andersen's second telling of the story also plants the idea that the girl's sadistic behavior is a reaction to an adult double bind: the constant inducements of guilt by her mother ("As a little child you often used to trample on my aprons; and when you're older I fear you'll trample on my heart"), and the persecutory servant-child identity she is forced to inhabit as a poor child in service to a rich family. Meanwhile, adult judgments continue to suffuse the narrative with what would, according to classical narratology, be seen as the evaluative perspective of "the narrator": "As she grew older she became even worse instead of better; but she was very pretty, and that was probably her misfortune. Because otherwise she would have been disciplined more than she was."

Whose judgmental perspective is this if not a narrator's? One can productively read it as the perspective of the "They say" (Galbraith 1989): the normative adult "lie-to-children" ideological perspective that creates cautionary tales in order to frighten children into obedience. This way of construing ideological perspective is supported by the way the story progressively kicks the pins out from under this judgmental position as we move deeper into the self perspective of the girl. Once she arrives in Hell, her punishment becomes so exotically grotesque—to stand like a stone in the Devil's anteroom for decades, sentient but immobilized— that most readers (judging by a class of university students and the [perhaps fictive] critics cited by Kathryn Davis in her novel *The Girl Who Trod on a Loaf*) "find the punishment excessive, given the nature of Inger's crime" (Davis 2003, 16), and begin to question how to construe the excessiveness of passages such as this:

> Worst of all was the dreadful hunger she felt. Could she stoop down and break off a bit of the bread on which she was standing? No, her back had stiffened, her arms and hands had stiffened, her whole body was like a statue of stone. She could only roll her eyes, but these she could turn entirely around, so she could see behind her,

and that was a horrid sight. Then the flies came and crept to and fro across her eyeballs. She blinked her eyes, but the flies did not fly away, for they could not; their wings had been pulled off, and they had become creeping insects. That was another torment added to the hunger, and at last it seemed to her as if part of her insides were eating itself up; she was so empty, so terribly empty.

"If this keeps up much longer, I won't be able to stand it!" she said.

But she had to stand it; her sufferings only increased.

Then a hot tear fell upon her forehead. It trickled over her face and neck, down to the bread at her feet. Then another tear fell, and many more followed. Who could be weeping for little Inger? Had she not a mother up there on earth? A mother's tears of grief for her erring child always reach it, but they do not redeem; they only burn, and they make the pain greater. And this terrible hunger, and being unable to snatch a mouthful of the bread she trod underfoot! She finally had a feeling that everything inside her must have eaten itself up. She became like a thin, hollow reed, taking in every sound.

She could hear distinctly everything that was said about her on the earth above, and what she heard was harsh and evil. Though her mother wept sorrowfully, she still said, "Pride goes before a fall. It was your own ruin, Inger. How you have grieved your mother!" Her mother and everyone else up there knew about her sin, that she had trod upon the bread and had sunk and stayed down; the cowherd who had seen it all from the brow of the hill told them.

"How you have grieved your mother, Inger!" said the mother. "Yes, I expected this!"

"I wish I had never been born!" thought Inger. "I would have been much better off. My mother's tears cannot help me now." (http://www.andersen.sdu.dk/vaerk/hersholt/TheGirlWhoTrodOnTheLoaf_e.html)

At this point in the narrative, the third capitulation, we have "occupied" Inger's body deep underground for several paragraphs. The vindictive glee we were encouraged to feel for Inger's karmically exorbitant punishment (analogous to how we feel in Roald Dahl's *Charlie and the Chocolate Factory* when Augustus Gloop gets sent up a pipe for the crime of eating chocolate in a chocolate factory) fades away, to be replaced by a palpable enargeic presence: what it is like to *be* her. In these two paragraphs, almost all the content is proprioceptive and haptic: hunger, stiffness, emptiness, flies crawling across her eyes, hot tears landing on her head. Even sight and sound are so magnified and near as to be tactile: hyperacute hearing of people's judgments, and her eyes turned round in her head to see her own ugliness. It is an extraordinary passage that succeeds powerfully by Jonathan Culler's definition: "it bring[s] about what it describes."[3]

The narrative grammar of the two paragraphs of this passage includes three questions that oscillate between reader-directed rhetoric (reminiscent of Socratic pedagogy) and the silent wondering of Inger herself: "Had she not a mother in the world?" The narrative coincides with Inger's experience to such an intimate degree at this point that the fiction takes on lyrical actuality: the deictic imaginary is pierced by a harmonics of the real (Greenblatt 1997, Schalkwyk 2004, Gumbrecht 2004). When the child self in Hell staunchly continues to resist even as it is eaten from within by the power of the universe, we cannot but feel, using Gerard Manley Hopkins's terms, the "instress" of this "inscape": "Each being in the universe 'selves,' that is, enacts its identity. And the human being, the most highly selved, the most individually distinctive being in the universe, recognizes the inscape of other beings in an act that Hopkins calls *instress*, the apprehension of an object in an intense thrust of energy toward it that enables one to realize specific distinctiveness" (Greenblatt, Ramazani, and Stallworthy 2012, 1514–15).

"The Girl Who Trod on a Loaf" enacts a child's suffering and redemptive emancipation from the thrall of cosmic justice—like an insect on a pin—thanks to the grace embodied in someone she never meets who, from childhood to the moment of her death in old age, holds the pilloried child Inger in her heart and forebears to judge. One suspects from the strength of this and other fictional testimony—as well as biographical evidence—that Andersen suffered not only near-death experiences but also curses of damnation and guilt and epiphanies of presence in which all judgments were transcended. That he has captured these experiences in short stories that have resonated with readers across translations and centuries indicates the power of the embodied felt sense from which he worked.

Conclusion

The insight that the deictic imaginary is a primary rather than a derivative semiotic function is supported by evolutionary theory of language, cognitive semiotics, philosophy of language, child language acquisition, and phenomenological accounts of writing and reading. Hamburger's *The Logic of Literature* asserts that fiction comes from a logic of creation rather than from a transitive logic of teller and told; this insight affords a more flexible, adequate, and accurate working model of the literary transaction and the profound experience it engenders.

The deictic imaginary emerges very early both in the history of humankind and in the individual life cycle—before the emergence of fully symbolic language. And in literature, this gift of the imaginary continues to be the means by which language itself is embodied and brought to life as imaginary presence. It is utterly confounding that the deictic imaginary develops so fully formed so early in human history and in individual development. Babies less than two years old indulge in imaginary creation before they speak in sentences, and our remote ancestors produced drama, poetry, and narrative as powerful as anything produced since. As Giambattista Vico observed in 1744, "men in the childhood of the world were by their nature sublime poets" ([1725] 2020, 86).

Notes

1. Though primal face-to-face address begins at birth (Trevarthen 2015), *I* and *you* as speech-role labels are late arrivals in native language acquisition (Bates 1990) in comparison with pointing words such as *that*, which are reliably among the first words acquired (Diessel 2013).
2. For a more extensive application of nonenunciative narratology to Samuel Beckett's work by four different scholars, see Banfield (2003), Moorjani (1990), Abbott (2013), and Barry (2008).
3. Culler's definition of successful performativity in the lyric—"the poem's success in bringing about what it describes" (2017, 131)—is also broadly applicable to literature.

References

Abbott, H. Porter. 2013. *Real Mysteries: Narrative and the Unknowable.* Columbus: Ohio State University Press.

Andersen, Hans Christian, and Maria Tatar. 2008. *The Annotated Hans Christian Andersen.* Translated by Julie K. Allen. New York: W. W. Norton.

Avery, Gillian, and Kimberley Reynolds, eds. 2000. *Representations of Childhood Death*. New York: Macmillan.

Banfield, Ann. (1982) 2014. *Unspeakable Sentences: Narration and Representation in the Language of Fiction*. Routledge Revivals.

———. 2003. "Beckett's Tattered Syntax." *Representations* 84 (1): 6–29. doi:10.1525/rep.2003.84.1.6.

Barry, Elizabeth. 2008. "One's Own Company: Agency, Identity and the Middle Voice in the Work of Samuel Beckett." *Journal of Modern Literature* 31 (2): 115–32. doi:10.2979/jml.2008.31.2.115.

Bates, Elizabeth. 1990. "Language about Me and You: Pronominal Reference and the Emerging Concept of Self." In *The Self in Transition: Infancy to Childhood*, edited by Dante Cicchetti and Marjorie Beeghly, 165–83. Chicago: University of Chicago Press.

Brandt, Line. 2013. *The Communicative Mind: A Linguistic Exploration of Conceptual Integration and Meaning Construction*. Newcastle-upon-Tyne: Cambridge Scholars Publishing.

Bühler Karl. (1934) 2011. *Theory of Language: The Representational Function of Language*. Translated by Donald Goodwin. Amsterdam: John Benjamins.

Chambers, Aidan. 2001. *Reading Talk*. Stroud, UK: Thimble Press.

Culler, Jonathan. 2017. *Theory of the Lyric*. Cambridge MA: Harvard University Press.

Davis, Kathryn. 2003. *The Girl Who Trod on a Loaf*. Boston: Back Bay Books.

Diessel, Holger. 2006. "Demonstratives, Joint Attention, and the Emergence of Grammar." *Cognitive Linguistics* 17 (4): 463–89. https://doi.org/10.1515/cog.2006.015.

———. 2013. "Where Does Language Come From? Some Reflections on the Role of Deictic Gesture and Demonstratives in the Evolution of Language." *Language and Cognition* 5 (2–3): 239–49. https://doi.org/10.1515/langcog-2013-0017.

Donald, Merlin. 1993. *Origins of the Modern Mind: Three Stages in the Evolution of Culture and Cognition*. Cambridge MA: Harvard University Press.

Dor, Daniel. 2017. "From Experience to Imagination: Language and Its Evolution as a Social Communication Technology." *Journal of Neurolinguistics* 43: 107–19. https://doi.org/10.1016/j.jneuroling.2016.10.003.

Elgrably, Jordan, and George Plimpton. 1984. "The Art of Fiction LXXVIII: James Baldwin." *Paris Review* 26: 49–82. https://www.theparisreview.org/interviews/2994/james-baldwin-the-art-of-fiction-no-78-james-baldwin.

Galbraith, Mary. 1989. "What Everybody Knew versus What Maisie Knew: The Change in Epistemological Perspective from the Prologue to the Opening of Chapter 1 in *What Maisie Knew*." *Style* 23 (2): 197–212.

Gendlin, Eugene T. 1997. *Experiencing and the Creation of Meaning: A Philosophical and Psychological Approach to the Subjective*. Evanston IL: Northwestern University Press.

———. 2018. *A Process Model*. Evanston IL: Northwestern University Press.

Genette, Gérard. (1986) 1993. "A Logic of Literature." Translated by Dorrit Cohn. In *Essays in Aesthetics*, 108–15. Lincoln: University of Nebraska Press.

Greenblatt, Stephen. 1997. "The Touch of the Real." *Representations* 59: 14–29.

Greenblatt, Stephen, Jahan Ramazani, and Jon Stallworthy. 2012. *The Norton Anthology of English Literature*. Vol. 2. New York: W. W. Norton.

Guetti, James. 1993. *Wittgenstein and the Grammar of Literary Experience*. Athens: University of Georgia Press.

Gumbrecht, Hans Ulrich. 2004. *Production of Presence: What Meaning Cannot Convey*. Stanford: Stanford University Press.

Hamburger, Käte. (1957, 1968) 1973, 1993. *The Logic of Literature*. 2nd ed. Translated by Marilynn J. Rose. Bloomington: Indiana University Press.

Haven, Cynthia. "David Lang's Postmodern Passion: 'It Is Not a Pretty Story.'" Book Haven. Accessed May 22, 2018. http://bookhaven.stanford.edu/tag/hans-christian-andersen/.

Hedrick, Robert E. 2018. "The Foundation of Vividness: The Epistemological Development of the Term *Enargeia* in Plato." Abstract. *CAMWS 2014*, 110th Annual Meeting. https://camws.org/meeting/2014/abstracts/individual/152.Enargeia.pdf.

Ionescu, Vlad. 2013. "Figural Aesthetics: Lyotard, Valery, Deleuze." *Cultural Politics: An International Journal* 9 (2): 144–57. https://doi.org/10.1215/17432197-2146075.

Kuroda, S.-Y. 2014. *Toward a Poetic Theory of Narration: Essays of S.-Y. Kuroda*. Edited by Sylvie Patron. Berlin: De Gruyter.

Kuzmičová, Anežka. 2013. "The Words and Worlds of Literary Narrative: The Trade-off between Verbal Presence and Direct Presence in the Activity of Reading." *In Stories and Minds*, edited by Lars Bernaerts, Dirk De Geest, Luc Herman, and Bart Vervaeck. Lincoln: University of Nebraska Press.

Lamont, George. 2005. "The Progress of English Verb Tenses and the English Progressive." Toronto: University of Toronto. http://homes.chass.utoronto.ca/~cpercy/courses/6362-lamont.htm.

Lassen, Henrik. 2006. "'. . . from a Swedish Tale by Andersen'—'The Little Match Girl' in America and the Topos of the Dying Child." In *When We Get to the End: Towards a Narratology of the Fairy Tales of Hans Christian Andersen*, edited by Per Krogh Hansen and Marianne Wolff Lundholt, 305–80. Odense: University Press of Southern Denmark.

McClary, Susan. 1997. "The Impromptu That Trod on a Loaf: Or How Music Tells Stories." *Narrative* 5 (1): 20–35.

Merleau-Ponty, Maurice. (1945) 1986. *Phenomenology of Perception*. Translated by Colin Smith. London: Routledge and Kegan Paul.

Mill, John Stuart. 1859. *Dissertations and Discussions* (version Google Play Books). London: Saville and Edwards. https://play.google.com/books/reader?id= Vz87aqaamaaj&printsec=frontcover&output=reader&hl=en&pg=gbs.pp8.

Moorjani, Angela. 1990. "Beckett's Devious Deictics." In *Rethinking Beckett*, edited by Lance St. John Butler and Robin J. Davis, 20–30. New York: Palgrave Macmillan.

Patron, Sylvie. 2011. "Enunciative Narratology: A French Specialty." Translated by Anne Marsella. In *Current Trends in Narratology*, edited by Greta Olson, 312–35. Berlin: De Gruyter.

Rakoczy, Hannes, Michael Tomasello, and Triciam Striano. 2017. "How Children Turn Objects into Symbols: A Cultural Learning Account." In *Symbol Use and Symbol Representation*, edited by Laura Namy, 69–97. New York: Lawrence Erlbaum.

Sartre, Jean-Paul. (1947) 2008. *What Is Literature?* Translated by Bernard Frechtman. New York: Routledge.

Schalkwyk, David. 2004. *Literature and the Touch of the Real*. Newark: University of Delaware Press.

Trevarthen, Colwyn. 2015. "Infant Semiosis: The Psycho-biology of Action and Shared Experience from Birth." *Cognitive Development* 36: 130–41. doi:10.1016/j.cogdev.2015.09.008.

Verhack, Ignace. 1978. "Wittgenstein's Deictic Metaphysics." *International Philosophical Quarterly* 18 (4): 433–44. doi:10.5840/ipq197818438.

Vico, Giambattista. [1725] 2020. *The New Science*. Translated by Jason Taylor and Robert Miner. New Haven: Yale University Press.

Weiner, Edmund. N.d. "Grammar in Early Modern English." *Oxford English Dictionary*. Accessed August 24, 2018. https://public.oed.com/blog/grammar -in-early-modern-english/.

West, Donna E. 2013. "Cognitive and Linguistic Underpinnings of *Deixis Am Phantasma*: Bühler's and Peirce's Semiotic." *Sign Systems Studies* 41 (1): 21–41. doi:10.12697/sss.2013.41.1.02.

Wittgenstein, Ludwig. [1922] 2010. *Tractatus Logico-Philosophicus*. Translated by C. K. Ogden. Project Gutenberg.

Zlatev, Jordan. 2005. "What's in a Schema? Bodily Mimesis and the Grounding of Language." In *Cognitive Linguistics Research from Perception to Meaning*, edited by Beate Hampe, 313–42. Berlin: Mouton. doi:10.1515/9783110197532.4.313.

———. 2012. *The Shared Mind: Perspectives on Intersubjectivity*. Amsterdam: John Benjamins.

11 Aesthetic Theory Meets Optional-Narrator Theory

LARS-ÅKE SKALIN

The optional-narrator theory has mainly been used in a criticism of the ubiquity thesis, mostly associated with the theory that may be called standard narratology. A detailed survey is found in Sylvie Patron's *Le Narrateur* (2009) and also in the introduction to a book edited by her, *Toward a Poetic Theory of Narration: Essays of S.-Y. Kuroda* (2014). My contribution to the topic is a discussion of literary fiction with relation to the narrator concept based on what I see as an "aesthetic/artistic" mode of reasoning (henceforth just "aesthetic," but still carrying also the meaning of "artistic"). I will do this by entering into dialogue with an important early exemplification of a repudiation of the ubiquity thesis: the well-known book by German literary theorist Käte Hamburger, namely *The Logic of Literature* ([1957, 1968] 1993). She explicitly states that her study of literature as an aesthetic art will show that the nature of such a phenomenon must be seen as something clearly different from what terms like "narrative" and "narration" indicate in contexts of nonfiction or factual accounts. She also declares that her mode of reasoning is based on linguistic theory. My own notion of the representational arts is entirely in line with her "difference" thesis, while a consequence of the larger scope of my object will be that my argument cannot be merely restricted to linguistic theory. This raises the following questions: Has our respective reasoning, which seems to have led to similar results as to the topic, focused on two aspects of what must be the same concept of that nonnarrated aesthetic object, or has our focus actually been on two different basic concepts that reject the pan-narrator idea from their particular aspects?

Hamburger presents her objective in the following way: "What follows is an attempt to extrapolate from the realm of general literary aesthetics a more specific logic of literature." That is, we will stay within the realm of literary aesthetics, but with focus on a "specific logic." This focal point is justified by "the special position which literature occupies within the realm of art" (1).

From my point of view, on the other hand, an important question is naturally the correlation between that method—investigating the "special position" of literature's logic—and a method that embraces also the other forms of the so-called fine arts (as we find in much of traditional aesthetic theory) or at least those which could be called "representational" art; for example, the Aristotelian version of mimesis. If the other forms are experienced as meaningful systems too, it would certainly indicate that they display some kind of logic. The method I am advocating could be seen as a variant of the mimetic method. I call it my "performance model," and I will describe its traits below.

First I will give a more explicit account of Hamburger's thesis. What, then, is "specific"? In other words, what directs Hamburger's "specific" method? Her answer is this: "*The logic of literature* qua *linguistic theory of literature has as its object the relation of literature to the general system of language.* The logic of literature is therefore to be understood in the sense of a theory of language." (Emphasis in the original.) Its basis is "a theory of statement [*Aussage*]" (3).

The treatise intends to demonstrate that there is an absolute boundary separating two linguistic systems, one of which is very large and the other very small in comparison. Hamburger's reasoning goes something like this: The very small system is represented by literature (but not by literature as a whole). There are only three categories: epic, drama, and lyric. Epic, which here should be understood as third-person narrative, along with drama, will be called *fiction*. These categories are defined by the unique property of being *nonreal*, the result of a *creative* language. The absolute opposite to the *nonreal*, naturally enough, is *reality*, represented by the system of language that marks our whole lives and is identified as the *formula of statement*. "Reality" should be understood as "nothing other than the reality of human life (of nature, of history, of mind), in contradistinction to what we experience as the 'content' of literary works; it designates the mode of being of human life as opposed to that mode of being which creative literature represents" (9).

The "formula of statement" has the following properties: In the role of senders we communicate with one another using a structural form that assumes a *statement-subject* with a *statement-object*. Accordingly, the core notion *statement* should be understood as the statement made by a subject about an object. This structural formula "permits us to recognize that not only the single statement, but also the whole of life which manifests itself in language, is described by the concept 'statement.'" Its opposite, the nonreal, manifests "the sole instance in the realm of language for which the statement formula is not valid, namely . . . narration in narrative literature" (31). (The meaning Hamburger applies to the terms "narration" and "narrative" in literature will become clear later.)

My aesthetic model has no problem accepting the relevance of this "otherness" thesis, not only for literature but also for the other representational arts. The structures of these forms are, according to the aesthetic point of view, built up by *motifs*, the building blocks functioning as catalysts of the intended effects of the given representations. And such instruments cannot possibly be serving the purpose of *statements* in the sense presumed by Hamburger here.

The Performance Model: Presentation and Self-Presentation in the Fine Arts

Drama, music, and dance are typical forms of art presented by factual, sensible actions we call "performances." Normally we think of a composer as being responsible for the artistic composition as such, and then the composed product being presented to an audience by professional (or sometimes amateur) performers, such as musicians, singers, dancers, and stage actors. But in what I call my specific "performance model," I go beyond this use of the term while still accepting its traditional function. As an "enlargement" of this use I suggest some "added pieces" (to allude to Hamburger's method in her grammar analysis), namely that many kinds of representational artworks—for example, the works of artists and composers—could be regarded as kinds of "performances." My reason for finding this unconventional use of the term workable is the following: The *function* of art is traditionally considered to provide a kind of entertainment, giving the peculiar kind of pleasure, which, for instance, Aristotle referred to as *oikeía hedoné* (see, for instance, his *Poetics*: 1459a16–20), associated with the particular kind of art actualized. We should take "pleasure" primarily as a technical term only, a word marking how one is willing to see the experience associated with what these forms of art offer; that is, what kinds of attention, attitude, and expectations are apt to result if this enjoyable game should turn out felicitously. Now, if we see these enjoyable experiences as intentionally *given* by artistic means made for just that purpose alone, in contrast to cases where we *find* pleasure in this or that activity, independent of its possible purpose or actual nature, the analogy with the performers' actions (in the ordinary sense—those of musicians, dancers, etc.) appears clear. This is so, if we believe that the compositions of artists, of whatever kind of art, are constructed by just those designs artists believe will produce those aesthetic experiences they want their works to engender—the function commonly referred to as the artworks' *expressive* power. So, this principle of the *self-presentational* constitution of the aesthetic works is in conformity with what I see as Hamburger's formulation: "The narration is the action, the action is the narration" (173); "the narrated is the narration and the narration the narrated" (189). The insight that the relation between act and content in manifestations of representational art is just one-place, not two-place or more, is an important element in an aesthetic theoretical approach (see, for instance, Goodman 1976, the section titled "Fiction"). This specific form is something I believe Aristotle intuited in Homer's epics: its motifs, or "mimesis-makers," are not recounted as information by someone, but are enacting themselves in self-presentation, more like the actions of the drama. Something similar may also be the intuition behind Benveniste's well-known nonnarrator statement in his explanation of the function of narratives in the aorist tense used in *histoire* as contrasted with *discours*: "As a matter of fact, there is then no longer even a narrator. . . . No one speaks here; the events seem to narrate themselves" ([1959, 1966] 1971, 208).

The Problem of the Narrator and the Ambiguity of the Terms "Narrative" and "Narration"

What portion of Hamburger's theory could the nonnarrator theorists be expected to agree with? The nonstatement nature of fiction, without doubt; the "non-communication" interpretation too, as Kuroda terms it; and possibly also Benveniste's claim, the "non-discourse" character, which rejects an I-you-relation.

Nonnarrator theorists may accept the following reasoning: Suppose "narrative" is understood in the ordinary sense, designating a teller telling about an object. Such an object will be something quite autonomous from the act of telling as such; it is not constructed by it. But a "narrative" in that sense cannot be valid for narrative fiction. The thesis most attacked by the nonnarrator representatives is probably that of a text-internal fictive narrator, an idea strongly advocated by standard narratology. What concept of "narrator" is assumed by such reasoning?

To illustrate it, I take a sentence from Winston Churchill's autobiography *My Early Life*: "I was just turning to Haldane to suggest that someone should scramble along the train and make the engine-driver reduce the speed, when suddenly there was a tremendous shock, and he and I and all the soldiers in the truck were pitched head over heels on the floor" (Churchill [1930, 1958] 1996, 245).

If we recognize the text as ordinary nonfiction narrative, we would say that the "I" in this sentence designates the agent telling about an event. Since the text is identified as "narrative" of the "text-type," we can call the narrative agent "the narrator," and since the book is identified as autobiographical, informing of its author's experiences, we can assert: "The author is the narrator." And this author and narrator makes statements that point out real things that actually are or were there, whether or not they are narrated. The receivers of the information may take interest in what attitude to these things the narrator seems to be willing to express, but since the objects pointed out are real things and the usual idea of the function of the narrative is to inform about these things, the receivers are permitted to form their own attitudes. If one accepts the thesis that literary fiction too, like any narrative communication, presents statements informing its receivers that this or that has happened, offering the opportunity to the receivers to try to make sense of the things they have been informed of, then the obligatory narrator would be self-evident.

Hamburger's topic, however, is not communication about what has happened. She says that the author—the maker of fiction—is its "narrator" of it. How should we understand such a claim? It has to do with the well-known ambiguity of the terms "narrative" and "narrator" in ordinary language. That the author is the narrator (*Erzähler*) means that he is the artist who, like the artists of other art forms, presents his literary artwork as something created by his artistic intention and competence:

"One may also say that the act of narration is a function, through which the narrated persons, things, events, etc. are created: the *narrative function*, which the narrative poet manipulates as, for example, the painter wields his colors and brushes" (136). Consequently, Hamburger's rejection of a "narrator" of literary fiction corresponding to the one we saw above in the Churchill example, is clear. The maker of fiction "does not narrate about persons and things, but rather he narrates these persons and things; the persons in a novel are narrated persons, just as the figures of a painting are painted figures. *Between the narrating and the narrated there exists not a subject—object relation, i.e. a statement structure, but rather a functional correspondence*" (136; emphasis in the original). Based on my aesthetic model I would perhaps question phrases such as "the narrated persons, things, events," asking if it should be understood as "persons" etc. narrated or told *about*. But the resolution to this tension comes when, further down on the same page, I read this: The author "does not narrate about persons and things, but rather he narrates these persons and things; the persons in a novel are narrated persons, just as the figures of a painting are painted figures." The "otherness" principle is obviously persistent.

The Grammatical Uniqueness of the Language of Narrative Fiction

Hamburger's well-known method, carried out mainly in the third chapter's instructive reasoning and examples, is built on features that enlarge traditional grammar with new pieces. Literary theorists and critics are familiar with them, which Hamburger summarizes in a short list: "the use of verbs of inner action with reference to the third-person, and derivable from this the narrated monologue [*erlebte Rede*], the disappearance of the narrative preterite's significance of designating past-ness, and the possibility (not necessity) created by this of its combination with deictic temporal, particularly future, adverbs. . . . They alone are elements which make fictional narration recognizable as a special verbal-grammatical phenomenon" (134). The most powerful element is probably that of the "epic preterite," a form that seems to point at something past, but instead its expressive function renders it to be experienced as a "here and now."

Take the following example from Hamburger, concerning a sentence from novel: "Mr. X was on a trip." Her interpretation is that that here we "can no longer pose the question as to When. . . . I learn from this, as a sentence occurring in a novel, not that Mr. X *was* on a trip, but that he *is* on a trip" (70). So, the conclusion is that a sentence occurring, for instance, in a historical or biographical work, the past tense "informs us of something past" while a sentence occurring in a novel in the past tense "depicts a 'present' situation" (70). We may say that the "here and now" could be attributed to a "Mr. X-representation" presented by the text. But in an aesthetic context, where the sentence functions as a picture, a mimetic motif, rather than a statement, it will present itself also to *the readers'* "here and now," which is where they are in their act of enjoying the progression of the performance.

Yet, within Hamburger's theory, the whole realm of literature is not to be understood as existing under the nonreal, the nonstatement, and the nonnarrator order. Lyric exists in the reality dimension, and a very specific condition is attributed to first-person narrative.

The first-person narrative should not be expected to exemplify the kinds of "added pieces" we find in the pure fiction. It manifests a structure that is not "narrative" in the sense used by the theory of the nonreal; rather, it could be seen as an account built up by some statement-subject. Hamburger presents a rather complex theory here. This subject is not a "fictional" narrator, since such a thing should be understood as a character within the fiction telling things to other characters. A "feigned" narrator, on the other hand, is expected to perform the kind of narration we associate with the artist giving us the story, but in this case one that is "invented" (see Hamburger [1957, 1968] 1993, 56–57, 327–30, 333–41). In my discussion of first-person narrative using Joseph Conrad's *Heart of Darkness* as an example, however, I will not strictly follow Hamburger's distinctions of different types but will adopt the more common usage chosen by literary critics and theorists. This is because the kind of literary structure I am interested in here is how the text's surface linguistic forms, which mostly correspond to *Aussage*, relate to what might be seen as the artwork's "deep-structure," the factor making aesthetic meaning available.

First-Person Narrative and the Problem of the Narrator

From the point of view of standard narratology, it would be an undeniable fact that a work such as *Heart of Darkness* exemplifies the property of a text-internal fictional narrator. It even posits two: narratologists might label one the "frame-narrator" and the other the "embedded." All novels and short stories in their view are narrated by text-internal narrators. They are necessarily overt in first-person narrative, but they may appear also in third-person works. In the latter, although the narrators may be covert, their existence must still be assumed. Hamburger rejects this model, but she sees the peculiarity of the language of first-person narrative as a symptom of a "narrative" counter to third-person narrative, that is, pure narrative fiction. The language characterizing first-person narrative is that used by statement-subjects in communicating reality-statements, because "the origins of first-person narration lie in the structure of autobiographical statement" (311).

Now, even if Hamburger might suggest more complex interpretation of the kind of first-person narrative exemplified by *Heart of Darkness*, she would agree that at least a large portions of the text's linguistic surface level exhibits a typical statement structure. To that point, the main character, who most literary theorists would call the "narrator," Charlie Marlow, actually volunteers for that role. On board the yawl *Nellie* on the Thames, waiting for the turn of the tide, he entertains his company with an account of some of his own remarkable past experiences.

Is the aesthetic performance model presented here compatible with Hamburger's thesis of the "absolute boundary" between the two types of literature—the first- and the third-person narratives—or will there be a conflict with it? If there is a conflict, it is grounded in the fact that her thesis does not square with the intuitions of many readers. Actually, Hamburger is conscious of people's hesitation about the decisive difference. Yet looking at her spelled-out argumentation, any reader must recognize at least one criterion presented: the *restrictions* that authors of such texts are plainly willingly submitting to. We can note that Marlow as fictive first-person narrator is made to accept the "laws" of the logic of language; it is not possible, for example, for him to inform his listeners about the inner life of the strange characters he has met. Therefore, such presence of such unconventional "unspeakable sentences," characterizing pure fiction, should not be expected in this text, if the rules of logical language are to be upheld consistently. And if these rules are followed, must not the reader's kind of attention be fundamentally different from the one working in fiction reading? Given her methodological point of departure Hamburger seems to think so. But is this a self-evident conclusion, or are there possible alternatives? Keeping in mind many readers' hesitation about the "absolute boundary" between the two literary types, I would like to explore this.

Hamburger has identified and described a surprising number of radical grammatical liberties used in third-person fiction. Thus, should one not try to test whether it is possible that grammatical experiments and radical liberties might cast light on first-person narrative as well? I will attempt to use some of what I see as cogent proposals from Hamburger herself as evidence in my argument.

Might the forms of first-person narrative be given another function than the linguistic structure seems to indicate, revealing "grammatical experiments" and "liberties" of a kind which causes the first-person variant to be experienced in a way that is compatible with that of third-person epic fiction? Let us consider some concrete examples.

Marlow's parts are constantly changing. One gives the impression of direct address to his audience on board the *Nellie*, and another one is more from the perspective we can connect with his "here and now position" in the situations he is assumed to be telling about. As readers, our focus is now on the motifs, the scenes themselves, not on his role on the ship as the narrator telling about what he has gone through.

The following example starts by what he sees after having got Mr. Kurz's station within sight: "I directed my glass to the house. There were no signs of life, but there were the ruined roof. . . . And then I made a brusque movement, and one of the remaining posts of the vanished fence leaped up in the field of the glass. You remember I told you I had been struck at the distance by certain attempts at ornamentation, rather remarkable in the ruinous aspect of the place" (Conrad [1899] 1995, 94). That the text takes us directly from his experience of what is seen into his turning to the audience on the *Nellie* seems to confirm the impression that this is Marlow's narrative account by statements in the genuine past tense of what happened to him back then; an epic preterite does not appear to be evident. Thus the statements of the assumed "embedded" fictive narrator are reported by the assumed "frame-narrator." The latter is supposed quoting both what he has heard told by Marlow about his experiences and also his own memories of what Marlow said to him and the others on deck when he asks them to remember what he has earlier said about "certain attempts at ornamentation."

There are also, however, many narrated episodes given different forms. For instance, the expedition to Kurtz's station has found the important man himself in bad condition and brought him on board its ship. He disappears after some time, however, and Marlow sneaks ashore to catch the fugitive.

"I came upon him, and, if he had not heard me coming, I would have fallen over him too, but he got up in time. He rose, unsteady, long, pale, indistinct, like a vapour exhaled by the earth, and swayed slightly, misty and silent before me; while at my back the fires loomed between the trees, and the murmur of many voices issued from the forest" (105).

It is certainly possible to read these sentences either as straight past tense or as epic preterite; either as a *narrating* Marlow, informing his audience about the situation, or as an *experiencing* Marlow as perceiving, thinking, and feeling in an artistically composed dramatic scene. For example: "if he had not heard me coming, I would have . . ." could very well be interpreted as a scene with him thinking this. It would be in harmony with, for example, his perceptions and the simile "like a vapour."

There is a reason one tends to adopt such a reading; I suggest that it has to do with an intuition about the purpose of such scenes, of the meaningful function of all the factors present in the novelist's text.

It is true that Conrad has mostly consented to the restrictions that go with the (surface) grammatical forms of first-person narrative. He can do so because it has not meant any restrictions for his real purpose, which is to write a novel: the writing can do its job as easily with this first-person variant as with the third-person one. So this is the provocative claim I hope to find convincing arguments for. But Marlow's "scenes" do not turn the whole structure of the novel into something else just because they expose a "scenic style" among the parts that look more like strict narrating. We must find a more conclusive device, which leads me to the notion of *themes*.

Are there "symptoms" of the "otherness" properties in the given structure besides those imitating a statement-subject with a statement-object? Here we come to the central point in my attempt to reason about representational art and how it functions, as I have suggested in the description of the performance model above. The model emphasizes the performance/showing structure of representational art, claiming that the purpose of its working constituents—according to traditional aesthetic theory—is to produce experience of its peculiar kind of "pleasure." The model's notion of the receiver's "aesthetic experience" claims to answer to the notion of the work's "expression"—an expression, I argue, that is not possible in the absence of the aesthetic factor I call a "theme."

I believe that my performance model is just as valid for Conrad's first-person novel as for one written in the third person. And this novel with an I is an artistic composition, the mimetic elements of which create the themes producing the emotion-laden effects answering to this composition's aesthetic purpose. Our experience is prepared prior to reading it by the novel's title: *Heart of Darkness*. The novel's "frame-narrator" describes the atmosphere like this: "The air was dark above Gravesend, and farther back still seemed condensed into a mournful gloom, brooding motionless over the biggest, and greatest, town on earth" (15). And this "narrator" brings the whole story to an end like this: "The offing was barred by a black bank of clouds, and the tranquil waterway leading to the uttermost ends of the earth flowed sombre under an overcast sky—seemed to lead into the heart of an immense darkness" (123–24).

The theme of darkness comes up in Marlow's parts by various symbolic features. The overarching symbolic action is the travel into the heart of darkness, an expedition from which we readers find our human world as a world of horror. This pessimistic effect, created by the various dissonant motifs, appears to dominate this artistic performance. There is, however, one faint glimpse of consonant representations: could something we dream of as civilization save us from our natural wildness, or is that dream also as absurd as everything else seems to be in what Marlow experiences in his confrontation with the colonizers? He tries to get an answer from the mysterious person Kurtz, whose inspiring idealist message is delivered with an irresistible rhetorical power. Marlow's meeting with him in his present condition is a shocking experience: the terrible revelation is that our human nature obviously does not find it impossible to cross the borderline into the un-human, as Kurtz. But the little glimpse of consonance does not come from Marlow, and it is not in the "frame-narrator's" concluding sentence about the sky that "seemed to lead into the heart of an immense darkness." Yet readers see the consonance, however, as symbolically represented by Kurtz's women, in images such as that of his native mistress stretching out her arms in display of grief beyond words when she realizes that Kurtz will be taken away from her. And a repetition of this kind of symbolic situation with a loving woman occurs, this time when Marlow visits Kurtz's "intended" in Brussels. He sees this woman, broken down by sorrow, stretching out her arms in a way that makes him remember the imposing black woman from Kurtz's station. An emotion-laden motif arises, a "chord" struck by Marlow's horrible memories of Kurtz, the man taken by the darkness in his desire to acquire the power of a god, yet when dying expressing the terrible insight of having crossed the borderlines between the human and un-human: "The horror! the horror!" However, the darkness chord given to Marlow is answered by the emotion-laden chord given to the woman: "Don't you understand I loved him—I loved him—I loved him!" (123). This chord serves as a contrast with the darkness, implying love, goodness, and the possibility of overcoming total selfishness; a chord that, even if paradoxical, affords a glimpse of our dreams for civilization. The theme is not a message but the conclusion of the genre exemplified by this novel: the artistic life-vision as a balance between moods of consonance and dissonance.

As readers we cannot possibly withstand the persuasive effects of the recognizable themes: they carry the work's intended expression and we accept our experience as answering to these expressive motifs with the moods associated with them. A first-person narrative, however, interpreted according to the statement-formula in Hamburger's definition, cannot produce such a direct aesthetic expression. Autobiographical narratives can relate horrible facts and express the teller's emotional reaction to them. We have a two-place relation to consider: the teller's attitude and the referents independent of it. In fiction created by the "narrative function" there is, as Hamburger emphasizes, only a *functional correspondence* between narrating and narrated. I take this interpretation to be a kind of endorsement of the comprehension that what makes such purely aesthetic themes possible is the one-place relation between these two factors.

First-Person Narrative and the "Substratum" Idea of the Narrator's Function

How could the first-person narrative structure, given by a language borrowed from the genre of autobiography, be turned into the art of literary fiction, as I have claimed above in denying Marlow's function as a statement-subject? To answer this question, I promised I would borrow a good explication from Hamburger herself.

At one point in the third chapter Hamburger tries to give a reason why readers can accept the grammatical liberties of epic fiction, and she chooses to take the lost temporality of finite verbs as an example. The surface form of the sentence is that of a statement; still, in narrative fiction we often find that the verb's meaning-content and its tense do not expose their usual relation, the *language form no longer directing our interpretation*. The form seems to imply a meaning-content regarding something that occurred in the past, but our actual experience in reading suggests that this temporal element is unimportant to us. How can we, as readers, still get the meaning-content right? Here is Hamburger's interesting solution: "Just as a painting cannot be painted in thin air, but rather must have a substratum, a wall or a canvas, so also must the act of narration in narrative literature proceed in a finite verb-form. Now the canvas, above and beyond the painting, has its own material value *qua* canvas. But as substratum of a painting, and therefore being subsumed within it, it loses this material value: as a painting, it is no longer a canvas as such. The same relationship applies to the tense of the finite verb" (108).

Thus ignoring the temporal dimension implied by the verb, we focus only on its *represented content*, since we expect this factor to carry the relevant story element. Hamburger quotes a sentence from *Anna Karenina*: "Everything was topsy-turvy in the house of Oblonsky" (109). The reader's experience will not be *when* everything was topsy-turvy but just that this condition *is the case* for the characters in their fictive here and now.

Could I use this for my argument that the first-person narrative may be open to a similar treatment of the surface language structure? What follows is my attempt to do so.

The story as narrated in the first-person form by a fictive narrator—in other words, its presentation in the style of autobiographical memories—is only a *justification function*. It justifies the *representations* present in the text—the novel's true aesthetic content—while the statement forms, which resemble those typically used by someone recounting facts, are nothing but "substratum." The form elements function as a *dummy* with regard to the function of the story as an artwork. When our reading intuitions have turned the surface forms into genuine novel functions, the work is understood as "narrated" by the poet performing the "narrative function," who creates the content like painters perform their aesthetic content on canvases or walls.

Marlow's autobiographical experiences as facts *told of* cannot constitute the point of the novel. The presented characters—the narrating ones as well as the others and even the very important Kurtz—do not embody the essence of what the novel is showing us when the first-person function is transposed into narrative fiction as art. They are all just *signs, mimesis makers, icons* whose aesthetic function is making up the artwork's *expression*. This highest structural level of the aesthetic game is directed straight toward *us*, the readers, to render the peculiar kind of experience this expression may offer. Again, my aesthetic performance model suggests that the icons' representational working constitutes the variation of the *themes* which, as have been claimed above, build up this aesthetic composition as a sequence of consonant and dissonant varieties. And the Greek notion of "musico-poetics" is still relevant: the themes create what in a way answers to the expressive power of "melodies" in music, which may induce in the receivers those variant moods that accompany the chosen genre. This reasoning certainly manifests more of *semiotics* than of strict language theory.

And it must be semiotics, if the theory of literature as art should be compatible with the Aristotelian mimesis theory Hamburger appears to take for granted. If we take the mimetic representations (the "semblances" in Hamburger's translation) as constituting the level of *icons* (in Peirce's sense), we may give the themes of the uppermost level the function of *symbols*. In Peirce's system, symbols are the linguistic signs, expressing a conventional meaning as our language does. It is true that literary fiction is not exactly "conventional" in the sense of "common." But it presupposes an agreement between artist and reader, because the theme level's meaning is *given* by what we intuit as a *rule-governed* system; aesthetic meaning is not something readers individually attribute to what is encountered in the text.

In my view, Hamburger's reasoning appears to disclose a theoretical dimension she has abstained from developing as a continuation of her linguistic method in defining the logic of literature. In aesthetic theory, such a continuation would connect once again with the dimension which, by necessity, constituted its point of departure: that of art's *purpose*. Yet Hamburger's examples show that her reasoning must truly be *based* on such a premise: the literary language game is a kind of rule-governed system we have already learned to master. Such an acquired "literacy" is the only reason why we indeed are doing the right thing when we pay no attention to certain linguistic forms in the text. Instead, we evidently transform these conventional signs of what Donald Davidson (1986) called a "prior language theory" into signs doing their unconventional jobs in a "passing," yet working, new "language theory" in order to get to the intended purpose of the said. Therefore, notwithstanding how clearly the action of a story seems to be told by a narrator in the function of a statement-subject presenting what has happened in a form we recognize from ordinary accounts of actual events, we do not let this form determine our reading experience. We cannot, in fact, because we started our reading already *prepared* with the basic rules applicable to such a language game. And Hamburger's reasoning reveals her familiarity with those rules. Actually, her many references to the methods of the fine arts, especially those of paintings, suggest that the aesthetic fundament of our methods displays our corresponding kind of intuitions.

The aesthetic-mimetic poetical game presupposes that mimesis elements produce a self-representing structure: art. Hamburger's linguistic analysis shows how grammatical divergences may signal a function beyond reality talk, art being an optional alternative. But the power to turn linguistic units into art is not given to grammar; it is in the rules of an aesthetic game.

With regard to our present topic—the optionality or ubiquity of the narrator—my dialogue with Hamburger's methods has tried to show their complexity. We cannot just refer to "the narrator" as if it were one well-defined object with intrinsic properties fulfilling the same role in any context. Instead, we encounter ambiguity and context dependence. We find the term "narrator" used as a method-internal function that seems to reveal the presence of several concepts rather than one consistent notion. The use of the term itself, however, may not engender theoretical problems, as both Hamburger's and my texts have possibly shown. Our reasoning may have made it likely that the lexical term "narrator" mostly functions as placeholder awaiting the concrete context whose peculiar rules of the game will make the intended meaning clear. The theoretical disagreements are not about the word but about the function it is given as designating a basic constituting concept in the asserted theory.

References

Aristotle. 1995. *Poetics*, edited and translated by Stephen Halliwell. Loeb Classical Library. Cambridge MA: Harvard University Press.

Benveniste, Émile. (1959, 1966) 1971. "The Correlations of Tense in the French Verb." In *Problems in General Linguistics*, 205–15. Translated by Mary E. Meek. Coral Gables FL: Miami University Press.

Churchill, Winston. (1930, 1958) 1996. *My Early Life*. New York: Simon and Schuster.

Conrad, Joseph. (1899) 1995. *Heart of Darkness*, with *The Congo Diary*, edited by Robert Hampson. London: Penguin.

Davidson, Donald. 1986. "A Nice Derangement of Epitaphs." In *Truth and Interpretation: Perspectives on the Philosophy of Donald Davidson*, edited by Ernest LePore, 433–46. Oxford, UK: Basil Blackwell.

Goodman, Nelson. 1976. *Languages of Art*. Indianapolis: Hackett Publishing.

Hamburger, Käte. (1957, 1968) 1973, 1993. *The Logic of Literature*. 2nd ed. Translated by Marilynn J. Rose. Bloomington: Indiana University Press.

Patron, Sylvie. (2009) 2016. *Le Narrateur: Un problème de théorie narrative*. Limoges, France: Lambert-Lucas.

———. 2014. "Introduction." Translated by Susan Nicholls. In *Toward a Poetic Theory of Narration: Essays of S.-Y. Kuroda*, edited by Sylvie Patron, 1–36. Berlin: De Gruyter.

12 The Vanishing Narrator Meets the Fundamental Narrator

On the Literary Historical and Transmedial Limitations of the Narrator Concept

KAI MIKKONEN

We do not have to look as far as medieval examples to notice the anachronism of the pan-narrator thesis, that is, the premise that every fictional narrative has a narrator as its unifying source of communication. Diachronic narratology, meaning the history of narrative forms, can meet serious challenges in this respect even in the context of the nineteenth-century novel. The impersonal, omniscient extradiegetic narrators are a case in point, insofar as we are to believe that such narrators are simultaneously part of the fiction and yet not part of the fictional world. Furthermore, more experimental examples of narrative transmission, such as R. L. Stevenson's *The Strange Case of Doctor Jekyll and Mister Hyde*, can problematize the postulation of a unifying impersonal narrator. The typologies of classical narratology cannot easily describe hybrid cases that feature several first-person narrators (Enfield, Lanyon, and Jekyll) but nevertheless tell much of the narrative through a focalized character (Gabriel John Utterson) without references to a narrator. Still another challenge in this historical context, and one that I will take as my point of departure here, is the strategic use of first-person narration in the beginning of an otherwise heterodiegetically related novel. This common nineteenth-century convention raises important questions about how to conceive the narrating instance in such examples.[1] In the latter part of this article, I will discuss the (ir)relevance of the narrator concept in the medium of comics by comparing the narrative strategies in two comic book adaptations of Alphonse Daudet's *Tartarin de Tarascon* (1872). Ultimately, the point of this comparison is to consider the general principles that apply to both the literary-historical and the transmedial argument for optional-narrator theory. This chapter thus aims to contribute to this approach in two ways: first, to develop the literary-historical and transmedial arguments that support it, and second, to discuss some of the principles that underpin these arguments.

The "Vanishing" Narrator

The nineteenth-century convention of an anonymous "I" or "We" narration in the novel's beginning is best known from some classical examples of realism, such as the collective "we narrator" in the first chapter of Flaubert's *Madame Bovary* (1857), who represents Charles Bovary's classmates, and the first-person narrator in the first two chapters of Charles Dickens's *The Old Curiosity Shop* (1841), an old gentleman who loves to take long walks around London. What can narratology make of these temporary narratorial roles? In principle, in both cases we have a homodiegetic narrator, who belongs to the world of his story, and who is personified to some extent, yet we can also note that the character's narratorial function seems to be overrun by other functions. In fact, the introducing "I" or "We" narration may not be easily distinguished from the convention of anonymous witnessing travelers, similarly used in various nineteenth-century novels but who are not narrators. The two devices have more or less the same function: they introduce the reader to the fictional world and its main character or characters through a subjective perspective and with a certain sense of the authority of a witness. Some well-known examples of the latter can be found in Stendhal's *Le Rouge et le noir* (1830), where a traveler visits the imaginary small town of Verrières, and in the second chapter of George Eliot's *Scenes of Clerical Life* (1857), where an anonymous traveler visits the fictional town of Milby in the English Midlands. Irene de Jong has classified such cases as a subcategory of the anonymous focalizer and related them to the hypothetical focalizer (2014, 316–17).

Here, the narratologist ought to be ready to pose the heretical question, Does it make much difference to distinguish between the disappearing *narrator* and the anonymous traveling *focalizer*? One might surmise, perhaps, that a first-person narrator's subjective viewpoint is more effective in introducing the main *character* and his or her immediate world, while the moving viewpoint of the anonymous traveler efficiently depicts the *milieu* from an outsider's viewpoint. Philippe Hamon, however, does not distinguish between these devices as to how they serve realist discourse as types of narrative concretization (or alibi). Hamon argues that both the "traveler" at the beginning of *Le Rouge et le Noir* and the "we" at the beginning of *Madame Bovary* "authenticate an act of speaking" and justify a "content by guaranteeing its origin" (1992, 174). By defining from the outset "a horizon of realist expectation," both also illustrate the importance of openings in literary realism (Hamon 1992, 175).

In *Discours du récit*, Gérard Genette discusses the transition of the narratorial status in similar examples as temporary infractions of implicit informational norms. Such norms concern, on the one hand, the narrator's relationship to the story and, on the other hand, the restriction of narrative information through focalization. The implicit narratorial norm to which Genette refers is the expectation of consistency regarding the main elements of the diegetic universe. For instance, when Gil Blas- or Watson-type narrators who are characters in the story that they tell momentarily disappear as characters, they can be expected to reappear at any time, since their existence in the narrative universe has already been established ([1972] 1980, 245). Genette mentions both discreet instances (*Bovary, Le Rouge et le Noir*) and some more obvious examples. Among the latter he counts Stendhal's *Lamiel* (1889, written 1839–41), in which the narrator leaves the story to become a man of letters. Furthermore, grammatical shifts in the hero's personal pronoun in Balzac's *Autre étude de femme* (1842) and Proust's *Jean Santeuil* (1952, written 1896–1900) suggest to Genette a kind of "narrative pathology" ([1972] 1980, 246) due to the violation of the narratorial status. Elsewhere, Genette's discussion of *alterations* (194–98), defined as isolated infractions of the informational norm established by focalization, admits the novelist's absolute freedom in restricting narrative information but at the same time insists on the persistence of the codes that are being transgressed, including the need for the continuing presence of a narrator.

Thus, for Genette, these infractions make apparent the norm that they transgress: the expectation that each story has a narrator, and, furthermore, that this narrator channels narrative information in a consistent way. The narrator's disappearance, however, can pose more serious theoretical challenges than Genette is willing to accept. If the witness narrator's "withdrawal" demonstrates that the narrator is, in fact, a literary device at the service of the plot, description, or focalization, rather than a fictional source of narration, then is it at all meaningful to perceive the device as a narrator? Consequently, if we insist that this is, indeed, one type of narrator, then how should we understand the relationship between the first narrator and the second, heterodiegetic narrator? This question seems necessary from a theoretical viewpoint but constitutes a purely theoretical dilemma. Let us now turn to another example of a vanishing narrator and unpack some of these concerns in more depth.

The Vanishing Narrator in Daudet's *Tartarin de Tarascon*

A parodic use of the device of vanishing narrator can be found in Alphonse Daudet's popular satire *Tartarin de Tarascon*, the first in a trilogy of novels that launched the adventures of the eponymous anti-heroic character, the chief "cap-hunter" in the small Provençal town of Tarascon. The novel begins with an anonymous first-person narrator who serves as the author's moving perspective and Tartarin's potential companion, and introduces the main character to the reader. The narrator visits Tartarin's home: "Although it is now some twelve or fifteen years since my first meeting with Tartarin de Tarascon, the memory of the encounter remains as fresh as if it had been yesterday" (Daudet [1872] 1997, 7). The narrator then describes the protagonist's garden, house, and interiors, including many weapons that hang on the walls. Finally, he introduces the protagonist himself, who is currently reading a book and smoking a pipe. The description then moves to the man, whose face is contorted in a pout, and finally concludes with a series of parodic attributes of the main character: "This man was Tartarin of Tarascon; Tartarin the intrepid, Tartarin the great—the incomparable Tartarin of Tarascon" (11).

In this introductory passage, the narrator clearly belongs to the world of his story. We can follow his movement through Tartarin's garden and sanctum where the antihero devours books on hunting trips, expeditions, and fictional adventures, yet the narrator exists in this world only as a moving eye. He does not engage in a conversation with Tartarin, and the protagonist does not seem to recognize his presence. After the beginning, the narrator's "eye" and "I" withdraw from the story, except for a few infractions. At the beginning of part 2 of the novel, the narrator is self-referential when he explains to his "dear readers" that he would like to tell the story as a great painter, who concentrates on the different positions of Tartarin's hat, his *chéchia*, during the sea voyage from France to

Algeria. At another point, the narratorial "I" gives the fleeting impression of having personally been present in the storyworld at an earlier stage. This occurs in a passage that relates how Tartarin "sings a duet," a segment from Meyerbeer's opera *Robert le Diable*, with Madame Bézuquet by roaring loudly "Non! Non! Non!" at regular intervals. Here, the narrator casts himself in the position of a former member of Tartarin's audience: "For my part, if I live one hundred years, I will always recall the great Tartarin approaching the piano with a solemn step" (21).

Otherwise, the narrator is absent from the fictional world. Is this "withdrawal" then another form of narrative pathology in the Genettian sense? This interpretation would seem an overstatement, since beyond the change of focalization, the tone of the telling does not change significantly. Whenever the narrator makes himself (I presume it is a "he") heard in the rest of the novel, his relationship to the protagonist remains similarly ambivalent, constantly alternating between empathy and admiration, and irony and mockery. Nonetheless, we have a theoretical problem. Daudet's novel is not a narratorless narrative, but the issue remains about the number and kind of the narrators, their relationship, and the overall significance of the narrator concept. At the outset, we have two different types of narrators or two distinct aspects of the same narrator. The first narrator is a character in the world of the story, even though "he" is a mere observer without a clear personality. The second is a heterodiegetic voice, not part of the fiction (except for a few infractions).[2]

Why should we call the second narrator a narrator rather than the author, or the author's invented storytelling persona? Here, the optional-narrator theorist might be tempted to conclude that there is no second narrator there due to the significant number of "objective" passages in the novel's later chapters. Tilmann Köppe and Jan Stühring (2015) have argued, convincingly, that we can avoid the narrator concept even in examples such as Nathaniel Hawthorne's short story "Rappaccinni's Daughter" (1844) that include various explicit indications of narrating instance. The Hawthorne story features, for instance, evaluations of the fictional facts, direct addresses to the reader, and temporal expressions that refer to a fictional act of narrating; that is, there are elements that could be attributed to a heterodiegetic narrator. For Köppe and Stühring, however, the agent of the narration is the author: "it is perfectly reasonable to assume that the person speaking to the reader is Hawthorne himself"

(2015, 36), whose intentions they also detect in the references to the narrative situation.[3]

In Daudet's novel, overall, the act of narration is much more personal and prominent than in Hawthorne's story. In fact, the references to the act of narration are so frequent in certain passages as to suggest a sense of an ongoing exchange, reminiscent of oral storytelling, between the storyteller and audience. Furthermore, in the latter parts of the novel, the narrator/author not only addresses the reader directly but also at times pretends to know how the audience reacts to his tale: "'Well, then!' you might say, 'since game is so rare in Tarascon, what do the Tarasconnais hunters do every Sunday?'" (16). Furthermore, he may "protest" against the readers' presumptions: "What did you expect?" (111) and "What do you want!" (151).

Other significant features may justify the use of the heterodiegetic narrator concept in this case. One is the ironic tone of the telling. For instance, a comment about Tartarin, such as the repeated mention of his audacity (*l'intrépide*), is often contradicted by something else that is related, or that happens, and that makes the attribution seem an exaggeration or simply wrong. Upon entering Tartarin's house, the first-person narrator has this to say: "From the outside, the house did not look like much. Nothing to indicate you were in front of the house of a hero. But when you went in, Heavens to Betsy! . . . From the cellar to the attic, the whole place looked heroic, even the garden!" (7–9). If it is not already odd to call someone's house and garden heroic, the irony of this description is underlined by the way in which the narrator/author explains how Tartarin's exotic plants, such as his cacti or baobab tree, were all very small in size, but still so admirable, and that all his weapons on display were arranged, polished, and labeled, "as in a pharmacy." The comment that he never would have dared to enter the house without the obliging cautionary cards on the walls next to the supposedly loaded weapons and poisoned arrows, is also wrought with irony. This suggests that the cards are only there to have a certain effect on the visitor.

Moreover, the narration is peppered with narratorial/authorial exclamations. These interruptions serve various purposes. They express empathy or pity for the protagonist (the frequent "*pauvre*" or "*malheureux*" Tartarin), emphasize a turning point in the narrative, and focus on storytelling as a performance. The exclamations also often contrast with the story's events to ironic effect, or poke fun at Tartarin's "heroic" self-image, as happens in the passage that describes Tartarin's precautions against his alleged enemies on his way to his club. Tartarin has self-appointed imaginary "enemies," and the narrator says that he is disappointed that he is never attacked by "them." The narrator exclaims, "But, alas! by a derision of destiny, never, ever, did Tartarin of Tarascon have the good luck to make a bad encounter. Not even a dog, not even a drunkard. Nothing!" (29). Tartarin's hunting trip to Algeria does constitute a real adventure of its own, but the reader soon becomes aware that the praise of any heroism in this endeavor should not be taken at face value.

The dynamic changes in the narrative tone might also justify the use of the narrator concept. Sometimes the narrator/author pretends to be as naïve or illusional as Tartarin, as happens during the initial visit to the antihero's home. The interesting question is whether the act of narration thus also becomes the target of irony. At least, there is much potential humor in the ambiguity vis-à-vis the witness narrator's knowledge and judgement. Later, however, the narrator/author reveals that he knows clearly more than the protagonist does, thus pointing out that Tartarin is disillusioned. Some narratorial judgments, or if you like, author's evaluations, invite the readers to consider the protagonist's illusions: "This is what Tartarin would have seen, if he had taken the trouble, but, entirely engrossed in his leonine passion, the man of Tarascon went straight ahead, without looking either to the right or to the left, the eye stubbornly fixed on his imaginary monster, which never appeared" (148). The narrator/author also claims near supreme authority over his character when he illustrates the contradictions in Tartarin's mind by presenting a dialogue between the separate personalities of "Tartarin-Quixote" and "Tartarin-Sancho."

Does it make sense, then, to refer to a narrator instead of the author, or are there still other possibilities? Daudet's novel treats storytelling as a kind of performance. Therefore, the reader needs to examine the way in which the story is told. Furthermore, part of the humor in this novel is that there is a narrating agent who alters his capacities, including the scope of his knowledge or judgment and his presence in the story, to create particular effects, such as to pretend to his protagonist that he may be similarly naive. Perhaps we could even say that the storyteller assumes some of the qualities of his protagonist.

Does the novel, in fact, have a narrator, separate from the author, at least in those parts of the story where narration can be characterized as a storytelling performance? Possibly, but that is not the only option. Even if it may be logical to say that there is a narrator in the story beyond the first chapter, it is not a given that this narrator is merely fictional or different from the real author. Perhaps we also need to decide whether there is one or several narrators. The inconsistencies in the narration complicate any reference to a narrator as the source of the discourse. It can certainly be said that the narrator is fictional when he implies that he has been present in the world of the story, yet is this a sufficient reason to say that he is fictional for the entire novel? A Genettian pan-narrator narratologist (if such a caricature is allowed) might want to posit various agents responsible for different functions in this regard, including the first anonymous homodiegetic narrator, and the subsequent, primarily heterodiegetic narrator, and then postulate hierarchical relations among these levels of narration. But this strategy might also make it more difficult to arrive at a historical understanding of the literary devices that are involved here. In fact, for anyone engaged in so-called diachronic narratology, it is worth asking whether it makes sense to begin the narrative analysis by engaging in a narratological categorization.

Nonetheless, to refer to the author as the narrator in this case is also potentially problematic, since then we would need to accept that Daudet, at times, pretends to belong to the story that he tells, and that he sometimes pretends to be someone other than who he is, acting out the role of an oral storyteller in a written narrative. Furthermore, the narrative voice alternates between reliable and unreliable moments.

The main conclusion that I must draw here is that the dynamic and inconsistent qualities of the narrating instance pose a challenge to both the narrator concept and the concept that the narrator equals the historical author. The fictional narrator concept is awkward here, especially if it is understood in the sense of "a specifiable inner-textual, highest-level speech or communication position functioning as the point of origin of the discourse" (Margolin 2014), but referring to the author as the narrator also does not seem to do justice to the complex effects of the storytelling performance. The solution that I prefer is to focus on the narrative and rhetorical effects of this performance, the multiplicity of voices at play in the text, including forms of narrative and narratorial instability, and perceive all these aspects in light of the author's choices for artistic and rhetorical reasons. One significant feature of the performance is the capacity to move among various positions of knowledge, attitude, judgment, and degrees of control over the story. Thus, the narrative agent pretends, for humorous purposes, to not always be in total charge of his narrative, that is, the agent is incapable of channeling any narrative information beyond what the protagonist knows and understands, and is unable to evaluate the facts of the fictional world any better than his character.

In addition, there is a literary historical advantage in perceiving the narrative agent in Daudet's novel in terms of the historical author's storytelling role rather than as a fictional narrator. Doing so may allow us to better conceptualize the author's intentions in creating such a protagonist and writing a story as a quixotic parody of popular nineteenth-century great hunters' stories. Typically, such stories emphasize the author's sincerity, honesty in description, and observations based on experience. Daudet meant his novel to be read against this background, such as Charles Laurent Bombonnel's best seller *Le Tueur des panthères, ses chasses* (1860), which describes in first-person mode the writer's panther hunting in Algeria in the 1850s, or Jules Gérard's *La Chasse au lion* (1855), also based on Algerian hunting experiences. Gérard was called the Lion Killer (*Tueur de lions*), the epithet used for Tartarin. Tartarin's self-importance and propensity for exaggeration is in full contradistinction to Bombonnel, who advances a rather modest image of himself in his hunting book; furthermore, Daudet's flamboyant and not always trustworthy narrative voice also creates a striking contrast here. Daudet emphasizes the parody by making Bombonnel a character in a comical scene, where Tartarin, who does not recognize the famous hunter, brags to him about having hunted with Monsieur Bombonnel "more than twenty times."

The Argument against the Graphic Narrator in Comics

Let us now move on to the transmedial argument against the pan-narrator concept to see if we can detect some shared principles with the above-discussed literary historical reservations. Here, I take as my starting point two graphic adaptations of *Tartarin de Tarascon* by Pierre Guilmard and Louisa Djouadi (2010), and Isabelle Merlet and Jean Jacques Rouger (2009). The noticeably different narrative strategies in the verbal narration of these comic books will allow me to evaluate the (ir)relevance of the narrator concept in third-person comics. Neither of these works employs the device of the introductory "vanishing" narrator. One probable reason for this is medium-specific: it is not common to picture a character-narrator in the images in the third-person context (though sometimes images depict the frame narrative or the narrator figure engaged in the act of telling). It is also relatively uncommon in this medium, especially in fictional comics, to use a consistent verbal narrative track that is situated outside the fictional world.

Narration in Merlet and Rouger's two-volume *Les aventures prodigieuses de Tartarin de Tarascon* relies, predominantly, on what is shown in the images and the characters' speech and thought representation (dialogue or short soliloquy).[4] The narratorial commentaries are rather infrequent, including short captions from one or two words to two sentences, in ten narrative boxes in volume 1 and eighteen narrative boxes in volume 2, spread evenly in the forty-eight-page-long albums. The beige background color of the boxes indicates that the source of the words is outside the fictional world. The commentaries serve various functions, many of which are highly conventional in longer formats of comics, and not only in the European comics album. The commentaries perform many narrative tasks. They indicate the present time and place, affirm the main character's identity ("That Sunday in 1865, Tartarin was not yet the popular hero that he would soon become"; translation mine); specify the passing of time between the panels ("Three weeks were still needed for (real) preparations"); mark repetition ("They would buy pipes. Dozens of pipes! A great gross of pipes!!"); confirm a turning point in the narrative ("Finally, one night . . ."); summarize recent events or the characters' sentiments ("More time passes, and the king remains in his kingdom. But in the small court, impatience grows!"), and cast the main character or the villagers in an ironic light ("I told you: he was the King!").

How can the reader conceive of the narrating instance behind the infrequent narratorial comments, indications, and statements? It seems counterintuitive to attribute these captions to a narrator. The comic book does not suggest a sense of a continuing voice or a narrator's continuing consciousness frame as a source behind the voice, nor is it conceivable that the same narrative agent would oversee the visual component of the story. Typically, in comics, and especially in third-person narration, captions serve limited purposes, and are subjected to the other means of narration such as the display of images (action, description, embodiment, etc.), and the representation of direct speech, as their prop and aid. Generally, in comics, the captions are often so simple as to be without tone.

Fig. 2. Tartarin is not happy about his life despite his many talents. Pierre Guilmard and Louisa Djouadi, *Tartarin de Tarascon*. Grenoble: Glénat, 2010, 4.

Pierre Guilmard and Louisa Djouadi's version of *Tartarin de Tarascon* employs much more verbal first-person narration. A narrative voice is heard on nearly every page of the album, and the comic features long passages with captions in every panel. The longest and most noticeable of these passages is the album's beginning: the first three and a half pages in the story include captions in all panels but one. Later, the passages with and without captions alternate in a steady rhythm. Most of the captions are citations from Daudet's novel, and often whole sentences are quoted verbatim. This technique aligns with the other adaptations in the Romans de Toujours series that try to maintain a sense of fidelity to the writer's language. Thus the tone of the verbal narration comes directly from Daudet's storyteller. I presume that another reason for using the first-person narrative voice in the beginning is rhetorical, and like the function of the vanishing narrators and focalizers in nineteenth-century novels, it introduces the reader to the fictional world and its characters.

Nevertheless, why does the narrative voice in this adaptation remain clearly less pervasive than in Daudet's novel? Perhaps the most evident explanation is the seminal role of visual showing and direct discourse without any reference to a narrator. In fact, after the introductory beginning, much of the narration is delegated to showing and speech/thought representation. In the passages without captions, the nonnarratorial "action and speech" passages move the story forward in their own right, and it is counterintuitive to imagine a narrating instance, a graphic narrator or a show-er, who would be their source. Another explanation is the limited number of words in the captions, which is partly due to the need to shorten the story in the adaptation but also is related to general medium-specific qualities, such as the default expectation that much of the story is told through images. Furthermore, beyond the beginning, the functions of verbal narration in the rest of Guilmard and Djouadi's album become further limited. While the Daudet-style interventions continue throughout the narrative, the more conventional "narratorial" indications of time passed, summary, and emphasis on the turning points in the plot become more frequent.

Another means of narration in Merlet and Rouger's adaptation that could potentially refer to a narrator are pictorial metaphors. These include, for instance, Tartarin's thought balloon that has the shape of the continent of Africa; the flames in his fireplace that turn into a menacing lion; the clouds over the approaching coast of Algeria that look like ferocious lions; the reflection of a sea horizon and crescent moon on his eyeglasses, and the clouds of imagination, showing the protagonist fighting with three lions in the air, as Tartarin begins his tall tale of his hunting adventure. All these instances illustrate something that Tartarin does not actually see but that he feels, thinks, or experiences, such as an emotion, or a preconceived notion. For instance, the Africa-shaped thought balloon that fills almost the whole panel where Tartarin is seen sitting on his bed, includes the words "Shipwrecks! Rheumatisms! High fevers! Quicksand! Elephantiasis! Plague!" This points out that Tartarin is overtaken by anxiety as he needs to make good on his promise to go hunt lions in Africa. His anxiety stems from preconceived notions about African diseases and fear of being shredded by the beasts.

Visual metaphors, which are based on the juxtaposition or fusion of pictorial elements from different conceptual frames, require that the reader first recognize and then process the different frames of meaning that are joined in comparison (such as the shape of Africa and the shape of someone's thoughts). They are not part of the reality of the fictional world, but rather they present an interpretation of the character's

Fig. 3. Tartarin gets anxious about having to go to Africa. Isabelle Merlet and Jean-Jacques Rouger, *Les aventures prodigieuses de Tartarin de Tarascon.* Paris: Delcourt, 2009, 1:30.

states of mind, emotions, attitudes, and conceptions for the reader's assessment. To understand their meaning, however, does not require the positing of a graphic narrator. In fact, we could apprehend them as non-narrated, comparable to the way in which Maria Nikolajeva and Carole Scott see the status of words (or what they call intra-iconic texts) that appear inside pictures in picture books and that comment on the primary narrative or provide an interpretive strategy (2001, 118). What suffices for comprehension is to recognize the function of the metaphorical elements, that is, the way in which the metaphors are *intended* to represent the character's mental state, emotions, and subjective perspective. This intention can be assessed from what is shown or narrated verbally and how these two relate to each other, without considering narratorial filtering. In the above example, the cues of that intention are predominantly visual: the perspective in the first frame of the citation makes the protagonist look smaller than his thoughts, and the expressive use of the thought balloon's shape further suggests that his anxiety intimately relates to, or is framed by, his perception of Africa. Furthermore, the immediately preceding frame, a close-up image that focuses on the protagonist's downcast eyes accompanied by the quotation *Je suis fichu*! ("I'm finished!"), orients the reader to the character's emotional state.

Here, the pan-narrator theorist might want to claim that the graphic style of comics, the drawing and showing of images in a certain way, or the interaction between visual and verbal style, indicates a source of narration, as in the arguments that have been voiced in relation to third-person narratives in prose fiction. One could then claim, to quote Monika Fludernik, that "in terms of readers' reactions to individual texts, the tendency to attribute stylistic features to a hypothetical narrator persona and/or character is a simple fact" (2001, 622). In this multimodal context, however, the "style means narrator" argument is weak for several reasons. Verbal style, for instance, is less indicative of a narrator since, with the exception of autobiographical comics and fictional autobiographies, authorial diction or the use of a continuous narrative verbal track has a more limited role in the medium. Another immediate challenge in this regard is the significance of the *relation* between the two modalities of words and images, as regards their potentially different ways of implying autodiegetic and heterodiegetic perspectives or the grammatical category of person. Therefore, it is also more difficult to make a case for the "second author" thesis in third-person comics than in modern prose fiction. In her reading of Thomas Mann's *Death in Venice*, Dorrit Cohn contends that an audible but impersonal narrator is "at the service of individual psychology" (1978, 26), and thereby develops her idea of "discordant narration," which refers to a heterodiegetic narrator who "audibly proclaims his or her subjective opinions" (2000, 307). While Cohn's careful analysis makes evident the complexities of voice in Mann's novella, we cannot generalize from it the usefulness of the "second author" thesis. In the multimodal medium of comics, the positing of such an instance is potentially even more problematic, given that it requires creating the illusion that the visual showing of the images is delegated to a narrator who is different from the author or authors. Moreover, any assessment of a person's grammatical status in this medium should take into consideration the importance of visual narration that may show the first-person narrator systematically from the outside.

In other words, another reason to doubt the "style-means-narrator" argument is that the stylistic features of drawing do not typically "vouchsafe" (to use Fludernik's word) the narrator's presence in comics. In graphic narratives, the default assumption is generally to attribute stylistic choices to the cartoonist, as an expression of the cartoonist's artistry, not to any narrator. Another commonly available option is to perceive style as the result of collective work and cooperation between the cartoonist, the writer, and the other artists involved (essentially, the penciller, the inker, the colorist, and the letterer). Moreover, stylistic choices can be perceived in relation to a particular genre, publication format, or production line.

Nevertheless, a comic may occasionally suggest that the narrator-character is fictively responsible, in whole or in part, for some of the images or the given graphic style. Some examples include David Mazzucchelli's graphic novel *Asterios Polyp* (2009), in which the narrator, the protagonist's stillborn twin brother Ignazio, points to a relief image of his brother and states that "THIS is Asterios Polyp," thus implying that he is showing the images; Matti Hagelberg's I-narrator in issue 18 of the comic book *Läskimooses*, who refers to the way in which he drew the images in the story; and the *Family Circus* strips where seven-year-old Billy takes over the drawing of his father's strip in his own naïve style. Morrison, Truog, and Hazlewood's *Animal Man* issue 5 includes a three-page "Gospel according to Crafty" that is drawn in the style of Looney Tunes and Merrie Melodies cartoons, thus suggesting that a character called Crafty may be its narrator *and* cartoonist. In the same installment of *Animal Man*, the visual depiction of the artist's fingers and pencil, which self-ironically stand for God in Crafty's gospel, suggest another ontological metalepsis that violates the distinction between different diegetic levels and their presumably distinct ontological domains.

The self-conscious play with narrative conventions in metaleptic infraction implies that what one sees and reads in the sequence is what the narrator-character fictionally presents to viewing. This is related to the perhaps more common instance of metalepsis in comics in which the images or visual style, or both, temporarily present a character's experience in the sense of an extended perception image, that is, the visual style, shape, color, or perspective of the image indicates a character's mental state. These include, for instance, several strips in the *Calvin and Hobbes* series that are shown according to Calvin's imagination, character Polza's visions that intercept the narration in Manu Larcenet's *Blast*, and Nao Brown's panic attacks in Glyn Dillon's *The Nao of Brown* (see Mikkonen 2017, 119–24, 190–91). Here, the reader is cued into thinking that what is seen is only true in terms of the character's experience, mental state, or imagination.

Such violations of ontological levels, however, do not justify the use of an implicit narrator concept. Rather, they call for careful attention to complexities in narrative transmission, since the selection of the images, their perspective, and graphic style may sometimes reflect a character's mind. In this respect, Seymour Chatman's conclusion that he draws from a brief analysis of the effects of voice-over narration in Alain Resnais's film *Providence* (1977) exemplifies the weakness of the pan-narrator assumption. While we may accept that viewers need to eventually surmise that the protagonist, expressed by novelist Clive Langham's voice-over, "is somehow constructing the images filling the screen" (1990, 133)—in other words, that the images are to some extent at the service of Langham's thoughts and fantasies—the conclusion that the voice-over narrator is replaced by "an impersonal extradiegetic narrator" (133) is problematic for various reasons. First, there is little justification for the kind of symmetry between different narrative media, on the level of narrative structure, that Chatman seeks. Chatman finds it "awkward" for "a general theory of narrative to say that some texts include the component 'narrator' and others do not" (133). Thus, the notion of a medium-independent narrator concept is deemed a precondition for transmedial narratology. Second, the concept of the impersonal cinematic narrator, who "is not a human being" but a theoretical construct, is a complicated schematic that seems of little use in actual narrative analysis. Various film theorists have questioned the idea that a cinematic narrator would present "the fictional events that are shown in images selected by the filmmaker" (Thomson-Jones 2007, 82) even if they may accept, to use Thomson-Jones's formulation, that films can draw the viewers' "attention to a kind of intelligence at work in visual narration" (85). Furthermore, perhaps the most important reason for this rejection is that the notion of the cinematic narrator requires us to distinguish between presentation and selection, and, furthermore, to attribute these actions to different agents (82).

Third, the positing of the cinematic narrator in films or the graphic narrator in comics not only multiplies the narrating agents but also postulates questionable hierarchies among these agents. Chatman, for instance, establishes a hierarchy among a possible voice-over fictional narrator, the general cinematic narrator to whom the voice-over is a cinematic device, and the implied author, to whom both the voice-over narrator and the cinematic narrator are instruments (1990, 133–34). For Thierry Groensteen, the hierarchy of narrating instances in comics is essentially that of acting narrators (*narrateur actorialisé*), such as narrator-characters; the reciting narrator, who is responsible for the captions; the "monstrator" (or show-er), who is responsible for showing the images, and the fundamental narrator, who controls the narrative whole and to whom all the previous agents are subjected (Groensteen 2011, 109–10; my critique in Mikkonen 2017, 131–36). Thus, such models shift attention to the relationship between the posited agents, and suggest that the study of these relationships is the true goal of narrative analysis.

Some General Arguments for Optional-Narrator Theory

Drawing on these literary historical and transmedial observations, we can identify some general pragmatic principles that speak in favor of the optional-narrator theory across both various media and historical periods. The first principle is the need to avoid the personalization of the narrative function by positing a narrator when none is needed. The rationale for this requirement is the potential to make narrative analysis more accurate, transparent, and self-aware. Thus, instead of constructing a narrator to make sense of the text, one can begin by making sense of the textual indications of a possible narrating instance and, subsequently, assess the need for positing any personalized narrating agent. The optional-narrator theory allows us to do just that: begin the analysis by first evaluating whether a fictional narrative has a fictional narrator (Köppe and Stühring 2015, 15).

The above-raised historical and medium-specific questions about Daudet's novel and its two adaptations highlight the essential pragmatic question, Why do we need to refer to a personalized narrating agent, who is responsible for the narrative, in the first place? The immediate response is that this is the case whenever there is sufficient reason to think that the person telling the story is not the one who crafted the story. In such cases the reader is prompted to pay attention to a narrating instance, who is make-believedly responsible for some significant degree of the narrating. In Genette's terms, therefore, "the narrating itself is implicated in the narrative" ([1972] 1980, 31); that is, the story draws attention to the when, where, and who of narrating, and demands an answer to the question of how the readers have access to the fictional world. But the optional-narrator approach allows that a narrator need not be posited before the question of the narrator's choices, as different from the actual writer's choices, becomes somehow relevant. This condition may further help us to ask more precise questions about the art of indirection, also involving instabilities of source and voice, in narrative discourse.

Another related principle is that lack of consistency in narrative agency can be important in itself: it can serve an artistic objective. For instance, whenever there is enough evidence to say that a narrative is at least partially fictionally narrated by a personalized narrator, we can nevertheless presume that this narrator does not have to be a consistent source of the whole narrative. We could also call this principle artistic "narratorhood": a fictional narrator is an artistic device that can be used for limited strategic purposes, even resulting in antinarrative textual effects (the disappeared narrator never returns) employed "inconsistently," or intermittently (see Walsh 1997, 507–8), to further a particular rhetorical purpose or artistic effect. Moreover, the representation of the act of narration can be subjected to functions other than narrating, such as creating a specific effect (humor, irony, suspense, curiosity, surprise), perspective taking, or a sense of storytelling performance that is as much the point of the narrative as the story told. The two comic format adaptations of Daudet's novel do not respond to the same narrative instabilities that I have identified in the novel. Nevertheless, Pierre Guilmard's version, like Daudet's novel, uses a strategic voice in the beginning to introduce the readers to the protagonist and the fictional world.

As much work in optional-narrator theory has shown, the problem of the pan-narrator theory is most evident in third-person narration. At the same time, however, it is crucial for optional-narrator theory to avoid making a sharp distinction between first-person and third-person narrative forms. One reason for this need is that the first-person narrative situation in fiction can also be highly inconsistent (with changes to third-person narration, for instance); include sentences whose words cannot have a source in the first-person narrator (see Nielsen 2004); or involve skillfully crafted ambiguities between author and narrator-character, as Genette has observed in relation to Proust and Stendhal. These instances of narratorial infraction, transgression of the knowledge frame, and ambivalent or composite voice make evident that not everything in the text can be understood as the fictional first-person narrator's communication.

Still another general reason, but perhaps less a principle, in favor of optional-narrator theory is the relevance of authorship and authorial intention in understanding the story. While the optional-narrator theories do not privilege the textual indications of authorial intention, or presume that such indications are always possible to detect, they provide a flexible approach to study the relationship between authors and narrating instance. One of the strongest cases, if not the strongest case, for using the narrator concept in the analysis of literary fictions is that of personalized narrators in realist fiction and modern prose who must be distinguished from the actual author. In this respect, the narrator concept is useful for combatting simplified interpretations in the vein of biographical criticism that equate narrator-characters, or other voices in the fiction, with the author. The introduction of the narrator concept in high school and university courses on literary analysis also offers an important means of illustrating the variety of narrative situations, voices and perspectives, and their complex relations in modern literature. But a real disadvantage of this approach is what Jonathan Culler calls "dubious naturalization," which makes the narrator the source of all the details in the story and subsequently evaluates all these details as the narrator's choices, and does so within a communicational model based on everyday storytelling situations, instead of perceiving them as the artist's choices that are made to create a specific effect in literary fiction (2018, 247–48).

Finally, optional-narrator theories offer a useful approach for investigating the relationship between narrative discourse, a particular genre and corpus, and a given medium. Transmedial narratology, which aims to develop the analysis of strategies of narrative representation across media (Thon 2016, xviii), should focus on the medium-specific differences, and transmedial similarities, in the way in which the act of narration may be delegated to a fictional source.[5] In this regard, one should especially try to avoid sweeping generalizations about narrative instance and agency based on a limited medium-specific corpus. For instance, while *some* visual narratives can imply that there is a narrator (or a kind of visual guide) by visual and stylistic means only, this possibility cannot justify the argument that there are *implicit* narrators in all visual narratives. Subjective style, or the tone of telling, do not necessarily imply that some impersonal narrator tells the story from a fictional point of view outside the story. Instead, stylistic choices can originate solely from the writer, the artist, or, as is also often the case in the medium of comics, collective authorship. In fact, we should consider the differences in commonsense assumptions about authorship in narrative media, such as comics and films, that are usually collectively produced and have collective authorship, since these assumptions influence the positing of both the narrator and the author concept. In visual or multimodal narration, in general, where narrators generally play a more limited role, it is also less evident how a possible confusion between author and narrator could take place. Optional-narrator approaches can help to develop the analysis of those textual features or contextual reasons that affect the choice of one option over another in narrative transmission.

Notes

1. For Genette, the narrating instance "refers to something like the narrating situation, the narrative matrix-the entire set of conditions (human, temporal, spatial) out of which a narrative statement is produced" ([1972] 1980, 31n10).
2. Still another unusual narrator in the novel is an old stagecoach that gets to tell a tale in a conversation with Tartarin.
3. Their discussion neglects some potential indications of narrator/author in Hawthorne's short story, such as gnomic statements, perspectival techniques, indirect discourse, and self-reference, but these features do not create a voice effect that could be compared to Daudet's novel.
4. One exception is the background story of Saint Martha, the monster Tarasque, and how the village of Tarascon was given its name, and that is told by a longer written passage on the first spread of volume 1.
5. Thon's term "non-narratorial representation" (attributed to authors or author collectives, 2016, 153) reflects the needs of transmedial narratology to compare the means of narration across different media. The term is, however, problematic for its dependence on the narrator notion, as it is defined by way of the narrator's absence, and for tying together a wide range of means of narration, which may play a more prominent role in their respective media than narrating through a narrator, including audiovisual representation in films or showing by images in comics.

References

Chatman, Seymour. 1990. *Coming to Terms: The Rhetoric of Narrative in Fiction and Film*. Ithaca NY: Cornell University Press.

Cohn, Dorrit. 1978. *Transparent Minds: Narrative Modes for Presenting Consciousness in Fiction*. Princeton: Princeton University Press.

———. 2000. "Discordant Narration." *Style* 34 (2): 307–16.

Culler, Jonathan. 2018. "Naturalization in 'Natural' Narratology." *Partial Answers: Journal of Literature and the History of Ideas* 16 (2): 243–49.

Daudet, Alphonse. (1872) 1997. *Aventures prodigieuses de Tartarin de Tarascon*. Paris: Librairie Générale Française.

———. (1872) 2018. *Tartarin of Tarascon*. Translated and illustrated by Robert Schoolcraft. New York: MS Books Publishing. Kindle.

Fludernik, Monika. 2001. "New Wine in Old Bottles? Voice, Focalization, and New Writing." *New Literary History* 32 (3): 619–38.

Genette, Gérard. (1972) 1980. *Narrative Discourse: An Essay in Method*. Translated by Jane E. Lewin. Ithaca NY: Cornell University Press.

Groensteen, Thierry. 2011. *Bande dessinée et narration (Système de la bande dessinée 2)*. Paris: Presses universitaires de France.

Guilmard, Pierre, and Louisa Djouadi. 2010. *Tartarin de Tarascon*. "Romans de toujours" series. Créteil, France: Éditions Adonis.

Hamon, Philippe. 1992. "On the Major Features of Realist Discourse." In *Realism*, edited by Lilian R. Furst, 166–85. London: Longman.

Jong, Irene J. F. de. 2014. "The Anonymous Traveller in European Literature: A Greek Meme?" In *Defining Greek Narrative*, edited by Ruth Scodel and Douglas Cairns, 314–33. Edinburgh: Edinburgh University Press.

Köppe, Tilmann, and Jan Stühring. 2015. "Against Pragmatic Arguments for Pan-Narrator Theories: The Case of Hawthorne's 'Rappaccini's Daughter.'" In *Author and Narrator: Transdisciplinary Contributions to a Narratological Debate*, edited by Dorothee Birke and Tilmann Köppe, 13–43. Berlin: De Gruyter.

Margolin, Uri. (2012) 2014. "Narrator." In *The Living Handbook of Narratology*, edited by Peter Hühn, Jan Christoph Meister, John Pier, and Wolf Schmid. http://www.lhn.uni-hamburg.de/article/narrator.

Merlet, Isabelle, and Jean-Jacques Rouger. 2009. *Les aventures prodigieuses de Tartarin de Tarascon*, 2 vols. Paris: Delcourt.

Mikkonen, Kai. 2011. "The Implicit Narrator in Comics: Transformations of Free Indirect Discourse in Two Graphic Adaptations of *Madame Bovary*." *International Journal of Comic Art* 13 (2): 473–87.

———. 2017. *The Narratology of Comic Art*. London: Routledge.

Nielsen, Henrik Skov. 2004. "The Impersonal Voice in First-Person Narrative Fiction." *Narrative* 12 (2): 133–50.

Nikolajeva, Maria, and Carole Scott. 2001. *How Picturebooks Work*. New York: Garland Publishing.

Thomson-Jones, Katherine. 2007. "The Literary Origins of the Cinematic Narrator." *British Journal of Aesthetics* 47 (1): 76–94.

Thon, Jan-Noël. 2016. *Transmedial Narratology and Contemporary Media Culture*. Lincoln: University of Nebraska Press.

Walsh, Richard. 1997. "Who Is the Narrator?" *Poetics Today* 18 (4): 495–513.

13   A Paradox of Cinematic Narration

PAISLEY LIVINGSTON

Consider the propositions expressed by the following three sentences:

(1) Some cinematic works are narrations.
(2) A work is a narration only if it has one or more narrators.
(3) Some of the cinematic works that are narrations have no narrator.

This collection of propositions is a paradox in the sense that there are reasons why each proposition appears to be sound when considered on its own, yet the collection is inconsistent.[1]

What reasons make the three propositions appear to be sound? Briefly, proposition (1) would appear to find ample support in the truism that many films convey stories *and are therefore narrations*. Expert opinion also supports (1). There are many excellent book-length studies on film narration, and these studies apparently have a real object.[2] As for (2), this proposition would appear to follow cogently from truisms about the nature of narratives and narrations, starting with the idea that in the absence of some narrating activity, there can be no narration. If we then ask who or what it is that narrates, the obvious reply is "narrators," which apparently leads to (2). Yet proposition (3) also appears to be sound. Some films obviously include bits of "voice-over" narration, but many others convey a story without using this device. Is there some other kind of narrator "had" by all of these narrative films? It is not immediately apparent that there is any such thing, from which it may seem to follow that there are some cinematic narrations without narrators. In other words, having a narrator may be "optional" to cinematic narration.[3]

In spite of these apparently good reasons supporting each of the three propositions, they are jointly inconsistent. Proposition (2) identifies having a narrator as a necessary condition for being a narration, while (3) maintains that some narrations have no narrator. So (2) and (3) obviously contradict each other.

How might this paradox be resolved? A genuine solution of a philosophical paradox requires us to restore consistency by replacing one or more of the propositions. It also requires an explanation of how it seemed to be the case that incompatible propositions were all true. One reason why it might wrongly appear that both (2) and (3) are true is equivocation. Perhaps one is thinking of a very broad sense of "narrator" when favorably entertaining (2), and of some narrower concept when assenting to proposition (3). If that is right, (2) and (3) should be replaced by propositions involving a single, defensible concept of narrators.

How, then, might "narrator" be explicated for the purposes of a revision of (2) and (3)? Given just how divisive theorizing on this topic has been, it may be prudent to take one's point of departure in examples that are highly or even entirely uncontroversial. It is widely accepted, for example, that in writing his *Confessions*, Augustine of Hippo narrated various events from his life, including his youthful fascination with the theatre. His narrational activities include writing the text of this autobiographical work and presenting it to future readers as a sincere and truthful account. Authoring a work in which he narrated a series of events in his life sufficed to make Augustine the narrator of that work.[4] There is nothing fictional about Augustine's narrational activities and achievements, which is not to say that everything he claimed was true.[5]

So here we have a first, uncontroversial kind of actual narrator, namely, the author of a narrative work. We can find many less elevated examples of the same kind in the realm of everyday utterances, such as "Paolo narrated the events of his journey in an email to his friend," and "The three eyewitnesses narrated how the accident occurred in strikingly incompatible ways."

Creating the text of a narrative is sufficient to being a narrator, but is it necessary? It would be if the only way to narrate something were to produce a written sequence of words. Yet that is not the case. Spoken narration also suffices, and it is generally allowed that images can also be used to convey a story. A comic strip devoid of verbal captions can be a narration.[6] The author of a silent film uses motion pictures to narrate the events in the lives of fictional characters. And so on. To generalize on the basis of these examples, we can say that a sufficient condition of being a narrator is actually creating some "vehicle" (a text, spoken discourse, sequence of images, etc.) that represents a story (i.e., situations and events). If this were also a necessary condition for being a narrator, only the actual authors of narrative utterances or works would be narrators. That, however, is not widely believed, as there are uncontroversial examples of a different kind of narrator.

One such example is provided by William Makepeace Thackeray's 1844 novel *The Luck of Barry Lyndon*. Thackeray, the actual author of the work, wrote the text of this novel in such a way that the reader is prompted to imagine that it is Barry Lyndon himself who has authored a first-person account of his life. In other words, it is *fictionally* true, or true in the story, that Lyndon is the writer or speaker of the tale, and he is so from the beginning to the end of the text. Lyndon is therefore what Gregory Currie calls a "controlling narrator" (1995, 265). This means it is fictionally true that the narrator is responsible for creating the entire text of the work. Controlling narrators can be contrasted to "partial" ones, who are fictionally responsible for authoring some parts of the work's expressive vehicle.

As for Lyndon's purpose in writing the narrative, Thackeray has Lyndon declare that "every word of this narrative of my life is of the most sacred veracity" (Thackeray [1844] 2001, 34). Thackeray obviously did not believe this statement, not only because Lyndon was just a figment of his imagination but also because this figment is to be imagined as a deeply mendacious character whose self-characterizations are frequently misleading. So here we have a case where there is a clear distinction between a work of fiction's actual narrator—the author—and its fictional narrator, the central character. This distinction makes a difference to the appreciation of the work. To appreciate this novel adequately, one must be attuned to the multiple ways in which the author's and fictional narrator's aims and perspectives diverge. The author, but not the fictional narrator, means for us to see through the narrator-character's flimsy excuses, boasting, and laughable rationalizations. The author's satirical performance resembles a skillful act of ventriloquism. The fictional narrator is like a puppet who is meant to betray his own unreliability while trying not to do so. As we sift through Lyndon's claims, we admire and enjoy Thackeray's insightful representation of this character's multiple foibles and vices.

This example illustrates the fact that in some works of fiction there is a significant difference between the actual authorial narrator and the fictional narrator. The actual author is responsible for making the expressive or communicative vehicle, such as a text or audiovisual display, by means of which some audience is invited, implicitly or explicitly, to imagine that such-and-such is the case.[7] The author fashions the vehicle in such a way that the audience is to imagine that there is some other figure, namely, a fictional narrator, who is at least partly responsible for the text's production. In this example, the division of labor between actual and imagined narrators is straightforward: whereas the author does not assert that the narrated events literally occurred in the actual world, the fictional narrator is imagined as relating events to us with the at least apparent conviction that they actually occurred.

Are there cinematic works of fiction where this kind of distinction between the authorial narrator and a fictional narrator readily applies? If we consider partial as opposed to controlling narrators, the distinction does apply well to many cases. Whenever there are bits of "voiceover" narration during the film, as is the case, for example, in many of Terrence Malick's films, there is one or more cinematic narrator, that is, whoever it is in the story who speaks these lines. Uptake of these partial narrator's utterances can be important to the appreciation of the work.

There are a few cinematic analogues to the *controlling* narrators in literary works. An early example is *David Holzman's Diary* (directed by Jim McBridge, 1967). What we see and hear in the audiovisual display is fictionally the autobiographical movie made by David Holzman, a character dreamt up by the actual author, McBridge. Another example is Vincent Lanoo's 2001 *Strass*, a work of fiction consisting of a nested nonfictional film about a theatre conservatory. With the exception of a disclaimer and the final credits, everything that is seen and heard in this work is meant to be the product of the documentarists whose filmmaking activities at the conservatory are partly depicted in the film.[8] This film clearly has fictional, controlling *filmmakers*, and unless one has a quite narrow understanding of narration (whereby narrating can only be done with words), it can be allowed that this film has a team of controlling *narrators*.

What are the implications of these elementary points for our task of reconsidering the paradox with which we began? Any cinematic narration that has an individual or collective author has by the same stroke at least one actual narrator. But do all cinematic narrations have authors? That question is controversial. It strikes me as ludicrous to deny that individually authored cinematic works exist. Collaborating authors can also function as joint narrators of a work. Yet there is also such a thing as accidental footage, such as what gets recorded when a cat inadvertently turns the device on with its paws. Perhaps it is good enough to say that cinematic *works*, as opposed to accidentally made images, necessarily have authors. Accidental audiovisual material could be appropriated and presented as a work, but that would require that someone acted in the role of author of the appropriation-art movie, the vehicle of which is "created" by being selected. One might protest that in such a case the appropriator-author does not actually narrate the events depicted in the video and so is not really a narrator. It would follow that there are narratorless video works. In any case, those who find that proposition (3) is at least apparently true are not likely to hold it to be true for the reason that there are some cinematic works having no authors. They are more likely to believe (3) because they note that many cinematic narrations lack a fictional, controlling narrator. That kind of narrator is indeed optional, and this is why (3) appears to be true.

A more capacious conception of narrators may come to mind when proposition (2), with its strong narration-narrator link, is considered. The thought might be charitably spelled out as follows:

(2′) A work is a narration only if it has one or more actual or fictional narrators, where a fictional narrator is fictionally responsible in the work for creating all or part of the narrational vehicle as a means to performing expressive or communicative actions.

Given (2′), in order to resolve the paradox, we also revise (3) accordingly:

(3′) For all cinematic works, w, where w is a narration, w has at least one narrator as required by (2′).

Given (2′) and (3′), coherence with (1) is regained.

This is a fairly "weak" solution given its generous disjunction allowing for either actual or fictional narrators, and given as well that the fictional ones need not be controlling narrators. Even so, although (1), (2′), and (3′) are consistent, it is not obvious that they are sound, and there is continued disagreement among experts in this regard. Some theorists assert, while others deny, that there are authorless works; some theorists deny, while others assert, that the use of a voice-over narrator suffices to give a cinematic narration a narrator in a suitably robust sense. Another source of ongoing disagreement is that some theorists believe that all cinematic narrations have a fictional narrator in some other, less-than-obvious sense. They think this kind of narrator is what makes (2′) true in a range of cases, whereas others would classify those cases as narrator-less narrations. It is also possible to argue, as I shall do below, that these less-than-obvious narrators are an undermotivated theoretical construction, and that the cinematic narrations in question have actual instead of fictional narrators. So it is at bottom a dispute over two different ways in which the conditions stated in (2′) and (3′) can be satisfied.

Here is an outline of a justification that is provided for the "less-than-obvious" narrators. This sort of narrator is a fictional entity, that is, one imagined appropriately in response to the work. As such, the narrational actions fictionally performed by this figure need not closely resemble what counts as narrating in the actual world, just as, for the sake of the story, the science and technology depicted in science fiction movies often depart radically from actual or even possible science and technology. The same can be said of what passes for medicine, psychology, university teaching, and so forth (the list is long) in many genres of cinematic fiction.

In what follows I shall critically explore this line of argumentation by discussing its possible application to an actual case. The example to which I turn in this regard is Roberto Enrico's celebrated *La rivière du hibou* (1961), a cinematic adaptation of the Ambrose Bierce story "An Occurrence at Owl Creek Bridge." Enrico's film is undoubtedly a narrative one. Moreover, it is a narrative with a deceptive twist. Readers who have yet to experience this work are forewarned that the following passages contain "spoilers." It is better to have seen the film (which is usually available on YouTube) before reading further.

At the beginning of the work, the spectator learns that the film's central character, Peyton Farquhar, has been captured by Union soldiers and is about to be hanged for spying. Viewers are shown the preparations for the hanging; they see that when the hanging is finally attempted, the rope breaks and Farquhar plunges into the river. Rapids carry him far away from his captors, and he makes his way through a forest to his home.

Just as Farquhar is about to reach the arms of his smiling wife, there is an abrupt cut to an image of Farquhar being hanged. The spectator is led to conclude that the elaborate escape that has taken up most of the film has only been a stylized representation of some hallucination or "vision" experienced by Farquhar just before his death. The spectator can rightly complain that he or she has been misled, but, on further viewings of the film, will likely remark that many clues along the way point to the conclusion that Farquhar's escape was merely a hallucination.[9]

These are uncontroversial facts about the film's narration. What is controversial is whether this film has a fictional narrator. Let's take a look at some reasons why one might favor a negative verdict on this score, in which case the likely conclusion would be that the narrating is done by the film's author, namely, Enrico and his team.

It seems quite clear, first of all, that Farquhar should not be taken as the narrator of his own story. He does not survive to tell the tale, nor is he narrating the relevant events to anyone as they unfold, since he is too preoccupied with trying to survive. If it is proposed that the film has a narrator because Farquhar narrates his escape to himself in his imagination (and that this is what the spectator somehow witnesses immediately), one may wonder what basis there is for such a conjecture. We see that Farquhar has very little time in which to fantasize about escaping; the vision or hallucination of his lengthy escape occurs in the very brief time between the beginning of his fall and the moment when the rope breaks his neck. He performs none of the basic actions required to generate an expressive vehicle that could be used to narrate anything.

If Farquhar is not the narrator of his own story, perhaps someone else in the domain of the story is. Yet this option is also problematic. Farquhar's "escape" is best understood to be a hallucination, a fleeting, perfectly private and subjective experience had in the instant prior to his death. How could anyone in the world of the story know that this condemned spy had such an illusory experience of escape? It could seem to follow that there is no fictional narrator of this narration.

The advocate of the less-than-obvious fictional narrator may object that this line of reasoning overlooks the different kinds of narrators that may satisfy the condition in (2′). The spectator of the film is not required to limit his or her inferences about the narrator to those that portray the narrator as a realistic character in the world of the story. The appreciator does not have to try to answer what Kendall L. Walton would call "silly questions" about how the story events could be known by a narrator.[10] All that is required is that it be *fictionally* the case that a narrator is at least partially responsible for the vehicle by means of which the narration is conducted. Perhaps it can be shown that such an imagining of a narrator's activity is warranted.

Here is a sketch of how that case might be made. First of all, it must be acknowledged that we do not have an immediate experience of the domain in which the story of Farquhar's execution occurs; instead we are selectively presented with images and sounds depicting a course of events in that realm.[11] Aspects of this presentation express a narrator's attitudes and rhetorical intentions. Detecting the latter need not give us a complex and plausible portrait of the narrator as a person but may nonetheless contribute crucially to the appreciation of the work. For example, the use of reaction shots and point-of-view shots at the outset of the film is clearly designed to signal Farquhar's concerns to the spectator. This cinematic rhetoric can, following Murray Smith (1995), be characterized as contributing to the viewer's "alignment" and "allegiance" with the protagonist. For example, the spectator is shown a shot of Farquhar as he raises his head and looks up to his left; this shot is followed immediately by a shot of what it is that has caught Farquhar's attention, namely, a soldier who has formed the noose and thrown it over the beam in preparation for the hanging. The editing structure thereby manifests the narrator's intention to promote the spectator's awareness of Farquhar's perspective and awareness. Other point-of-view and reaction shots allow us to infer that Farquhar is looking about, trying to identify avenues of escape. Shots depicting the direction of his gaze are followed by shots of the well-armed soldiers who stand on guard to block the way. Such narrational strategies are again indicative of a narrator's intention to direct the spectator's attention to Farquhar's concerns.

The narrator's expressive devices include deliberately arranged relations between the images and recorded sounds. For example, as Farquhar runs through the forest, we hear a raucous drumroll, which pauses now and then when the exhausted Farquhar pauses to catch his breath. We are not meant to imagine that the character hears this snare drum: there are no such sounds in the woods through which Farquhar runs, nor is he imagining or hallucinating this jazzy drum performance, which would be hopelessly anachronistic given the historical setting of 1860–64. The drumroll can be read as another of the narrator's expressive devices. It is the narrator who would have us compare the exhausted Farquhar's hectic flight through the woods to the syncopated clatter of the drumroll. If one is of the opinion that uptake of musical expressivity requires imagining an expressive persona, it might be added that that persona too plays a narrator's role in the film. Whether it is a matter of one or two narratorial agencies at this point is hard or even impossible to determine, which could be a problem for this account. The advocate of the less-than-obvious narrator may prefer to say that this is one of the "spots of indeterminacy" that the prudent appreciator does not try to fill in (just as Ingarden recommends; [1937] 1973, 293). Suffice it to imagine that somehow the narrator presents a drum performance that expresses the hectic and frenetic quality of Farquhar's flight.

Continuing in this vein, we may conjecture that it is the narrator who directs our gaze, along with Farquhar's, to the marvel of a spiderweb at the moment when he revels in being alive and wants to appreciate everything in God's creation. And it is the narrator who toys with our credulity in the film's final sequence. Having seemingly made his way back to his plantation, Farquhar rushes toward his smiling wife, somehow not quite reaching her. The narrator then cuts to a similar shot in which Farquhar is again shown running toward his wife; he covers the same ground, this time getting even closer to her. This kind of shot is repeated several times, and then, abruptly, the narrator cuts to a shot of Farquhar's hanging, forcing the viewers to draw the bleak conclusion that the entire escape was an illusion.

The foregoing remarks were meant to provide a sample of the ways in which a narrator-tracking approach to the film's narrational strategies can contribute to a fine-grained appreciation of the work. If that is indeed the right approach, this film is consistent with (2′), which does not require a controlling narrator. Instead, this is a case where some of the work's expressivity is attributed to a largely indeterminate and partial fictional narrator.

It may be objected, however, that this "specimen" of appreciation does not really establish that the film should be understood as having a fictional storyteller who is distinct from the author and fictionally responsible for partially creating the narration's vehicle. There are serious problems with the imaginative project this approach requires. Some of the imaginings it requires are irrelevant to an adequate appreciation of the work, and it fails to support other results that are required by an adequate appreciation.

To develop these criticisms, we note first of all that the putative narrator was described above as using shots, cuts, and recorded sounds to convey not only story events but also attitudes toward them. This is perfectly appropriate given that the appreciator's task was to describe the expressive and rhetorical devices of a cinematic work, the vehicle of which indeed manifests shots, cuts, and other cinematic devices. Does the appreciator's reference to these cinematic items entail that the narrator is to be imagined as a filmmaker of some sort? One would think so, yet that would be highly problematic because it leads the appreciator back to silly questions. It is unproblematic to imagine, when reading Thackeray's novel, that a character such as Barry Lyndon has put pen to paper and written out his life story, so that we can cogently think that this is what we are reading. What, however, is the corresponding story to be told about the sequence of black-and-white motion picture images that are the putative narrator's vehicle in *La rivière du hibou*? There is no good reason to imagine that the narrator is a magical figure who has somehow used moving pictures to report on some actual episode in the 1860s, including the contents of a man's private hallucination. If we rule out that kind of imaginings, the fictional narrator would have to be like the actual director in having made and edited motion picture images of actors playing their scripted roles in the requisite locations. Yet here is where the author/narrator division of labor breaks down, since the postulated fictional narrator becomes a mere replica of the author—in this case the filmmakers. Enrico and his crew, we know, are responsible for the making of the work's audiovisual display. As the film is a work of fiction, Enrico and his crew use motion picture shots and recorded sounds to prompt and guide us to make-believe or imagine that in the Civil War period there was a Peyton Farquhar who hallucinated his escape, and so on. Enrico and his crew are responsible for the narrational design of the work, and in particular, for its deceptive "twist." So why, if our goal is to appreciate this work adequately, *must we also* imagine that there is a nebulous narrator who has made some analogue of the actual film's audiovisual display and who presents it to us? Note that (2′) requires no such redundant and far-fetched imaginative conjecture about a fictional narrator's efforts and achievements. That, once more, is an option that need not have been taken by Enrico and his cast and crew.

As opposed to engaging in a problematic imaginative project whereby we conjure up a fictional narrator who resembles the actual filmmakers, we should instead prefer an approach to appreciation that directly refers to the actual filmmakers, since it is their achievement that is the principal object of appreciation. Such an approach allows us to appreciate some elements of the film in ways that the fictional narrator approach cannot. For example, working in the early 1960s, Enrico chose to make the film using black-and-white stock. Various artistic motivations can be evoked, including a desire to have the look of the film resonate with that of well-known grainy, black-and-white Civil War photographs taken by Mathew Brady and his many assistants. We might choose to attribute similar motives to a fictional narrator/filmmaker whom we might imagine, but our decision could not be "right" in this case because it could also be coherently imagined that the imaginary filmmaker was operating in a world where only black-and-white film existed, so the use of black and white would not in that case have manifested any artistically significant choice. That was not, however, the world in which the film was actually made, and the appreciator has good reason to situate his or her assessment of the film in that actual world.

Consider as well the drumroll that was mentioned above as an instance of the fictional narrator's expressive activity. Like the other non-diegetic music in the film (most importantly, the "Living Man" song that charmingly underscores Farquhar's joyful moments), this part of the soundtrack is certainly inconsistent with the thought that the film gives us unmediated or direct access to the contents of Farquhar's private hallucination, since this music is not plausibly understood as figuring within that hallucination. So to identify this as nondiegetic sound seems the appreciator's only option. Yet it does not follow that we have sufficient reason to imagine that the sound is being presented to us by a fictional narrator of some sort. Such imaginings are, of course, logically possible. Yet our appreciation of the work's cinematic artistry is in no way enhanced if we imagine that some mysterious narrator figure with unknown powers is "somehow" presenting everything that we see and hear in the audiovisual display. If we were really to take that imaginative fancy seriously, our attention would be drawn in entirely the wrong direction. Instead of trying to make conjectures about a narrator's activity by scrutinizing the features of the audiovisual display, such as composition within the frame, sound-image relations, implicit camera positions and movement, and montage, it is better to appreciate these features for what they really are, namely, the product of the actual filmmakers' art.

I conclude with a recapitulation of the main points in my argument. That many cinematic works are narrations is uncontroversial even if we have no definitive or sharp explication of "narrative" and "story." *Ladri di biciclete* is a narration, *L'avventura* is a narration, *Pickpocket* is a narration, and so on. It is also widely thought that a narration is an activity that requires a narrator. "No narrator, no narration" looks to be a truism. Yet with regard to some cinematic narrations, it is far from obvious that there is a narrator. These three apparent truths are incompatible, so we have a paradox to resolve.

The proposed solution requires a disambiguation of the term "narrator." Two distinctions that genuinely matter to appreciation are actual versus fictional narrators, and within the latter, controlling versus partial ones. The necessity condition in (2) can be defended as long as two other conditions obtain: (i) it is allowed that the actual author can be the narrator, and (ii) it is assumed that all narrational works have an author. Yet as fictional narrators are also an option having genuine importance for the appreciation of a range of narrative works, a disjunctive condition is to be preferred, whence the proposed revisions labeled (2′) and (3′). Proposition (3) as stated at the outset is false, whereas (2) is expanded to include either the actual or a fictional narrator.

Some theorists are tempted by the thesis that all works of cinema that are fictional narrations have a *fictional* narrator. Putative support for this claim is found in the idea that approaching cinematic narrations in this manner is the way to appreciate certain features of their expressivity and design. Such an approach is explored and tested with reference to Enrico's *La rivière du hibou.* Although it is possible to imagine that a mysterious narratorial figure is somehow responsible for expressive cuts, camera movements, and sound-image relations observed in the audiovisual display, describing the narrator as a kind of filmmaker raises unanswerable and irrelevant questions about such things as the narrator's relation to specific motion picture technologies. It is hard to see how the narrator's manipulation of cinematic devices is to be appreciated in the absence of even a moderately determinate grasp of how the narrator's mediation of the story events is achieved. The more accurate and detailed the description of that mediation, the more the narrator's function collapses into that of the actual filmmakers. This dilemma is defeated when we revert to an approach to appreciation that refers instead to the actual filmmakers and their achievement in an actual context of cinematic production. If recourse to a fictional narrator is an option not taken by the actual filmmakers, the spectators and appreciators would do well to follow their lead.

Notes

1. For background to this conception of paradoxes, see Sainsbury (2009).
2. For a start, see Bordwell (1985) and Chatman (1978). I survey some of the literature on narrative in Livingston (2009, 2013).
3. Consider an early remark by George M. Wilson: "The usual elaboration of the literary concept [of point of view] depends essentially upon a concept of narrator which doesn't have an obvious counterpoint in the case of film. We simply have no clear, general idea of film narrative being rendered by a kind of 'visual' narrator in the required sense" (1976, 1027). For Wilson's more recent survey of the topic, see "Seeing through the Imagination in the Cinema" (2013).
4. For narration by actual authors as opposed to fictional narrators, see Livingston ([2001] 2013), Gaut (2010, 199ff.), and Wilson (2011, 111).
5. For background on authorship, see Livingston (2016, 2009a, 2005).
6. On the narrator in comics, see Kai Mikkonen's article in this volume (editor's note).
7. For more on this conception of fiction, with references to various thinkers who have developed and defended this approach, see Livingston (2005).
8. For more on this example, see Livingston (2003).
9. For a longer discussion of this aspect of the film, see Livingston and Ponech (2016).
10. For Walton on silly questions, see *Mimesis as Make-Believe* (1990, 174–82), and *In Other Shoes* (2015, 28–33).
11. For probing explorations of the "face-to-face" account and various sorts of more or less determinate "mediation" accounts, see Wilson (2011, 1986) as well as Livingston (2013).

References

Bordwell, David. 1985. *Narration in the Fiction Film*. London: Methuen.
Chatman, Seymour. 1978. *Story and Discourse: Narrative Structure in Fiction and Film*. Ithaca NY: Cornell University Press.

Currie, Gregory. 1995. *Image and Mind: Film, Philosophy, and Cognitive Science*. Cambridge: Cambridge University Press.

Gaut, Berys. 2010. *A Philosophy of Cinematic Art*. Cambridge: Cambridge University Press.

Ingarden, Roman. (1937) 1973. *The Cognition of the Literary Work of Art*. Translated by Ruth Ann Crowley and Kenneth R. Olsen. Evanston IL: Northwestern University Press.

Livingston, Paisley. (2001) 2013. "Narrative." In *Routledge Companion to Aesthetics*, edited by Dominic McIver Lopes and Berys Gaut, 340–50. 3rd ed. London: Routledge.

———. 2003. "Artistic Self-Reflexivity in *The King Is Alive* and *Strass*." In *Purity and Provocation: Dogma 95*, edited by Mette Hjort and Scott MacKenzie, 102–10. London: British Film Institute.

———. 2005. *Art and Intention: A Philosophical Study*. Oxford, UK: Clarendon.

———. 2009a. *Cinema, Philosophy, Bergman: On Film as Philosophy*. Oxford: Oxford University Press.

———. 2009b. "Narrativity and Knowledge." *Journal of Aesthetics and Art Criticism* 67 (1): 25–36.

———. 2013. "The Imagined Seeing Thesis." *Projections* 7 (1): 139–46.

———. 2016. "Authorship." In *The Routledge Companion to Philosophy of Literature*, edited by Noël Carroll and John Gibson, 173–83. London: Routledge.

Livingston, Paisley, and Trevor Ponech. 2016. "Philosophy with a Twist: *La rivière du hibou*." *Contemporary Aesthetics* 5: n.p.

Sainsbury, R. M. 2009. *Paradoxes*. 3rd ed. Cambridge: Cambridge University Press.

Smith, Murray. 1995. *Engaging Characters: Fiction, Emotion, and the Cinema*. Oxford, UK: Clarendon.

Thackeray, William Makepeace. (1844) 2011. *The Luck of Barry Lyndon*. Auckland: Floating Press.

Walton, Kendall L. 1990. *Mimesis as Make-Believe: On the Foundations of the Representational Arts*. Cambridge MA: Harvard University Press.

———. 2015. *In Other Shoes: Music, Metaphor, Empathy, Existence*. Oxford: Oxford University Press.

Wilson, George M. 1976. "Film, Perception, and Point of View." *Modern Language Notes* 91: 1026–43.

———. 1986. *Narration in Light: Studies in Cinematic Point of View*. Baltimore: Johns Hopkins University Press.

———. 2011. *Seeing Fictions in Film: The Epistemology of Movies*. Oxford: Oxford University Press.

———. 2013. "Seeing through the Imagination in the Cinema." *Projections* 7 (1): 155–71.

Bibliography

Andersson, Greger. 2001. *The Book and Its Narratives: A Critical Examination of Some Synchronic Studies of the Book of Judges*. Örebro, Sweden: Universitetsbiblioteket.

———. 2009. *Untamable Texts: Literary Studies and Narrative Theory in the Books of Samuel*. New York: T. and T. Clark.

———. 2013. "The Problem of Narratives in the Bible: Moral Issues and Suggested Reading Strategies." In *Narrative Ethics*, edited by Jakob Lothe and Jeremy Hawthorn, 59–72. Amsterdam: Rodopi.

Andersson, Greger, Per Klingberg, and Tommy Sandberg. 2019. "Introduction: Sameness and Difference in Narratology." *Frontiers of Narrative Studies* 5 (1): 11–16.

Andersson, Greger, and Tommy Sandberg. 2018. "Sameness versus Difference in Narratology: Two Approaches to Narrative Fiction." *Narrative* 26 (3): 241–61.

———. 2019. "A Reply to Mari Hatavara and Matti Hyvärinen." *Narrative* 27 (3): 378–81.

Badiou-Monferran, Claire. 2012. "Autour des connecteurs: La phrase pseudo explicative des fictions narratives d'Ancien Régime est-elle une 'phrase sans parole'?" *Le Français moderne* 1: 104–20.

Badiou-Monferran, Claire, and Delphine Denis. 2012a. "Enjeux de l'hypothèse non communicationnelle du récit de fiction pour les corpus de la première modernité." *Le Français moderne* 1: 1–14.

———, eds. 2012b. Special issue, "Le narrateur en question(s) dans les fictions d'Ancien Régime: Récits parlés, récits montrés," *Le Français moderne* 1.

Banfield, Ann. (1982) 1995. *Phrases sans parole: Théorie du récit et du style indirect libre*. Translated by Cyril Veken. Paris: Le Seuil.

———. (1982) 2014. *Unspeakable Sentence. Narration and Representation in the Language of Fiction*. London: Routledge Revivals.

———. 2005. "No-Narrator Theory." In *Routledge Encyclopedia of Narrative Theory*, edited by David Herman, Manfred Jahn, and Marie-Laure Ryan, 396–97. London: Routledge.

———. 2019a. *Describing the Unobserved and Other Essays: Unspeakable Sentences after "Unspeakable Sentences,"* edited by Sylvie Patron. Newcastle upon Tyne, UK: Cambridge Scholars Publishing.

———. 2019b. *Nouvelles phrases sans parole: Décrire l'inobservé et autres essais*, edited by Sylvie Patron. Translated by Nicole Lallot, Jean-Marie Marandin, and Sylvie Patron. Saint-Denis, France: Presses universitaires de Vincennes.

Barbauld, Anna Laetitia. (1804) 1959, 1977. "Life of Samuel Richardson, with Remarks on His Writings." In *The Correspondence of Samuel Richardson*, 1: vii–ccxii. London: Lewis and Rodem. https://babel.hathitrust.org/cgi/pt?id= mdp.39015002712563;view=1up;seq=29. Reprinted as "Three Ways of Telling a Story?" In *Novelists on the Novel*, edited by Miriam Allott, 258–60. 2nd ed. London: Routledge and Kegan Paul.

Benveniste, Émile. (1959) 1966, 1990. "Les relations de temps dans le verbe français." In *Problèmes de linguistique générale*, 1: 237–50. Paris: Gallimard.

———. (1959, 1966) 1971. "The Correlations of Tense in the French Verb." Translated by Mary E. Meek. In *Problems in General Linguistics*, 205–15. Coral Gables FL: Miami University Press.

Birke, Dorothy. 2015. "Author, Authority and 'Authorial Narration': The Eighteenth-Century English Novel as a Test Case." In Birke and Köppe 2015b, 99–111.

Birke, Dorothy, and Tilmann Köppe. 2015a. "Author and Narrator: Problems in the Constitution and Interpretation of Fictional Narrative." In Birke and Köppe 2015b, 1–12.

———, eds. 2015b. *Author and Narrator: Transdisciplinary Contributions to a Narratological Debate*. Berlin: De Gruyter.

Bordwell, David. 1985. *Narration in the Fiction Film*. Madison: University of Wisconsin Press.

———. 2008. "Afterword: Narrators, Implied Authors, and Other Superfluities." In *Poetics of Cinema*, 121–33. London: Routledge.

Boyd, Brian. 2017. "Does Austen Need Narrators? Does Anyone?" *New Literary History* 48 (2): 285–308.

Brenkman, John. (2000) 2005. "On Voice." *Novel: A Forum on Fiction* 33 (3): 281–306. Reprinted in *Essentials in the Theory of Fiction*, edited by Michael J. Hoffman and Patrick D. Murphy, 411–44. 3rd ed. Durham NC: Duke University Press.

Brinton, Laurel. 1980. "Represented Perception: A Study in Narrative Style." *Poetics* 9 (2): 363–81.

Brooke-Rose, Christine. 1988. "La controverse sur le discours indirect libre: Ann Banfield vs les littéraires." In *Théorie, littérature, enseignement* 6: 77–89.

———. 1990. "Ill Locutions." In *Narrative in Culture: The Uses of Storytelling in the Sciences, Philosophy and Literature*, edited by Christopher Nash, 154–71. London: Routledge.

———. 1991. "Illocutions." In *Stories, Theories, and Things*, 63–80. Cambridge: Cambridge University Press.

———. 1999. "Narrating without a Narrator." *Times Literary Supplement* 4058 (December 31): 12–13.

———. 2002. *Invisible Author: Last Essays*. Columbus: Ohio State University Press.

Butor, Michel. (1961) 1964. "L'usage des pronoms personnels dans le roman." *Les Temps modernes* 178: 936–48. Reprinted in *Répertoire II*, 61–72. Paris: Minuit.

Carroll, Noël. 2006. Introduction to part 4, "Film Narrative/Narration." In *Philosophy of Film and Motion Pictures*, edited by Noël Carroll and Jinhee Choi, 175–84. Malden MA: Blackwell.

Chatman, Seymour. 1978. *Story and Discourse: Narrative Structure in Fiction and Film*. Ithaca NY: Cornell University Press.

Culler, Jonathan. (1974) 2006. "The Elusive Narrator." In *Flaubert—The Uses of Uncertainty*, 109–22. Ithaca NY: Cornell University Press. Reprinted in *Flaubert: The Uses of Uncertainty*, 99–115. Aurora CO: Davies Group Publishers.

———. 1984. "Problems in the Theory of Fiction." *Diacritics* 14 (1): 2–11.

———. (2004) 2006. "Omniscience." *Narrative* 12 (1): 22–34. Reprinted in *The Literary in Theory*, 183–201. Stanford: Stanford University Press.

———. 2018. "Naturalization in 'Natural' Narratology." *Partial Answers* 16 (2): 243–49.

———. 2019. "Narrative Theory and the Lyrics." In *Cambridge Companion to Narrative Theory*, edited by Matthew Garrett, 201–16. Cambridge: Cambridge University Press.

Currie, Gregory. 1995. "Unreliability Refigured: Narrative in Literature and Film." *Journal of Aesthetics and Art Criticism* 53 (1): 19–23.

———. 2010. *Narratives and Narrators: A Philosophy of Stories*. Oxford: Oxford University Press.

David, Davies. 2010. "Eluding Wilson's 'Elusive Narrators.'" *Philosophical Studies* 147 (3): 387–94.

Denis, Delphine. 2012. "De quelques scrupules sur le style narratif: Du Plaisir théoricien du récit 'désintéressé.'" In Badiou-Monferran and Denis 2012b, 45–54.

———. 2015. "Historien ou narrateur? Vers une approche non communicationnelle du récit de fiction à l'âge classique." In *La Représentation de la vie psychique dans les récits factuels et fictionnels de l'époque classique*, edited by Marc Hersant and Catherine Ramond, 21–29. Leiden, Netherlands: Brill/Rodopi.

Duchan, Judith F., Gail A. Bruder, and Lynn E. Hewitt, eds. 1995. *Deixis in Narrative: A Cognitive Science Perspective*. Hillsdale NJ: Lawrence Erlbaum Associates.

Edholm, Roger. 2018. "The Narrator Who Wasn't There: Philip Roth's *The Human Stain* and the Discontinuity of Narrating Characters." *Narrative* 26 (1): 17–38.

Galbraith, Mary. 1995. "Deictic Shift Theory and the Poetics of Involvement in Narrative." In Duchan, Bruder, and Hewitt, 19–59.

Gaut, Berys. 2004. "The Philosophy of the Movies: Cinematic Narration." Chap. 13 in *The Blackwell Guide to Aesthetics*, edited by Peter Kivy, 230–53. Hoboken NJ: Wiley-Blackwell.

Hamburger, Käte. (1957) 1968. *Die Logik der Dichtung*. 2nd rev. ed. Stuttgart: Ernst Klett Verlag.

———. (1957, 1968) 1973, 1993. *The Logic of Literature*. 2nd ed. Translated by Marilynn J. Rose. Bloomington: Indiana University Press.

———. (1957, 1968) 1986. *La Logique des genres littéraires*. Translated by Pierre Cadiot. Paris: Le Seuil.

Hansen, Per Krogh, Stefan Iversen, Henrik Skov Nielsen, and Rolf Reitan, eds. 2011. *Strange Voices in Narrative Fiction*. Berlin: De Gruyter.

Herman, David. 2012. "Authors, Narrators, Narration." In David Herman, James Phelan, Peter J. Rabinowitz, Brian Richardson, and Robyn Warhol, *Narrative Theory: Core Concepts and Critical Debates*, 44–50. Columbus: Ohio State University Press.

Hersant, Marc. 2011. "Usages du discours direct chez Voltaire: Discours rapportés et discours créés dans les *Mémoires pour servir à la vie de M. de Voltaire, écrits par lui-même* et *Candide*." In *Les Discours rapportés dans les récits fictionnels et historiques des XVIIe et XVIIIe siècles*, edited by Marc Hersant, Marie-Paule Pilorge, Catherine Ramond, and François Raviez, 203–20. Arras, France: Artois Presses Université.

———. 2015a. *Voltaire: écriture et vérité*. Leuven, Belgium: Peeters.

———. 2015b. "Saint-Simon omniscient de lui-même: La 'Note Saint-Simon' des *Notes sur tous les duchés-pairies*." In *La Représentation de la vie psychique dans les récits factuels et fictionnels de l'époque classique*, edited by Marc Hersant and Catherine Ramond, 145–59. Leiden, Netherlands: Brill/Rodopi.

Hersant, Marc, and Catherine Ramond. 2015. Introduction to *La Représentation de la vie psychique dans les récits factuels et fictionnels de l'époque classique*, edited by Marc Hersant and Catherine Ramond, 5–18. Leiden, Netherlands: Brill/Rodopi.

Kania, Andrew. 2005. "Against the Ubiquity of Fictional Narrators." *Journal of Aesthetics and Art Criticism* 63 (1): 47–54.

———. 2007. "Against Them, Too: A Reply to Alward." *Journal of Aesthetics and Art Criticism* 65 (4): 404–7.

Kawashima, Robert S. 2004. *Biblical Narrative and the Death of the Rhapsode*. Bloomington: Indiana University Press.

Köppe, Tilmann, and Jan Stühring. 2011. "Against Pan-Narrator Theories." *Journal of Literary Semantics* 40 (1): 59–80.

———. 2015. "Against Pragmatic Arguments for Pan-Narrator Theories: The Case of Hawthorne's 'Rappacini's Daughter.'" In Birke and Köppe 2015b, 13–43.

Kuroda, S.-Y. 2012. *Pour une théorie poétique de la narration*, edited by Sylvie Patron. Translated by Cassian Braconnier, Tiên Fauconnier, and Sylvie Patron. Paris: Armand Colin.

———. 2014. *Toward a Poetic Theory of Narration: Essays of S.-Y. Kuroda*, edited by Sylvie Patron. Berlin: De Gruyter.

Livingston, Paisley. (2001) 2002. "Narrative." In *The Routledge Companion to Aesthetics*, edited by Berys Gaut and Dominic McIver Lopes, 275–84. 2nd ed. London: Routledge.

Meindl, Dieter. 2004. "(Un-)reliable Narration from a Pronominal Perspective." In *The Dynamics of Narrative Form: Studies in Anglo-American Narratology*, edited by John Pier, 59–82. Berlin: De Gruyter.

Mikkonen, Kai. 2010. "Le narrateur implicite dans la bande dessinée. La transformation du *style indirect libre* dans deux adaptations en bandes dessinées de *Madame Bovary*." *Image & Narrative* 11 (4): 185–207.

———. 2017. *The Narratology of Comic Art*. London: Routledge.

Mirguet, Françoise. 2009. *La Représentation du Divin dans les récits du Pentateuque. Médiations syntaxiques et narratives*. Leiden, Netherlands: Brill.

Morreall, John. 1994. "The Myth of the Omniscient Narrator." *Journal of Aesthetics and Art Criticism* 52 (4): 429–35.

Murphy, Terence Patrick. 2012. "Defining the Reliable Narrator: The Marked Status of First-Person Fiction." *Journal of Literary Semantics* 41 (1): 67–87.

Olsen, Jon-Arild. 2004. *L'Esprit du roman: Œuvre, fiction et récit*. Bern: Peter Lang.

———. 2005. "Film, fiction et narration." *Poétique* 141: 71–91.

Patron, Sylvie. 2005a. "Describing the Circle of Narrative Theory: A Review Essay." Translated by Viviane Cox and Sylvie Patron. *Style* 34 (4): 479–88.

———. 2005b. "Le narrateur et l'interprétation des termes déictiques dans le récit de fiction." In *De l'énoncé à l'énonciation et vice-versa: Regards multidisciplinaires sur la deixis/From Utterance to Uttering and Vice Versa: Multidisciplinary Views on Deixis*, edited by Daniele Monticelli, Renate Pajusalu, and Anu Treikelder, 187–202. Tartu, Estonia: Tartu University Press.

———. 2006. "Sur l'épistémologie de la théorie narrative (narratologie et autres théories du récit de fiction)." *Les Temps modernes* 635–36: 262–85.

———. (2006) 2008. "On the Epistemology of Narrative Theory: Narratology and Other Theories of Fictional Narrative." Translated by Anne Marsella. In

The Traveling Concept of Narrative, COLLEGIUM: *Studies across Disciplines in the Humanities and Social Sciences,* edited by Matti Hyvärinen, Anu Korhonen, and Juri Mykkänen, 118–33. http://www.helsinki.fi/collegium/journal/volumes/volume_1/. Reprinted in *Phantom Sentences: Essays in Linguistics and Literature Presented to Ann Banfield,* edited by Robert Kawashima, Gilles Philippe, and Thelma Sowley, 43–65. Bern: Peter Lang.

———. (2009) 2016. *Le Narrateur: Introduction à la théorie narrative.* Paris: Armand Colin. Reprinted as *Le Narrateur: Un problème de théorie narrative.* Limoges, France: Lambert-Lucas.

———. (2010) 2019. "The Death of the Narrator and the Interpretation of the Novel: The Example of *Pedro Páramo* by Juan Rulfo." *Journal of Literary Theory* 4 (2): 253–72. Reprinted in Patron 2019c, 13–29.

———. 2011a. "Discussion 'Narrator.'" Translated by Susan Nicholls. In *The Living Handbook of Narratology,* edited by Peter Hühn, John Pier, Wolf Schmid, and Jörg Schönert. University of Hamburg. http://wikis.sub.uni-hamburg.de/lhn/index.php/Talk:Narrator.

———. 2011b. "Enunciative Narratology: A French Speciality." Translated by Anne Marsella. In *Current Trends in Narratology,* edited by Greta Olson, 312–35. Berlin: De Gruyter.

———. 2011c. "Homonymy, Polysemy, and Synonymy: Reflections on the Notion of Voice." Translated by Susan Nicholls. In Hansen et al. 2011, 13–36.

———. (2011) 2015. "La mort du narrateur et l'interprétation du roman. L'exemple de *Pedro Páramo* de Juan Rulfo." In *Théorie, analyse, interprétation des récits/Theory, Analysis, Interpretation of Narratives,* edited by Sylvie Patron, 147–82. Bern: Peter Lang. Reprinted in Patron 2015c, 25–52.

———. 2012. "Introduction." In S.-Y. Kuroda, *Pour une théorie poétique de la narration,* edited by Sylvie Patron, 7–51. Paris: Armand Colin.

———. (2012) 2014. "Introduction." Translated by Susan Nicholls. In *Toward a Poetic Theory of Narration: Essays of S.-Y. Kuroda,* edited by Sylvie Patron, 1–36. Berlin: De Gruyter.

———. (2012) 2015c. "Phrases sans parole. À propos d'une histoire d'amour du XXe siècle." CMLF 2012, Third World Congress of French Linguistics, July 4–7, 2012, Lyon, France. http://www.shs-conferences.org/index.php?option=com_articleandaccess=doianddoi=10.1051/shsconf/20120100206andItemid=129. Reprinted in Patron 2015c, 125–46.

———. (2012) 2015c. "Phrases sans parole. À propos d'une histoire d'amour du XXe siècle." *Textuel* 67: 209–26. Reprinted in Patron 2015c, 125–46.

———. (2012) 2015c. "Les récits de fiction antérieurs à la deuxième moitié du XIXe siècle: Des instances de réfutation pour les théories poétiques de la narration?" *Le Français moderne* 1: 15–31. Reprinted in Patron 2015c, 95–112.

————. (2012a) 2019. "[Interview with] Sylvie Patron." Translated by Susan Nicholls. In *Narrative Theories and Poetics: 5 Questions*, edited by Peer F. Bundgaard, Henrik Skov Nielsen, and Frederik Stjernfelt, 159–69. Copenhagen: Automatic Press/VIP. Reprinted in Patron 2019a, 77–85.

————. (2012b) 2019. "Narrative Fiction Prior to 1850: Instances of Refutation for Poetic Theories of Narration?" Translated by Susan Nicholls. *Amsterdam International Electronic Journal for Cultural Narratology* 6. http://cf.hum .uva.nl/narratology/a11_sylvie_patron.htm. Reprinted as "Narrative Fiction before 1850: Instances of Refutation for Poetic Theories of Narration?" in Patron 2019a, 63–76.

————. (2013) 2019a. "Unspeakable Sentences: Narration and Representation in Benedetti's 'Five Years of Life.'" Translated by Susan Nicholls. *Narrative* 21 (2): 243–62. Reprinted in Patron 2019a, 86–104.

————. 2015a. "Entretien." In Patron 2015c, 113–23.

————. 2015b. "Homonymie, polysémie et synonymie: Réflexions sur la notion de voix." In Patron 2015c, 73–94.

————. 2015c. *La Mort du narrateur et autres essais*. Limoges, France: Lambert-Lucas.

————. 2015d. "Théories de l'absence de narrateur/théories du narrateur optionnel: Étude critique de quelques propositions récentes. Pour une histoire des concept en théorie narrative." In Patron 2015c, 165–86.

————. 2017a. "Deux livres sur la représentation de la conscience dans le récit. Essai de narratologie comparée." *Vox Poetica*. http://www.vox-poetica.com/t/ articles/patron2017.html.

————. 2017b. "Les catégories narratologiques et la (non-)distinction oral-écrit dans la théorie narrative (narratologie et autres théories du récit de fiction)." In *Narrativité, oralité et performance: Actes du colloque du RRENAB 2014*, edited by Alain Gignac, 19–42. Leuven: Peeters.

————. 2017c. "Two Books on the Representation of Consciousness in Narrative: An Essay in Comparative Narratology." Translated by Melissa McMahon, with the collaboration of Sylvie Patron. *Poetics Today* 38 (4): 695–715.

————. 2018. "Unspeakable Images: On the Interplay between Verbal and Iconic Narration in Benedetti's 'Cinco años de vida.'" Translated by Melissa McMahon, *Narrative* 26 (1): 39–62. Reprinted in Patron 2019a, 105–19.

————. 2019a. *The Death of the Narrator and Other Essays*. Trier, Germany: Wissenschaftlicher Verlag Trier.

————. 2019b. "Images sans parole: À propos d'une histoire d'amour du XXe siècle." In *Le Désir demeuré désir. Mélanges offerts à Franck Bauer*, edited by Chantal Liaroutzos and Christian Nicolas, 331–50. Caen, France: Presses universitaires de Caen.

———. 2019c. "Introduction." In Ann Banfield, *Describing the Unobserved and Other Essays: Unspeakable Sentences after "Unspeakable Sentences,"* edited by Sylvie Patron, 1–33. Newcastle upon Tyne, UK: Cambridge Scholars Publishing.

———. 2020. "No-Narrator Theories/Optional-Narrator Theories: Recent Proposals and Continuing Problems; Toward a History of Concepts in Narrative Theory." Translated by Melissa McMahon. In *Contemporary French and Francophone Narratology*, edited by John Pier, 31–53. Columbus: Ohio State University Press.

———. Forthcoming. "Narrator." Translated by Melissa McMahon. In *Fictionality in Literature: Core Concepts Revisited*, edited by Lasse Gammelgaard, Simona Zetterberg Gjerlevsen, Louise Brix Jacobsen, Richard Walsh, James Phelan, Henrik Skov Nielsen, and Stefan Iversen. Columbus: Ohio State University Press.

Pettersson, Anders. 1990. *A Theory of Literary Discourse*. Lund, Sweden: Lund University Press.

Philippe, Gilles. 2000a. "Centre énonciatif et centre interprétatif. L'analyse linguistique et l'interprétation du roman." *Études romanesques* 6: 37–52.

———. 2000b. "L'ancrage énonciatif des récits de fiction. Présentation." *Langue française* 128: 3–8.

———. 2000c. "Les divergences énonciatives dans les récits de fiction." *Langue française* 128: 30–51.

———. 2002. "L'appareil formel de l'effacement énonciatif et la pragmatique des textes sans locuteur." In *Pragmatique et analyse des textes*, edited by Ruth Amossy, 17–34. Tel-Aviv: University of Tel-Aviv.

Pieper, Vincenz. 2015. "Author and Narrator: Observations on *Die Wahlverwandtschaften.*" In *Author and Narrator: Transdisciplinary Contributions to a Narratological Debate*, edited by Dorothy Birke and Tilmann Köppe, 81–97. Berlin: De Gruyter.

Reitan, Rolf. 1999. "Balzac Fælde—Who Can Tell the Dancer from the Dance?" *Kritik* 142: 63–72.

———. 2003. "Kun et snit. Om synsvinkler og fokaliseringer." Aarhus: Institut for Nordisk Sprog og Litteratur ved Aarhus Universitet, "Nordisk Instituts Publikationsserie."

Romberg, Bertil. 1962. *Studies in the Narrative Technique of the First-Person Novel*. Translated by Michaël Taylor and Harold H. Borland. Stockholm: Almqvist and Wiksell.

Sandberg, Tommy. 2019. "The Critique of the Common Theory of Narrative Fiction in Narratology: Pursuing Difference." *Frontiers of Narrative Studies* 5 (1): 17–34.

Searle, John R. (1975) 1979. "The Logical Status of Fictional Discourse."
In *Expression and Meaning: Studies in the Theory of Speech Acts*, 58–75.
Cambridge: Cambridge University Press.

Segal, Erwin M. 1995a. "A Cognitive-Phenomenological Theory of Fictional
Narrative." In Duchan, Bruder, and Hewitt, 61–78.

———. 1995b. "Narrative Comprehension and the Role of Deictic Shift
Theory." In Duchan, Bruder, and Hewitt, 3–17.

Skalin, Lars-Åke. 1991. *Karaktär och perspektiv: Att tolka litterära gestalter i det
mimetiska språkspelet*. Stockholm: Almqvist and Wiksell International.

———. 2003. "Den onödige berättaren: En fiktionologisk analys." In *Berätteren,
en gäckande röst i texten*, edited by Lars-Åke Skalin, 85–119. Örebro, Sweden:
Örebro Universitet.

———. 2011. "How Strange Are the 'Strange Voices' of Fiction?" In Hansen et
al. 2011, 101–26.

———. 2019. "The Art of Narrative—Narrative as Art: Sameness or
Difference?" *Frontiers of Narrative Studies* 5 (1): 35–56.

Spearing, A. C. 2005. *Textual Subjectivity: The Encoding of Subjectivity in
Medieval Narratives and Lyrics*. Oxford: Oxford University Press.

———. 2012. *Medieval Autographies: The "I" of the Text*. Notre Dame IN:
University of Notre Dame Press.

———. 2015. "What Is a Narrator? Narrator Theory and Medieval Narratives."
Digital Philology 4 (1): 59–105.

———. 2019. "Narration in Two Versions of 'Virginius and Virginia.'" *Chaucer
Review* 54 (1): 1–34.

Thomson-Jones, Katherine. 2007. "The Literary Origins of the Cinematic
Narrator." *British Journal of Aesthetics* 47 (1): 76–94.

———. 2009. "Cinematic Narrators." *Philosophy Compass* 4 (2): 296–311.

Thon, Jan-Noël. 2014. "Toward a Transmedial Narratology: On Narrators in
Contemporary Graphic Novels, Feature Films, and Computer Games." In
Beyond Classical Narration. Unnatural and Transmedial Challenges, edited
by Jan Alber and Per Krogh Hansen, 25–56. Berlin: De Gruyter.

———. 2016. *Transmedial Narratology and Contemporary Media Culture*.
Lincoln: University of Nebraska Press.

Walsh, Richard. (1997) 2007. "Who Is the Narrator?" *Poetics Today* 18 (4): 495–
513. Reprinted as "The Narrator and the Frame of Fiction" in *The Rhetoric
of Fictionality: Narrative Theory and the Idea of Fiction*, 69–85. Columbus:
Ohio State University Press.

———. 2010. "Person, Level, Voice: A Rhetorical Reconsideration." In
Postclassical Narratology: Approaches and Analyses, edited by Jan Alber and
Monika Fludernik, 35–57. Columbus: Ohio State University Press.

Walton, Kendall L. 1990. *Mimesis as Make-Believe: On the Foundations of the Representational Arts*. Cambridge MA: Harvard University Press.

Wartenberg, Thomas E. 2007. "Need There Be Implicit Narrators of Literary Fiction?" *Philosophical Studies* 135: 89–94.

Wistrand, Sten. 2012. "Time for Departure? The Principle of Minimal Departure—a Critical Examination." In *Disputable Core Concepts of Narrative Theory*, edited by Göran Rossholm and Christer Johansson, 15–44. Bern: Peter Lang.

Wolff Lundholt, Marianne. 2008. *Telling without Tellers: The Linguistic Manifestation of Literary Communication in Narrative Fiction*. Copenhagen: Medusa.

Wolterstoff, Nicholas. 1980. *Works and Worlds of Art*. Oxford, UK: Clarendon Press.

Contributors

Greger Andersson is a professor of comparative literature and the leader of the research environment Narration, Life, Meaning at Örebro University, in Sweden. He is also a lecturer in Old Testament studies at Örebro Theological Seminary. Andersson has published on the application of narratology as an analytical method to biblical studies and on religious groups and their continuous negation of meaning when it comes to issues like homosexuality, baptism in the spirit, and illness and healing. Some of his recent publications are "Stories about Humans in a Complicated World: The Narratives of the Hebrew Bible," in *God and Humans in the Hebrew Bible and Beyond*, edited by David Willgren; with Tommy Sandberg, "Sameness versus Difference in Narratology: Two Approaches to Narrative Fiction," in the journal *Narrative*; "The Charge against Classical and Post-Classical Narratologies 'Epistemic' Approach to Literary Fiction," in *Narrative Theory, Literature, and New Media*, edited by Mari Hatavara et al.; "The Problem of Narratives in the Bible: Moral Issues and Suggested Reading Strategies," in *Narrative Ethics*, edited by Jakob Lothe and Jeremy Hawthorn; and "To Live the Biblical Narratives: Pentecostal Autobiographies and the Baptism in the Spirit" in the journal *PentecoStudies*.

Brian Boyd is a University Distinguished Professor of English at the University of Auckland. He has published much on Vladimir Nabokov, and on art and literature from the Paleolithic and Homer to the present; on American, Brazilian, English, Greek, Irish, New Zealand, Polish, and Russian literature; on fiction, nonfiction, drama, verse, comics, film, translation, and adaptation; on literary and art theory, linguistics, and philosophy (epistemology, ontology, politics); and on the relations between the arts, humanities, and sciences. Among his recent books are *On the Origin of Stories: Evolution, Cognition, and*

Fiction; the coedited *Evolution, Literature, and Film: A Reader*; *Stalking Nabokov*; *Why Lyrics Last: Evolution, Cognition, and Shakespeare's Sonnets*; the coedition and cotranslation of Nabokov's *Letters to Véra*; the coauthored *On the Origin of Art*; and the coedition of Nabokov's *Think, Write, Speak*. His "Does Jane Austen Need Narrators? Does Anyone?" in *New Literary History* is closest to the concerns of this volume. His work has appeared in twenty-one languages and won awards on four continents.

John Brenkman is a Distinguished Professor of Comparative Literature and English at the City University of New York Graduate Center and Baruch College. He is the coordinator of the critical theory certificate program at the CUNY Graduate Center and directs the US-Europe seminar at Baruch. His publications have engaged a wide variety of topics in literary, cultural, and political theory. *Mood and Trope: The Rhetoric and Poetics of Affect* is published by the University of Chicago Press. Previous work includes *Culture and Domination*; *Straight Male Modern: A Cultural Critique of Psychoanalysis*; and *The Cultural Contradictions of Democracy: Political Thought since September 11*. His current project is "James the Minimalist: An Essay on the Late Novels."

Jonathan Culler was a fellow in French at Selwyn College, Cambridge, then a university lecturer and fellow in French at Brasenose College, Oxford, before moving to Cornell University in 1977, where he succeeded M. H. Abrams as the Class of 1916 Professor of English. A former president of the American Comparative Literature Association, chair of the New York Council for the Humanities, and secretary of the American Council of Learned Societies, he is a fellow of the American Academy of Arts and Sciences and of the American Philosophical Society. He is the author of *Flaubert: The Uses of Uncertainty* and numerous books on contemporary critical theory, including *Structuralist Poetics: Structuralism, Linguistics, and the Study of Literature*; *On Deconstruction: Theory and Criticism after Structuralism*; and *The Literary in Theory*. His *Literary Theory: A Very Short Introduction* has been translated into twenty-six languages. His latest book is *Theory of the Lyric*. His work in narratology includes chapters in *Structuralist Poetics* and *Literary Theory: A Very Short Introduction*; "Story and Discourse in the Analysis of Narrative" in *The Pursuit of Signs: Semiotics*; "Problems in the Theory of Fiction" in the journal

Diacritics; "Omniscience" in the journal *Narrative*; and "Narrative Theory and the Lyric," in *The Cambridge Companion to Narrative Theory*, edited by Matthew Garrett.

Mary Galbraith is a lecturer in the Department of English at San Diego State University. She specializes in literary representations of childhood self, theory of the novel, and theory of auteur picture books. Her publications include "Meditation on *The Polar Express*"; "What Everybody Knew versus What Maisie Knew: The Change of Epistemological Perspective from the Preface to Chapter 1 of *What Maisie Knew*" in the journal *Style*; "Pip as 'Infant Tongue' and as Adult Narrator in Chapter 1 of *Great Expectations*" in *Infant Tongues: The Voice of the Child in Literature*, edited by Elizabeth Goodenough, Mark A. Heberle, and Naomi Sokoloff; and "Deictic Shift Theory and the Poetics of Involvement in Literature" in *Deixis in Narrative: A Cognitive Science Perspective*, edited by Judith F. Duchan, Gail A. Bruder, and Lynne E. Hewitt.

Marc Hersant is a professor of eighteenth-century French literature at New Sorbonne University. A specialist in the writing of historiography, memorialists, the dialogue between history and fiction, the writing of the self, and conceptions of truth in the classical era and their discursive treatment in literary and nonliterary texts, his publications include *Le Discours de vérité dans les Mémoires du duc de Saint-Simon*; *Voltaire: Écriture et vérité*; *Saint-Simon*; and *Genèse de l'impur: L'Écriture carcérale du marquis de Sade* (forthcoming). He has also written articles on Monluc, Tallemant des Réaux, Perrault, Cardinal de Retz, Madame de Staal-Delaunay, Marivaux, Diderot, and Rousseau as well as on Proust, Cohen, and Genet. He has edited or coedited many collective works, including *Retour à Bakhtine? Essais de lectures bakhtiniennes*, with Chantal Liaroutzos; *Le Sens du passé, pour une nouvelle approche des Mémoires*, with Jean-Louis Jeannelle and Damien Zanone; *La Représentation de la vie psychique dans les récits historiques et dans les récits fictionnels de l'époque classique*, with Catherine Ramond; and *Tout Saint-Simon*, with Marie-Paule de Weerdt-Pilorge and François Raviez.

Robert S. Kawashima holds a joint appointment in the Department of Religion and the Center for Jewish Studies at the University of Florida. Before joining the faculty of the University of Florida, he was a faculty fellow at UC Berkeley and a Dorot assistant professor and faculty fellow in the Skirball Department of Hebrew and Judaic Studies at New York University. He has written on various aspects of the Hebrew Bible—linguistic, literary, legal—as well as on Homer, literary theory, and most recently, Proust. He is the author, most notably, of *Biblical Narrative and the Death of the Rhapsode*, and the coeditor, with Gilles Philippe and Thelma Sowley, of *Phantom Sentences: Essays in Linguistics and Literature Presented to Ann Banfield*.

Paisley Livingston is a professor emeritus of philosophy at Lingnan University in Hong Kong and a visiting professor of philosophy at Uppsala University. He taught previously at the University of Copenhagen, Aarhus University, and McGill University. He has published various papers and books in aesthetics, including *Art and Intention*; "History of the Ontology of Art," in the *Stanford Encyclopedia of Philosophy*; and *Cinema, Philosophy, Bergman*.

Kai Mikkonen is a professor of comparative literature at the University of Helsinki, Finland, and a life member of Clare Hall College, University of Cambridge. His main research and teaching interests include nineteenth- and twentieth-century French and British literature, travel writing, graphic narratives and comics, multimodality, and theories of narrative and fiction. He is the author of *The Narratology of Comic Art*; *Narrative Paths: African Travel in Modern Fiction and Nonfiction*; *Kuva ja sana* (Image and Word in Interaction); and *The Plot Machine: The French Novel and the Bachelor Machines in the Electric Years 1880–1914*, as well as various articles in periodicals such as *Style*, *Poetics Today*, *Partial Answers*, *Narrative*, *Word & Image*, *Image & Narrative*, *Studies in Travel Writing*, and the *Journal of Literary Semantics*.

Sylvie Patron is a lecturer and research supervisor (*maîtresse de conférences habilitée à diriger des recherches*) in French language and literature at the University of Paris, France. A specialist in the history and epistemology of literary theory, she has published *Le Narrateur: Introduction à la théorie narrative*, reprinted as *Le Narrateur: Un problème de théorie narrative*; and *La Mort du narrateur et autres essais*. An English version of the latter has recently been published: *The Death of the Narrator and Other Essays*. Patron has also edited or coedited *Théorie, analyse, interprétation des récits/Theory, Analysis, Interpretation of Narratives*; *Life and Narrative: The Risks* *and Responsibilities of Storying Experience*, with Brian Schiff and A. Elizabeth McKim; and *Introduction à la narratologie postclassique: Les nouvelles directions de la recherche sur le récit*. She is the author of numerous articles, published in both French and English, on the narrator and other problems in narrative theory. She has also translated several articles on linguistics and narrative theory into French and edited S.-Y. Kuroda's *Pour une théorie poétique de la narration*, translated by Cassian Braconnier, Tiên Fauconnier, and Sylvie Patron (English version: *Toward a Poetic Theory of Narration: Essays by S.-Y. Kuroda*); and Ann Banfield's *Nouvelles phrases sans parole: Décrire l'inobservé et autres essais*, translated by Nicole Lallot, Jean-Marie Marandin, and Sylvie Patron (English version: *Describing the Unobserved: Unspeakable Sentences after "Unspeakable Sentences"*). She was president of the International Society for the Study of Narrative in 2020 and serves presently as past president.

Vincenz Pieper is a research fellow in the Institute of German Studies at Osnabrück University, in Germany. He is the author of *Philologische Erkenntnis: Eine Untersuchung zu den begrifflichen Grundlagen der Literaturforschung*. His other publications include "Narratologie und Interpretation. Ein Beitrag zum besseren Verständnis von Kleists Erzählungen," in *Kleist-Jahrbuch*; "Author and Narrator: Observations on 'Die Wahlverwandtschaften,'" in *Author and Narrator: Transdisciplinary Contributions to a Narratological Debate*, edited by Dorothee Birke and Tilmann Köppe; "Was heißt es, eine fiktionale Erzählung zu verstehen? Überlegungen am Beispiel von 'Der Tod in Venedig,' 'Der Erwählte' und 'Felix Krull,'" in *Der Geist der Erzählung: Narratologie bei Thomas Mann*, edited by Jens Ewen, Tim Lörke, and Regine Zeller.

Lars-Åke Skalin is a professor emeritus of comparative literature at Örebro University, in Sweden. He has worked on literary and narrative theory for several years, an endeavor that started with his book *Karaktär och perspektiv: Att tolka litterära gestalter i det mimetiska språkspelet* (Character and Perspective: Reading Fictional Figures in the Mimetic Language-Game). He is the editor of Örebro Studies in Literary History and Criticism with issues such as *Fact and Fiction in Narrative: An Interdisciplinary Approach* and *Narrativity, Fictionality, and Literariness: The Narrative Turn and the Study of Literary Fiction*. He has taken a particular interest in how a theory of narrative fiction

relates to a general theory of narrative, with focus on how aesthetic/
artistic perspectives come into the picture.

A. C. Spearing is a life fellow of Queens' College, Cambridge, and
William R. Kenan, Jr., Professor Emeritus of English, University of
Virginia. He was previously Reader in Medieval English Literature at
the University of Cambridge. His books on medieval literature include
Criticism and Medieval Poetry; *The Gawain-Poet: A Critical Study*;
Medieval Dream-Poetry; *Chaucer: Troilus and Criseyde*; *Medieval to
Renaissance in English Poetry*; *Readings in Medieval Poetry*; *The Cloud
of Unknowing and Other Works*; and various editions and collabora-
tive works. Among his publications on narrative theory are *Textual
Subjectivity: The Encoding of Subjectivity in Medieval Narratives and
Lyrics*; *Medieval Autographies: The "I" of the Text*; "What Is a Narrator?
Narrator Theory and Medieval Narratives," in *Digital Philology*; and
"Narration in Two Versions of 'Virginius and Virginia,'" in *Chaucer
Review*.

Index

Page locators in italics refer to illustrations.

autobiography, 226, 229, 233, 234, 235, 251, 260, 262. *See also* memoir-novels; nonfiction narratives

Autre étude de femme (Balzac), 240

Les aventures prodigieuses de Tartarin de Tarascon (Merlet and Rouger), 247, 249–50, *250*

Avery, Gillian, 211

Bachelard, Gaston, 6

Bakhtin, Mikhail, 144, 211

Baldwin, James, 208

Bally, Charles, 9, 121

Balzac, 94, 112, 115, 127n15, 240

Banfield, Ann: definition of narration, 146n5; on distinction between writing and speech, 131; "expressive" constructions of, 137; linguistic arguments of, 8, 9, 10, 112, 113, 120, 121, 122, 123, 134, 143; narrative theory of, 1, 111, 114, 123, 124, 203; on narrators' existence, 132, 143; on narrator types, 3, 12; and nonreflective consciousness, 26

Barbauld, Anna Laetitia, 37, 109, 117

Bareis, J. Alexander, 2

Barthes, Roland: concept of narrator, 22, 145; criticism of, 79–80, 82; on "death of author," 144; on literary discourse, 147n15; mentor of, 147n16; method of analysis, 77; on narrative communication, 8, 9; on tense use in novels, 90

Bathsheba, 155–57, 159, 160, 162

Baudry, Jean-Louis, 80, 81

Beardsley, Monroe, 76, 77, 78, 83

Benjamin, Walter, 147n17

Benveniste, Émile: academic background of, 147n16; definition of historical enunciation, 146n5; on dis-tinction between writing and speech, 131; on French verb tense, 121, 133, 134, 135; on function of narratives, 225; and syntactic features of Bible, 24; on "you" presupposing "I," 142

Bernstein, Leonard, 42

Bible: "classical" portion of, 146n2; narrative theory applied to, 24–25, 150, 151, 156, 167; narrator concept in, 156, 161, 162, 171; narratorless stories in, 151, 162; poetry in, 142; storytellers in, 154–55; voice in Deuteronomistic History section of, 158. *See also* Classical Biblical Hebrew; *and specific books*

The Biblical Narrative (Sternberg), 154–55

Bierce, Ambrose, 264

biography, 42, 57, 228

Birke, Dorothee, 5

"The Black Cat" (Poe), 90

Black Panthers, 42

Blake, William, 210

Blanche of Lancaster, 173–74

Blast (Larcenet), 252

Bombonnel, Charles Laurent, 246

The Book of the Duchess (Chaucer), 25, 166, 168, 173–80

Booth, Wayne, 79, 81, 90, 125, 127n13

Bordwell, David, 12, 42

Boyd, Brian, 5, 19, 24, 82–84, 180n2

Brady, Matthew, 269

Brenkman, John, 16, 24

Brooks, Cleanth, 38

Browning, Robert, 38

Bühler, Karl, 205

Calvin and Hobbes, 252

Cambridge, England, 80

Candide (Voltaire), 6, 187, 191, 196

Canterbury Tales (Chaucer), 166

Cervantes, Miguel de, 94, 95, 109, 167

characters: access to fictional world through, 15, 58–59, 102, 239, 240; authors' presentation of, 48–50, 57–58, 68, 92, 93, 118, 190, 191, 194, 196, 227, 255, 261; in comics, 246–47, 250, 252; in Homer's epics, 143, 144; of Leo Tolstoy, 63, 65, 67; as narrators, 13, 20, 26, 37–38, 49, 50n5, 56, 57, 69n4, 73, 74, 93, 108, 109, 111, 112, 114, 116, 117, 118, 124, 125, 126n4, 150, 162, 229, 235, 238, 242, 244, 246, 252–53, 255, 261, 265; and omniscient narrators, 44–46; in optional- and pan-narrator theories, 16, 123, 153; in Sade narratives, 186–89; as speakers in poetry, 38, 171–73, 178; speech of, 135, 206; as storytellers, 54; of Voltaire's third-person narratives, 185

Charlie and the Chocolate Factory (Dahl), 216–17

La Chasse au lion (Gérard), 246

Chatman, Seymour: on authors' roles, 46–47, 59, 77–79; comic strip narrative analysis by, 50n5; criticism of Wayne Booth, 81, 82; on film presentation, 42; on narrators as presenters, 48; on necessity and function of narrator, 68n1, 85n2; and *telling* and *showing*, 29n17; on voice-over narration, 253

Chaucer, Geoffrey, 25, 166, 168, 173–80

children's literature, 210, 215, 217

Chomsky, Noam, 10

Chronicles, Book of, 163n3

Churchill, Winston, 226

cinema: as form of narration, 270; medieval romances compared to,

170, 171; narrative theories applied to, 3, 11–15, 18, 27, 47, 253; presence or absence of narrators in, 42–43, 50n7, 259–60, 262–65, 267, 271, 271n3; *telling* and *showing* in, 29n17

Classical Biblical Hebrew: books in, 146n2; grammar and syntax in, 133–43, 146, 146n7; and optional-narrator theory, 24–25, 132; relationship to poetry, 142. *See also* Bible

Classical era, 108

close reading, 85n1

Cohn, Dorrit, 7, 73, 79, 85n2, 251

comics, 11, 13, 27, 42, 50n5, 238, 246–47, 255, 260. *See also* jokes

Coming to Terms (Chatman), 47, 78, 79

communication: in biblical stories, 154–55; in discourse, 134; in films, 43, 47, 263; linguistics of, 56, 120, 122, 123, 204; in medieval literature, 173; by narrative, 8–10, 20, 42, 47, 50n1, 103, 113, 151, 152, 162, 196–97, 225, 226; nonverbal, in optional-narrator theory, 26. *See also* language

Complaint of the Black Knight (Lydgate), 175

Confessions (Augustine of Hippo), 260

Confessions of Felix Krull (Mann), 74

Conrad, Joseph, 27, 228, 231

Contes étranges (Sade), 185

Courtès, Joseph, 206

Crane, Ronald, 81

Crébillon, Claude-Prosper Jolyot (de), 191, 198n9

Les Crimes de l'amour (Sade), 184, 198n17

Culler, Jonathan, 6, 18, 23, 93–94, 217, 218n3, 256

Cummings, E. E., 39

Currie, Gregory, 261

Dahl, Roald, 216

Dällenbach, Lucien, 125

Daphnaïda (Spenser), 175

Daudet, Alphonse, 27, 238, 241–46, 248, 249, 254, 255, 257n3

David (biblical figure), 155–62

David Holzman's Diary (McBridge), 262

Davidson, Donald, 236

Davies, David, 13, 14, 15

Davis, Kathryn, 215

Death in Venice (Mann), 85n2, 251

deictic imaginary, 205, 206, 207, 209, 214, 217, 218. *See also* imagination

Delon, Michel, 185, 199n20

Derrida, Jacques, 76

Deuteronomy, Book of, 140, 141, 158

Dickens, Charles, 239

diēgēsis, 143, 144

Dillon, Glyn, 252

Discours du récit (Genette), 111, 240

discourse: description of, 133–34; differentiation from narration, 139, 141, 142, 225; in epics, 143, 144; in optional-narrator theory, 24; Roland Barthes's idea of literary, 147n15; speech patterns and grammar in, 138; stories as effects of, 168; verb tenses in, 134–37, 146n9. *See also* language; speech

Djouadi, Louisa, 246, 248, 249

Döblin, Alfred, 110

Donald, Merlin, 205

Don Quixote (Cervantes), 109

Dor, Daniel, 57, 58, 205

drama, 84, 223, 224, 225. *See also* plays

dramatic narrators, 11

dramatic speaker, 77

écriture, 79

Edholm, Roger, 125

L'Education sentimentale (Flaubert), 112

Edward III, 173

ekphrasis, 26, 208, 209, 210, 212

Elective Affinities (Goethe), 19

Eliot, George, 49, 110, 239

Emaré, 168

Emma (Austen), 19, 20, 57–58, 94

enactivism, 83–84

English language, 9, 28n4, 113, 121, 123, 168, 205–6. *See also* Middle English

English literature, 20, 25, 166, 184

énoncé/énonciation. See enunciation

Enrico, Roberto, 264–65, 268–69

enunciation: function of, 91–92; in *Great Gatsby*, 97; as key category of discourse, 104, 105; in Sade narratives, 186, 187, 194; stages of, 108–9; theories of, 107, 108, 112–13, 121, 125, 206, 209, 210

enunciative realism, 185

epics, 109, 142, 143, 144, 225, 230, 231, 234

epistemology, 107, 205, 206, 207

Ermatinger, Emil, 118

Eveline (Joyce), 77

Exodus, Book of, 135, 141, 142

factual narrative. *See* nonfiction narratives

The Family Circus (Keane), 252

fictional narratives: authors as narrators of, 38; authors' role in, 55, 56, 60, 74–75, 102–3, 116, 117, 123, 227; categories of, 111–13, 168, 223; for children, 210; distinction from nonfiction, 150–51; dualist conception of, 116, 119, 120; in first- and third-person, 179, 190, 229; imagination in, 57–59; language of, 203; methods of analysis of, 112, 114; modes of, 109; presence or absence of narrators in, 48, 49; relation to real world, 43, 68, 74, 172, 188, 190, 196–97; temporality and subject in, 91; tense in, 190. *See also* cinema; novels; short stories

fictional narrators: access to fictional world through, 15; of biblical stories, 155, 160; creation of, 2, 126; definition of, 28n2; in film, 262, 267–70; in first- and third-person narratives, 16; genres without, 42; historical perspectives on, 19–21; implied authors as, 41, 253; imposed narrators in, 54–55; language use by, 10, 11, 14; in poetry, 23; presence or absence of, 1, 4, 5, 22, 43, 48, 85, 222, 236; relationship to author and reader, 261, 262; theories about, 13, 24, 75, 125, 264–66; transmedial comparison of, 253. *See also* narrators

fictional worlds: access to, 14–15, 17, 56, 61–62, 102, 239; of comics, 247, 248, 255; existence of narrator in, 152–54, 187, 242; genres belonging to, 39; imagination in, 58–60; in "Little Match Girl," 212; narrators' knowledge and disclosure of, 44, 48, 64, 241–42, 246, 255; uniqueness of, 67

Fielding, Henry, 109, 110

Fitzgerald, F. Scott, 24, 95–101

Flaubert, Gustave, 94, 112, 122, 239, 240

Fludernik, Monika, 111, 114, 167, 179, 251

Fokkelman, Jan P., 156

free indirect style, 9, 121, 122

French language: communication of narrators in, 9, 113, 123; comparison to Middle English, 175; description of fiction genre in, 168; narrative

strategies in, 27; theses on Homer in, 147n16; use in novels, 90; verb tense in, 121, 133–35, 137, 141, 143; in *War and Peace*, 61, 62, 63

French literature, 5, 20, 184

French poststructuralism, 79, 80, 81

French school, 107

French structuralism, 38

Friedemann, Käte, 22, 110, 111, 116–18

Froissart, Jean, 175, 179

fundamental narrator. *See* pan-narrator theory

Galbraith, Mary, 26

Gaut, Berys, 12, 13, 14

Genand, Stéphanie, 185

Gendlin, Eugene, 208–10

Genesis, Book of, 25, 132, 137, 138, 141, 157–58, 160, 161

Genette, Gérard: concept of narrator, 22, 118–20, 123; on equivalents of structural analysis, 85n1; on factual and fictional narrative, 102; influence of, 125; on narrative communication, 9, 20; on narratorial status, 240; on omniscient narrators, 7; relation to linguistic reasoning, 120–21; theory of fictional narrative, 111–12, 190, 203, 254, 255, 257n1

Gérard, Jules, 246

Gilgamesh, 142, 143

"The Girl Who Trod on a Loaf" (Andersen), 26, 210, 213–17

Goethe, Johann Wolfgang von, 19

Goldsmith, Oliver, 109

Good Samaritan, parable of the, 25, 151, 153–54, 160, 161

grammar. *See* linguistics

The Great Gatsby (Fitzgerald), 24, 95–101

Greimas, Algirdas Julien (A. J.), 206

Job, Book of, 214
John of Gaunt, 169, 173–74, 177
jokes, 53–54, 171. *See also* comics
Jong, Irene J. F. de, 239
Joshua, Book of, 136, 140, 141, 142, 146n2
Joyce, James, 77
Judges, Book of, 139–40, 142, 146n2, 158
Justine (Sade), 187, 191, 195, 197n6

Kania, Andrew, 8, 13, 14, 15, 17, 56
Kawashima, Robert S., 10, 24–25
Kayser, Wolfgang, 38, 110–12, 118
"The Killers" (Hemingway), 18, 45, 46
King Horn, 25, 167–76, 181n6
Kings, Books of, 132, 136, 138, 140, 141,
    146n2, 158
Kittredge, George Lyman, 177
Klein, Lillian, 158
Klein, Ralph W., 157
Klingberg, Per, 18
Köppe, Tilmann, 5, 13–16, 28nn4–5,
    56, 123, 242
Korthals Altes, Liesbeth, 19
Koskimies, Rafael, 118
Kundera, Milan, 95
Kuroda, S.-Y.: on distinction between
    writing and speech, 131; linguistic
    arguments of, 8, 9, 10, 112, 113, 122–
    23; narrative theory of, 1, 111, 114,
    123, 124, 203; nonreportive style,
    26; on omniscient narrators, 7–10,
    28n13; origin of term *narrator theo-
    ry of narration*, 28n5

Lamb, Charles, 115
Lamiel (Stendhal), 240
Landy, Joshua, 79
Langham, Clive, 253
language: acquisition of, 204, 207,
    218n1; authors' use of, 72, 73, 76–78,

80–85, 91, 93; and consciousness,
26; of first-person narratives, 229;
function in literature, 56, 57; in
Holy Sinner, 73; of narrative systems, 150, 155; narrative theories
about, 115, 203–8, 210, 218; noncommunicational uses of, 5, 10; in
novels, 103; in performance model,
224; poststructuralist and enactivist approaches to, 83–84; process
model and taxonomy of, 208–9;
real acts of fiction through, 74; as
speech, 131. *See also* Classical Biblical Hebrew; communication; discourse; English language; French
language; linguistics; speech;
speech acts; voice
*The Languages of Criticism and the
    Sciences of Man* (Rosolato), 104
Lanoo, Vincent, 262
Larcenet, Manu, 252
Läskimooses (Hagelberg), 252
Lassen, Henrik, 211
Legend of Good Women (Chaucer),
    178, 179
legislative texts, 10
Lely, Gilbert, 185
Leviticus, Book of, 141
The Lily of the Valley (Balzac), 115
linguistics: of biblical authors, 141;
    in epics, 142, 143, 144; and French
    verb tense, 133–34; and grammar,
    139, 227, 231; history of, 112–13; and
    narrator theories, 3, 4–5, 8–10,
    107, 120, 121, 122, 124, 222, 223, 234;
    symbolism in, 235, 236. *See also*
    language
Lips, Marguerite, 121
The Literary Work of Art (Ingarden),
    75–76

speech patterns and grammar in, 137–38; verb tenses of, 24, 134–37, 146n9, 190. *See also* voice-over narration

narration, first-person: in comics, 248; competing theories about, 203; in historical fiction, 185; language structure in, 230, 234–35; literary structure of, 228, 231, 232, 233

narration, heterodiegetic: description of, 112; in epics, 142; existence of narrator in, 152, 251; and language use, 10, 131; in optional- and pan-narrator theories, 3, 4, 123; in *Tartarin de Tarascon*, 242, 243, 245; voice effects in, 150

narration, homodiegetic, 3, 10, 111–12, 123, 131, 143, 239, 245

narration, third-person: in comics, 247, 251; grammar and syntax in, 227, 230; literary structure of, 231, 232; relationship to first-person narratives, 26, 184, 187, 255; Sade works as, 185, 190

Narrative Discourse Revisited (Genette), 121

narrative forms, 11, 12, 38, 144

narrative theory: history of, 107–8, 238–39; terminology of, 226. *See also* optional-narrator theory; pan-narrator theory

narratology: of children's literature, 215; definition of, 1, 28n1; of fictional narratives, 89, 102–3, 105, 150–53, 155, 156; foundational principles of, 203; and history of narrator concept, 113, 120; linguistic arguments in, 120–22; of medieval narratives, 167, 180; optional-narrator theory in, 222; pan-narrator theory in,

28n6, 111, 238; research in, 114; scientific status of, 108; structuralist view of, 77–79; of textual analyses, 159, 161–63

narratology, transmedial: language in, 11, 123; narrator concept in, 253, 257n5; optional- and pan-narrator theories in, 3, 5, 13, 27, 254, 256–57

narratorless narrative: in biblical texts, 151, 154, 158, 159, 162; in comics, 248–50; definition of, 2, 132; example of, 59; in film, 270; in *King Horn*, 171, 173; in transmedial narratology, 257n5. *See also* no-narrator theory

narrators: adult judgment of, 215; authors' choice to use, 46–47, 49, 186, 190; concept of, 21, 25, 27, 89–90, 108–11, 113–19, 123–26, 126n5, 132, 145, 151, 162, 222, 226, 236, 238, 256, 260; disappearance of, 240, 241, 246; knowledge and disclosure by, 45, 49, 64, 65, 172, 177, 179, 246; in language frames, 150–51; in narrative history, 144; necessity and function of, 37, 41, 47, 48, 51n11, 53, 56, 61, 62, 64, 65, 67, 68n1, 69n3, 85n2, 108, 110, 114–15, 117, 118, 123, 132, 159–60, 239–41, 253–55, 260–61, 268–71, 271n3; as presenters, 48, 56, 62, 143, 144, 243, 253, 254, 266–68; relationship to author and reader, 59, 67, 90–91, 103, 104, 105, 244–45, 251, 260–61; text-internal, 227–28; theoretical assumptions about, 152–53. *See also* dramatic narrators; fictional narrators; nonfictional narrators; storytellers

narrators, impersonal, 12, 17

narrators, implied, 9, 18, 53, 131, 256

narrators, imposed, 23, 54, 55, 56

narrators, omniscient: as ad hoc hypothesis, 5, 9–10; authors as, 38;
in biblical texts, 25, 156, 157, 159; in
Great Gatsby, 96; in *King Horn*, 171;
knowledge and disclosure by, 44–
46, 93–94; problems of, 17, 18, 44,
171–72; as product of pan-narrator
theory, 4, 7–8

narrators, "reticent," 18

narrators in first-person narratives:
attributions to, 10; in *Book of the
Duchess*, 174; concept of, 21, 22,
101–2, 109, 111, 112, 113, 119–21, 125,
127n15; creation of, 1; distinction
from authors, 37, 38, 116, 117, 261;
Edgar Allan Poe's use of, 90; in
epics, 142; function of, 47, 239;
Geoffrey Chaucer's use of, 166, 168,
174–76, 178, 179; John Searle's theory
about, 29n16, 120; in *King Horn*, 172,
173; linguistics of, 122; in literary
history, 25; in novels, 96–99, 101–2,
191, 229, 238, 246; in optional- and
pan-narrator theories, 3, 8, 9, 16, 21,
118; in *Tartarin de Tarascon*, 241–43;
Toni Morrison's use of, 92; truth
effect of, 115; types of, 38. *See also* I,
experiencing and narrating

narrators in third-person narratives: and authors, 48, 90–91, 118,
125; concept of, 22, 116, 119, 246;
contradictions of, 17; examples of
unmediated, 25; in free indirect
style, 9, 122; history of, 37–38, 111;
in Homer's epics, 143, 144; knowledge and disclosure by, 7, 44, 47,
49, 73; language use by, 10, 113, 122,
123, 206; in medieval literature, 167;
narrative category of, 112; in novels,

89, 95–99, 101–2, 185, 229; in op-
tional- and pan-narrator theories,
3, 4, 16

necessary narrator. *See* pan-narrator
theory

Nehemiah, Book of, 25, 157, 160, 161

New Criticism, 37, 38

The New Justine (Sade), 195, 197n6

Nielsen, Henrik Skov, 12

Nikolajeva, Maria, 250

no-narrator theory, 2, 225–26

nonfictional narrators, 4, 8, 15–17

nonfiction narratives: distinction
from fiction, 150–51; imagination
in, 57; by Leo Tolstoy, 63; narrators
of, 260, 262; separation of author
from narrator in, 42, 43, 102–3, 157,
158. *See also* autobiography; biography; historical narratives

*Nouvelle critique ou nouvelle impos-
ture* (Picard), 79

novels: definition of genre, 185; drama
in, 116; historical arguments associated with, 19, 89; medieval romances compared with, 170; mode
of storytelling in epistolary, 54, 109;
narrative theory applied to, 167,
180n1; narrator concept in, 21, 27,
37, 47, 89, 102–3, 113, 229; narrators
in, 98, 99, 109, 119, 126n4, 127n15,
185, 191, 198n8, 229, 231, 232, 238,
239, 246; omniscient narrators in,
93–94; optional-narrator theory in,
1, 24, 89; thesis on rise of, 147n17;
voice and time in, 90, 92, 97, 99,
103–5, 145, 228; Voltaire's dislike of,
198n18. *See also* fictional narratives;
memoir-novels

Numbers, Book of, 139–40; narration
and discourse in, 135–36

obligatory narrator. *See* pan-narrator theory

O'Brien, Tim, 93

"Occurrence at Owl Creek Bridge" (Bierce), 264

Odyssey (Homer), 142–44

The Old Curiosity Shop (Dickens), 239

ontological-gap argument, 14–15

"On Voice" (Brenkman), 24

optional-narrator theory: biblical examples of, 132, 139; contrast with pan-narrator theory, 2–3, 6, 51n11, 101, 102, 123, 124, 132, 222, 255; definition of, 1, 28n4, 132; in films, 27, 259; historical arguments associated with, 26, 27, 107, 144, 145, 254; language and consciousness in, 26, 113, 134; poststructuralist approach to, 24, 72; in storytelling, 53; transmedial application of, 256–57; types of narrators in, 48, 116, 117, 150, 242; versions of, 47

Örebro School, 18–19

"Oxford philosophy," 80

pan-narrator theory: arguments against, 4–5, 13–15, 21, 23, 27, 123, 152, 222, 253; authors in, 18–19, 45, 48, 118; in comics, 250–51; contrast with optional-narrator theory, 2–3, 6, 51n11, 101, 102, 123, 124, 132, 222, 255; definition of, 2, 28n5; in different works of single author, 61, 67–68; in fiction and nonfiction, 150, 151; historical arguments associated with, 5, 19–22, 107–8, 124, 126, 238; imposed narrators in, 54; inconsistency of fictional narrator in, 16–17, 123, 255; on narrators' omniscience, 44; in novels, 61–62, 89; popularity of, 48, 114, 123;

and readers' imagination, 60; relationship to narratology, 111; students' understanding of, 49; tense in, 133; transmedial application of, 246

Parry, Milman, 145, 147n16

Patron, Sylvie, 37, 72, 101–2, 132, 150, 196, 209, 210, 222

Pauvert, Jean-Jacques, 185

Peanuts (Schulz), 42

Peirce, Charles S., 235

Pelckmans, Paul, 195

Pentateuch, 146n2

Père Goriot (Balzac), 112

Petersen, Julius, 7

Petsch, Robert, 110, 118

Phelan, James, 19, 69n3

Picard, Raymond, 79

Pieper, Vincenz, 19, 20, 24, 69n4

Plato, 108, 143, 207

plays, 47. *See also* drama

Poe, Edgar Allan, 90, 105n1

poetic theories, 50n1

Poetik (Scherer), 73

poetry: discourse in biblical, 141, 142; narrators in epic, 142–44; presence or absence of narrators in, 23, 37, 49, 116, 142, 171; shifters in, 91–92; speakers in, 38, 40, 45, 76, 77, 179–80; speech acts in, 43; successful performativity in, 218n3

poets: choice and arrangement of words by, 40–41, 45, 46; creation of narrators, 1; distinction from speakers, 39, 49, 76; historical arguments associated with, 19; implied authors compared with, 72; modes of presentation by, 73–74, 119, 197; as narrators, 25; storytelling styles of medieval, 166, 167, 168. *See also* authors

writing: by authors, 72, 75–77, 80–82, 84–85, 91, 105n2; distinction from speech, 131–32, 134, 138; readers' interaction with, 206, 208

Writing Degree Zero (Barthes), 90, 145

Zipfel, Frank, 3, 8, 10, 13–17, 28n7, 29n18, 75, 180n1

Zlatev, Jordan, 205

To order or obtain more information on these or other University of Nebraska Press titles, visit nebraskapress.unl.edu.

Lightning Source UK Ltd.
Milton Keynes UK
UKHW010252290421
382821UK00001B/28